CONSTRUCTIVISM IN FILM

GENERAL EDITORS

Henry Breitrose, *Stanford University*
William Rothman

ADVISORY BOARD

Dudley Andrew, *University of Iowa*
Garth Jowett, *University of Texas at Houston*
Anthony Smith, *British Film Institute*
Colin Young, *National Film School*

OTHER BOOKS IN THE SERIES

Paul Clark, *Chinese Film*
Sergei Eisenstein, *Nonindifferent Nature* (trans. Herbert Marshall)
Paul Swann, *The British Documentary Film Movement, 1926–1946*

CONSTRUCTIVISM IN FILM

The Man with the Movie Camera
A Cinematic Analysis

VLADA PETRIĆ

CAMBRIDGE
UNIVERSITY PRESS

Published by the Press Syndicate of the University of Cambridge
The Pitt Building, Trumpington Street, Cambridge CB2 1RP
40 West 20th Street, New York, NY 10011-4211, USA
10 Stamford Road, Oakleigh, Melbourne 3166, Australia

First published 1987
First paperback edition 1993

Printed in the United States of America

Library of Congress Cataloging-in-Publication Data
Petric, Vladimir.
Constructivism in film.
(Cambridge studies in film)
Filmography: p.
Includes bibliography and index.
1. Chelovek s kinoapparatom. 2. Vertov, Dziga,
1896–1954 – Criticism and interpretation. I. Title.
II. Series.
PN1977.C452225P48   1986   791.43'023'0924   86–12893

A catalogue record for this book is available from the British Library.

ISBN 0-521-32174-3 hardback
ISBN 0-521-44387-3 paperback

Contents

Preface   vii

Acknowledgment   xii

I   **Dziga Vertov and the Soviet avant-garde movement**   1

The *kinok*s   1

The constructivist tradition   5

"Art of fact"   13

Struggles with NEP   21

Vertov and Mayakovsky   25

Futurist and formalist expression   35

Educating the masses   44

The Vertov–Eisenstein Controversy   48

Vertov's difficult years   60

The demise of the Soviet avant-garde   62

II   **Thematic meaning of *The Man with the Movie Camera***   70

Experiment in cinematic communication   70

Segmentation of the film's structure   72

A "difficult" movie   78

Reactions to the camera   81

Self-referential associations   82

Ideological implications   84

Negation of narrative   91

Disruptive–associative montage   95

Social and political commentary   107

The nature of the film image   110

Cinematic illusion   113

Point of view   119

III   **Formal structure of *The Man with the Movie Camera***   129

A mathematics of facts   129

Shot composition and visual design   130
Phi-effect and kinesthesia   139
Intervals of movement   148
Subliminal propulsion   155
Oneiric impact of intervals   164
Optical music   176
Movement versus stasis   184
Structural recapitulation   188
Ideology of graphic patterns   196
A cornerstone of world cinema   199

Appendix 1   Introductory statement of the film   201

Appendix 2   Annotated bibliography of Vertov's writings
(published articles)   203

Appendix 3   Annotated filmography of Vertov's work,
1918–1954   213

Appendix 4   Biographical sketch of Vertov's career,
1896–1954   221

Appendix 5   Selected bibliography   229

Notes   237

Frame enlargements   249

Plates   308

Index   319

Preface

For a brief period in its cultural history, the USSR enjoyed a unique marriage of liberal artistic expression and generous government support. Immediately following the October Revolution, Soviet artists felt free to engage in the most original and controversial of experiments, including those which clashed with the official party line. Those few years of ideological freedom and creative enthusiasm gave birth to some outstanding avant-garde achievements that still inspire artists worldwide to express themselves in ways uncompromised by artistic conventions or political dictates.

Dziga Vertov was one of the most unorthodox artists in the Soviet avant-garde movement, in both his style, exhibited by his documentary films, and his concept of cinema as a social force and as a medium for artistic expression. Inspired by constructivist and futurist ideas, Vertov saw cinema as an autonomous art and conceived of a film as a "building" made of numerous units (shots) and appropriate "architectural" procedures (shooting techniques), the meaning and impact of which were to be determined by the image composition, juxtaposition of shots, and cinematic integration of all components, including the narrative.

An inspirational force behind the group of film enthusiasts known as the *kinok*s, Vertov struggled to prove that film is a universal language of expression, intelligible to all people regardless of national borders because it is capable of constructing "sentences" and "phrases" that convey ideas more powerfully than any other means of communication. He considered the camera to be the instrument an artist could use to penetrate the essence of external reality. Identifying himself as a worker among other workers, Vertov regarded his movies as "productive objects," or "film-things," intended to help the audience – workers, peasants, and ordinary citizens – to see "through and beyond" the appearance of mundane reality. He believed that cinema as a revolutionary force could affect the mass consciousness and incite people to reject bourgeois melodramas (photoplays), which Vertov, echoing Marx, labeled "an opiate for the people." At the same time, he wanted to demonstrate the cinema's exceptional power, which could be used as an educational means to build the new society.

Vertov's most radical achievement and his masterpiece, *The Man with the Movie Camera*, is based on the constructivist concept known as "art of fact." This nonfiction (unstaged) film, as its credits specify, is "an experiment in the cinematic communication of visible events, executed without the aid of intertitles, without a script, without theater, without sets and actors." It introduces numerous innovative stylistic features through its genuine montage structure, which challenges conventional narrative movies as well as traditional documentary filmmaking. Destined as early as its first screening to be controversial in every respect, yet to make a profound mark on world cinema, Vertov's work has exerted tangible influence on such directors as Jean Rouch, Richard Leacock, Frederick Wiseman, Roberto Rossellini, Jean-Luc Godard, Satyajit Ray, Andrzej Wajda, Dušan Makavejev, Stan Brakhage, Don Pennebaker, Bruce Conner, and Jonas Mekas. Particularly intriguing is the relationship between Vertov's "Film-Eye" method and "The Camera Eye" section in Dos Passos's fiction *USA*, to whom Vertov refers in his diary. (While this book was in press, I learned of the study entitled *In Visible Light: Photography and the American Writer*, soon to be published by Oxford University Press, in which Carol Shloss dedicates an entire chapter to Vertov's influence on Dos Passos.)

A close examination of the film's key sequences reveals the structural complexity of *The Man with the Movie Camera* on both thematic and cinematic levels. The relationship between its diegetic meaning and its cinematic execution is often so intricate that one needs to view the film – or parts of it – repeatedly, and with the help of an analyst projector or editing table. Only by so elaborately scrutinizing the film's structure can one understand its complexity (just as one rereads passages of Joyce's *Ulysses* in order to appreciate its dense literary style). The use of the analyst projector is particularly necessary to detect those shots consisting of only one or a few frames that otherwise remain imperceptible, even after repeated viewings. Furthermore, the viewer is expected to be acquainted with the specific historical, political, economic, geographical, and environmental facts referred to throughout the film, all of which possess subtle ideological and psychological implications.

Chapter I outlines Vertov's position in relation to constructivism, futurism, formalism, and suprematism, the leading avant-garde movements in the Soviet Union of the 1920s. Vertov's association with the group of artists and intellectuals gathered around Mayakovsky's journal *LEF* is examined in terms of how Mayakovsky's poetic works influenced Vertov to write deconstructed stanzas and to lay out his film scripts poetically. In both endeavors he followed Mayakovsky's style as well as his practice of graphically displaying lines on the page in a collagelike style.

Although the participants in the Soviet avant-garde movement were unified by their aversion to bourgeois art, this unity did not preclude divergent tendencies within the same artistic trend, as well as conflicting attitudes among the individual artists and theorists. One such disagreement is exemplified by the dispute between Vertov and Aleksei Gan, the most militant of the constructivists, who strove for new revolutionary art and insisted on its being politically responsible to society. Even more controversial were the debates Vertov had with Sergei Eisenstein concerning the "true" nature of documentary cinema, the ideological function of montage, and the role of actors in staged (fictional) films.

With the eventual victory of socialist realism, officially proclaimed as the only "correct" approach to art, and their ensuing disappointment with the New Economic Policy (NEP), which encouraged the production of entertainment movies, Vertov and Mayakovsky realized the impossibility of fulfilling their revolutionary ideals. As the suppression of the avant-garde movement reached its peak in the early 1930s, Vertov's cinematic experimentation was proclaimed "unsuitable" and considered undeserving of support from the Ministry of Cinematography. Attacked by the orthodox film critics for being "formalistic" and therefore "inaccessible" to the masses, Vertov gradually sequestered himself from public life, while his films were removed to the state archive's vault.

Chapter II offers a thematic reading of *The Man with the Movie Camera* through in-depth examination of presented "life-facts" and their function within the thematic context, as well as the film's overall montage structure. To facilitate analysis of the sequences and individual shots, a breakdown of the film's basic themes is presented at the chapter's beginning. This segmentation emphasizes the thematic units as defined by the montage reconstruction of the recorded events.

To substantiate the ideological reading of key sequences, each analysis is accompanied by a shot-by-shot breakdown and illustrated by frame enlargements. Quotations from Vertov's theoretical writings are used to illustrate particular stylistic and theoretical features, or to justify the conclusions drawn later in this book. The "Film-Eye" method, the "Film-Truth" principle, the "Theory of Intervals," and the concept of disruptive–associative montage are discussed according to the Marxist belief in a dialectical contradiction that imbues all events in the material world. The chapter ends by systematically examining the film's different points of view, specifying their diegetic and structural functions.

Chapter III contains a formal analysis of selected sequences that best illustrate Vertov's directorial style and clearly elucidate his theoretical concepts, which are sparingly defined in his writings. Accompanied by frame enlargements and diagrams, the formal analysis shows how Vertov applied to cinema many basic constructivist principles, among them the idea that the artistic process is analogous to industrial production – hence the term "Productive Art."

In collaboration with his wife, Elizaveta Svilova (the Editor in the film), and his brother, Mikhail Kaufman (the Cameraman in the film), Vertov tried to establish cinematic equivalents of certain concepts developed by the formalist poets and suprematist painters, influences of which are most evident in those semirepresentational shots and montage sequences composed of only one or two frames, generating unique kinesthetic energy through cinematic abstraction. Vertov's most original experiments with subliminal montage grew, apparently, from his theoretical interest in the psychology of perception as well as his practical exploration of recording sound and movement, performed during his study at the Psycho-Neurological Institute in St. Petersburg.

Close structural examination of *The Man with the Movie Camera* reveals cinematic values that cannot be properly perceived nor seriously studied when the film is projected at regular speed: the most fascinating optical resolutions in this film are hidden within its complex montage structure. This fact alone suggests the extent of originality and modernism pervading Vertov's method. His last silent film marks the peak of Vertov's creative imagination, which was at odds with all facets of the traditional directorial style, every aspect of established shooting technique, and conventional editing rules. He fought uncompromisingly against the common practice of using the camera merely to record the other arts, or, equally, to register everyday events superficially.

Chapter III ends with an analysis of the three basic graphic patterns (vertical, horizontal, and circular) prevailing in most shot compositions throughout the film. Integrated by montage, these patterns attain an optical "pulsation" that – on the screen – transforms recorded "life-facts" into representationally ambiguous imagery, thus defying the spectators' customary perception of reality and its interpretation. With such remarkable cinematic features, *The Man with the Movie Camera* continues to challenge orthodox filmmaking, reject literary/theatrical theories of the medium, and demonstrate that cinema is an autonomous means of expression – "a higher mathematics of facts."

The appendixes provide necessary documentation for the three chapters and serve as reference material for the reader. They include the following:

1. the introductory statement as presented in the film's opening credits,
2. an annotated bibliography of Vertov's articles,
3. an annotated filmography of Vertov's work,
4. a biographical sketch of Vertov's career, and
5. a selected bibliography related to Vertov's work in general.

Frame enlargements (with numbers corresponding to the figures and plates marked throughout the book) are reproduced at the end as a separate section. They were realized by my assistant, Barry Strongin, who photographed the frames of a 16mm print projected on the screen by an analyst projector. Computer illustrations were drawn by Steve Eagle. The shot descriptions are quoted from the shot-by-shot breakdown executed by the author and Roberta Reeder (a copy of the complete breakdown is housed at the Harvard Film Archive). The index was compiled by Renata Jackson.

Acknowledgment

The completion of this book would not have been possible without the assistance of many people who participated in the preliminary research, close cinematic analysis, and final literary editing of the text.

To avoid the risk of excluding any of the students, colleagues, and friends who – in one way or another – generously contributed to this endeavor (which, with few breaks, spanned almost a decade), I will, sincerely and wisely, follow Vertov's example and assign myself the role of "author-supervisor of the experiment" carried out by numerous *kinoks*.

Without the help of the *kinoks*, Vertov would not have been able to realize his projects; similarly, my goals embodied in this work would never have been accomplished without the help of those who deeply believed in it, collaborated with me, and provided encouragement when it was most necessary.

V. P.

CHAPTER

I

**Dziga Vertov
and the Soviet
avant-garde movement**

> It is far from simple
> to show the truth,
> yet the truth is simple.
> — Dziga Vertov

The *kinok*s

The decade after the October Revolution unleashed one of the most exciting periods in Russian art. Although the majority of the artists remained committed to the forms of expression dominant before the revolution, the avant-garde groups in search of ways to express the needs and goals of the newly liberated working class chose forms and subjects as innovative and experimental as the times. These revolutionary enthusiasts met a serious challenge in the attitudes of the traditional artists, as both groups strove to define theoretical concepts for the artist's role in the new Soviet state, and as numerous factions of the avant-garde adopted varying and often mutually conflicting ideological positions. The resulting differences of opinion did not, however, prevent the avant-garde artists from collectively promoting artistic experimentation and freedom of expression. This was particularly evident in cinema, which was considered the most powerful means of communication and expression.

Spurred on by avant-garde experiments taking place in other arts, Dziga Vertov envisioned the development of an unconventional cinematic mode that could be universally understood. To accomplish this he demanded that fellow filmmakers get rid of literary and theatrical conventions in order to create a new form of cinema that would engage the moviegoer's "dormant" consciousness and foster an active mental participation both during and after the screening. He proclaimed as

1

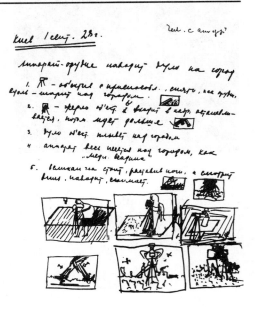

Dziga Vertov and a page from
his shooting diary, dated "Kiev,
1 Sept. 28," which shows one
of the shot breakdowns for *The
Man with the Movie Camera*.
The constructivist drawing is
by I. Galadzhev.

the most urgent task the need to replace bourgeois melodramas with
revolutionary newsreels reflecting everyday life. Vertov surrounded himself with a group of collaborators whom he called the "*kinoks*" [*kinoki*], a neologism that reflected their ardent dedication to film.* The
members of the *kinoks* were young cameramen, editors, technicians,
and animators, including Mikhail Kaufman, Vertov's brother who, in
addition to playing the "protagonist," served as the cameraman for
The Man with the Movie Camera, and Vertov's wife, Elizaveta Svilova,
the film's editor, who played herself in that role.†

Vertov, Kaufman, and Svilova formed the Council of Three [*Soviet
troikh*] – "the higher organ of the *kinoks*" [*visshii organ kinokov*] –
which bore responsibility for the production policy of the cooperative.
The *kinoks* promulgated and defended their views with idealistic zeal,

---

* Vertov's neologism "*kinok*" is constructed from two words: "*kino*" (film) and "*oko*" (a de-
rivative suffix that makes an agent out of a verb). In addition, "*oko*" is an archaic word for
"eye." His other, though rarely used, term for *kinoks* – "*kinoglazovtsy*" – employs the modern
word for "eye" ("*glaz*").
† Besides Vertov, Kaufman, and Svilova, the *kinoks*' group included Ivan Beliakov, cameraman; Petr Zotov, cameraman and editor; Il'ia Kopalin, editor; Alexandr Lemberg,
cameraman; Boris Frantsisson, animator; and Boris Barantsievich, technician.

insisting on a sharp distinction between the traditional fictional film and the new proletarian newsreel. As a member of the Council of Three, Svilova derided the directors of entertainment films as those "who do not understand that the newsreel can also be edited, and who do not know that documentary films are more important and more exciting than photoplays with actors, because the newsreel shows life that cannot be imitated by actors."[1] She concluded her statement with a question: "If one photographs a real worker and an actor playing a worker, which is better? The impersonating actor or the real man? Unquestionably the latter!"[2] Svilova's answer clearly reflected the *kinoks*' desire to free film of the theatrical conventions it had acquired while becoming "artistic," an evolution which led cinema to become merely a recording device for the performing arts.

To promote the *unstaged film*,* the *kinoks* organized special traveling cinemas known as "agit-trains" [*agitpoezd*] and regularly visited villages without movie theaters. Their efforts were instrumental for the state's effectiveness in propagandizing new political ideas: by bringing newsreels to the peasants in distant rural areas, the *kinoks* introduced film to people who had never before seen moving pictures. The extent of the *kinoks*' activities among the peasants and workers was documented in two of Vertov's newsreels, *Instructional Steamer*, also known as *Red Star* (1920), and *The Agit-Train*, also known as *VTSIK* or *On the Bloodless Military Front* (1921). It may seem contradictory that although the workers' newsreels were made for ordinary Soviet people, the *kinoks* considered themselves members of "an international movement that marched in step with the world proletarian revolution,"[3] as they wanted their films to have a worldwide distribution. Explaining the essentials of the "Film-Eye" method, Vertov urged the newly recruited *kinoks* to use their skills in confronting the world at large and to focus on everyday life while "pushing art to the periphery of our consciousness."[4] In addition to Vertov, only Aleksei Gan and Vladimir Mayakovsky were so explicit in declaring their cosmopolitan feelings soon to be proscribed by the party as a "betrayal" of the revolution.

To understand fully how Vertov applied the constructivist concept of "making an art-object" to film, it is necessary to compare his work and his theoretical views with the achievements of other Soviet avant-garde artists, especially those whose experimentation was intended to revolutionize art. Vertov believed that the camera should not disturb the natural course of events during shooting, and therefore he advised his *kinoks* to record the "life-facts" [*zhiznennyi fakty*] "as they are" so

---

* The term "unstaged film" [*neigrovoi fil'm*], meaning a film which excludes actors, in contrast to the term "staged film" [*igrovoi fil'm*], which includes actors, has a specific ideological connotation in Vertov's theory of documentary cinema.

that, with this basis, montage could then create the "film-facts" [*kino-fakty*]. This does not mean that the "film-fact" should remain structurally unchanged through the editing process. As numerous sequences of *The Man with the Movie Camera* prove, they are built on the constructivist principle of an ideational juxtaposition of different materials to produce a more meaningful structural whole.

Vertov claimed that the *staged film* was antithetical to the spirit of the revolutionary times which required the cinema's goals be in direct political alignment with those of the new socialist reality. As a strategy for achieving this, Vertov proposed the principle of "Film-Truth" [*kino-pravda*]. Upon this basis he conceived a series of newsreels under the same title, which also alludes to the first Bolshevik daily newspaper, *Pravda* ("Truth"), founded by V. I. Lenin in 1912. From this there emerged his "Film-Eye" [*kinoglaz*] directorial method, which, according to Vertov, was capable of penetrating beneath the surface of external reality in order to show "Life-As-It-Is" [*zhizn' kak ona est'*] on the screen. By shooting "life-unawares" [*zhizn' v rasplokh*], the *kinoks* fostered an undramatized cinematic presentation of reality that was caught unawares and subsequently restructured through montage, a creative procedure Vertov believed could capture the fleeting moments of reality that otherwise escape observation. He demanded that the "*kinok*-engineer" use his or her camera as an omnipotent eye to reorganize the visible world, by revealing many processes inaccessible to the naked eye, processes made visible only through the "montage way of seeing," through the "recording of movements composed of the most complex combinations."[5]

Vertov's intention to merge the human and the mechanical eye led toward two essentially disparate goals, and inevitably produced a dialectical contradiction within the "Film-Truth" principle. In their newsreels, the *kinoks* sought both to preserve the notion of "Life-As-It-Is" and to express a new vision of reality. This contrariety was blunted by the two-pronged effect of the "Film-Eye" method which, on the one hand, dealt with "life-facts" as they appeared in external reality and, on the other, employed all available cinematic devices to recreate a new visual structure (the "film-thing"), not only phenomenologically different from its prototype but far more revealing than reality itself. On the basis of these precepts, one can conclude that Vertov's concept of truth − however concerned with "life caught unawares" − is not identical with objective truth, not even with truth as it is initially recorded on the celluloid strip.

To understand fully Vertov's significance within the worldwide avant-garde trends of the 1920s, it is not only necessary to explore how he was influenced by other unorthodox artists but also how his theories and practice inspired others. Vertov, of course, was not the sole Soviet revolutionary filmmaker who rebelled against traditional art forms, yet his works represent one of the most innovative expressions of this protest. A comparative analysis reveals that, although Vertov was influenced by futurism, suprematism, and formalism, his most experimental films incorporate various principles of the constructivist method, particularly its attitude toward the creative process.

The constructivist tradition

The constructivists, whose ideas represent the most sophisticated aspect of the Soviet avant-garde, viewed the artist as an "engineer" whose duty was to construct "useful objects," much like a factory worker, while actively participating in the building of a new society. One of the more suitable means of artistic production was the relatively new medium of film, an art form that, given its ability to convey messages to vast audiences and its capacity to reconstruct all components of natural movement, had an immense appeal for the constructivist artists: they considered it the most powerful tool available to educate the people. In this context, film should serve a dual purpose: to assist the technological revolution and environmental transformation by replacing the bourgeois mentality with a socialist consciousness and to emancipate art by focusing on the needs and responsibilities of the emerging working class.

Perhaps the most articulate definition of constructivism was put forth in the famous "Realist Manifesto" (1922) issued by the brothers Naum Gabo and Antonin Pevsner. Representing the more aesthetic wing of this movement, they wrote that "art is the realization of our spatial perception of the world," and that the artist "constructs his work as the engineer builds his bridges and the mathematician establishes his formulas of the orbits."[6] Vertov was equally preoccupied with exploring the possibilities of cinema as the "art of imagining the movements of objects in space within a conception of a rhythmic and aesthetic whole brought in accordance with the specific properties of the photographed material as well as the inner pace of each separate element."[7] *The Man with the Movie Camera* vividly exemplifies this constructivist attitude applied to filmmaking, as its key sequences achieve a high degree of visual dynamism often by intercutting abstract shots (including black or transparent frames) within otherwise representational segments of the film. As will be documented later, Vertov's dynamic and subliminal montage was considered shocking and mischievous by most contemporary critics and filmmakers, including Sergei Eisenstein, who failed to recognize the revolutionary significance of *The Man with the Movie Camera*.

It was the futurist literary tradition in prerevolutionary Russia that stimulated the constructivists' enthusiasm for technology in the early days of the Soviet state. Admiration for machines is evident in futurist paintings by Malevich, Goncharova, and Rozanova, whereas an appreciation of pure geometrical forms is dominant in Malevich's suprematist works. This is equally true of avant-garde Russian photography and film. Vertov's youthful experiments with recording sound and motion pictures attest to his inborn fascination with machinery, its "stupendous power" and the beauty of its forms. He was so thrilled by technology that he once declared: "Our artistic vision departs from the working citizens and continues through the poetry of the machine toward a perfect electrical man.... Long live the poetry of moved and moving machines, the poetry of levers, wheels, steel wings, the metallic clamor of movement and the blinding grimace of the scorching electric current."[8] This vision is best exemplified in the camera work of Vertov and Kaufman, as their footage depicting machines and bridges are often reduced to elaborate constructions silhouetted against burning furnaces or clear sky, structures transmuted by means of montage or optical devices into graphic imagery inspired by industrial design. Vertov's enthusiasm for factories and metal constructions can also be related to the "aesthetics of the machine" as elaborated by the Italian futurists. Their manifesto, "The Futurist Cinema" (1916), proclaimed the supremacy of cinema over all other art forms and described the uniqueness of cinematic language, which, although somewhat similar, substantially differs from that of painting and photography:

Cinema is an autonomous art. Cinema must therefore never copy the stage; being essentially visual, cinema must, above all, fulfill the evolution of painting, detach itself from reality, from photography, from the graceful and solemn; it must become antigraceful, deforming, impressionistic, synthetic, dynamic, freewording.[9]

Most of these qualities can be applied directly to Vertov's work, particularly to *The Man with the Movie Camera,* in which the best sequences clearly demonstrate the distinction between still photography and the freeze-frame, animation (stop-trick) and the motion picture, the image on the film strip and the image on the screen-within-the-screen, thus acknowledging the uniqueness of the cinematic process.

The rhythms of the working man and of machines play an important role in constructivist theater, particularly in the work of the most innovative Soviet theater director, Vsevolod Meyerhold.* Inspired by the

---

* Immediately after the October Revolution, Meyerhold was among the first theater directors to offer his services to the new government; nonetheless his theater was closed in 1938, and one of the greatest revolutionary theater directors became an outcast. Only the venerable Stanislavsky befriended him, making him director of the Stanislavsky Opera Theater. But in 1939, soon after Stanislavsky died, Meyerhold was at once arrested and executed by the KGB, while his wife Zinaida Raikh was subsequently found brutally murdered in their apartment.

analytical study of time and motion related to efficiency in manufacturing operations done by Frederick Winslow Taylor, the American industrial engineer, Meyerhold developed a theory of "biomechanics," which applied the "mechanics of movement" to the stage mise-en-scène. Certain actions – such as shooting an arrow or slapping a face – were reduced to sets of elementary gestures to be, almost balletically, performed by actors in a dramatic context. A similar fascination with the rhythm of machinery and the physical motion of factory workers is manifest in Vertov's early works, the *Film-Truth* series (1922–5), as well as in his films *Forward March, Soviet!* (1926) and *One Sixth of the World* (1926). In *The Man with the Movie Camera*, the dynamic presentation and kinesthetic simulation of machines is heightened by a formal reiteration in the film's montage. Through different pictorial designs, Vertov creates a geometrical interplay of gears, pistons, rods, and wheels in horizontal and vertical movement, or he juxtaposes cars and trolleys moving horizontally against the dispersed vertical flow of milling pedestrians. Like the symbolic mise-en-scène in Meyerhold's biomechanical stage performances, various passages in *The Man with the Movie Camera* explore abstract patterns of movement in the production process; shots of stopping and starting machines, handles being pulled, levers falling, cigarettes being packaged, and ore being mined all convey the mechanical aesthetic with great expressiveness. And by comparing industrial movements with those of athletes, Vertov suggests that machines also possess an expressive visual beauty. Similarly, the motion picture apparatus is equated with the human being as it suddenly begins to "walk" on its own accord: the camera is seen from an anthropomorphic point of view.

The constructivist theater had a "deconstructing" attitude toward the organization of the dramatic performance: instead of viewing a play as an inviolable entity, the performance was considered a "product" composed of many different components the "director-engineer" must arrange according to his or her understanding of the staged event. Meyerhold, for example, often shifted scenes and acts, changing their order and breaking them into numerous shorter episodes, thereby increasing the overall tempo of the dramatic action and providing a mise-en-scène with greater visual impact. In 1922, he staged Aleksandr Ostrovsky's *The Forest,* the chronology of which he intentionally ignored, rearranging the original text according to the principle of dramatic montage. Although he hardly altered the original dialogue, the actual five acts became thirty-three episodes shuffled and demarcated with pantomime interludes to lend contrasting mood and pace. The deconstructed composition of *The Man with the Movie Camera* is based on the same constructivist as well as futurist principle of creating a nonsequential structure that reflects the essence of an urban environment and the dynamism of a technological age.*

Vertov's early concept of montage, even before 1920, drew extensively on the constructivist concept of mechanical rhythm. In 1919, he wrote that all filmmakers must treat the film footage — the recorded "life-facts" — according to their ideological views, expressing their personal attitudes toward the realities presented in the individual shots then restructured through montage. On this point, Vertov differed with most of the other Soviet futurist and constructivist artists, who insisted on the absolute dominance of "facts" in art, and sought to eliminate any subjective interpretation. Vertov was less inclined to restrict his filmmaking to such a factual approach and instead strove to achieve a balance between an authentic representation and "aesthetic" reconstruction of the external world. In doing so, he merged his "Film-Truth" principle of respecting the authenticity of each separate shot with his "Film-Eye" method, which requires a cinematic recreation of events through editing. This dialectical synthesis underlies the construction of the most dynamic sequences in *The Man with the Movie Camera,* especially the formal design of the shots (see Chapter III) and the suppression of their representational outlook by the reduced duration of their appearance on the screen. Even Lev Kuleshov, who at the beginning of his film career was strongly influenced by futurist and constructivist ideas, and who, in 1922, wrote that the "essence of film lies in its composition, as well as in the alteration of the photographed pieces/shots," that "for the organization of impressions it is not important what is shot in a given piece, but how the pieces in a film alternate with one another, how they are structured,"[10] even he complied in practice with a more orthodox concept of montage and shot composition than one might expect after reading his theoretical essays. Vertov repeatedly emphasized that theory and practice should be united: in his manifestos (often conceived as introductions to his films), he emphasized the *kinoks'* duty to prepare the audience for a novel visual experience provided by the camera's "geometrical extraction of movements"[11] from external reality.

Constructivist theory exerted considerable influence on avant-garde architecture, especially in the works of Mozes Ginsburg, the Vesnin brothers, and Vladimir Tatlin.† Concerning themselves more with

---

* For more information on Meyerhold's theory of "biomechanics" and its relationship to "Taylorism," see Edward Braun, *The Theater of Meyerhold* (New York: Drama Book Specialists, 1979).
† For more information on Russian avant-garde architecture, see Anatole Kopp, *Town and Revolution,* trans. T. Burton (New York: George Braziller, 1970). Characteristically, like all other avant-garde achievements, those architectural styles that were most revolu-

structure than with decoration, these architects sought to expose the architectonic shapes expressive of functional aspects rather than to cloak a form with columns or other structural embellishments. The most extraordinary expression of this "purism" was Tatlin's unrealized Monument to the Third International, which he proposed in 1920. This colossal structure was envisioned to be twice as tall as the Empire State Building, with certain parts designed to move during the course of a year or a month, while the uppermost cube was to complete a full rotation around its axis each day. In designing the monument, Tatlin followed the formalist concept of "baring the device" [obnazhenie priema] whose basic function was to make the viewer conscious of the architectural structure and the attached elements moving within its space as components unto themselves, rather than as prefabricated units creating a generically functional whole.*

Vertov's attitude toward cinema, as evidenced in The Man with the Movie Camera, stems from a similar commitment to the examination of the mechanisms at work within a film. In an attempt to explicate his concept of cinema as the "art of organizing the movement of objects in space," Vertov underscored not only the movement of objects before the camera through rhythmic fragmentation but also the movements of the recording apparatus itself – the movie camera. Just as Tatlin strove to convey the building's relation to the passage of time, Vertov decided to reveal the multifaceted procedure of cinematic creation to the audience by showing the camera directly recording events, and by acquainting the viewer with the processes of editing and projecting film images. Thus, the viewer's attention is shifted from the object being recorded to the actual process of recording the "life-fact," substantially increasing the spectator's awareness of the cinematic devices being employed. Whether it is lighting, montage, camera angle, fast or slow motion, freeze-frame, flicker effect, or any other technique, the manifestation of the actual filmmaking forces the viewer to acknowledge the motion picture as reconstructed reality rather than its representational reflection.

Annette Michelson points to the similarity between Vertov and two other filmmakers of the period, Jean Epstein and Laszlo Moholy-Nagy.[12] Epstein's call for "the revision of perception," as well as his

tionary at the beginning of the 1920s (especially "rational functionalism") were declared "bourgeois" at the beginning of the 1930s and replaced by the clumsy Stalinist pseudo-classical style.

* "Baring the device" [obnazhenie priema] is a formalist principle intended to make the perceiver aware of the expressive means unique to the given medium, and thus direct the perceiver's attention to the nonnarrative aspect of the work, its formal structure. See Viktor Shklovsky's definition in his seminal article, "Art As Device" [Iskusstvo kako priem], included in Poetics: A Collection of Articles On the Theory of Poetic Language II [Poetika: Sbornik po teorii poeticheskogo iazyka II] (Petrograd: 1919), pp. 101–14.

particular interest in slow motion as "a new range of dramaturgy," and Nagy's concept of the camera as a "supplement of the eye," as well as his rejection of "dramatic action," have, indeed, much in common with Vertov's theoretical views. Yet the most evident kinship between Vertov and Moholy-Nagy can be found in the structure of Nagy's 1922 film script, *Dynamics of a Metropolis*,[13] written in a typical constructivist manner. The presentation of concrete details depicting factories, buildings, and traffic in a big city, the indication of shooting angles, montage pace, and camera movement, even the graphic display of lines in Nagy's script, all this is reminiscent of Vertov's unrealized scripts cited later in this chapter.

The constructivist photomontage is based upon the principle of self-reference, and it precedes the emergence of self-referential cinema. In the early 1920s, Aleksandr Rodchenko produced extraordinary photomontage compositions with snapshots of everyday events that either he or someone else had taken and subsequently combined into new photographic structures. The freedom to deconstruct the individual photographs and reconstruct them into a new order allowed Rodchenko to go beyond the customary meanings derived from ordinary stills. *The Man with the Movie Camera* draws on the same principle: the newsreel shots are used in it as "basic material" [*osnovnoi material*] transformed through a "montage way of seeing" [*montazhnoe vizhu*] or a "concentrated seeing" [*kontsentrirovannoe vizhu*] into a new cinematic vision. But Vertov did not limit his cinematic vision to the visual aspects of reality. As a complement to the "Film-Eye" [*Kinoglaz*], he introduced the "Radio-Eye" [*Radioglaz*] method, which implies the "montage way of film-hearing" [*montazhnoe kinoslyshu*] and which acknowledges Vertov's concept of montage as a dual "cinematic organization" [*kinoorganizovanie*] of the "Film-Eye" and the "Radio-Ear" [*Radioukho*].[14]

Rodchenko's concept of photomontage relates to *The Man with the Movie Camera* in yet another important respect. Like other constructivists, Rodchenko emphasized the self-referential aspect of the photograph achieved by the dualistic relationship between the image's content and the means by which the image is constructed. He suggested that the photographer should find the most expressive viewpoint that would alert the viewer to the potential of the medium.[15] Implicit in this approach is the formalist method of "defamiliarization," which entails depiction of a familiar environment in an unusual way, thus provoking the viewer to experience an unconventional perception of the world. Inspired by Rodchenko's work as well as by similar experiments in formalist poetry, Viktor Shklovsky invented the self-referential terms "making-it-difficult" [*zatrudnenie*] and "making-it-strange" [*ostranenie*].* In his article "Art as Device," Shklovsky explains that the poetic structure should be "difficult" and "strange" in order to stimulate the reader to discover subtle and often unlikely meanings that are obscured by the convention of everyday speech.[16] In line with this principle, Rodchenko's most experimental photographs employ extreme low-angle shots of buildings, smokestacks, bridges, trees, and contrasting photographic texture, often with unusual light-_ng, that would transform ordinary objects into symbolic visual signs. John Bowlt notes that it is possible "to infer that Vertov borrowed some of Rodchenko's photographic methods... [for] his extreme camera angles... in *The Man with the Movie Camera.*"[17] This observation is reiterated by Camilla Gray who links Rodchenko's "constructivist photographic method" to Vertov's film style, "for example, in the catching of movement at its height... [and] the movement of maximum drama obtained by a typically constructivist low-angled shot."[18] Vertov's films do abound with low-angle shots and graphic compositions that emphasize the architectural aspects of the photographed object and emphasize its dynamic features.

Rodchenko collaborated with Vertov on several of the *kinoks'* projects, including the production of two posters, one for the *Film-Eye* series (1924), the other for *One Sixth of the World* (1926). The two men first met while contributing to Aleksei Gan's constructivist journal *Kinofot* in 1922. It is reasonable to suspect that, as the designer of several issues of the journal *LEF*,† Rodchenko "showed the path of revolutionary Soviet cinema to Dziga Vertov, Lev Kuleshov, and Sergei Eisenstein," as suggested by Viktor Shklovsky.[19] In addition, Rodchenko was responsible for the eccentric graphic layout of Vertov's early manifesto, "*Kinoks*. Revolution," published in *LEF* near the end of 1923. One year earlier, Rodchenko designed the unconventional intertitles in the *Film-Truth* series, as indicated in an unsigned article on constructivism published in *LEF:*

---

* The concept of "making-it-strange" [*ostranenie*] can be related to Brecht's principle of "alienation" [*Verfremdungseffekt*]. This similarity in their theoretical attitudes supports the claim that Brecht developed his concept of alienation under the infuence of Russian formalist theory.

† LEF stands for the "Left Front of Art" [*Levii front iskusstva*]. The journal *LEF* first appeared in a series of seven issues (March 1923–August 1924), with Vladimir Mayakovsky as the editor-in-chief. The second series, consisting of twelve issues, retitled *Novyi LEF* [*The New LEF*], ran from January 1927 through December 1928. Mayakovsky continued to function as the editor-in-chief of the new series only for the first seven issues, after which Sergei Tretyakov succeeded him. Mayakovsky left the journal due to his disagreement with the group regarding the question of joining RAPP, an official organization including traditionally oriented writers, most of them ardent proponents of socialist realism. For more information about socialist realism see Marc Slonim, *Soviet Russian Literature* (New York: Oxford University Press, 1964).

Rodchenko conceived the intertitles as an intrinsic part of the film itself, designing them according to the needs of montage and the script. He introduced three new ways of using intertitles: plastering them grossly enlarged in a haphazard fashion across the screen, using contrasting styles, and animating the letters spatially, so that the written text becomes an organic part of the film instead of its deadspot.[20]

The anonymous writer of this article points to Rodchenko's innate feeling for rhythm, which is also an essential feature of Vertov's montage style. Vertov and Svilova carefully developed each sequence of *The Man with the Movie Camera* according to "its own rhythm stolen from no one . . . [and] through the actual movement of real things,"[21] while he and Kaufman used various shooting devices to make their shots visually dynamic and of high contrast, often emphasizing the particular graphic pattern dominating the frame.

In 1923, El Lissitzky and Ilya Ehrenburg launched the idea of "art as an object" [*iskusstvo kak veshch'*], claiming that "every organized work – whether it be a house, a poem, or a picture – is an object directed toward a particular end which is calculated not to turn people away from reality, but to summon them to make their own contributions to social life."[22] To promulgate this socioaesthetic attitude, they founded the journal *Veshch'/Gegenstand/Object* (1922) whose title indicates the international aspiration of the movement. Following the constructivist ideas in his photographic experiments, Lissitzky often depicted mechanical tools as part of the photograph's graphic design; for example, "The Constructor" (1924), his self-portrait, is composed of several superimpositions of a head, hand, and compass, symbolizing the constructivist view of the artist as engineer, while the head is surrounded by a circular shape, which suggests a unification between the mind of man and the tools he employs. In *The Man with the Movie Camera*, an almost identical conjunction between the worker and the machine is achieved by a superimposition of the smiling face of a working woman and the circular form of a rotating spindle machine. Throughout the film, circular graphic forms recur in many of Vertov's and Kaufman's shots depicting the industrial environment, communication, and city traffic. In close-ups of the camera lens and the human eye (sometimes both present at once), the circular form takes on a metaphorical meaning as it reiterates the constructivist belief that the amalgamation of human and mechanical forces can "decipher the visible world as well as the invisible."[23] With this belief, Vertov urged his *kinok*s to handle the camera as an extension of their bodies and senses (an attitude accepted by certain modern experimental filmmakers). The same attitude pervades Vertov's 1923 manifesto "*Kinok*s. Revolution" in which, identifying himself with the camera, Vertov exclaims: "I, a machine, am showing you a world, the likes of which only I can see.... My road leads toward the creation of a fresh perception of the world.... I decipher, in a new way, a world unknown to you."[24]

The unorthodox use of the camera and even more unconventional approach to montage allowed Vertov, Kaufman, and Svilova to construct what Vertov termed the "autonomous film-thing" or the "absolute vision" conveyed by every existing optical means – above all by "the camera experimenting in space and time."[25] The ultimate result of this attitude was *The Man with the Movie Camera,* a work in which Vertov integrated his "Film-Eye" method with the "Film-Truth" principle, and produced the most constructivist film in the history of cinema, an achievement – conceptually and creatively – ahead of its time.

"Art of fact"

The *kinoks'* ideas and achievements attracted the attention of constructivist critics, most of whom hailed cinema as *the* medium of the modern age. The most militant among them was Aleksei Gan who founded the first Soviet film journal, *Kinofot* (1922), and used it as a platform for propagandizing his extreme views of cinema as a "factual" art. Appealing to the Soviet constructivist artists in his book *Constructivism* (1922), Gan contended that the first task confronting artists in the new society was "to educate the workers to accept art as an active social force, and to help them come to grips with the everyday problems that rise at every turn of the revolutionary road."* Expanding this extremely political attitude toward art, Gan wrote another essay six years later, entitled "Constructivism in Cinema," outlining the political function cinema should play in society:

Film which demonstrates real life in a documentary manner – not theatrical film playing at life – that is what the new cinematic production should be.... But it is not enough to link individual moments of episodic phenomena of life through montage. The most unexpected accidents, occurrences, and events are always connected organically with the fundamental root of social reality.... Only on this basis can one construct a vivid film of dynamic and concrete reality that substantially departs from the superficial newsreel.[26]

This proclamation led Vertov to name Gan "the first shoemaker of Russian cinema" [*pervyi sapozhnik ruskoi kinematografii*], an occupation he deemed more honest than that of an "artist of Russian cinema" [*artist russkoi kinematografii*] or of "the priests of art" [*zhretsy iskusstva*] who continued to dominate the Soviet film industry. Vertov found

---

* Aleksei Gan, *Constructivism [Konstruktivizm]* (Tver: Tver'skoe izdatel' stvo, 1923), p. 54. The book is reprinted by Edizione de la Scorpione (Milano, 1977). In addition to being the editor of the journal *Kinofot,* Gan also made a documentary film, *The Island of the Young Pioneers [Ostrov Pionerov,* 1924], depicting the life of juvenile deliquents [*besprizornye*] in a working youth camp.

no distinction between so-called manual and creative work: he claimed that "honest filmmakers" produce equally useful objects, "just as do carpenters [*plotniki*] and cobblers [*sapozhniki*]."[27] In contrast, he ridiculed the traditional film directors, calling them "shoeshiners" [*chistilniki sapog*] who "superficially polish" everyday reality, "overcasting the [viewer's] eyes and mind with a sweet fog."[28]

It is reflective of their shared attitudes toward graphic art and visual arrangement that the design of Gan's *Constructivism* was identical to Rodchenko's layout for Vertov's manifesto "Kinoks. Revolution," published one year later in *LEF* (1923). The use of varying type fonts and the boxing of important portions of the article on the page reflect a futuristic inclination toward stylistic excess, as well as a constructivist tendency to link content – in an extricable way – with visual presentation, which shapes the message of the text in its own manner. By focusing on the stylistic rendition and formal arrangement of the text, Gan strove to communicate his ideological tenets according to which artistic "products" should, above all, serve the needs of the people. The same political commitment was to be required of all socialist "workers in art," including filmmakers who where expected to produce "things" in no way exceptional or distinct from those made by factory workers. Vertov took a similar view in referring to documentary films as "film-things," which he likened to buildings, while discussing his *Film-Truth* series:

Film-Truth is made of material as a house is made of bricks. Using bricks, one can make an oven, the Kremlin wall, and many other things. From the filmed material [shots], one can construct different film-things. Just as one needs good bricks to make a good house, so one needs good film material to organize a good film.[29]

Vertov's equation of film shots to bricks and his comparison of the filmmaker to the mason can be seen as an expansion of Gan's idea that the photographed events must be used as "masonry" for building the new society through the reorganization of reality according to political needs and the filmmaker's ideological standpoint. Obviously, Vertov's term "film-thing" [*kinoveshch*] is different from Eisenstein's term "film-image" [*kinoobraz*], which implies not only the montage juxtaposition of the shots but primarily their pictorial execution according to the principles of the plastic arts. The "Film-Eye" method, however, is exclusively concerned with the process of montage, whereas the photographic execution (the process of capturing "life-unawares") constitutes the "Film-Truth" principle.

The publication of Gan's *Constructivism* coincided with the appearance of Vertov's most important project, the *Film-Truth* series which opened on June 5, 1922, introducing a radically new concept of newsreel production. In his 1922 article "Cinematograph and Cinema," Gan stated that the cinematograph, as a mechanical tool, had been "constantly exploited" in bourgeois society for recording theatrical events; hence, he demanded that, in the new socialist environment, it be used as a "creative vehicle for witnessing everyday life, a conscious extension of the proletarian state."[30] Only with such an ideological attitude toward the cinematographic apparatus, insisted Gan, could the filmmakers produce authentic cinema [kinematografiya]. In his most important essay, "Long Live the Demonstration of Everyday Life" (1923), he immediately singled out Vertov's Film-Truth series as a genuine demonstration of "kinematografiya," praising it as an exemplary cinematic expression of the constructivist worldview, objectively demonstrating the technical qualities of cinema through the "direct recording of actual socialist processes and their dynamics without the outside aid of the high-priests of absolute art." At the same time, Gan urged the kinoks to "construct films based on reality and, by means of montage, to extract the maximum truth from life-facts presented on the screen."[31]

Gan saw "kinematografiya" as the ideal medium to utilize what he called tectonics ("the essential component of the constructivist method"), which could allow artists to escape from the "dead end of traditional arts' aestheticizing professionalism," and move instead toward active artistic expression reflective of an "overall communist construction."[32] At first sight, it seems that the concept of tectonics was incongruous with the suprematist insistance on the nonobjective, abstract, and self-referential aspects of art/work and its articulation on the basis of composition, volume, interrelationship of masses, speed and direction of movement; yet, suprematists fought against the traditional roster of the arts on the same front as constructivists, repelling worn-out aesthetic concepts through elaborate and scientifically founded formal research. Gan's tectonics actually represented one of the three constructivist principles (together with "textures as forms of supply" and "construction laws as forms of surface resolution") and were directly related to the ideological context of dialectical materialism and its function in the reconstruction of society – from capitalist to communist.

Every social structure, inevitably, must have its own "constructive tectonics," and cinema is capable of playing a major role in the transition from one social order to another. In post revolutionary Russia, to achieve the type of cinema that could contribute to the ideological struggle, it was necessary, above all, to develop a new theoretical concept based on an aesthetic attitude totally different from that which governed the obsolete bourgeois film. Gan was fully aware that it was "hard to erase 'art' from the screen," because general audiences had been for centuries "mesmerized," their brains atrophied, by bourgeois photoplays. Consequently, he found Vertov's work to be in the proper spirit with the constructivist view, especially the *Film-Truth* series no. 13, in which not only the visual aspect was in accordance with "cinema of fact," but even intertitles, produced by the constructivist Rodchenko, were conceived as "objects." What follows is Gan's — obviously constructivist — interpretation of *Film-Truth* no. 13:

LENIN
All over the screen.
The screen word!
Speaking film
in cinematic language.
Titles like electric wires,
like conductors that illuminate
reality on the screen.

And all that we see in focus,
all that happens on the streets,
the squares, the windows, posters.
And we hear as they
CHEER
all, all, all

TO THE $\dfrac{\text{IN} \mid \text{TER}}{\text{NATI} \mid \text{ONAL}}$

and proletarian
OCTOBER.
And we see airplanes and, at the same time, watch from them the earth below, but the earth flies as there appear streets and houses seen from another view, and newspapers with words of comrade

Trotsky, words that have both spatial and temporal meaning:

"We exist, but they do not recognize us."
"We fight, and fight not to the life, but to the death, while we do not hide anything."
Graves in Astrakhan, shovels bury

the bodies of our heroes fallen at

LENIN
Vo ves' ekran.
Ekrannoe slovo!
Govoriashshii kinematograf
kinematograficheskim iazykom.
Nadpis' kak elektricheskii schnur,
kak provodnik cherez kotoryi
pitaetsia ekran svetiashcheisis
deistvenost'iu.
I my sve - vidim v fokuse,
kak zhili i kak zhivut ulitsy,
ploshchadi, vitriny, plakaty.
I slyshim kak oni
ZOVUT
vsekh, vsekh, vsekh

K $\dfrac{\text{MI} \mid \text{RO}}{\text{VO} \mid \text{MU}}$

k proletarskomu
OKTIABRIU.
I my vidim aeroplany i odnovremenno smotrim
s nikh vniz na zemliu, a zemljia bezhit,
nesutsia v novom plane ulitsy, doma, gazety
i chetkaia s prostranstvennym smyslom i vremennym
taktom slova tovarishcha Trotskogo:

"My sushchestvuem, a oni nas ne zamechaiut."
"My borimsia i borimsia ne na zhizn', a na smert' i ne skrivaem nichego."

Groby v Astrakhani, lopaty zasypiaiushchie tela
tela nashikh pogibshchikh geroev v

Kronshtadt, for a moment the banners	Kronshtate, sklonennye znamena v moment
are at half-mast in Minsk. We take	pogrebennii v Minske. My snimaem golovnye
off our hats. Moscovites, standing	ubory. Eto delaiut moskvichi na naberezhnoi
on the Moskva River, do the same.	Moskvy-reke.
Again, scores of banners and throngs	Snova znamena vrest i ljudi stremitel'no
of people flood into Red Square.	idut ko Krasnuiu ploshchad'.
A portrait of Barbolin, the worker	Portret rabochego Barbolina, ubitogo u
killed in 1917.	1917 godu.
A placard comes closer:	Naplivaet plakard:
"Glory to the partisans!"	"Slava bortsam!"
Then a slow montage unfolds our	A dal'she razvorachivaetsia v spoko- inom montazh
achievements and our victories	nashie zavoevaniia, nasha pobeda i
and our unyielding alliance to	nashe nekolebimoe ravnenie na
the machine.	mashinu.
Yes, cinema is great stuff!	Da, velikoe delo kinematografiia!
Splendid is the *Film-Truth*.	Horoshaia trinadtsataia Kino-Pravda.[33]

Gan's description of Vertov's newsreel perfectly reflects both the constructivist way of expressing ideas (note the montagelike presentation of the events seen on the screen) as well as the dynamic structure of Vertov's *Film-Truth* series (note how various events, occurring in different places, are juxtaposed on an associative principle to convey an ideological message). One can rightly assume that this literary way of conveying images as connotative signs had an inevitable influence on the formation of Soviet montage concepts. Even the graphic presentation of this and other articles in Gan's *Kinofot* were designed with a strong emphasis on the constructivist concept of typography: the meaning of words can be enhanced and expanded by the way they are designed and laid out on the page.

The Soviet film scholar Tamara Selezneva contends that Gan's struggle for "cinema of fact" played a major role in the evolution of early Soviet film theory, and that — although the relationship between Vertov and Gan was later frought with a number of disagreements regarding the function of ideology in art — "they always stuck together in their resistance to the 'threat' of narrative cinema, which they discredited as masquerading itself in the form of newsreels, particularly in the work of Eisenstein."[34] Gan's radical attitude toward art coincided with the style of Vertov's early newsreels, but soon the ideological distance between the two men became evident. Gan retained his extreme view of cinema as an aggressive political force, whereas Vertov modified the militancy of his stance, especially with respect to cinematic language, as he showed an interest in the structural and aesthetic aspects of the medium. Yet, as Selezneva points out, despite the ideological rift, Gan and Vertov continued to share a common opposition to staged films, particularly those that used nonprofessional actors. In 1923, Gan denounced fictional, narrative, illusionistic, and "fabricated art" in the most belligerent manner:

> Let us release our speculative energy and transform the healthy bases of art into the field of practical construction.... We declare ourselves irreconcilable with Art since it is intrinsically linked with theology, metaphysics, and mysticism ... Death to ART.[35]

Gan condemned the "enemies" of socialist art as a reactionary force that sought to aid in the evasion of reality rather than in its confrontation. "Art of fact" was to replace traditional art tainted with such escapism, which − "through film mesmerization" − paralyzed the conscious (mental) activity of its consumers. A similar fervor characterized the slogans Vertov espoused early in his career. Addressing the *kinok*s at the June 9, 1924, conference of their cooperative, Vertov exclaimed "the Babylonian tower of art will be destroyed by us."[36] From the beginning, he considered fictional movies antithetical to the development of a true "cinema of fact," and, like Gan, rejected the rearrangement of events (mise-en-scène), which, according to Vertov, reduces the film to a "surrogate of life" [*surogaty zhizni*]. True reality, he contended, should not reside in "photoplays, [which] tickle nerves, but in 'Film-Eye,' [which] helps one to see."[37] To exemplify this statement, he drew a symbolic distinction between "Petrushka" and "Life" − the former implying the artificiality of the theater, the latter representing the actual domain of cinema.* Vertov's manifesto "*Kinok*s. Revolution," which was aimed at initiating a new direction in the Goskino production company, clearly outlined similar goals for the revolutionary cinema:

> From today on, there will be no need for the
> psychological and detective drama.
> From today on, cinema will not need theatrical
> productions recorded on a film strip.
> From today on, there will be no more representation
> of Dostoevsky or Nat Pinkerton.

---

* Vertov, " 'Film-Eye' − Petrushka or Life" (1926) [*Kinoglaz − Petrushka ili zhizn'*], Articles, p. 90. This is a separate part of the article "Film-Eye," which contains several additional parts under different titles. Petrushka is a popular character in the Russian puppet theater whose name symbolizes theatrical artificiality.

Everything will be included in the new concept of
newsreels.
. . .
The "Film-Eye" is challenging the visual
presentation of reality as seen by the human eye.
The "Film-Eye" is proposing its own way of seeing.
The *kinok*-editor is organizing a new perception of
life's moments for the first time.[38]

The original version of this manifesto, published in *LEF* (no. 3, 1923),
includes an epigraph summarizing more emphatically Vertov's critical
view on Russian film: "I simply want to state that everything we have
produced in cinema until now has been one-hundred percent wrong,
that is to say, absolutely contrary to what we had and have to do."[39]
As one can see, together with Gan, Rodchenko, and Mayakovsky, Vertov was convinced that Soviet cinema needed to be revitalized with a
revolutionary vision, and that this should be accomplished by rejecting the theatrical conventions used to present reality on the screen.

Another important constructivist critic with an acute understanding
of both the theoretical and practical aspects of documentary cinema
was Viktor Pertsov, whose essays (published in *LEF*) established his
reputation as one of the most analytical Soviet film theorists of the
1920s. In his famous article " 'Play' and Demonstration" (1927), Pertsov compares Vertov's films to those of Esther Shub,* another important Soviet documentary filmmaker:

Vertov's film *One Sixth of the World* and Shub's *The Fall of the Romanov Dynasty* and *The Great Road* represent genuine agitational journalism expressed
in a cinematic language. The authentic non-aesthetic impact of these films de-
rives from the real facts which comprise the films' structures. If the cinematic
juxtaposition of facts stimulates emotions, it does not mean that these emotions in and of themselves transform facts in a non-authentic aesthetic structure. We know that in staged films the impact on the audience is provided by
various dramatic devices; however, in unstaged film journalism, the impact is
provided by the rules of rhetoric. It is not a coincidence therefore that Vertov
conceives his films on an oratorical principle. He is a true cinematic orator
who makes his point in the manner dictated by the intrinsic power of the se-

* Esther (Esfir) Shub began her film career as an editor (adaptor) of foreign films distributed in the Soviet Union. Her method of editing had a substantial influence on both
Vertov and Eisenstein. In turn, she claimed that although she had learned many things
from Eisenstein, she considered herself "Vertov's pupil, regardless of our disputes and
disagreements." Shub demonstrated great mastery in her three major compilation films,
The Fall of the Romanov Dynasty [*Padenie dinastii Romanovikh*, 1927], *The Great Road*
[*Velikii put'*, 1927], and *The Russia of Nicholai II and Lev Tolstoi* [*Rossia Nikolaia II i
Lev Tolstoi*, 1928]. Shub's memoirs and articles are collected in the book *My Life – Cinema* [*Zhizn' moia – kinematograf*] (Moscow: Iskusstvo, 1972). More information about
Shub and her work can be found in my article, "Esther Shub: Cinema is My Life," *Quart-
erly Review of Film Studies*, no. 4 (Fall 1978), pp. 429–56.

lected facts, thus building a structure which holds the attention of the audience. . . . To edit facts [montage] means to analyze and to synthesize, not to catalogue.[40]

Pertsov's explanation of Vertov's method demonstrates his understanding of the two crucial aspects of Vertov's work: first, the evident ontological authenticity of each separate shot ("the non-aesthetic impact of the shot"), and second, the montage organization of the footage ("building a structure"), by which the filmmaker reconstitutes the spatiotemporal aspect of reality and conveys his message ("makes his point") while "holding the attention of the audience." It is difficult to find a more precise and equally sensitive elaboration of Vertov's directorial style even in contemporary critical literature.

Vertov's films drew the attention of another constructivist critic affiliated with the *LEF* circle, Sergei Ermolinsky, who emphasized the different attitudes in early Soviet "cinematographic journalism" that stemmed from the methods of "montage analysis and synthesis" as practiced by Vertov and Shub. Ermolinsky noted that Shub assembled footage as she found it in film archives, whereas Vertov *de*constructed the footage in order to achieve a new meaning and to convey his viewpoint. Shub's editorial strategy, Ermolinsky concluded, can be described as a faithful preservation of original newsreels – hence the long and unbroken (continuous) sequential takes in her films accompanied by descriptive intertitles. According to Ermolinsky, "the documentary shot was for Shub the actual goal," while "for Vertov it was always a means."[41] A further distinction between the two filmmakers, Ermolinsky contended, was the difference in their attitudes toward the film image as recorded by the camera. Vertov "threw himself on the given material, cutting it into numerous pieces, thus subordinating it to his imagination, while Shub regarded each piece [shot] as to a self-sufficient, autonomous entity."[42] Ermolinsky's astute analysis substantiated his characterization of Shub and Vertov as the two most significant documentary filmmakers of the silent era. From today's perspective, it is clear that Shub was the initiator of the "compilation film" genre, whereas Vertov was the precursor of the modern cinéma vérité style in its most genuine form.

To encourage a greater critical appreciation of cinema, the journal *Novyi LEF* organized panels that addressed the specific role of film in society. The most exemplary of these discussions was published in the December 1927 issue of the journal, under the title *"LEF* and Film." The panel, which included Osip Brik, Sergei Tretyakov, Viktor Shklovsky, and Esther Shub, reached the consensus that the controversy between staged and unstaged film constituted "the basic issue of contemporary cinema."[43] They concluded that Vertov and Shub produced "true cinema of fact," as opposed to Eisenstein who moved to-

ward "cinema of fiction." Tretyakov summarized the discussion, noting that ontological authenticity in cinema should be measured by the extent to which reality is presented and/or transformed on the screen:

Based on the degree of transformation, filmed material falls into three basic groups. First, candidly filmed material, i.e. facts caught unawares; second, arranged material, i.e. events found in reality and molded by the filmmaker to a certain extent; and third, staged material, i.e. dramatic and narrative situations that are pre-scripted and then entirely acted out before the camera. The candid shots are, without exception, caught "off guard." Such is Vertov's "Life-Caught-Unawares." One can find a minimum of deformation in it, which does not mean that candidly filmed material lacks its own gradations of transformation.[44]

This summary reveals the subjectivity with which even the most committed advocates of "factual art" viewed the cinematic "deformation" of life's raw material; yet, subjectivity was allowed so long as it helped enhance the film's ideological meaning. According to the *Novyi LEF* panelists, only Vertov and Shub presented reality on the screen candidly, whereas Ermler, Pudovkin, and Eisenstein distorted reality to the point of misrepresenting life, a practice that became, as Mayakovsky termed it, "disgusting" and "outrageous," referring to the quasi-documentary presentation of Lenin in Eisenstein's *October*.[45]

In another discussion published in *Novyi LEF* of April 1928, Vertov's film *The Eleventh Year* and Eisenstein's *October* were directly compared. The panel, which called itself "The *LEF* Ring" (implying an "arena" of ideological contest), composed of Brik, Pertsov, and Shklovsky, unanimously proclaimed Vertov's film "outstanding" for its straightforward rendering of "life facticity" and "historial accuracy." At the same time, *October* was characterized by Brik as "Eisenstein's hopeless effort to jump over his own head."[46] The remark was meant to sting, since Brik condescendingly referred to Eisenstein as the "young director," although he was thirty, and *October* was his third film. But neither was Vertov immune to the panel's harsh criticisms, especially in Shklovsky's remarks stating that Vertov's insertion of metaphorical intertitles in *The Eleventh Year* not only incurred redundancies ("doubling the data") but also obscured the film's ideological meaning ("blurring the message"). The panelists concluded their discussion by establishing guidelines for "cinema of fact" (the unstaged film) as opposed to "cinema of mesmerization" (the staged film).

Struggles with NEP

The *LEF* critics adamantly opposed entertainment cinema even after Lenin had introduced the NEP policy,* which encouraged commercial film production and promoted the import of foreign trivial melodra-

* NEP stands for "New Economic Policy" [*Novaia ekonomskaia politika*], defined during

mas. As the editor of *Novyi LEF,* Tretyakov stated that during the NEP period American entertainment movies had a "devastating effect" on Soviet film. While in the early twenties the great American classic filmmakers inspired Kuleshov, Pudovkin, and Eisenstein to develop new revolutionary montage concepts, near the end of the decade many Soviet directors began to imitate Hollywood's conventional production, thus "contributing to a Pickfordization and Fordization of the workers' way of life."[47] This metaphorical warning went unheeded, however, because Lenin, suddenly, had concluded that a "reasonable dose" of entertainment films could function as an effective panacea for the masses, adding variety to the film repertory while yielding greater profits. The formula for achieving an appropriate "balance" between entertainment films and newsreel propaganda became known as the "Leninist Proportion,"* which commercial distributors immediately took as an excuse for making concessions to popular taste. With its obvious eclecticism, the Leninist Proportion contained contradicting suggestions, one demanding that Soviet film production "should begin with newsreel," and the other stating that if "good newsreels and serious educational films exist, then it doesn't matter if some useless film of the more or less usual sort is shown to attract an audience."[48] Naturally, the producers and distributors grabbed the second suggestion while almost totally neglecting the first one. As a result, experimental filmmaking became extremely difficult, while the NEP audience [*nepmanovska auditoriia*] was coddled by cheap imported films, much to the chagrin of the *kinoks* and the *LEFists.*[49]

Vertov's diaries reveal how he continued to urge his *kinoks* to make films with pertinent ideological substance in order to "give proletariats of all countries the opportunity to see, hear, and understand each other better."[50] Not surprisingly, the Leninist Proportion proved to be at odds with Vertov's ideals about revolutionary cinema, but his concept of documentary film was equally antagonistic to Stalin's promotion of blatant political propaganda. Consequently, Vertov put forth a new "proportion" in his 1939 article "In Defense of the Newsreel," emphasizing the necessity to establish legitimate "rights" for both staged and unstaged films, to support the production of films concerned with documentary presentation, and to proscribe "intermediating" [*promezhutechnoi*] and "typage" [*tipazh*] films.[51] Vertov intentionally used the

Lenin's famous speech at the Tenth Congress of the Communist Party (March 1921) when he declared: "We are in a condition of such poverty, ruin, and exhaustion of the productive powers of workers and peasants that everything must be set aside to increase production." Quoted in George Vernadsky, *A History of Russia* (New Haven: Yale University Press, 1954), p. 323.
* Anatoly Lunacharsky claimed that Lenin "emphasized the necessity of establishing a definite proportion between entertainment and educational movies" at the meeting they held in January 1922. *About Film [O kino]*, (Moscow: Iskusstvo 1956), p. 4.

terms "intermediating cinema" and "typage" to focus his criticism of Eisenstein who had introduced them to film theory while applying basic principles of documentary cinema to his staged films. The *LEF* critics considered this method inappropriate for "cinema of fact," thus supporting Vertov's criticism of Eisenstein's films as "staged films in documentary trousers."[52] Mayakovsky attacked Eisenstein's concept of typage publicly, denouncing this "most shameful method" of depicting historical personalities on the screen.*

Vertov's contempt for the NEP policy is understandable: he saw it as detrimental to the development of Soviet documentary cinema for which he had fought all his life. Since the Leninist Proportion represented yet another impediment to the growth of the "cinema of fact," Vertov proposed another "balance" in which newsreels and documentary films should constitute forty-five percent of all films distributed, educational and scientific films should make up thirty percent, and entertainment films should account for no more than twenty-five percent.[53] Needless to say, this suggestion hardly received any attention; actually, it had little hope for realization because the NEP mentality, enforced by the state, prevailed in film companies. With unconcealed bitterness, Vertov wrote in his diary:

The official voice of our [state] cinematography, the *Proletarian Film,* issued the following order: either make a transition to the staged film, make your mothers and fathers cry and get rid of your documentary cinema, or we shall destroy you with administrative measures [*unichtozhim vas administrativnimi merami*].[54]

This entry, written one year after the completion of *Three Songs about Lenin* (1934), reflects the frustration Vertov felt during the production and distribution of the film, in spite of its topic and the workers' enthusiastic response immediately after the Moscow opening. In the same section of the diary, symbolically entitled "About My Illness" (1935), Vertov openly revealed the inconveniences endured in the course of making the Lenin film:

The actual shooting in Central Asia took place under the most abnormal circumstances. We worked in constant danger of typhus, with a lack of transportation, and with irregular wages. Often we did not eat for three days, and sometimes we had to repair clocks for the local villagers in order to earn a meal without bread. We had to function covered with flea powder from head to toe, or rubbed with a greasy, smelly liquid which irritated our skin but saved us from the flies. Yet, all the time, we preserved our patience, retaining a strong will, because we did not want to give up. We decided to endure and fight to the finish.[55]

---

* See also note 127.

The difficulties continued throughout the editing of the film, and although Vertov's diary does not provide details about it, there is no doubt that the film was severely censored, since all the archival footage with Trotsky, Zinoviev, Kamenev, and Radek were cut from the final print. Even three years after the film was completed, Stalin personally ordered that an additional 700 feet be inserted at the end, "showing how Stalin was continuing Lenin's work."[56]

All these difficulties, however, did not shake Vertov's confidence that *Three Songs about Lenin* would reestablish documentary film as the most suitable method for reconstructing the revolutionary past and for conveying "Revolutionary Truth." In reality, his expectations were met with a paradoxical resistance. In his article "The Last Experiment," Vertov expressed his fear that the Lenin film was the last experiment of the "Film-Eye" method, since the Soviet film repertory was dominated by "entertainment movies" [*uveselitel'nye kartiny*] and by "translated films" [*perevodnye fil'my*], that is, films that "imitate the languages of theater and literature." Consequently, all the creative attempts at making "original films" [*fil'my originali*] and "author's films" [*avtorskie fil'my*] were "neither financially supported nor artistically encouraged by the government."[57] Surprisingly, on January 11, 1935, one week after his article appeared in *Literaturnaia gazeta*, Vertov received the Order of the Red Star.* However, the fact remains that after *Three Songs about Lenin*, Vertov was not able to make a major film, although he continuously offered his scripts to the Ministry of Cinematography.

By the end of 1938, Vertov had resigned himself to the realization that cinematic experimentation was no longer possible in the Soviet Union and that his own work in the Soviet film industry was considered – by the officials – as "inappropriate." He wondered at one point whether "in this situation" he could reasonably justify "fighting for his personal principles unscrupulously" as most of his colleagues did in order to work in their profession:

Can one conform to whatever modes, the habitual abominable modes – shameful, humiliating, and disgraceful methods – which hypocrites and imposters use all the time? I obviously cannot. . . . As long as I search for truth by means of truth alone.[58]

Similar moral dilemmas haunted Vertov until the end of his life: his initial pursuit of "truth" as a conscious effort to reveal "Life-As-It-Is" had grown into an ethical issue concerning freedom of expression in a

---

* The Order of the Red Star is the third one in the hierarchy of Soviet state honors, the Order of Lenin being the highest of all. Vertov received the honor at the celebration taking place in the Bolshoi Theater, January 11, 1935. Eisenstein received an even less important honor (People's Artist). For more information about this event, see Leyda (*Kino*, p. 319), who participated in the ceremony.

society that was beginning to stifle all individual accomplishments that did not comply with political dictates. As with all true artists, Vertov could not sacrifice his artistic freedom for political pragmatism, and he found himself isolated from the film community.

Vertov and Mayakovsky

From his student days, Vertov was fascinated by Mayakovsky's poetry, his innovations in language and prosodic style – especially his experiments with auditory effects and the musical rhythm of poetic structure. While studying psychology at the Psycho-Neurological Institute in Petrograd, Vertov had expended great effort, examining in practice the effects of direct sound recordings of auditory signals. Much like Mayakovsky, Vertov explored the expressive possibilities of sound and its role in the creation of what he called "a new type of art – the art of life as it is – that could contribute to the unstaged documentary film and the newsreel."[59] Also at this time, Mayakovsky delivered public readings in various cities including Petrograd; hence, it is no surprise that Mayakovsky's revolutionary poetry became inspirational to Vertov's research on aural comprehension and visual perception.

A brief autobiographical sketch reveals how Vertov's experiments with sound led him to his interest in cinema, as he began to understand that the two media – radio and film – were closely related. Reflecting on those days of youthful experimentation, Vertov emphasized his fascination with the possibility of "capturing" the auditory and visual aspects of everyday life:

From my childhood, I was interested in various means for making documentary recordings of the exterior world of sound through montage, stenographic recordings, phonographic recordings, etc. In my "Laboratory of Hearing," I created documentary compositions as well as literary-musical montages of words. I was particularly interested in the possibilities of the motion picture camera, its capacity to register segments of life as a true chronicle and newsreel of vanishing and irrevocable events occurring in reality.[60]

The act of recording as well as rearranging the perceptual elements of the visual and auditory world was of paramount importance for Vertov. His early experiments, in which recorded sounds were cut up and restructured according to musical rhythm, bear a striking resemblance to the linguistic theories and experiments done by the Soviet formalists, especially their investigation of poetic structure, the musical function of words, and the subliminal impact of syntax. The formalists' discoveries and their subsequent theories concerning the auditory dynamics of prosody helped futurist poets to realize that the resonance of the arranged words could alter and expand the thematic meaning of a stanza so much that a poem could be fully grasped only when read aloud in an appropriate tone of voice and at a particular pace. Similarly, as the forthcoming analysis of the montage structure of *The Man with the Movie Camera* will prove, it is the tempo of visual changes occurring on the screen that makes this film such an exciting visual experience. Many of these optical beats are not directly perceptible because their impulses are below the threshold of consciousness, but even though the spectators react to them subliminally, these impulses contribute to the sequence's meaning.

The rhythmic organization of words to achieve a musical impact in poetry was of exceptional importance to Mayakovsky as well. In his essay "How to Make Verses" (1926), he emphasized the precedence not only of line length but also of the "transitional words" that connect one line with the next. Mayakovsky urged his fellow poets to take advantage of all the formal possibilities available to them, or, as he put it, to give "all the rights of citizenship to the new language, to the cry instead of the melody, to the beat of drums instead of a lullaby."[61] If a poem was intended to reflect the dynamism of the new technological age, then, Mayakovsky insisted, its style and, even more, its formal structure should be equally "energetic"; otherwise, the poem would merely echo the mawkish and oldfangled [*staromodnii*] conventions of a symbolist-romantic imagination, only to function on the thematic level. The opening stanzas of "Morning" (1912), an early poem in which Mayakovsky isolates various objects from the external world, clearly illustrates the poet's search for a rhythm that is expressive and musical at the same time. The structuring of the lines, some of which consist of only one or one-and-a-half words (!), is reminiscent of Vertov's use of a single frame as a shot or montage unit. In both cases the result is an intensified prosodic or cinematic rhythm.

The morose rain looked askance.	Ugriumyi dozhd' skosil glaza.
And beyond	A za
the well-defined	reshetkoi
grillwork	chotkoi
of the wires' iron through –	zhelezhnoi mysli-provodov
a featherbed.	perina.
And on	I na
it	nee
lightly rest	vstaiushchikh zvezd
the feet of awakening stars.	legko operlis' nogi.
But the per-	No gi-
dition of lanterns,	bel' fonarei
of tsars	tsarei
with the crown of burning gas	v korone gaza
for eyes	dlia glaza
made it painful to take	sdelala bol'noi

| the odorous bouquet of | vrazhduiuschii buket |
| boulevard prostitutes. | bulvarnykh prostitutok.[62] |

In his analysis of this poem, Edward Brown points out that Mayakovsky achieves his rhymes by matching the last two syllables in paired lines, thus building a unique metric beat.[63] Unlike traditional poets, Mayakovsky also creates rhymes by splitting words and placing each half in a different line; this draws the reader's attention to the vocalistic sounding of a word; it also energizes its meaning within the thematic context, which takes on a new, auditory significance. Rather than restrict himself to traditional poetic forms, Mayakovsky expanded the stylistic features of his poetry, much as Vertov was preoccupied with experimenting with image and sound to form his unique cinematic style. Instead of letting the narrative restrictions dictate the arrangement of shots and relationship between sequences in *The Man with the Movie Camera,* Vertov and Svilova based their editing decisions on graphic and visual features, juxtaposing shots in such a way that their compositions match graphically, and only when perceived as part of an overall cinematic structure do these shots reveal their full meaning within the thematic context. This principle of editing, developed from Vertov's "Theory of Intervals,"* draws a lot from the constructivist concept of film as a "building" comprised of many bits and pieces whose ultimate meaning depends on the interrelationship between various components. Applying this concept to silent cinema, Vertov achieved a high degree of cinematic abstraction through the "battle" of different visual structures and movements, producing a "kinetic impact," the basis of *kinesthesia,*† the most unique experience that cinema can provide. He later extended the idea of intervals to his sound films, especially *Enthusiasm,* in which one can detect a contrapuntal relationship not only between image and sound but also between various sounds juxtaposed to each other. Vertov's "Theory of Intervals," aimed at creating primarily visual impulses by "a movement between the pieces [shots] and frames,"[64] has many features in common with the "Rhythmicosyntactic Theory" as defined by Osip Brik in his famous essay "Contributions to the Study of Verse Language."[65] Both theories suggest that the rhythmic beat of a poem or a sequence

---

* Vertov formulated his "Theory of Intervals" as early as 1919, although it was published two years later as part of the "We" manifesto. Later, Vertov elaborated the theory in his article "From 'Film-Eye' to 'Radio-Eye' " (1929). The most important aspect of this theory is its emphasis on the perceptual conflict that occurs between two adjoining shots as the result of cutting "on movement," so that the sequence functions like a musical phrase, with its rhythmic ascent, peak, and decline.

† In his "We" manifesto, Vertov uses the term "kinetic resolution" [*kineticheskoe rezreshenie*], but he actually had in mind what is known today as the kinesthetic impact. For an explanation of this term, as well as the notion of "kinesthesia," see Slavko Vorkapich, "Film as a Visual Language and as a Form of Art," *Film Culture* (Fall 1965), pp. 1–46.

not only supports the thematic meaning but acts as an autonomous structure with its own impact and signification.

Among Vertov's papers in his Moscow archive, there is a "deconstructed" poem that testifies to Vertov's fascination with Mayakovsky's syllabic meter. Written in the mid 1920s, the poem employs a metric pattern typical of Mayakovsky's early poetry (especially "Morning"), with split words that enforce the musical structure of the rhymes. Titled "Mouths Are Gaping Through the Window," the poem is dedicated to the thousands of children who were dying of hunger in drought-stricken areas:

The field is	Pole	
bare.		golo.
Bodies are everywhere	Tel	
as after a snowstorm.		metelitsa.
The year	God	
like a sacrificial lamb		tel'tsem
fell		v grob
into the grave		leg.
Hun-	Go-	
-ger		-lod
long-	do-	
-lasting.		-log.
Mountains of	Gory	
grief.		goria.
While the city looks like		Gorod
a rainbow		radugoi.
I throw	Gorem	
my burning pain		goriu
into the city's		gorodam
face.		v upor.[66]

The alliterative use of entire words ("*gorem*," "*goriu*," "*goro*dam") or only their separate syllables ("go-*lod*," "do-*log*"), the splitting of words ("hun-ger"; "long-lasting"), and their treatment as autonomous lexical units with pertinent signification, and especially the graphic distribution of verses on the page, are clearly influenced by Mayakovsky's metric patterns. The poem can also be related to the formalist principle by which the rhythmic flow of the lines should reveal per se the respective situation or the poet's emotional state, as each word or its severed part triggers an image linked to another image-word in the manner of montage. The aggressive tone of Vertov's poem is paralleled by the staccato pace of its deconstructed lines, a principle Vertov often uses in the climatic portions of his films, by "scattering" the segments of the same shot throughout the sequence.

Mayakovsky produced complex poetic images by breaking up common syntax and by forcing the reader to abandon the rational search for a sequential order and thematic progression in poetry. Similarly, Vertov relied on the intricate juxtaposition and inversion of filmed fragments (shots) with the intention of disrupting the film's linear development and thwarting the reader's narrative expectations. Yuri Lotman's analysis of Mayakovsky's technique emphasizes the innovative and rhetorical figures that make Mayakovsky a most individual poet, a statement one can apply to Vertov with respect to cinema.* Both artists used innovative "communicative structures," whether in words or in images, to transpose the "life-facts" into a new vision of external reality that corresponded to their subjective perception. Above all, they shared an uncompromising attitude toward artistic creation in general, struggling − to the end of their lives − for the legitimate right of the artist to experiment in all media, to search constantly for new expressive means, and to interpret reality according to a personal world view. Vertov saw this search for a novel poetic expression as an exciting confrontation of creative forces.

In his poem "Conversation with a Tax Collector about Poetry," Mayakovsky refers to his rhymes as "a barrel of dynamite" and calls the poetic line "a fuse that's lit" and when "the line smoulders, / the rhyme explodes − / and by a stanza / a city / is blown to bits."[67] In an almost identical fashion, Vertov's and Svilova's cutting produces optical "explosions" at the juncture of two shots. Their juxtaposition of different visual compositions and their insertions of unexpected light flashes (optical pulsations) correspond to Mayakovsky's arrangement of stanzas to shock the readers, to engage them in a novel and unconventional perception of the external world. Mayakovksy talks about the "extracted" and "distilled" tropes, just as Vertov talks about the "concentrated way of seeing and hearing." In his youthful poems, Vertov demonstrated great fascination with futurist rhetoric. In one of these humorous epigrams dedicated to cinema and in opposition to the exploitation of the medium by the commercial entrepreneurs, Vertov unabashedly imitated similar epigrams by Mayakovsky. Intended as a proclamation of the *kinoks*' view of contemporary cinema, this 1917 short poem also informs us about Vertov's early interest in the psychology of perception.

---

* Yuri Lotman is one of the leading contemporary Soviet semiologists involved in extensive research on the relationship between media and the message. His study of cinema, *Film Semiotics and Problems of Film Aesthetics* [*Semiotika kino i problemy kinoestetiki*] (Tatlin: Eesti raamat, 1973), has been translated into English by Mark Suino under the title *Semiotics of Cinema*, published in the series *Michigan Slavic Contributions*, no. 5 (Ann Arbor: University of Michigan, 1973).

Not "Pathé," nor "Gaumont,"	Ne "Pate," ne "Gomon,"
Not this, not about this.	Ne to, ne o tom
The apple should be seen as Newton saw it.	N'iutonom iabloko videt'.
Open eyes to the Universe.	Miru glaza.
So that the ordinary dog	Chtob obychnogo psa
By Pavlov's eye can be seen.	Pavlovskim okom videt'.
We go to the movies	Idem v kino
To blow up the movies,	Vzorvat' kino,
In order to see the movies.	Chtoby kino uvidet.[68]

Vertov's brother, Mikhail Kaufman, explained that this poem was written "in reaction to a popular ad for the 'Pathé Newsreel,' which claimed to know everything and to see everything. . . . Dziga made fun of this ad by indicating that the 'Pathé Newsreel' sees very little and thinks even less."[69] The last three lines of the poem, however, have a broader meaning: they reveal Vertov's revolutionary idea about the "cinema of fact" rising from the ashes of the old movie dramas. His mention of Pavlov, with whose work he was certainly familiar and whose classes he might have attended at the Psycho-Neurological Institute, indicate Vertov's interest in behaviorist concepts of art. One can argue that from the idea of "Pavlov's eye" emerged Vertov's "Film-Eye," with its power to unveil the external world not in a conventional manner (à la "Pathé" or "Gaumont"), but through an analytical penetration into the internal structure of visible reality where, he believed, the true meaning of things and events is concealed. As unsophisticated and simplistic as Vertov's ruptured lines may be, they can be compared to Mayakovsky's own "movie-poems" in which he mocked traditional art and the type of filmmaking the *kinok*s denounced. In the early 1920s, Mayakovsky wrote a short but emphatic poetic aphorism, "Film and Film," which glorified the revolutionary cinema and condemned bourgeois photoplays (film melodramas) by distinguishing between film as entertainment and as an engaged social force:

For you cinema is spectacle	Dlia vas kino – zrelische
For me – a view of the world	Dlia menia – pochti mirosozertsanie
Cinema – conductor of movement	Kino – provodnik dvizheniia
Cinema – innovator of literature	Kino – novator literatury
Cinema – destroyer of aesthetics	Kino – razrushitel' estetiki
Cinema – fearlessness	Kino – besstrashnost'
Cinema – sportsman	Kino – sportsmen
Cinema – distributor of ideas.	Kino – rasseivatel' idei.[70]

Mayakovsky wrote these lines in 1922, at the time when Vertov's *Film-Truth* series had already attained considerable popularity. At this juncture it should also be noted that Mayakovsky had shown quite a different attitude toward film *before* the revolution. In his first article on cinema, written in 1913, Mayakovsky questioned whether contem-

porary theater could survive competition from the cinema, and postu-
lated that theater should learn from film how to rid itself of the artificiality and lifelessness of sets. Claiming that cinema can only
"imitatively register movements in real life," Mayakovsky believed that
film would "open the way to the theater of the future and to the actor,
unfettered by a dead backdrop of a painter's set."[71] Evidently, the
young Mayakovsky regarded cinema as a medium whose sole capacity
was to reproduce exterior events, as opposed to the theater which possessed the ability of interpreting reality with poetic license. Like many
other artists of the period, Mayakovsky failed to recognize the possibility of cinema as an autonomous medium, an art form with a unique
means of expression. Vsevolod Meyerhold adhered to a similar attitude
and, in his 1913 essay on film and theater, stated that cinema was a
"shining example of obsession with quasi-verisimilitude," and contended that film was of "undoubted importance to science, but when it
is put to the service of art, it senses its own inadequacy and labors in
vain to justify the label of art."* After the revolution, however, both
Meyerhold and Mayakovsky changed their attitude toward cinema and
involved themselves directly in film production. Their prerevolutionary
scorn for cinema agreed with the common belief that film was unworthy of the title "art"; it also attested to the atmosphere in which the
Soviet avant-garde filmmakers had to work and promote their unorthodox ideas and experimental works.

In his second article, "The Destruction of the Theater," published
the same year (early 1913), Mayakovsky continued to describe film as
"a cultural means for the emancipation of the theater."[72] Even in his
third essay on cinema (published in late 1913), Mayakovsky maintained a distrust of film as an art form:

Can cinema be an independent art form? Obviously no.... Only an artist can
extrapolate the images of art from real life while cinema can act merely as a
successful or unsuccessful multiplier of the artist's images. Cinema and art
are phenomena of a different order.... Art produces refined images while cinema, like a printing press, reproduces them and distributes them to the remo-

* Vsevolod Meyerhold, *Meyerhold on Theatre*, trans. and ed. by Edward Braun (New
York: Hill and Wang, 1969), pp. 34–5. In 1915, Meyerhold also claimed that "the film as
it exists today is entirely inadequate and my attitude toward it is negative" (Leyda, *Kino*,
p. 81). That same year, Meyerhold directed his first film, *The Picture of Dorian Gray*
[*Portret Doriana Greia*], based on Oscar Wilde's work, which is considered to be "the
most important Russian film made previous to the February Revolution" (Leyda, *Kino*, p.
82). Unfortunately, this and the other Meyerhold film, *The Strong Man* [*Sil'nyi chelovek*,
1916], are lost. In 1925, Meyerhold planned to direct a film based on John Reed's *Ten
Days That Shook the World* for Proletkino, but the project was never realized. In 1928,
he was assigned to direct the historical epic *Twenty-Six Commissars*, which was subsequently directed by Nikolai Shengelaia in 1932. As an actor, Meyerhold appeared in *The
Picture of Dorian Gray*, *The Strong Man*, and *The White Eagle* [*Belyi orel*, 1928], directed
by Yakov Protazanov.

test parts of the world.... Hence cinema cannot be an autonomous art form. Of course, to destroy it would be stupid; it would be like deciding to do away with the typewriter or telescope because they do not relate to theater, literature, or Futurism.[73]

In the same article, Mayakovsky addressed the question: "Can cinema provide an aesthetic experience?" This time his response was affirmative, yet without any theoretical substantiation for his position. After a brief discussion of what he considered essential to art, Mayakovsky reiterated his previous claim that "at its best, cinema can only have a scientific or merely descriptive function."[74]

Mayakovsky's failure to appreciate the new medium and to anticipate its creative potentials seems strange in retrospect, especially because his initial disdain for cinema was not much different from the acrid note Tsar Nicholas II wrote along the margin of a 1913 police report:

I consider cinema to be an empty, totally useless, even harmful form of entertainment. Only an abnormal person could place this farcical business on a par with art. It is complete rubbish, and no importance whatsoever should be attributed to such idiocy.[75]

However obsolete today, the above quotations illustrate to what extent cinema was considered inferior to the other arts in Russia, both by artists and laymen. Even more than in other European countries, film in Russia was reduced to the level of fairground entertainment, which discouraged the young artists from participating in its development and emancipation. Such was the climate in which Vertov arrived with his revolutionary ideas regarding cinema as "the art of inventing movements of things in space" and "the ordered fantasy of movement."[76] Initially contemptuous of cinema as an art form because of his practical and enthusiastic involvement in the theater – one of the most developed and highly esteemed art forms in tsarist Russia – Mayakovsky reconsidered his negative attitude toward film only after he became acquainted with the works of Soviet revolutionary filmmakers such as Shub, Vertov, and Eisenstein. He even embraced cinema as his own expressive means: in 1918, he wrote three scripts and played leading roles in the subsequent films, while his critical writing about cinema revealed an increasing awareness of the distinction between film as entertainment and film as an art form.*

---

* Mayakovsky wrote eleven scripts altogether, although only three were produced. These three are: *The Young Lady and the Hooligan* [*Barishnia i khuligan*, 1918], based on the novel *Coure* by Edmondo d'Amicis; *It Cannot Be Bought for Money* [*Ne dlia deneg rodivshisia*, 1918] based on Jack London's *Martin Eden* (with Mayakovsky in the title role); and *Shackled By Film* [*Zakovannaia filmoi*, 1918], with Mayakovsky again playing the lead. The first and most popular film was directed by Evgeni Slavinsky, the other two by Nikandr Turkin. All of Mayakovsky's scripts appear in *Complete Works*, XII, pp. 7–212, 481–7.

During Mayakovsky's editorship of *LEF,* numerous discussions were organized about the nature and function of documentary cinema. Mayakovsky supported Vertov and Shub in denouncing the tide of commercial production prevailing during the NEP era; the *LEF* group believed that the promotion of entertainment movies jeopardized the role of revolutionary artists in Soviet society and worsened the already low cultural level of the masses. Mayakovsky wholeheartedly joined Vertov in his intention to change the common audience's consciousness about cinema. His support was clearly demonstrated in his humorous movie-poem "Film and Film" placed right above a photograph of Vertov in *Kinofot,* the journal dedicated to revolutionary art and edited by the enfant terrible of constructivism, Aleksei Gan, who was equally outraged over the importation of trivial movies from Germany, France, and the United States during the NEP years.

The *kinoks'* most difficult problem was to find theaters for screening their films, since at that time distributors, misinterpreting Lenin's idea of "proportion," established a strictly economic policy for showing films, a policy favoring profit-making movies. Despite this obstacle, Vertov urged his *kinoks* not to be discouraged by the lack of understanding from politicians, producers, and film distributors, but instead to hold to their revolutionary ideas in fighting the prevailing bourgeois mentality in cinema:

Although our newsreels are boycotted by both the film distributors and the bourgeois or semi-bourgeois audiences, this fact should not force us to comply with the habitual taste of a philistine audience. To the contrary, it should prompt us to change the audience.[77]

Vertov seized every opportunity to denounce "the ruthless money-grabbing profiteers" of the Soviet import companies, just as Mayakovsky used the official film congresses (organized by *Narkompros*) to attack the "commercial mentality" of Soviet film producers and distributors. Under Mayakovsky's leadership, *LEF* became a stronghold of critical and often vitriolic reactions against NEP policy. In its April 1923 issue, *LEF* published Tretyakov's famous article "*LEF* and NEP," in which he pointed out that NEP existed for one of two reasons: either as a vehicle for "restoring the old bourgeois attitudes towards art," or (according to the official definition) as a "temporary step that will make true art possible in the future."[78] For Tretyakov, Mayakovsky, Shub, and Vertov, there was no doubt about which of the two evaluations of NEP's role in art was the more appropriate. With their revolutionary eagerness, they rejected any compromise that was against their artistic conviction and their love for "cinema of fact." Vertov was above all enraged at the economic contradictions brought about by the NEP policy, not only in the cinematic world but also in overall living conditions. This is evident from his unpublished poem, "Mouths Are Gaping Through the Window," whose first part has already been quoted. The closing stanzas even more vehemently cry out against social injustice by condemning the stores fully stocked in the cities while hungry children die in the country:

NEP! Screw thy cafés and catafalques,	NÈP! Tvoiu-kafe-katafalk,
Carriages full of candies and violets!	Konfekt i fialok fiakr!
Children's cries – be a knot in thy throat!	Detskogo krika – oskolok v kadyk!
Take the cakes from thy mouth!!	Torty-to-iz gorla vytashchi!!
Mouths are gaping through the window!	Rty u vitrin.[79]

The avant-garde's resistance to and criticism of the NEP was extremely risky, since it meant disagreement with the party line. But despite this danger, Vertov and Mayakovsky continued to be vocal partakers of the anti-NEP attitude, romantically believing that the artist's voice might change the situation. On October 15, 1927, Mayakovsky declared publicly that "Soviet cinema is utterly archaic and based on obsolete aesthetics which have nothing in common with contemporary Soviet life."[80] The following year he published the famous poetic epigram "Film and Wine" (in Russian the two words rhyme: *kino* and *vino*), poking fun at the state company Sovkino for producing films ("*kino*") like wine ("*vino*"), and declaring that the company's bosses possessed minds not unlike those of "wine traders."[81] Supporting the truly revolutionary filmmakers, Mayakovsky used both his prestige and his rhetoric to discredit the NEP officials who made decisions about film production. He urged "Communism . . . to free film from the hands of the speculators" and advised "the Futurists to purify the putrid water – the sluggishness and immorality in art," because "without this, we shall have their imported two-step from America or a perennial eyes-full-of-tears à la Mozhukin. The first is a bore. The second even more so."[82] In actuality, Mayakovsky and Vertov could do little to change the NEP practice of making profit on movies, even less to improve popular taste. Against their attitude stood not only the official policy but also the Soviet equivalent of the Hollywood "dream factory,"* which thrived under the NEP auspice and produced a new type of sociorealist melodrama.

The comparison between Vertov and Mayakovsky shows the extent to which these two artists were concerned with the formal aspect of the creative process and with the involvement of the masses in that

* "Dream factory" [*fabrika snov*] is the term Shklovsky used to deprecate Hollywood productions, contrasting it with the term "Film factory" [*kinofabrika*], which described the practice of Soviet revolutionary filmmakers.

process as well, be it literary or poetic production. Their preoccupation with the auditory-visual structure and specific expressive means was so profound that their political commitments, let alone their obligations to the party, became of secondary importance. For such an "individualistic" behavior they had to pay a price, which turned out to be more emotionally devastating than they could foresee. With all their ideological radicalism, neither Vertov nor Mayakovsky ever placed political dogma above their personal artistic visions and their humanistic attitude toward freedom of expression. And if there is a Soviet contemporary of Vertov to whom he should be compared, both ideologically and psychologically, it could only be Mayakovsky. To equate Vertov with Trotsky ("cinema's Trotsky"[83]) seems unjustifiable. Whereas Trotsky valued political doctrine above all else during *and* after the time he possessed political power, Vertov and Mayakovsky always held their artistic visions and art in general above politics, defending uncompromisingly freedom of expression. It is therefore more appropriate to call Vertov the "Mayakovsky of cinema."

Futurist and formalist expression

A mutual aversion toward the staged film (photoplay) led Vertov and Mayakovsky to arrive at identical definitions of "cinema of fact." The actual source of this concept was Mayakovsky's "factual poetry," which inspired Vertov to formulate his "Film-Eye" and "Radio-Eye" methods. His first article on Mayakovsky's poetry (written in early 1934) openly imitated the rhetorical style of futurist proclamations, emphasizing the infuence of Mayakovsky on the *kinok*s: "Mayakovsky is 'Film-Eye.' He sees what the human eye does not see. 'Film-Eye,' like Mayakovsky, fights against the clichés of the world's film production."[84] Vertov's next article (written near the end of 1934) reiterated his enthusiasm for Mayakovsky, especially the auditory impact of his poetic language. Pointing to Mayakovsky's prosody as the source of his cinematic vision, Vertov wrote: "The unity of form and content which dominates folk art is equally striking in Mayakovsky's poetry. Since I have been working in the field of poetic documentary cinema, both Mayakovsky's poetry and folk songs have had an enormous influence on me."[85] Vertov's emphasis on the unity of form and content explains his concern for rhythmic structure (dominant in folk songs) as well as poetic imagery (evident in Mayakovsky's verse), which are the most significant features of *The Man with the Movie Camera,* especially its symphonic montage structure.

After studying Mayakovsky's essays on poetic expression while trying to imitate his versification, Vertov strove for a "cinematic poetry" devoid of conventional narrative linearity and the theatrical presentation of reality. In his diary, Vertov refers to himself as a cinematic poet: "I am a writer of cinema. I am a film poet. But instead of writing on paper, I write on the film strip."[86] Reflecting back on his earlier work, he confirms that he "discovered the key to recording documentary sounds while analyzing the musical rhythms of Mayakovsky's poems." Eisenstein also recognized the Soviet avant-garde cinema's debt to Mayakovsky, particularly to his method of deconstructing rhymes in order to achieve stronger auditory and visual effects and new meanings. In his essay "Montage 1938," Eisenstein wrote that Mayakovsky "does not work in lines...he works in shots, verses... cutting his lines just as an experienced film editor would construct a typical film sequence."[87] Both Eisenstein's "Montage of Collisions" and Vertov's "Montage of Intervals," preoccupied with the shots' formal structure, parallel Mayakovsky's concern for the words' syntactical relation and their inflection. *The Man with the Movie Camera* went farther than any other silent film in linking shots with the intention to create a musical structure, to produce a poetic impact, and to provoke subliminal responses in the viewer.

Another device integral to Mayakovsky's poetic technique is the condensation of thematic elements in which one character represents an entire social class, or one fragment of reality evokes a set of associations in the reader's mind. In the "Friends" section of "About This," Mayakovsky depicts the decadent atmosphere of a reception given by the "new bourgeoisie" through a few select details: the raven-guests, trivial conversation, bubbling champagne, and the two-step (which in the Soviet Union at the time connoted Western licentiousness). In his *Strike* (1924), Eisenstein used symbolic details in depicting (unmasking) negative characters by superimposing the emblematic close-ups (the owl, the fox) over the faces of his *typages* (nonprofessional actors chosen according to their facial features). In contrast, Vertov did not adhere to such a direct – and quite histrionic – visual symbolism; instead, he always showed real people within their natural environment, engaged in their usual activities (workers in mines, bureaucrats in offices, peasants in markets or on farms, old people in churches, derelicts sleeping among garbage, ladies in beauty parlors, children in amusement parks, drunkards in pubs and streets, athletes on fields, and the omnipresent cameramen). What makes these people representative of their class, occupation, mentality, and psychological attitude is the fact that they are "caught" by the camera when their true nature exposes itself fully, even if they instantly realize they are being filmed. It is the juxtaposition between the people (mostly shown in close-up) and the action they are involved in or the environment in which they function that generates the authors' comment on the "characters" and

their actions. Through montage, Vertov and Svilova succeed in com-
municating the complex meaning of "the boisterous ocean of life," into
which the Cameraman "throws himself," capturing things "unawares"
so that "life's chaos gradually becomes clear,"[88] and the essence of the
visible world becomes apparent.

The "Film-Eye" method, whose basic goal was to make possible a
"cinematic sensation of the world" [*kinooshchushchenie mira*] and
whose basic technique was to "extract" (Vertov's term) the most revealing images from thousands of feet of film, is analogous to the process
of "creative mining" (Mayakovsky's term) in poetry. Referring to this
process in the "Conversation with a Tax Inspector about Poetry," Mayakovsky writes: "Poetry's / also radium extraction. / Grams of extraction / in years of labour. / For one single word, / I consume in action /
thousands of tons / of verbal ore."[89] In fact, Vertov quotes these lines
in his diary, stating that this was the style he wanted to follow in his
films, and not "the path of the poets whose lines hit the viewer (!) as
the arrow of a cupid-lyre chase."[90] This, "organic" repulsion of conventional, trivial, and entertainment art was both the source of Vertov's
and Mayakovsky's creative energy and their critical acrimony.

Vertov's published – but unrealized – scripts (particularly those
written between 1935 and 1940) most clearly reveal his concern for poetic impact and formal structure. Referring to them as "musical/poetic
films without magic or talisman,"* Vertov expected his readers to
"see" the described images, and even to "edit" them into an imaginary
montage structure! The ruptured and seemingly isolated lines, the
contrapuntal organization of words, the concatenation of terse sentences, the musical flow of phrases, and the specified photographic
viewpoint (angle), all of these do indeed inspire the reader of Vertov's
scripts to envision the described situations. The introductory paragraph of the script "A Girl Plays the Piano," with its unusual graphic
arrangement of sentences, parallels Mayakovsky's technique of laying
out lines (or shots) by underscoring graphically outstanding details.
After a brief "overture" that explains the basic intention of this "scientific and fantastic cinematic poem," Vertov's script begins just like a
poem:

---

* Vertov, "A Girl Plays the Piano" (1939) [*Devushka igraet na roiale*], *Articles*, p. 288. In
several of his other scripts, Vertov shows a particular interest in various aspects of the
life and the social position of women in the Soviet Union. Among these scripts are "She"
[*Ona*, 1939], "The Girl Composer" [*Devushka-kompozitor*, 1936], "Song of a Girl" [*Pesnia o devushke*, 1936], and "The Letter from a Girl Tractor Driver" [*Pismo traktoristki*,
1940]. Also, his third sound film, *Lullaby* (1937), deals with women and is therefore
subtitled "A Song to the Liberated Soviet Woman."

A girl is playing the piano	Devushka igraet na roiale
She is watched	Na nee smotrit
through the open windows of a	
terrace	skvoz' raskrytye okna terrasy
by a starry night.	zvezdanaia noch'.
The Moon illuminates her hands.	Luna osveshchaet ee ruki.
The Moon illuminates the keyboard.	Luna osveshchaet klavishi.
And to her it seems not sounds	I ei kazhetsia, chto ne zvuki,
but rays of distant, invisible worlds,	a luchi nevidannykh dalekikh mirov,
rays of glimmering stars	luchi mertsaiushchikh zvezd
that sing from under her fingers.	poiut iz-pod ee paltsev.[91]

Even without a profound analysis of this text and its structure, one can realize that Vertov's goal is to create a musical rhythm with words. Each sentence rhythmically correlates with the next, so much so that in order to be fully apprehended the phrases must be visualized. Prosodically, the structural arrangement of rhymes is reminiscent of Mayakovsky's technique, whereas the imaginistic presentation of nature and landscape may be related to other poets Vertov admired, Whitman among them.* The next passage from the same script requires the reader to participate even more imaginatively in "extracting" a series of images from a literary description:

This could take place on a significantly lesser planet,
let us say the Moon.
     But the surrounding setting would not change.
     This means only gravity would change.
     Actually,
             on the tennis court,
                 on the basketball court,
             in the gymnastic compound,
                 on all the spaces which meet
                     her eyes,
                         strange things occur:
all the players do not run,
     but glide floating.

Eto moglo by imet' mesto na znachitel'no men'shei planete,
skazhem na Lune.
     No obstanovka krugom ne izmenilas'.
     Znachit, izmenilos' tol'ko tiagotenie.
     Deistvitel'no,
             na tennisnom korte,
                 na basketbol'noi ploshchadke,

---

* In his diary written during World War II, after describing the difficulties he faces in persuading the administration to approve his new project, Vertov suddenly begins to write in a highly emotional manner ("The poetry of science.... The poetry of space.... The poetry of unheard numbers...."), and quotes several lines from Walt Whitman's *Song of Joys. Articles*, "Notebooks" (February 1, 1941), p. 234.

v gimnasticheskom gorodke,
na prostranstve, kotoroe obkhvatyvaet
ee glaz,
proizkhodiat strannie veshchi:
vse igraiushchie ne begaiut.
a plavno porkhaiut.[92]

Because of their position within the line, the words themselves appear to "glide," thus inviting the reader to experience the line's "tonal glissando" as a stimulant in envisioning the events in "slow motion." The rhythm of the sentences is constructed in such a way as to enhance the mood of the event while at the same time suggesting a particular montage pace to be achieved in the process of editing. Indeed, it is a pity that Vertov was not allowed to realize this and other scripts he conceived in the later period of his career. The lexical use of the words and their syntactic order in these scripts indicate that he sought to expand his "Film-Eye" method as well as the "Film-Truth" principle by developing more symbolic montage "figures," and by allowing rather stylized mise-en-scène and shot compositions. One wonders how the last few "shots," as described in the script "A Girl Plays the Piano," would appear on the actual screen, if Vertov had been permitted to shoot them:

The universe	Vselennaia
looks	smotrit
with the eyes of the stars	glazami zvezd
at the girl,	
	na devushku,
dreaming at the piano.	mechtaiushchuiu za roialem.[93]

The futurists' and formalists' unprecedented concern for stylistic (formal) aspects and expressive modes of art stemmed from their belief that form and structure can produce their own meaning, which is as important as the narrative context. Vladimir Markov, who personally participated in the Russian futurist movement throughout the 1920s, explains that the main goal of the futurist poets like Mayakovsky was "to make the word the real protagonist of poetry, and, more importantly, to insist consciously and aggressively that poetry grows out of the word."[94] The cubo-futurists in particular were concerned with the value, function, and aesthetic impact of the "word as such," not only in poetry but also in "fine prose." In her analytical comparison of Vertov's work with Soviet futurist poetry, Anna Lawton points to A. Kruchenykh's 1913 futurist poem "Pomada" [*Pomade*/Lipstick], whose stanzas (e.g., *"dyr buv shchyl"*) are composed of newly constructed words without any meaning, in the typical manner of the "Zaum language." According to Lawton, "the images [shots] in this poem are liberated from any kind of causal relationship [diegetic editing] and arranged in rhythmic segments" [sequences], thus "endowing the text [film] with a new and fresh meaning based on analogical relationships [associative editing] – a meaning which relies on the participation of the reader's [viewer's] intuition."[95] As one may see from the words suggested in the brackets, this statement can be applied almost verbatim to Vertov's film *The Man with the Movie Camera*, by replacing the terms describing literature-poetry with ones pertinent to cinema. Indeed, it is difficult to find a filmmaker who believed as strongly as Vertov in the importance of individual shots as the foundation of the film's ontological integrity. Like the futurist poets, Vertov knew that in order to fully exploit the potentials of the (cinematic) medium, it was necessary to prevent narrative and theatrical conventions from shackling the kinesthetic impact of the film. This does not mean that Vertov did not draw on other media whenever he felt they could contribute to the overall unity of a sequence; yet he did insist that these "borrowed" elements be fully transformed into new cinematic values that, when properly integrated, would become an organic part of the cinematic vision of reality.

With all their concern for the formal aspect of artistic creation, Mayakovsky and Vertov demonstrated an equal interest in political content whenever they found it necessary. They saw great possibility and appeal in the use of political cartooning as a means of visual communication. During the Russian Civil War, Mayakovsky personally designed hundreds of widely distributed political ROSTA posters for the Russian Telegraph Agency.[96] In many respects, the graphic style of these cartoons resembles animated segments that Vertov incorporated in his early *Film-Eye* series, especially in terms of the treatment of characters and the simplicity of their pictorial execution. The use of the instantly identifiable types (e.g., "the worker," "the bureaucrat," "the bourgeois imperialist") and characteristic settings (e.g., "the factory," "the office," "the mine") made Mayakovsky's cartoons accessible to largely illiterate audiences. Vertov's cartoon insets in the *Film-Eye* series were also intended to convey a political message to the masses in the most understandable manner, through simplified graphics in motion. Ironically, it is in these segments of his films (which are the least cinematic) that Vertov succeeded in being the most "accessible" to the masses, those same masses that – to his great disappointment – proved totally unresponsive to his idea of the "ultimate language of cinema" as demonstrated in *The Man with the Movie Camera*.

The futurists' admiration for the technological age is the major theme of Mayakovsky's "hymns" to factories and machines. He saw the steel constructions as a challenge to the pastoral scenes glorified by the traditional poets, especially the symbolists and ego-futurists* whom Mayakovsky ridiculed as being soaked in sentimental laments and sobs. Mayakovsky urged the revolutionary poets to write about common people, "those thousands of street folks," students, prostitutes, salesmen, and workers "who are creators within a burning hymn / the hymn of mills and laboratories."[97] His enthusiasm for the mechanical age erupted in its full fervor during his 1925 visit to the United States, where he wrote his ode to the Brooklyn Bridge which, together with his ode to the Eiffel Tower, best illustrates the futuristic preoccupation with technology:

What pride	Ia gord
I take	vot etoi
in that mile of steel,	stal'noiu milei,
and from it arose	zhiv'em v nei
my living vision	moi videniia v staliu-
the struggle	bor'ba
for construction	za konstruktsii
instead of style,	umesto stilei
the stern calculation	raschet survovoi
of steel	gaek
precision.	i stali.[98]

The relationship between the futurists and the formalists was on one level harmonious and on another antagonistic. They shared the identical view of art as a "device" artists must learn to use properly, that is, within the constraints of a given medium; they mutually disagreed with the proponents of socialist realism and especially with its insistence on politicizing art. Of course, futurists promulgated their own political views concerning artistic creation that considerably differed from the party's interpretation of Marx and dialectical materialism. In fact, there were many diverse ideological tendencies among futurists, all of them incompatible with the party's demand that its members follow the prescribed ideological trend regardless of personal opinion. In contrast, formalists were ideologically disengaged; they concentrated predominantly on the structural, linguistic, and formal aspects of artistic work. In this respect, they had much in common with constructivists who were equally preoccupied with form and structure in art. All three groups, however, were fascinated with the current technological revolution and modern industrial environment. Futurists wrote poems about factories and machines; constructivists painted abstract geometrical forms inspired by a mechanical world or

---

* Mayakovsky used to attack the ego-futurist poets publicly, especially their leader, Igor Severianin (Lotarev), who was prolific and extremely popular before the revolution. Severianin emigrated to Estonia in 1919, and even after the Soviets occupied that land, he continued to publish in the USSR.

built sculptures that were creative replicas of the machine; formalists helped poets discover the melody and rhythm of language, the dynamic structure of words and stanzas that can echo the mechanical beat of factories and machines. The widespread practice of photographic collage became even more dramatic when motion pictures were combined into sequences that generated optical rhythms and mechanical movement unattainable in still-photography.

From a structural position, *The Man with the Movie Camera* can also be seen as an ode to the industrial revolution reflected in each and every aspect of the daily lives citizens lead in a great city that is persistently watched and scrutinized by the "Film-Eye." Emphasizing the structural beauty of machines, extolling the workers' zeal, and empathizing with ordinary citizens performing their duties, this film is one of the truly artistic documents about a technological – as well as social – transformation. Yet, given the circumstances under which it was made, as a cinematic achievement this film is more a statement about the future than a record of actual socioeconomic conditions. What Vertov and Mayakovsky conceived and dreamed of as an ideal social order or as a novel art structure was largely suppressed by the major ideology in practice; restrained in their creative drives, they could only hope that future generations would recognize their works as genuine avant-garde achievements and revolutionary artistic visions.

The practice of producing a musical rhythm by selecting (or constructing) words according to their "sounding" was essential for the formalist poets (and critics) gathered around the OPOYAZ society.* Dedicated to the "scientific inquiry into literary technique," OPOYAZ introduced the concept of a transcendental (transrational) poetic language known as "Zaum,"[99] meaning "beyond the rational." Comprised of the combination of sounds that do not represent concrete words, but which are constructed on musical principles to evoke feelings and imply abstract ideas, Zaum poetry grew out of suprematist painting, particularly its concept of the emotional impact of colors. The basic premise of the Zaum movement was that all art should be free from its subservience to thematic meaning so that sounds, colors, movements, and nonrepresentational shapes sustain their autonomous associations and pure aesthetic function. In actual poetic achievements, the alternation of various auditory beats, according to a symphonic pat-

---

* OPOYAZ stands for "Society for the Study of Poetic Language" [*Obshchestvo izucheniia poeticheskogo jazyka*], founded in Petersburg in 1916. It included some of the most significant formalist poets and theorists, such as Yuri Tynianov, Osip Brik, Boris Eikhenbaum, Viktor Shklovsky, and Vladimir Zhirmunsky. The members of this society differed markedly in their literary preferences, although futurists considered its "Formalist method as the key element in the study of art." Victor Erlich, *Russian Formalism: History – Doctrine*, p. 47.

tern, approximates the structure of so-called concrete music and is associated with the sounds of working machines and mechanized factories. Examples of such a mechanistic rhythm, achieved through the repetitive use of words with one or two syllables, are poems by the greatest and most controversial of Zaumists, Velemir Khlebnikov, who inferred that a poem "is built of words as the constructive units of the edifice"; accordingly, in his dramatic poem "Snake Train," he made up words based on the Russian linguistic root *"um"* [mind], to evoke certain feelings and to achieve a musical beat:

Deum.	Deum
Boum.	Boum.
Koum.	Koum.
Soum.	Soum.
Poum.	Poum.
Glaum.	Glaum.
Noum.	Noum.
Nuum.	Nuum.
Vyum.	Vyum.
Bom! Bom! Bom!	Bom! Bom! Bom!
It's a loud toll in the bell of the mind.	Eto bol'shoi nabat v kolokol uma.
Divine sounds flying down from above	Bozhestvennye zvuki, sletaiushchiesia
At the summons of man.	sverkhy na prizyv cheloveka.*

One can find a direct relationship between certain nonrepresentational shots and optical pulsations in *The Man with the Movie Camera* and the "verbal flashes" or "syntactical drumming" achieved through the rhythmic beats of vowels and syllables in Zaum poetry. Explaining how he conceived his film *Three Songs about Lenin* "in the style of folk-song images," Vertov stated that he also created "verbal concatenations in the manner of Zaum,"[100] both as part of the spoken commentary and written intertitles. Vertov's practice of using the "flicker" (achieved by repeatedly inserting a single black, gray, or transparent frame between various shots) produces a unique perceptual sensation in the viewer. Given the irritating impact of the flickering effect employed even more emphatically in *The Man with the Movie Camera*, it is clear why this film, which challenges human perception and rejects a traditional approach to art, has been attacked by the orthodox critics as mere optical pyrotechnics. But the futurists immediately understood Vertov's experiment and wholeheartedly defended his film as an outstanding avant-garde achievement.

Aesthetically, Vertov's theory and practice in many respects comply

* Velemir Khlebnikov, *Snake Train,* trans. Gary Kern (Ann Arbor: Ardis, 1976), p. 77. Published in 1922 (written between 1920 and 1921), Khlebnikov's *Zangezi* was produced in the theater of the Museum of the Materialist Culture in Petrograd, 1923, under the direction of the constructivist painter and sculptor, Vladimir Tatlin.

with the futurist's, suprematist's, and formalist's belief that every artist should express his or her ideas within the specificity of the given medium and without making concessions to popular taste. Just as Mayakovsky dedicated his poetic talent to changing the traditional prosodic structure, Vertov decided to create an international visual language understood by all people regardless of national boundaries. In his article "The Forward Looking," Fevralsky discusses the conceptual relationship between Vertov and Mayakovsky, particularly the way they use "cinematic" devices to present the "characters" in their films/ scripts:

Vertov's film-poems were conceived according to Mayakovsky's poetical tradition. The visual concept of *The Man with the Movie Camera* has many contiguous points with Maykovsky's script *How Do You Do?*, written in 1926. Mayakovsky's protagonist is "The Man with the Pencil," i.e. the poet, as Vertov's protagonist is "The Man with the Movie Camera." Like Vertov, Mayakovsky insists on using "specific cinematic devices" instead of replacing them by other means of expression. It is an attempt to apply documentary style to a narrative film script.[101]

Fevralsky also points to other thematic and formal similarities in the works of the two artists. Commenting on the treatment of Lenin in Vertov's film *Three Songs about Lenin* and Mayakovsky's poem "Vladimir Ilyich Lenin," Fevralsky emphasizes Mayakovsky's concern for the historical documentation of the presented events. This insistence on historical accuracy was in line with constructivist ideas about "art of fact," which required the artists not to falsify the actual matter, but to register it faithfully before putting it into a new context – requirements almost identical to the demands Vertov assigned to his *kinoks*.

Educating the masses

Accessibility to the masses was a problem Mayakovsky and Vertov tried to resolve in an uncompromising yet painful way. Believing that the masses could be gradually educated to understand and appreciate unconventional means of expression, both men eagerly experimented with a novel structural relationship between words and images. In their revolutionary romanticism, they tended to overlook the masses' inability to appreciate avant-garde art and experimentation. Even after they became aware of this fact, they did not yield to popular taste, but continued to demand that the masses change their attitude toward art! Mayakovsky expressed his criticism of popular taste openly – and often with aggressiveness – at many public meetings. Reacting rather disdainfully to the repeated accusation that his poetry was "difficult," he would instantly reply: "I agree that poems must be understood, but the reader must be understanding as well. . . . You must finally learn to appreciate complex poetry. . . . You cannot say, 'If I don't understand a poem, then it is the writer who is the fool.' "* Vertov, who claimed that he "has never considered Mayakovsky incomprehensible or unpopular,"[102] responded almost identically to the allegations that his films were "inaccessible" to the masses when he wrote: "If the NEP audience [*nepmanovskaia auditoria*] prefers dramas of kisses and crime [*potseluinye ili prestupnye dramy*], it does not necessarily mean that our work is inappropriate; it may well mean that the mass audience is still unfit and incapable of understanding it" [*ne goditsia publika*].[103]

Paraphrasing the Marxist view of religion in his "Simplest Slogans," Vertov stated that "film-drama is an opiate for the people,"† and insisted that "it is necessary to distinguish between being popular and pretending to be popular."[104] Given the political and cultural circumstances, Vertov and Mayakovsky proved to be excessively idealistic in their intention to educate the masses. Just as their vision of the ideal socialist state was utopian, their belief in the substantial change of the masses' artistic taste was impractical. However, true artists and humanists are expected to dream of far-reaching ideals; hence it seems scandalous to call such visions "idiotic and ugly,"[105] as Raymond Durgnat does in referring to Vertov's ideas of society.

The concern for the cultural sophistication and education of the masses was part of the constructivist's activism, which counted on the audience's participation in the creation of the artistic meaning rather than on the passive consumption of art. To encourage such a participation, the "artistic products" were intentionally made strenuous and self-referential, in keeping with the formalist device known as "making-it-difficult,"‡ thereby forcing the audience to search for a more

---

* Herbert Marshall, *Mayakovsky* (London: Dennis Dobson, 1965), p. 66. According to Marshall, only five days before committing suicide, Mayakovsky presented a lecture at the Plekhanov Institute of Economics in Moscow and, among others statements, responded to criticism of his poetry as being "difficult" in the following way: "In fifteen or twenty years, the cultural level of the workers will be raised so high that all my works will be understood. . . . I am amazed at the illiteracy of this audience. I never expected such a low cultural level from the students of such a high and respected educational institution." p. 71. Quoted from *Literary Chronicle of Mayakovsky*, ed. V. Katanyan (Moscow: The State Publishing House of Artistic Literature, 1956), p. 406.
† Vertov's aphorism appears as the third section (entitled "Simplest Slogans") of his 1926 statement "Provisional Instructions to 'Film-Eye' Groups" [*Vremennaia instruktsiia kruzhkam kinoglaza*], *Articles*, p. 96. The statement contains nine "instructions," and the first one reads: "Film-drama is an opiate for the people!" [*Kino-drama – opium dlia naroda!*].
‡ Among the three formalist concepts, the idea of making a work of art "difficult" to understand was most criticized by the proponents of socialist realism. For more information about "estrangement," "*otstranenie*," "*zatrudnenie*," and "*obnazhenie priema*," see Victor Erlich, *Russian Formalism: History – Doctrine*, pp. 145–63.

rarefied meaning in the given work, and to enjoy aspects of artistic creation beyond the narrative ones. The practice of making the structure of an artistic product "difficult" also meshed with the formalist principle of "baring-the-device" in order to reveal how reality is aesthetically transformed into art through the process of construction [*stoitel'nyi protsess*]. Vertov adhered to this principle throughout the production of *The Man with the Movie Camera*, hoping that it would "open the masses' eyes" toward film as an autonomous art. Unsurprisingly, his belief proved to be premature, as his most avant-garde films have had to wait more than half a century to be fully appreciated, and even then only by certain film scholars.

By adopting such an uncompromising attitude toward cinema, Vertov made himself vulnerable, especially to those critics who stood for the principles of socialist realism which catered to the popular taste in promoting political ideas. At the same time, there was a contradiction in Vertov's attitude: on the one hand, he believed that film should educate the masses; on the other, he constantly challenged popular taste. Almost every *Film-Truth* series featured a specific filmic device – from reverse to accelerated motion, from associative editing to jump cuts – often with the intention that the viewers use their full intellectual acuity if they wanted truly to understand the film. Thus, especially in his later work, Vertov alienated himself from the masses by being too demanding, an attitude he was aware of without feeling guilty or obliged to follow party orders:

One of the chief accusations leveled at our method is that we [the *kinoks*] are not understood by the masses. Well, even if you accept the fact that some of our works are difficult to understand, does it mean that we are not supposed to create any serious work? That we must abandon all exploration in cinema? If the masses need simple agitation and polemical pamphlets, does it mean that the masses do not need serious essays by Engels and Lenin? What if a Lenin of the Soviet Cinema appears among us and he is not permitted to work, because the products of his creation are new and inaccessible?[106]

This statement, reminiscent of Mayakovsky's response to the criticism concerning the "impenetrability" of his verses, parallels Shub's defense of the artist's right to produce "difficult" works. In her reply to Shklovsky's objection that Dovzhenko's film *Ivan* (1932) was not accessible to the masses, Shub wrote:

Not long ago Mayakovsky was also criticized for being incomprehensible to a large audience. Bearing this in mind, today's critics have no right to say: "This is an important work of art, but it is a failure as an achievement." This is unacceptable. The task of a true critic is to create the climate for such "difficult" works of art. Whenever an important work of art is created, the critic's duty is to help it with his pen so that a temporarily incomprehensible work soon becomes comprehensible to everybody.[107]

What a wise attitude toward avant-garde creation and its inaccessibility to the masses! Mayakovsky also used his authority to support the avant-garde artists whose works were criticized for not taking into account popular taste and current political needs. At a conference designated "Theater Policies of the Soviet Government," Mayakovsky publicly denounced the party's decision to ban Mikhail Bulgakov's play *The Days of the Turbins** as politically "inappropriate":

I consider the politics of suppression absolutely pernicious.... No, art must not be suppressed.... What shall we achieve by suppression? Only that such literature will be distributed around the corner and read with even greater satisfaction as I have read poems by Yessenin in manuscript form.[†]

However vocal, Mayakovsky's cry for creative freedom remained futile. A few days before his suicide,[‡] he sardonically admitted to the victory of bourgeois aesthetics in Soviet art. Exhausted and depressed, he saw numerous signs of the avant-garde's collapse in the government's repeated attempts to suppress unorthodox achievements and to promote consumer products for both political and commercial purposes. In what was his last public appearance, Mayakovsky attacked the bourgeois mentality in art, in a tone humorous and nostalgic at the same time:

All those Venuses of Milo with their lopped off arms, all that Greek classical beauty, can never satisfy the millions who are entering into the new life of our noisy cities, and who will soon be treading the path of revolution. Just now, however, our chairwoman offered me a sweet with the label Mosselprom on it. Above the label there is the same old Venus. So, what we've been fighting

---

* *The Days of the Turbins [Dni turbin]* is a stage adaptation of Bulgakov's famous novel *The White Guard [Belaia gvardiia,* 1925]. It was produced by the Moscow Art Theater in 1926 with great success. But after a short run, the performance was banned. Disappointed, Bulgakov personally appealed to Stalin, asking for permission to emigrate. Stalin told him (over the phone) that he could not leave the country, and promised to lift the ban on the play; this soon occurred, but only for a short period of time. A few years later, another great Soviet avant-garde writer, Yevgeny Zamyatin – the author of *We,* the fascinating and prophetic satire on a futuristic totalitarian society – was also forced to request permission to leave Russia, which Stalin granted him in 1931. Zamyatin emigrated to France, but lived in total seclusion and died in Paris six years later. His and Bulgakov's contemporaries, however – Valentin Katayev, Vsevolod Ivanov, and Veniyamin Kaverin – sacrificed their literary talents to become hacks, manufacturing whatever was required in the shape and style demanded by the party.
† Marshall, *Mayakovsky,* p. 45. Mayakovsky drew parallels between Bulgakov and Yessenin because Yessenin's poetry was also criticized as "defeatist" and was banned for a considerable period of time. Yessenin hanged himself on December 17, 1925, in a Leningrad hotel.
‡ Mayakovsky shot himself on April 14, 1930, in Moscow.

against for twenty years apparently has become victorious. And the lopsided beauty is being circulated among the masses, appearing even on candy wrappers, poisoning our brain and destroying *our* idea of beauty all over again.[108]

Mayakovsky's bitterness reflects his inability to change the state of Soviet art and to improve the mental inertia of the masses for whose enlightenment both he and Vertov had devoted their talents. Disillusioned, they saw no future for their avant-garde experimentation, and therefore had no motivation for further contributing to a culture they found stale. The psychological burden of this realization took its toll in them: Mayakovsky soon ended his life, and Vertov became a recluse who gradually lapsed into a state of apathy.

The Vertov–Eisenstein controversy

It is clear today that, together with Eisenstein, Vertov's work as well as his ideas about film represent the most revolutionary contribution not only to Soviet but also to world cinema. Although their aesthetic and theoretical concepts differ in many respects, their writings are all relevant to the understanding of cinematic language. Vertov fought for authentic cinematic expression throughout his career, while Eisenstein — especially in the later part of his life — extended his theoretical research to film modes that embrace other arts, particularly literature and theater. In contrast, Vertov made no concession whatsoever to theatrical (staged) and fictional (literary) film, remaining both in theory and practice firmly committed to documentary, nonfictional cinema. Even in his unrealized scripts, that include prearranged mise-en-scène, Vertov made sure that every situation he envisioned would correspond as closely as possible to what he considered "a faithful copy" [*tochnaia kopiia*] of the given "life-facts."

That Eisenstein and Vertov adopted different approaches to film is hardly surprising: Eisenstein came to cinema from theater, whereas Vertov was involved in cinematic experimentation from the very beginning of his career. Their conflicting attitudes regarding the aesthetic value and social function of cinema reflect in many ways the conceptual and ideological discord characteristic of Soviet revolutionary art throughout the 1920s. A comparative examination of their theoretical disagreements provides further insight into the evolution of Soviet art in general. It reveals the extent to which the development of Soviet avant-garde film depended on experimentation in other media and was influenced by the theoretical and aesthetic concepts of the revolutionary critics.

Viktor Shklovsky, in his booklet *Their Genuineness* (1927), was the first to compare Vertov and Eisenstein. He praised Vertov's early *Film-Truth* series, but exhibited a clear preference for the shot composition and pictorial stylization of Eisenstein.[109] Reiterating his standpoint in a more recent monograph on Eisenstein (published in 1973), Shklov-sky supported Eisenstein's critique of Vertov's "Film-Truth" principle. He agreed with Eisenstein's statement that Vertov used montage to make "essentially static shots simulate movement,"[110] and although admitting that Vertov's theories influenced Eisenstein's early films, he maintained that Eisenstein "had gone much further" in his montage experiments. Shklovsky's critique of Vertov is challenged by the mod-ern Soviet film theorist Sergei Drobashenko, who infers that the two filmmakers influenced each other equally, and that both materialized their theoretical ideas in a unique way.[111] Another contemporary Soviet theorist, Tamara Selezneva, draws a similar conclusion in her discus-sion of the problem of staged and unstaged cinema. In her book *Film Thought of the 1920s* (1972), Selezneva states that Eisenstein and Ver-tov were equally important as creative figures within their respective domains.[112]

Eisenstein expressed his initial disagreement with Vertov shortly after he began to attend the *kinok*s' workshop.* Since he was prepar-ing to redirect his artistic career from theater to film, Eisenstein tried to learn about techniques of shooting and editing. In his memoirs, Vertov recalls his encounters with Eisenstein before *Strike* (1924) was made, at the time Eisenstein used to visit the *kinok*s' workshop:

At that time [1918 to 1924], Sergei Mikhailovich Eisenstein still respected the *kinok*s; he used to attend every single screening at which we discussed the *Film-Truth* series. But although we respected his mind and talent, we were not grateful to Sergei Mikhailovich. We had constant fights with him, because we felt that his concept of "intermediating cinema" [*promezhutochnoi*] (this term is not mine, but Eisenstein's) impeded the advancement of documentary film. In contrast, we considered that the application of the documentary method to the staged film was unnatural [*protivoestestvennyi*].[113]

The term "intermediating cinema," as the core of the controversy, im-plies a mixture of "staged" and "unstaged" film, a hybrid scheme Ver-tov flatly rejected. Eisenstein, however, saw in the stylized mise-en-scène and the expressive shot composition (especially the lighting) "a conscious and active remaking [*perekraivanie*] of reality, not so much reality in general, but every single event and each specific fact."[114] Ver-tov considered such a directorial method incompatible with the "re-cording of facts, classification of facts, dissemination of facts, and agitation with facts."[115]

---

* Eisenstein's first film experience was associated with the *kinok*s' group. The camera-man Boris Frantsisson shot Eisenstein's movie *Glumov's Diary* [*Dnevnik Glumova*, 1922] as part of the Proletkult Theater's production of Ostrovsky's *The Wise Man*, while Vertov was assigned as the "artistic instructor" (although Eisenstein claims that Vertov soon left the shoot). Conceived as a "parody on the idea of Pathé newsreels" (Eisenstein, *Se-lected Works* II, p. 454), this short film (about 160 feet) was later included in *The Spring Film-Truth* [*Vesennaia kinopravda*], May 1923.

Eisenstein repeatedly stated that he was not influenced by the "Film-Eye" method, nor by any of Vertov's early newsreels. But his close friend Esther Shub recalls that Eisenstein admitted this influence, if not publicly, then at least under a particular circumstance:

Eisenstein, who otherwise disavowed the influence of Vertov on his film *Strike*, admitted with the frankness of a great artist – not only to me personally, but also to his students in VGIK – that one of the best sequences in *Battleship Potemkin*, the gathering of the people around Vakhulchik's dead body, was conceived under the direct inspiration of Vertov's *Leninist Film-Truth*.[116]

There is no doubt that the relationship between Vertov and Eisenstein was tense, despite various attempts to make it look incidental. Elizaveta Svilova, in her 1976 recollections about her husband, tried to illustrate the "friendly" relationship between the two men with an episode in which Eisenstein was depicted as "bursting with his impression" while "telling me what exceptional success *Symphony of the Don Basin* received in England"[117] (from which Eisenstein had just returned in early 1931). If this was true, then it seems strange that, having had such enthusiasm about the international success of Vertov's film, Eisenstein never mentioned it in his writings nor analyzed the film's unique audiovisual structure, which in many respects substantiated Eisenstein's own theory of sight and sound counterpoint. Svilova obviously wanted to tone down the existent controversy when she wrote:

In the later period, Vertov and Eisenstein argued a lot about creative problems, but they nevertheless preserved good personal relations. Their polemics, in fact, sharpened their theoretical views, and they actually enjoyed their discussions. After all, they rejoiced in each other's successes, and accepted them with pleasure, not with jealousy.[118]

This statement can be taken only as a circumstantial gesture, unsupported by what one finds in Eisenstein's writings about the *kinoks*, especially in his attitudes toward *The Man with the Movie Camera*, which to the end of his life he considered "mischievous."

The theoretical disagreement between Vertov and Eisenstein stems, by and large, from their divergent definitions of "ontological authenticity"* in cinema, that is, the extent to which the viewer accepts an event presented on the screen as actually taking place in the real world. In his book *The Phenomenon of Authenticity* (1972), Sergei Drobashenko finds Eisenstein's polemics with Vertov centered so much on this issue

---

* "Ontological authenticity" implies that the motion pictures projected on the screen have a unique associative power that evokes in the viewer's consciousness – by a code of perceptual recognition – a sensorial notion of reality as well as a strong feeling that the events, characters, and the environment exist as a real world, in spite of the fact that the cinematographic projection consists merely of light, shadows, and sound waves.

that "Eisenstein's entire theory and practice in the 1920s (and even much later) was subordinated to a single goal and to one overriding idea, which was to find the best expressive means and *stylized devices* capable of jarring the viewer's psychology"[119] [italics mine]. Pointing directly to the theoretical dispute between the two filmmakers, Drobashenko concludes:

Eisenstein accused Vertov's films of having insufficient purposeful intention in commenting upon the filmed event.... therefore, he considered Vertov's work as primitive impressionism and a dispassionate representation of reality.[120]

According to Drobashenko, this argument reveals two different if not irreconcilable concepts of "cinema of fact." Eisenstein did not believe that the camera – a mere instrument in the filmmaker's hands – was capable of penetrating reality or revealing the hidden meaning of everyday events, as Vertov, Shub, Gan, and other constructivists contended. Drobashenko further infers that Eisenstein rejected the idea that a film image per se could achieve any substantial impact on the viewer unless sufficiently stylized *before* and *after* the shooting. In contrast, Vertov had a complete trust in the camera's power to "unveil those aspects of the filmed event which otherwise cannot be perceived."[121] This penetrating and revelationary capacity of the camera was the basis of the "Film-Truth" principle, which Eisenstein considered an artistically useless, purely mechanical device.

Eisenstein defined the representational character of the film image as the "shot's tendency toward complete immutability rooted in its nature";[122] in order to counteract the shot's faithfulness to reality, Eisenstein opted for techniques – expressionist lighting, histrionic acting, exaggerated makeup, and symbolic mise-en-scène – which reduced the ontological authenticity of the shot. Vertov opposed all those "histrionic" interventions, believing that the true nature of cinema resides in the camera's capacity to uncover the hidden aspects of reality, which must be caught unawares before they are aesthetically reconstructed through montage. Whenever he abandoned this principle by rearranging the events in front of the camera (as in some segments of the *Film-Eye* series, *One Sixth of the World,* and *The Man with the Movie Camera*), Vertov never concealed the fact that the photographed people were aware of the presence of the camera. The candid recording of "life-facts" was Vertov's primary principle substantiated throughout *The Man with the Movie Camera,* which presents the actual making of the film as yet another "life-fact." Here, the Cameraman appears on the screen in a double "role": he is a worker (who makes a film), as well as a citizen participating in daily life, whether by shooting on location or by posing for another camera.

Rejecting the "Film-Truth" principle, Eisenstein criticized Vertov's shots as "static" and "lacking metaphorical implications," and expressed his intense dissatisfaction with the "Film-Eye" method as a "disguising" device:

By structuring images of authentic life (as the post-Impressionists use authentic colors), Vertov weaves a pointillist picture emphasizing the external dynamism of events in an attempt to disguise the virtually static presentation of events on the screen.... Thus by recording the outer dynamics of the facts, [Vertov] neglects the inner dynamism of the shot [*vnutrikadrovaia dinamichnost'*], which actually is nothing but the beautification [*grimirovanie*] of the stationary shots.[123]

Eisenstein made these remarks shortly after the completion of his *Strike* (1924), at the time he was experimenting with the ideological function of montage. Criticizing the "Film-Truth" principle, Eisenstein claimed that it did not have "enough ideological power" because Vertov "selected only those facts from the outside world which *impressed* the filmmaker, and not those with which he should plough up the viewer's psyche" [*perepakhivaiut ego psikhiku*].[124] This criticism was most painful for Vertov, whose ultimate goal was to change the viewers' conventional perception by "shaking" their minds, not merely by "impressing" them optically, but by challenging their customary way of seeing.

Eisenstein felt that only through the stylistic modifications of photographed objects and events could the viewers' attitudes be affected; therefore, from the very beginning, he found the "Film-Eye" method ideologically inadequate. He was joined by Viktor Shklovsky in devaluating Vertov's method, especially his way of presenting newsreel footage. In his 1926 article "Where is Dziga Vertov Marching?" Shklovsky tried to discredit the *kinoks'* rejection of actors and staged events:

"Film-Eye" rejects the actor, believing that by doing so it separates itself from art. However, the very act of selecting images is an artistic gesture and the result of conscious will.... In the *Film-Eye Series,* cinema is not achieving a new level of artistic expression, but merely narrowing the old one. In the films made by the *kinoks,* photographed events are impoverished because they lack an artistic bias in their relation to the objects.[125]

From today's perspective, it is difficult to understand Shklovsky's uncompromising rejection of Vertov's work, especially when one knows that the *kinoks* produced two outstanding newsreels, *Forward March, Soviet!* (1926) and *One Sixth of the World* (1926), which were far superior to the contemporary newsreel, and marked a turning point in the evolution of documentary cinema.

Politically, Vertov differed from Eisenstein in various subtle, yet important, respects. Both opposed the party's control of art, but when directly faced with official demands to alter the ideological content of their works, they reacted differently. Confronted with the choice between his own artistic integrity and subservience to the party, Eisenstein did agree to include an apotheotic (and Stalinistic) finale in *Ivan the Terrible, Part Two* (1946/58), while Vertov intrepidly refused to make any such concessions. When pressed by the party to reedit his 1937 film *Lullaby* (dealing with the emancipation of Soviet women), he firmly declined to do so, and subsequently a mutilated version of the film was released *without* Vertov's consent. The same occurred a few months later with the compilation film *Sergo Ordzhonikidze* (1937), whose completed version was "altered against [my] will," as Vertov stated in his "Diaries."* Furthermore, he demonstrated great courage to disapprove of the political appendix to *Three Songs about Lenin,* which was nevertheless attached to the film by the production company in order to present Stalin as equal, if not superior, to Lenin.

The use of the nonprofessional actor [*naturshchik*] was yet another theoretical point on which Vertov and Eisenstein disagreed. The concept of "typage,"[126] according to which the nonprofessional actors in a film should be chosen according to their physiognomy, their facial expressions, and physical stature, is an important aspect of Eisenstein's theory. In keeping with the strict distinction between documentary and fictional cinema, Vertov was against the inclusion of any *artificial* ingredients in documentary films and, conversely, any *quasi-authentic* elements in fictional films. He believed that the two film genres could develop fully only if each explores its own specific means of expression – a theoretical extension of his concept of autonomous cinema "without the aid of theater and literature." Consequently, he considered the use of nonprofessional actors in staged films as incompatible with the notion of "life-fact" because such a practice "impedes the evolution of the documentary film....[Since] newsreels have their own path of development, [and] the staged films should not follow the same path, the inclusion of the newsreel technique into the organism of staged cinema is simply unnatural."[†]

In numerous articles and "collective discussions," the *LEF* journal fully supported Vertov's view, and when Eisenstein chose an ordinary worker to play the role of Lenin in *October,* all of the *LEF* critics de-

* In his diaries (at the beginning of 1945), Vertov states that *"Three Songs about Lenin"* was acknowledged one year after the film was completed. *Lullaby* was forcibly butchered during the editing and given very little coverage in the press. Undated, unpreserved, it was finally destroyed. *Sergo Ordzhonikidze* was ruined in the course of reediting and endless revisions. *Articles,* p. 263.
† Vertov, "In Defense of Newsreels," *Articles,* p. 153. In the same text, Vertov complains that at a 1939 film conference "all the speakers avoided the question about the newsreel film, [and]...talked only about 'artistic' [staged] cinema, [as if] we are not artists, not creative workers."

cried his decision. Osip Brik refuted Eisenstein for being "totally insensitive to the historical truth,"[127] and for using the "most shameful
method" to betray "historical facts." Mayakovsky was equally scathing
in his objection to Eisenstein's casting the worker Nikandrov for the
role of Lenin, and – in contrast – praised Vertov's and Shub's methods
as *the* appropriate way of presenting the October Revolution and its
leaders on the screen. In his 1927 article "On Film," Mayakovsky attacked Eisenstein and his production company (Sovkino) for "drama-
tizing the Revolution" in a "disgusting manner," while pointing to the
"workers' revolutionary newsreels" produced by the *kinok*s as the "correct approach to history." Referring to *October* as "the staging of Lenin
by various Nikandrovs and the like," Mayakovsky wrote:

It is disgusting to see a person imitating poses and gestures resembling those
of Lenin. Behind all these appearances one feels nothing but emptiness and a
total lack of thought. A comrade was perfectly right in saying that Nikandrov
may resemble Lenin's numerous statues, but not Lenin himself.[128]

In his 1928 public speech "Paths and Politics of Sovkino," Mayakovsky
was even more sarcastic when he alluded to Eisenstein's film:

I promise that I will boo and throw eggs at this fake Lenin, even at the most
solemn moment, whenever it may be. For this is outrageous! Under the name
of Eisenstein, Sovkino is giving us a counterfeit of Lenin, i.e., a certain Nika-
norov or Nikandrov – who knows his name! Sovkino must take blame for this,
because it refuses – just as it did in the past – to understand the importance
of newreels. No wonder we buy our own newsreel footage from America in dollars.*

Naturally, Mayakovsky came out in support of Vertov's use of archival
footage as the proper alternative to Eisenstein's method; he felt Vertov's approach ideally suited the cinematic reconstruction of historical
events. Objectively, Mayakovsky's criticism of the "outrageous" imper-
sonation of Lenin's character prevented him from recognizing other
unique features in *October,* especially its "intellectual" and "overtonal"
montage, both of which have many touching points with Vertov's theories.†

Historically, the theoretical difference between Vertov and Eisenstein emerged from the time their first theoretical essays appeared in

---

* Mayakovsky, "Paths and Politics of Sovkino" (1927) [*Puti i politika Sovkino*], Complete
Works, XII, p. 359. Referring to the newsreel footage that had to be bought "from America in dollars," Mayakovsky had in mind the fact that Shub, in order to complete her
compilation films, had to purchase the original footage about prerevolutionary Russia
from American distributors who initially bought it from various individuals during and
immediately after the revolution.
† The forthcoming close analysis of the major sequences in *The Man with a Movie Camera* will demonstrate how, in their practical achievement, Vertov and Eisenstein arrived
at similar montage resolutions.

the same June 1923 issue of *LEF*. Eisentein's article, "Montage of Attraction," dealt with his theatrical staging of Ostrovsky's *Enough Simplicity in Every Wise Man* (in the Proletkult Theater), and focused on
the mise-en-scène as a theoretical issue.[129] Vertov's article, *"Kinoks.
Revolution,"* addressed only cinema by declaring "war" on staged
films. Inspired by the constructivist concept of art, Vertov introduced
the first sophisticated theory of montage[130] one full year before Eisenstein became involved in cinema. From that moment, the rivalry between the two men grew bitter; and although it was Eisenstein who
resorted to political insinuations, Vertov was not above mudslinging
either, even though his attacks were not as prompt or systematic.* Perhaps Eisenstein would not have been so critical of Vertov had Mayakovsky and the other *LEF*ists not been so steadily supportive of Vertov's cinematic concepts and achievements.

Eisenstein's most elaborate theoretical disagreement with Vertov appeared in his essay "On the Question of a Materialist Approach to
Form" (1924), which begins as a formal analysis of *Strike* and develops into a dissection of Vertov's views of cinema. In the introduction,
Eisenstein reluctantly admits the importance of the *Film-Truth* series
in the development of Soviet cinema, while almost simultaneously
stating that "the formal structure and method of realizing *Strike* are
antithetical to the *Film-Eye* series."[131] The central theme of the essay
can be read as an ideological denouncement of Vertov's failure both
to explore the "act of seeing" and to avoid "impressionistic
representation"[132] of reality. Concluding his essay, Eisenstein states
ironically that cinema does "not need a 'Film-Eye,' but 'Film-Fists' [*ki-
nokulaki*]!"[133] This was Eisenstein's direct political allusion in his criticism of the *kinoks*. Apparently, Vertov's article "The Factory of Facts,"
published two years later in *Pravda*, was a delayed response to Eisenstein's criticism. Accepting the play with words, Vertov launched neo-
logistic counterterms – "fists of facts" [*kulaki faktov*], "lightning of
facts" [*molnii faktov*], and "hurricanes of facts" [*uragani faktov*] –
while urging the *kinoks* to treat "film witchcraft" [*kinokolodovstvo*]
and "film mystification" [*kinomistifikatsiia*][134] as antithetical to cinema. True revolutionary cinema, Vertov stated in his article, is "neither
FEKS, nor the 'Factory of Attraction' as conceived by Eisenstein, nor
the factory of kisses and doves.... Simply, it is the Factory of Facts.
Recorded facts. Sorting facts. Disseminating facts. Agitating with

---

* In two of his articles, Vertov directly claimed that his "Film-Eye" method and his
"Film-Truth" principle influenced Eisenstein. In " 'Film-Eye' about *Strike*" ["*Kinoglaz*" o
"*Stachke*"], printed in *Kino* (March 24, 1925), Vertov stated that *Strike* was the first attempt at applying the *kinoks* method to staged cinema. In "The Factory of Facts,"
printed in *Pravda* (July 24, 1926), he wrote that the *Film-Eye* series inspired Eisenstein
to shoot the mass sequences in both *Strike* and *Battleship Potemkin*.

facts. Propagating with facts. Fists of facts."[135] Vertov also requested that staged films with actors and dramatized events "stay away" from "cinema of fact," while referring to Eisenstein's films *Strike* and *Battleship Potemkin* as "isolated examples" that "inappropriately" adopt the "Film-Eye" method to fictional cinema. Obviously, Vertov's intention was to identify Eisenstein with one of those orthodox film directors who exemplified what Vertov defined as "the factory of grimace, i.e., an association of all kinds of theatrical moviemakers, from Sabinsky to Eisenstein."* Undoubtedly, this was Vertov's most caustic remark.

The "Theory of Intervals," as a conceptual basis of the "Film-Eye" method, was the core of the Vertov-Eisenstein controversy. In "The Fourth Dimension in Cinema," Eisenstein attacked the "Theory of Intervals" as the failing point of *The Eleventh Year* (1928), a film "so complex in the way its shots are juxtaposed that one could establish the film's structural norm only with a 'ruler in hand,' that is, not by perception but only by mechanical [metric] measurement."[136] When *The Man with the Movie Camera* was released, Eisenstein used the same tactics to underrate Vertov's method by describing the accelerated shooting and slow motion used extensively in the film as "mere formalistic jackstraws and unmotivated camera mischief."[137] This can be seen as a latent political accusation in light of the party's current engagement in ridding art of "eccentricism" and "formalism." Whether Eisenstein's attacks were motivated by personal bias or whether they happened to be unconscious side effects of a professional debate carried out in a politically charged atmosphere is a matter for speculation. Nonetheless, the rumors about Vertov's stubbornness, craziness, and personal quirks – which were at odds with the party's idea of an obediant "socialist artist" – may have been supported by Eisenstein who, at that time, did not realize he would soon fall prey to a similar pressure from the condemnation of his "eccentric" directorial style, as well as his "personal" interpretation of the historical events and his "ideologically inappropriate" presentation of contemporary life circumstances.[†] It may be only a coincidence that Eisenstein's article "What

---

* Vertov, "The Factory of Facts" (1926), *Articles,* p. 88. Cheslav Sabinsky was a set designer at the Moscow Art Theater, who turned to film before the revolution and made a series of studio-made spectacles. He continued to direct photoplays, mostly taken from literary and dramatic texts such as *Mumu* (based on Turgenev's story) and *Katerina Izmailova* (based on Leskov's novel), and produced numerous films until he died in 1941.

† In his statement about the "mistakes" of *Bezhin Meadow [Bezhin lug]*, 1937, Eisenstein explained: "Mistakes of generalization divorced from the reality of the particular occur just as glaringly in the methods of presenting the subject.... Philosophical errors lead to mistakes in method. Mistakes in method lead to objective political error and looseness. ...A detailed scrutiny of all the consecutive scenes fully revealed to me my wrong approach to this subject. The criticism of my comrades helped me to see it." The entire statement is reprinted in *Sergei M. Eisenstein* by Marie Seton, pp. 372–7.

Lenin Gave to Me" (1932) appeared during the period of the ideological "purification" of Soviet art ordered by Stalin. Denouncing the *kinok*s as the "Talmudists of pure film form" and the "Talmudists of
'Film-Truth' documentary" [*talmudisti chistoi kinoformy i talmudisti
'kinopravdy' dokumentalizma*],[138] Eisenstein made an overt political allusion that, by its implication, could only aggravate the *kinok*s' standing because the term "Talmudist" belonged to the vocabulary used by
Stalin and Zhdanov[139] in their attacks on the artists and their work
considered ideologically incorrect and hence deserving of punishment.

But Eisenstein's attitude toward Vertov and his *kinok*s was inconsistent and unpredictable. In his essay "Pantagruel is Born" (1933), Eisenstein acknowledged the contribution Vertov's *Film-Eye* series had
made to Soviet cinema by stating figuratively that "Soviet sound cinema was born not from the ear, but from the eye of the silent film (and
perhaps even from the 'Film-Eye')."[140] Not long after this article, Eisenstein reversed his stance and condemned the "Film-Eye" method for its
"formal excesses" [*formal'nye ekstsesy*], which he labeled a "peculiar
type of film-schizophrenia" [*kino shizofreniia*].[141] Claiming that Vertov's cinematic style suffered from "a hypertrophy of montage which
detracts from the representational aspect of the shot,"[142] Eisenstein totally dismissed Vertov's contributions to the theory of montage, and he
often quoted *The Man with the Movie Camera* as an example of the
"misemployment" of cinematic technique, a film unworthy of scholarly
attention. Then, at the time *Three Songs about Lenin* became interna-
tionally acclaimed, Eisenstein suddenly showed considerable interest
in Vertov's film, which Mayakovsky and the *LEF* critics used to
counteract Eisenstein's method and practice of presenting historical
figures on the screen. In his rather opportunistic article "The Most Important of the Arts" (1935), whose title was obviously "inspired" by
Lenin's famous statement about cinema, Eisenstein wrote that "together with Kuleshov's experiments, Vertov's *Film-Truth* series and
Film-Eye series offer profound views and insights into our contemporary society."[143] In the article "Twenty" (1940), Eisenstein retreated to
his earlier critical position which objected to the newsreel footage of
the *Film-Truth* series for "lacking a proper concept in its montage organization."[144] After World War II there was another vacillation in Eisenstein's attitude toward Vertov: the *Film-Eye* series, which he
initially found "problematic," became "important" again! In the article
"About Stereoscopic Film" (1948), he admitted for the first time that
Vertov's newsreels successfully melded documentary authenticity with
the maker's own view of the world: "What we see on the screen is the
result of Vertov's personal view; hence his films represent not only objective reality, but also Vertov's own cinematic self-portrait."[145]

The theoretical differences between Vertov and Eisenstein are best exemplified in their attitudes toward the role of sound in cinema. From the beginning of his career, Vertov was fascinated with the possibilities of sound, particularly synchronous sound recording. His belief that the sound film camera is capable of unveiling the substance of reality is significant when one realizes that in the Soviet Union at that time the technical equipment for direct sound recording was extremely primitive.* Eisenstein, on the other hand, remained skeptical of sync-sound as a creative device for a long period of time. When Vertov was enthusiastically writing about the "auditory facts" out of which the "Radio-Eye" could compose a "cinematic symphony," Eisenstein was warning filmmakers about the "dangers" of sound cinema in his famous 1929 "Statement,"[146] which, in essence, was antagonistic to the inclusion of sound in cinema in general, and only on a secondary level discussed the concept of sight-and-sound counterpoint. In contrast, Vertov proved receptive to sound cinema long before it was technically feasible, and he produced the first Soviet full-length unstaged sound film, *Enthusiasm* (1930), with the intention of abolishing "once and for all the immobility of sound recording equipment ... confined within the walls of the film studio."[147] At the same time, Eisenstein, lecturing at home and abroad, claimed that "the hundred percent talking film is nonsense."[†] *Enthusiasm* upheld Vertov's contention that the direct recording of sound on location had enormous expressive possibilities, especially in creating "the complex interaction of sound and image."[148] Most importantly, Vertov's experimentation with sync-sound took place *after* the appearance of Eisenstein's 1929 "Statement about the Future of the Sound Cinema." Released in the fall of 1930, long before Pudovkin's first sound film project, *Deserter* (1933), was completed, *Enthusiasm* has remained the most creative experiment in the early use of sync-sound.[‡]

---

* Vertov explained his concept of sound cinema in various articles. One of the earliest, " 'Film-Truth' and 'Radio-Truth' " (1925), urged the *kinok*s to "campaign with facts not only in terms of seeing but also in terms of hearing." In "Film has Begun to Shout" [*Kino zakrichalo,* 1928], he introduced the idea of applying the principle of "Film-Truth" to the recording of natural sound. In "Watching and Understanding Life" [*Bachti i chuti zhitiia,* 1929], Vertov anticipated the principle of sync-sound shooting at a time when it was considered impossible. In "The First Steps" [*Pervye shagi,* 1931], he acknowledged the principle of direct sound recording with portable sound equipment and expanded the idea of sight-and-sound counterpoint. At the Conference of Workers in Sound Film (held in the Summer of 1933), Vertov delivered a report urging the sound engineers (who resisted recording sound on location) to develop a portable sound recording system capable of "instantly capturing the sound in the street simultaneously with photographing the image of the event."
† In his lecture delivered at the Sorbonne (February 17, 1930), Eisenstein declared: "I believe that the hundred per cent talking film is nonsense, and I hope that everybody agrees with me." *Selected Works,* I, p. 553. The title of the lecture was "The Principles of the New Russian Film" [*Printsipy novogo ruskogo fil'ma*].
‡ Although both are based on the principle of asynchronism, *Deserter* and *Enthusiasm*

The fact that the release of the "Statement" preceded Vertov's preparatory work for *Enthusiasm* has led some critics to consider the film a response to Eisenstein's concept of sound cinema. Vertov, however, claimed that another statement, written also in 1929, motivated him to produce the first Soviet sound film, a project which he had looked forward to undertaking for quite some time.[149] He referred to an article written by the sound-film engineer Ippolit Sokolov, who insisted that sound should be "recorded entirely in the studio" to ensure the "aesthetic relationship between the sound and the image."[150] Discussing the auditory aspect of the sound track, Sokolov maintained that "auditory reality is essentially non-phonogenic."[151] On the basis of this contention, he claimed that it is "impossible to capture 'life unawares' with the microphone, because unorganized and random noises occurring in reality make a true cacophony of sound, literally a feline concert" [*bukval'no koshachii kontsert*].[152] Evidently, Solokov's conclusion was in direct opposition to Vertov's "Film-Truth" principle as well as his "Radio-Ear" method, both of which favored sound captured candidly as an auditory "life-fact."

Sokolov's statement "The Potential of Sound Cinema" in many ways echoes Eisenstein's rejection of sync-sound, warning the filmmakers that "sound recording on a naturalistic level, i.e., sound which faithfully corresponds to movement on the screen, will destroy the culture of montage."[153] This complied with most filmmakers and theorists of the silent era who intrinsically opposed sound, but at the same time it enraged those who tried to demonstrate that "sounds captured at random" *could* become expressive components of the cinematic structure, and even function as "music" of a different sort.* In his 1931 article "The First Steps," written immediately after the completion of *Enthusiasm,* Vertov explained:

The beginning of work on *Enthusiasm* was preceded by the "theory of the feline concert" [*teoriia koshacheo kontserta*], as defined by Ippolit Sokolov. It was also motivated by some foreign and domestic authorities who rejected the possibility of recording sound for the newsreel. Hence *Enthusiasm* resulted from the negation of this negation.[154]

Vertov's vanguard achievement in sound cinema was conditioned by a whole range of factors, both theoretical and personal: his longstanding experimentation with auditory perception as an inevitable part of the "montage way" of seeing *and* hearing was meant to func-

---

treat sound differently: while Pudovkin's sound track can stand apart from the picture as a musical structure of its own, Vertov's sound track is closely related to – and integrated with – the image, thus commenting on the shots emotionally and ideologically.

* See Lucy Fisher, *"Enthusiasm:* From Kino-Eye to Radio-Eye," *Film Quarterly,* no. 2 (Winter 1977), pp. 25–34. Fisher suggests some fifteen different uses of sound in Vertov's film.

tion as "a transition from silent to sound cinema in the domain of the newsreel and unstaged films."[155]

It is interesting to compare the ways in which the two most avant-garde Soviet films were received by the press and critics: *Enthusiasm* was attacked by Soviet critics for being "eccentric" and "anti-proletarian,"* but it received overwhelmingly favorable reviews in Europe and the United States; *The Man with the Movie Camera* was equally misinterpreted and rejected both in the Soviet Union and abroad. Eisenstein, who might have been expected to defend these films for their unorthodox structure on both visual and auditory levels, remained either antagonistic or reserved: he derided *The Man with the Movie Camera* as "formalistic" play, and failed to mention *Enthusiasm* in any of his numerous essays about the relationship between image and sound.

Vertov's difficult years

Excluding personal grudges that may have come into play, the Vertov–Eisenstein controversy testifies to the divergent interests and opposing theoretical views among the leading figures of the Soviet avant-garde movement in the 1920s. Official ideologists exploited these internal divisions to encroach on the freedom of artistic expression and to subordinate the artists' integrity to the pragmatic goals of the party. Those who opposed the dogma of socialist realism were pronounced "unsuitable" and denied full participation in the artistic community; those who adhered to the canonized doctrine were given special treatment. As a member of the former category, Vertov was made to feel abandoned and useless. He became aware of the support being accorded to other filmmakers, while he was consistently prevented from realizing his own projects. From 1935 to 1939 he submitted numerous manuscripts to the *Soiuzkino* film company, but received no favorable replies, a fact that left his mood cramped and forlorn:

It is impossible to assure my comrades of the necessity for me to work. . . . If they only would ask me to make films with the same persistence as they ask comrade Eisenstein, I would certainly be able to turn the world around. But nobody has asked me to do anything.[156]

---

* After criticizing *The Man with the Movie Camera* as "futile, self-infatuated trickery," Lebedev attacked *Enthusiasm* from the same orthodox position, in his article "For Proletarian Film Journalism" [*Za proleterskuiu kinopublitsistiku*], Literatura i iskusstvo, no. 1 (November 1931), pp. 15–16. Vertov responded to the Lebedev criticism in general in "The Complete Capitulation of Nikolai Lebedev" [*Polnaia kapitulatsiia Nikolaia Lebedeva*], Proleterskoe kino, no. 5 (May 1937), pp. 12–13.

The situation worsened in the ensuing years, and Vertov gradually withdrew into himself. "I do not isolate myself – I am isolated – nobody invites me anywhere any more," he complained in the early 1940s.[157] Later the same year, a lengthy documentary film to celebrate the twentieth anniversary of Soviet cinema (Our Cinema) was made without mentioning Vertov whatsoever!* The apparent futility of his attempts to make films finally exhausted him, and in 1941 he wrote: "I am sick and tired of everything, I do not understand anything that is going on. I have no energy left to cope with my enemies' intrigues, and I am afraid to look behind the screen."[158] By this time Vertov had reached the point of no return. He felt his "nervous system [had] been completely ruined by endless procedures of approval and disapproval, agreement and disagreement."[159]

Tragically for the history of cinema, he spent the remainder of his life supervising newsreel production at the Central Studio for Documentary Films,[†] amid working conditions that were antithetical to his youthful dreams about a "truly socialist" film production cooperative similar to his kinoks' workshop. To paraphrase Mayakovsky, everything Vertov and his kinoks had fought against and considered bourgeois suddenly appeared victorious, while their idea of unspoiled beauty and their vision of a revolutionary art had been destroyed all over again.[‡] Vertov's and Mayakovsky's careers metaphorically reflect the destiny of the Soviet avant-garde: at the height of their creative energy they were scarred by disappointment, as the impossibility of putting into practice their revolutionary ideals became clear, and as their creative achievements were constantly rejected by the state as well as by the masses. Their initial unreserved faith in the new government "of" and "for" the working class was shattered by a subsequent realization that their achievements were judged only according to current political needs, and that their expectation of the masses' appreciation of the avant-garde art was naively idealistic. The precariousness of remaining faithful to his own beliefs and the impossibility of expressing

---

* Our Cinema, Twentieth Anniversary of the Soviet Cinema [Nashe kino, dvatsatiletie sovetskogo kino, 1940] was a full-length documentary made by Fedor Kiselev in honor of the twentieth anniversary of Soviet cinema. It was composed of sequences from "the most important Soviet films," but never mentioned Vertov's work. Vertov points to this injustice in his diary entry of February 12, 1940, Articles, p. 228.
† Vertov's last documentary film, The Oath of Youth [Kliatva molodykh, 1944], was completed just before the end of World War II. From that period until his death (1954), Vertov was entirely engaged in supervising the production of the official newsreel series News of the Day [Novosti dnia], altogether fifty-five issues, produced by the Central Studio for Documentary Films. Although the credits identify Vertov as "author-director," his actual role was rather editorial, since all the essential decisions had to be made by the official and political board of the production studio.
‡ See note 108.

freely his cinematic vision had a devastating effect on Vertov; he expressed this frustration in poetic terms through lines found among his notebooks and unfinished manuscripts:

Arrived as a youngster of medium height	Prishel iunoshei srednego rosta
To Malyi Gnezdnikovskii, no. 7	v. Malyi Gnezdnikovskii, 7.
Proposed the "Film-Truth,"	Predlozhil kinopravdu.
It seemed simple.	Kazalos' by, prosto.
No. Not at all.	Net. Ne sovsem.
Here begins a long story.	Zdes' nachinaetsia dlinnaia istoriia.
In this story History will be clarified.	V etoi istorii razberetsia Istoriia.[160]

Indeed, history did clarify Vertov's "story," albeit unfavorably for him, as well as for Mayakovsky and other Soviet avant-garde artists, many of whom were persecuted by Stalin for being too candid in voicing their personal views about life, society, and art.

Mayakovsky's life ended tragically: shortly after he publicly expressed his discontent with the NEP policy and its negative impact on popular culture, he committed suicide. But Mayakovsky was "dead" long before he destroyed himself physically on April 14, 1930. Ten years later, reflecting upon the relationship between the artist and society, Vertov cried out: "Is it possible to die not from physical but from creative hunger?" And immediately he gave the inevitable answer: "It is possible."[161] However, despite his irrevocable situation, Vertov never even contemplated the idea of leaving the Soviet Union. Like Mayakovsky, he felt that he must remain on his native soil – in life or death!

The same question haunted the entire Soviet avant-garde throughout the 1920s, as its creative potential – initially manifested without any limitation – became increasingly suppressed by political terror. Faced with hopeless prospects, most of the artists complied with the party's demands; others could not do so even when their very existence was threatened. Vertov belonged to those revolutionary artists who felt unjustly prevented from satisfying their "creative hunger," a hunger stronger than the survival instinct. Therefore, it is of no surprise that he considered himself "dead" before his actual passing.

The demise of the Soviet avant-garde

As the danger of engaging in any form of nonconformist artistic endeavor became more apparent, disillusionment crept into the Soviet art community. Anxiety reached a critical point in the late 1920s when the most prominent avant-garde artists were denouced by *Narkompros** as

* *Narkompros* stands for the People's Commissariat of Education [*Narodnyi komissariat prosveshcheniia*], headed by Anatoly Lunacharsky from 1917 to 1929.

"ideologically unsuitable." Consequently, traditional artists who had fortified within RAPP,* the stronghold of socialist realism, took absolute control of Soviet art, whereas those who disagreed with RAPP policy had little choice but to rescind their ideological stance or to lapse into silence. According to Vahan Barooshian, the demise of the Soviet avant-garde was accelerated by their attempt to "deemphasize the role of ideology in art† and their disagreement with the dogma of socialist realism. As the pressure to bend to the party line increased, schisms between the proponents of pluralism in artistic expression and the pragmatic followers of socialist realism became critical.

By the end of the 1920s, the internal ideological shakedown had taken its toll on the strength of the avant-garde movement, which gradually yielded to mounting political pressure. Even Mayakovsky shied away from his initial radicalism, and in 1929 he founded REF (Revolutionary Art Front), intending to merge *LEF* with RAPP and thus postpone the extinction of the avant-garde. Unlike his earlier statements, Mayakovsky's speech at the first REF meeting stressed the "primacy of [political] aims over content and form," emphasizing that "only those literary means which lead to Socialism are correct."[162] Although he did not specify what he meant by "correct" literary means, it is reasonable to assume that he referred to the directives stipulated by the party. However conciliatory, Mayakovsky's speech satisfied neither the RAPP ideologists nor his avant-garde friends who, like Brik, took his action as a betrayal of futurism.[163] Mayakovsky's failure to reconcile the two antagonistic ideologies exacerbated his disillusionment with an environment in which one group of artists was promoted at the expense of the other and evaluated exclusively on political grounds.

Vertov's diaries from that period reveal that he was increasingly confronted with obstacles that thwarted his creative energies. After returning from London, where *Enthusiasm* had received overwhelming praise (Charlie Chaplin described the film as "one of the most exhilarating symphonies"‡), Vertov encountered difficulty in acquiring distri-

---

* RAPP (founded in 1928) stands for the Russian Association of Proletarian Artists [*Russkaia assotsiatsiia proletarskikh pisatelei*]. With their traditional attitudes toward the arts, the members of this organization, by and large, believed in the central position of party ideology in literature. Many of RAPP's concepts were later developed into the dogma of socialist realism.
† Vahan Barooshian, "Russian Futurism in the Late 1920s: Literature of Fact," *Slavic and East European Journal*, no. 1 (Spring 1971), p. 43. Barooshian emphasizes that the most active contributors to *Novyi LEF* were both militant and exclusive in their demand that traditional art be abandoned altogether in the name of "art of fact."
‡ Vertov, "Notebooks" (November 17, 1931), *Articles*, p. 173. The original statement reads: "Never had I known that these mechanical noises could be arranged to sound so beautiful. I regard it [*Enthusiasm*] as one of the most exhilarating symphonies I have heard. Mr. Dziga Vertov is a musician. The professors should learn from him and not quarrel with him. Congratulations. Charles Chaplin." Initially, the statement was pub-

bution for his newly completed Lenin film. It may seem strange that a film that glorified the legendary communist leader was surreptitiously denied major distribution. The actual reason: Stalin was unsatisfied with the film because it ignored what he thought was his role in the October Revolution.* In his diary of May 17, 1934, Vertov describes the party's indifference regarding the promotion of his film, which had a demoralizing effect on him:

It is almost four months since *Three Songs about Lenin* was completed.... The agony of waiting. My entire being is tense – like a drawn bow. Anxiety – day and night.... They managed to exhaust me completely.[164]

Expressing his growing frustration at the government's reluctance to promote the distribution of his film, he wrote two days later: "I do not know whether I am a human being or a 'schema' invented by my critics."[165] On November 9, 1934, after the film had finally been released in a few neighborhood theaters in Moscow, Vertov learned about the film's overwhelming success in the United States. Yet this fact had little influence on the Soviet distributors, even after the official press conceded that *Three Songs about Lenin* was an international success. Consequently, Vertov's diary notes became increasingly grim and desperate, as he repeatedly accused the Soviet bureaucracy of purposely disregarding his new proposals. In a diary entry written at the end of 1939, Vertov quoted Saakov (a functionary at the Ministry of Cinematography) as warning him: "You must act as we tell you to do, or you will not be allowed to work in cinema anymore."[166] Unwilling to comply with orders, Vertov turned to script writing, vowing to "work with the pen if it is not possible for me to work with the camera."[167]

The Man with the Movie Camera was plagued with even greater problems. In spite of the acclaim it had received in the domestic and international press, the film was withheld from the broad audience Vertov had particularly wanted to reach. The paradoxical situation continued: following the premiere of the film in Moscow, *Pravda* wrote that "rarely was an audience so attentive as during the screening of this film,"[168] and recommended that *The Man with the Movie Camera* be shown widely among Soviet theaters. Again, one would expect that a recommendation coming from such an authoritative organ would automatically be followed and put into practice. However, although the positive review appeared in the party newspaper, the suggestion for the film's wide release went unheeded by the distributors. Their bureaucratic attitudes were fostered by the champions of socialist realism, among them Nikolai Lebedev who attacked Vertov's work as

lished in the German journal *Film Kurrier*. In addition to this acknowledgment of *Enthusiasm*, Chaplin included it in his list of the best films made in 1930 (responding to a questionnaire organized by *The London Times*).

* In 1938, the film was reedited to include Stalin's speech on Lenin and the October Revolution.

"confused, formalistic, aimless, and self-satisfied trickery,"* prompt-
ing the distributors to shelve the film. As a result, *The Man with the
Movie Camera* was, on the one hand, praised by the official reviewers,
and on the other, criticized by the party ideologists whose opinion was
meant to be the "working policy" for the "money-hungry" distributors
who readily withdrew *The Man with the Movie Camera* from the large
theaters – a fact which distressed Vertov enormously, as his friend
Sergei Ermolinsky recalls:

Most critics accused the film of being too formal and eccentric without ever
realizing that its "eccentricity" was aimed at discovering a new and genuine
cinematic expression.... I met Vertov after the first few screenings near Pushkin Square and found him depressed, which he did not attempt to conceal....
Generally, he was a reserved person who did not easily express his emotions,
but this time he said to me: "It didn't work, it did not!" The situation was thus
more difficult for him since the very concept of this film was so dear and important to him.[169]

Obviously, Vertov found himself in a most peculiar position since
the leading newspapers and journals supported his film, emphasizing
the originality and significance of his experiment. For example, *Vechernaia Moskva* (January 22, 1929) heralded Vertov as one of "the greatest innovators of Soviet and world cinema whose work is virtually
unknown to Soviet audiences," and recommended that "*The Man with
the Movie Camera* be circulated widely."[170] *Kino-Gazeta* (February 19,
1929) was critical of the fact that "the Moscow theaters have not as yet
ordered a single copy of this film, although it was completed last November."[171] In the Ukraine, where the previews of *The Man with the
Movie Camera* were particularly successful, the problems with the general distribution of the film were no different. *Vechernii Kiev* (March 9,
1929) making veiled references to party bureaucracy, asked the following embarrassing questions:

Who has the right to say, and who dares claim, that Vertov's film lacks social
value, that it is incomprehensible, inaccessible, etc.? Whom did they ask? Did
they conduct a poll? In what cities? With what kind of people? Clear the way
for Dziga Vertov![172]

Kino i kul'tura (no. 4, March–April 1929) was most vehement in criticizing the narrow-minded bureaucracy, claiming that the "distribution
companies continue a policy implemented by pre-Revolutionary petty

---

* Nikolai Lebedev's attack on Vertov and his *kinoks* appeared in his article "For A Proletarian Film Journalism" [*Za proleterskie kinopublitsistiki*], Literatura i iskusstvo, 1931,
no. 9–10. Almost word for word, he reiterated the attack in his *Survey of the History of
Silent Film in USSR: 1918–1934* [*Ocherk istorii kino SSSR: nemoe kino, 1918–1934*]
(Moscow: Iskusstvo, 1965), claiming that "in *The Man with the Movie Camera*, it is virtually impossible to find any logic in the succession of the shots" (p. 206).

bosses," and that "to Vertov's disadvantage, they make profits for mediocre imitators, unaware that without Vertov, Soviet cinema would wither away."[173] Vertov personally took part in this struggle for the distribution of *The Man with the Movie Camera*. On March 12, 1929, he sent the following letter to *Kinogazeta:*

Instead of answering countless enquiries about the fate of *The Man with the Movie Camera,* let me inform the editorial staff, which promptly acclaimed the appearance of my film, as well as all of the friends who supported it on numerous occasions both in Moscow and the Ukraine, that *The Man with the Movie Camera* (released in November of last year) has not reached major theaters in Moscow or Leningrad so far (i.e., after five months) simply because it was shelved and boycotted by all means available to the film distributors, while you, comrades, at the same time were asking when the film would be shown. Evidently, this will cease to occur only when the opinion of the public and the press becomes more relevant than the opinion of those who run our distribution companies, whose taste is on the level of movies like *Six Girls Behind the Monastery Walls.**

However, it soon became clear to Vertov that the large audience as well was incapable of grasping the complex structure of his film, and that the masses had tastes identical to those of the film distributors; hence, the labeling of *The Man with the Movie Camera* as "inaccessible" and "formalistic" was all the more painful for him. Yet he did not make self-debasing apologies for "political errors"[†] (as Eisenstein did in 1936 and 1937), even after the most virulent party spokesman, A. Fedorov-Davydov, discredited Vertov as an "idol" of foreign "decadent" critics:

It is not accidental that this film received the greatest recognition abroad by the aesthetes belonging to European avant-garde cinema. They welcome Vertov's complete retreat from a realistic reflection of reality to an empty and fruitless play with form underscored by the philosophy of rejection of an objective perception of the world.... However, [Vertov] does not understand the whole reactionary, anti-realistic essence of *The Man with the Movie Camera.*[174]

---

* Roshal', *Dziga Vertov*, pp. 200–4. *Six Girls Behind the Monastery Walls* or *Six Girls in Search of Night Shelter* [*Shest devushek kotorye za monasterskoi stenoi ili Shest devushek ishchut pristanishcha*] is a commercial German melodrama [*Sechs Madchen suchen Nachtquartier,* 1927] directed by Hans Behrendt. It was shown in seven leading Moscow theaters during March and April of 1929, with extensive promotion. Vertov's letter, dated March 12, appeared in the March 19, 1929 issue of the journal *Kinogazeta.*
† Although Eisenstein had ideological problems with his earlier films, the real crisis occurred during the work on *Bezhin Meadow* [*Bezhin lug*], based on Turgenev's story. It was Boris Shumyatsky, a mediocre administrator of Soviet cinematography, who elaborated Stalin's criticism of Eisenstein's concept of peasant life. After several "corrections" of the script and inspections of the rushes, the entire project was canceled, and Eisenstein had to expose his "mistakes" publicly, See *Sergei M. Eisenstein* by Marie Seton (New York: A. A. Wyn, 1960), pp. 351–78. About Stalin's interference during the editing of *October*, see Herbert Marshall's *Masters of Soviet Cinema* (London: Routledge & Kegan Paul, 1983), pp. 191–200.

Following this type of defamation (in early 1936), Vertov's already precarious position in the Soviet cinema became even more aggravated. All his projects for new films and anticipated experiments were turned down by the officials: he was simply "written off" as a creative force in the Soviet cinema. Consequently, his diaries were filled with grim thoughts, and his articles lacked theoretical weight, dealing more and more with his growing depression:

Nobody requires anything of me. Therefore, it is difficult for me to talk. But, nevertheless, I will not give up. I will try once again to convince my comrades of the necessity for me to work.... They say that I do not know how to admit my mistakes. That is true. But I want to correct my mistakes by creating films which will be more accessible to the masses.[175]

Rather than a recantation of his works' ideological content, this desperate statement is a result of Vertov's frustration over the proletariat's inability to appreciate his avant-garde work. "There is nothing more terrible for an artist than to see his creative work misunderstood and destroyed,"[176] wrote Vertov in 1944, referring both to the masses and the officials who discarded his films as politically inept. Seen within the flood of other artists' ideological renunciations, Vertov's readiness "to correct [his] mistakes" seems pathetic. Unable to realize his numerous projects at the time of his creative peak, exhausted by humiliation and political pressure he could neither overcome nor surrender to, he was left at the mercy of the "obsequious" bureaucrats and political "mediators" [posredniki] who impeded his creativity, following the official directive to crush every filmmaker who did not meet current political dictates. The following note written during World War II at Alma-Ata in Kazakhstan (where the Soviet film industry had been relocated) summarizes Vertov's agony:

Most of my projects have not borne fruit, have not been finished. Nobody picked them up, hence they rotted. I have no powerful friends, nobody to go to for support.... Nobody wants to help me. Everybody is afraid of losing his head. But I am not afraid of losing mine.[177]

Unfortunately, individual courage was not a quality the political bureaucrats appreciated: they proclaimed him "stubborn" and treated him as an impediment to the "positive" evolution of Soviet cinema, while his work was disregarded by the film historians and theorists long before his death in 1954. Even when it became evident that Vertov's method exerted substantial influence on numerous documentary filmmakers such as Jean Rouch, Mario Ruspoli, Richard Leacock, Lionel Rogosin, and other representatives of the "cinéma-vérité," the "direct cinema," and the "candid-eye" concepts of shooting,[178] the Soviet film critics insisted that Vertov's place in world cinema was insignificant. Nikolai Abramov exemplifies this disdainful attitude toward Vertov, and *The Man with the Movie Camera* in particular, by stating: "This film, just like other pseudo-innovative films by foreign 'avant-garde' filmmakers, failed to exert the slightest influence on the development of the expressive means of cinema. Like all the films of this kind, it remained barren, with undeveloped characters that quickly pass over the screen, loaded with images of scandalous sensations, incapable of enriching, in any way, a living and growing art."[179] However, Jean Rouch, in his introduction to Georges Sadoul's 1971 monograph on Vertov, fully acknowledges Vertov's influence on the contemporary non-fictional cinema. Comparing Vertov with such great innovators in art as Marinetti and Apollinaire, Rouch metaphorically describes the avant-garde significance of Vertov's masterpiece:

The Man with the Movie Camera is an anxious provocation of the man who decided to make a film which we have not yet been able to understand completely and, for this very reason, which has continued to surprise the spectators over the past forty-two years.[180]

Faced with the political repression that expanded near the end of the 1920s, most of the Soviet avant-garde artists became cautious about expressing their nonconformist views. But for Vertov, to compromise his cinematic experimentation and free artistic expression was unthinkable, totally alien to his creative and ethical standards. This period of inactivity and frustration is reflected in his theoretical writings, which lost all the visionary style that characterized the *kinoks'* proclamations of the early 1920s. Stalin's crackdown on the avant-garde throughout the 1930s completely stifled creative exploration in all areas of Soviet art.* As Jean Laude explains, the party's initial ideological criticism of formalism turned into a general threat against the Soviet avant-garde:

In the USSR, the Zhdanov Report, the defeat of *LEF,* and the state takeover of ideology were to mark the moment from which the term formalism, which in the first place had been polemical, came to designate counter-revolutionary design.[181]

Following Zhdanov's notorious report at the Party Congress in 1936, "Zhdanovism" [*Zhdanovshchina*] took over – confirming that the dogma

---

* Ideological pressure in the Soviet Union had varying intensity and repercussions depending on the economic and political situation. The attack on constructivism and futurism was initially launched in 1922, when the Central Committee issued a letter entitled "About the Proletkult," which stated that "under the guise of 'proletarian culture' the artists grouped around *LEF* present to the people decadent bourgeois views of philosophy (Machism), while in the domain of art they offer poor taste and perverse ideas to the workers." *About the Soviet Party Press: Collection of Documents* [*O partiinoi i sovetskoi pechati: sbornik dokumentov*] (Moscow: Pravda, 1954), p. 221. Ernst Mach was an Austrian physicist and philosopher whose subjective idealism Lenin severely criticized in his work *Materialism and Empirio-Criticism* (1909).

of socialist realism was definitively accepted as the only "correct" way of dealing with art and culture. The party's stringent policy "to reduce all tendencies in art to a single one" engaged the entire bureaucratic apparatus "to institutionalize *its own* truth."[182] Such a dogmatic attitude was at odds with Vertov's life-long quest for truth, not only in art but in life as well.

Inevitably and ironically, one of the most innovative Soviet avant-garde artists was officially considered "counterrevolutionary" and "reactionary." Given these circumstances, a film like *The Man with the Movie Camera* would automatically become a target of the Zhdanovist and Stalinist critics who accused it of being a "formalist," "antirealistic," and "fruitless play" with images, thereby incompatible with what was considered to be "the straight road that leads toward Socialism."

The official criticism of his work and suppression of his numerous creative plans alienated Vertov from his colleagues, even his friends. He became totally withdrawn and depressed; his diaries and notebooks from that period are bleak, often bewildered. He refers to himself as if to another person, suspicious of everybody and everything: "What an injustice is concealed in the recent treatment of Vertov who is threatened with an ultimatum – either accept Sisyphean toil or face the accusation of being idle."[183]

Not surprisingly, he felt that "Sisyphean labor is torture – useless, aimless, painful, and grueling work,"[184] wholly adverse to his creative nature. He helplessly cried: "How can one explain intolerance of the talented and support of the mediocre?"[185] For Vertov, such a situation was a bitter personal blow; for the Soviet avant-garde in general, it was a clear sign of its eventual defeat.

Experiment in cinematic communication

From the beginning of his career, Vertov's goal was to break the literary/ theatrical conventions of cinema in order to attain an autonomous film language based on specific visual devices unique to the nature of the medium. Considering the camera a technological vehicle capable of recording "life-unawares" and recognizing montage as the means by which one could create the genuine "film-thing," Vertov and his *kinok*s dreamt of a newsreel that would not merely present "Life-As-It-Is" but also stimulate viewers to participate in the "associative construction" of the projected images. The result of this attitude is *The Man with the Movie Camera,* a film so radically different from both the traditional fictional and documentary film genres that even those who sympathized with Vertov's experimentation could neither understand its extraordinary significance nor fully appreciate its unorthodox cinematic structure.

The film's introductory credits (see Appendix 1) describe *The Man with the Movie Camera* as a cinematic presentation of visual events "without the aid of intertitles, without a script, without sets and actors," an "experiment in cinematic communication" intended to develop "an ultimate language of cinema based on its total separation from the language of theater and literature." Vertov identifies himself as the "Author-Supervisor" of the experiment, and calls his film "an excerpt from the diary of a cameraman," referring to his brother, Mikhail Kaufman (the "protagonist" in the film). The third person cooperating on the production of the film is Elizaveta Svilova, Vertov's wife, shown at the editing table, classifying footage and putting shots together in montage units.

Functioning as the Council of Three* for the *kinok*s, Vertov, Kaufman, and Svilova could be considered the collective authors of *The*

* See Chapter I, note 1.

Man with the Movie Camera. But the credits clearly assign the role of "Chief Cinematographer" to Mikhail Kaufman, and the function of "Assistant Editor" to Elizaveta Svilova, implying that Vertov was in charge of the entire production and therefore should be regarded as the sole "author" of the film. Vertov emphasized that he prepared for this project "through all the previous experiments of the 'Film-Eye' method,"[1] and that his ultimate goal was to present "the facts on the screen by means of 100 percent cinematic language."[2] Hence, *The Man with the Movie Camera* should be studied as the expression of Vertov's essential theoretical views on cinema. For Kaufman, however, this film's complex structure was a failure and disappointment. In a 1979 interview, recalling how the Council of Three decided to make a film that would exemplify the *kinoks'* method, Kaufman only repeated his initial doubts:

We needed a film theory and film program expressed in a purely cinematic form. I suggested such an idea to Vertov, but it could not be realized at the time. . . . Well, we finally had to break off shooting, and Vertov started editing. I was very disappointed then. Instead of a film which had been thought out, what came out was actually only its first part. And it was terribly overloaded with events which were, from my point of view, very intrusive.*

Kaufman's disappointment proves that he failed to grasp the uniqueness of the film's "overloaded" structure even long after the project was completed. Furthermore, innovation and experimentation had never excited him, as one can see from his traditional documentary *In Spring*, produced immediately after the completion of *The Man with the Movie Camera*. Therefore, it seems unjustified to claim that "the structure of Mikhail Kaufman's 1926 documentary film *Moscow . . .* seems to have influenced both Walter Ruttmann's *Berlin: Symphony of a Great City* (1927) and Vertov's *The Man with the Movie Camera*," as Annette Michelson insists.[3] Even a superficial comparison of the two films reveals that the structure of Vertov's film is light-years ahead of the conventional manner in which Kaufman depicts a city.

To facilitate the close study of *The Man with the Movie Camera*, it is useful to break up the film's diegetic evolution into separate segments so that the narrative function of each thematic unit can be easily discerned. The film's overall montage structure, which Vertov called "the film's indissoluble whole," develops around a central theme – that of the Cameraman performing his daily routine in an urban environment – and is built by juxtaposing events occurring in di-

* In his interview published in *October,* no. 11 (Winter 1979), Mikhail Kaufman also implies that he "suggested" to Vertov in 1924 the idea of making a film that would express "a Kino-theory and a Kino-program in cinematic form" (p. 55). Vertov, however, never mentioned this in his writings.

verse locations and at different times, all unified by the ideological connotation of the photographed "life-facts."

The appearance of the Cameraman as the protagonist and the thematic grouping of the selected events lends to *The Man with the Movie Camera* what one might call a "surrogate narrative." However, although the viewer is temporarily prompted to follow certain diegetic threads, "there is little possibility of fantasizing about what happened before the film's beginning or after its end, only of thinking through the paradigm of its construction."[4] This observation implies that the thematic meaning of the sequences depends exclusively on the structural relationship of the connected shots and the filmic devices employed during shooting, editing, and laboratory processing. The film's overall meaning ought to be sought in the photographic execution and montage structure of its recorded and subsequently concatenated shots. Mikhail Kaufman states that he and Vertov "accumulated an enormous number of devices of all sorts which were supposed to be revealed in *The Man with the Movie Camera*...as a means to an end,"[5] whereas Vertov describes *The Man with the Movie Camera* as a film that is not merely "a sum of recorded facts," but a "higher mathematics of facts,"[6] which permeated all stages of this production. Consequently, the ideological meaning of the film should be discerned from the relationship between the cinematic form and the thematic connotation of the film material (footage).

Segmentation of the film's structure

In his 1926 article "*Kinoks* and Montage,"[7] Vertov specifies different stages of montage (the organization of shots according to their basic function; an overall familiarization with the material in order to detect the correct connecting shots; the establishment of major themes and discovery of smaller motives; and finally, the reorganization of the entire material in the most appropriate cinematic manner), all of which can be discerned in the fifty-five segments of *The Man with the Movie Camera.*

Structurally, *The Man with the Movie Camera* consists of four parts: the Prologue (2 min. 45 sec.), Part One (33 min. 12 sec.), Part Two (27 min. 50 sec.), and the Epilogue (7 min. 5 sec.).

The Prologue introduces the film's major topic (the Cameraman with his camera) and the environment (the movie theater that reappears in the Epilogue). The Prologue concludes with the orchestra's performance, indicating that the screening of the film has started. Part One depicts an early morning urban setting; it follows the Cameraman's activity, introduces the Editor, and develops the themes of birth, marriage, and death. Part Two begins with various kinds of labor and culminates in sequences showing machines in operation, sports events, and a musical performance executed with spoons and bottles, all in the presence of the Cameraman as he witnesses "Life-As-It-Is." The Epilogue, a brief coda, brings the viewer back to the movie theater in order to recapitulate the diegetic as well as cinematic elements of the entire film recorded by the "Film-Truth" principle and restructured by the "Film-Eye" method.

The segmentation of a film in which narrative development is not conceived as the basis of its thematic structure can be nothing but arbitrary. The two existing (published) segmentations of *The Man with the Movie Camera* present filmic units according to different principles. Croft and Rose base their segmentation on a thematic/structural concept that divides the film text into seven sections:

"A Credo" (shots 1–4),

"Introduction: The Audience of the Film" (shots 5–67),

"Section One: Waking" (shots 68–207),

"Section Two: The Day and Work Begin" (shots 208–341),

"Section Three: The Day's Work" (shots 342–955),

"Section Four: Work Stops, Leisure Begins" (shots 956–1,399), and

"Coda: The Audience of the Film" (shots 1,400–1,716).[8]

Another segmentation of the film's thematic development, this one by Bertrand Sauzier, published in his essay "An Interpretation of *The Man with the Movie Camera,*"[9] contains ten segments noting 1,712 shots, as opposed to 1,716 shots specified in the Croft–Rose segmentation. This discrepancy in the number of shots indicates the difficulty of delineating cuts between shots often consisting of only a few – usually highly abstract – frames.*

The segmentation proposed here contains fifty-five units with 1,682 shots, excluding the "shots" that consist of transparent or black leader and blurred or decomposed images without any representational signification.

What follows is a specific thematic segmentation of the film (16mm print), indicating the number of shots and their duration within each sequence (based upon a projection speed of eighteen frames per second):

CREDITS: 1,765 fr., 1 min. 38 sec.

BLACK SCREEN: 16 fr. (1,766–1,781).

---

* There also exists an in-depth transcription of *The Man with the Movie Camera* in Seth Feldman's *Dziga Vertov: A Guide to References and Resources* (Boston: G. K. Hall, 1979), pp. 98–110; however, Feldman presents an extensive and detailed description of shots in the film, rather than an analytical segmentation into sections or sequences.

PROLOGUE: 5 sequences, 66 shots, 3,967 fr. (1,782–5,748), 3 min. 45 sec.

I.   *Introduction*: 4 shots, 502 fr. (1,782–2,283), 28 sec.

II.   *Movie Theater*: 17 shots, 1,280 fr. (2,284–3,563), 1 min. 11 sec.

III.   *Arrival of the Audience*: 10 shots, 879 fr. (3,564–4,442), 49 sec.

IV.   *Preparation*: 21 shots, 846 fr. (4,443–5,288), 47 sec.

V.   *Performance*: 14 shots, 460 fr. (5,289–5,748), 26 sec.

PART ONE: 19 sequences, 491 shots, 47,813 fr. (5,749–53,561), 44 min. 20 sec.

VI.   *Morning*: 62 shots, 5,555 fr. (5,749–11,303), 5 min. 15 sec.

VII.   *Awakening*: 37 shots, 3,277 fr. (11,304–14,580), 3 min. 1 sec.

VIII.   *Vagrants in the Street*: 14 shots, 1,248 fr. (14,581–15,828), 1 min. 10 sec.

IX.   *Washing and Blinking*: 24 shots, 1,798 fr. (15,829–17,626), 1 min. 40 sec.

X.   *Street Traffic*: 18 shots, 3,006 fr. (17,627–20,632), 2 min. 47 sec.

XI.   *Factory and Workers*: 36 shots, 3,276 fr. (20,633–23,908), 3 min. 2 sec.

XII.   *Travelers and Pedestrians:* 11 shots, 1,926 fr. (23,909–25,834), 1 min. 47 sec.

XIII.   *Opening Shutters and Stores*: 18 shots, 2,668 fr. (25,835–28,502), 2 min. 28 sec.

XIV.   *Vehicles and Pedestrians*: 14 shots, 1,874 fr. (28,503–30,376), 1 min. 44 sec.

XV.   *Ladies in a Carriage*: 22 shots, 2,726 fr. (30,377–33,102), 2 min. 31 sec.

XVI.   *Arrested Movement*: 6 shots, 936 fr. (33,103–34,038), 52 sec.

XVII.   *Editing Room*: 38 shots, 3,506 fr. (34,039–37,544), 3 min. 20 sec.

XVIII.   *Controlling Traffic*: 7 shots, 423 fr. (37,545–37,967), 24 sec.

XIX.   *Marriage and Divorce*: 35 shots, 7,726 fr. (37,968–45,693), 7 min. 9 sec.

XX.   *Death, Marriage, and Birth*: 16 shots, 1,890 fr. (45,694–47,583), 1 min. 45 sec.

XXI.   *Traffic, Elevators, and Cameraman*: 18 shots, 2,192 fr. (47,584–49,775), 2 min. 2 sec.

XXII.   *Street and Eye*: 77 shots, 500 fr. (49,776–50,275), 28 sec.

XXIII.   *Accident on the Street*: 15 shots, 1,418 fr. (50,276–51,693), 1 min. 19 sec.

XXIV.   *Fire Engine and Ambulance*: 23 shots, 1,868 fr. (51,694–53,561, 1 min. 44 sec.

PART TWO: 27 sequences, 855 shots, 40,021 fr. (53,562–93,582) 37 min. 10 sec.

XXV   *Various Kinds of Work*: 53 shots, 3,037 fr. (53,562–56,598), 2 min. 49 sec.

XXVI.   *Manufacturing Process*: 31 shots, 1,598 fr. (56,599–58,196), 1 min. 29 sec.

XXVII.   *Working Hands*: 73 shots, 1,876 fr. (58,197–60,072), 1 min. 44 sec.

XXVIII.   *Mine Workers*: 9 shots, 1,387 fr. (60,073–61,459), 1 min. 17 sec.

XXIX.   *Steel Workers*: 16 shots, 1,876 fr. (61,460–63,335), 1 min. 44 sec.

XXX.   *Power Plant and Machines*: 23 shots, 2,784 fr. (63,336–66,119), 2 min. 35 sec.

XXXI.   *Cameraman and Machines*: 152 shots, 875 fr. (66,120–66,994), 49 sec.

XXXII.   *Traffic Controller and Automobile Horn*: 28 shots, 989 fr. (66,995–67,983), 55 sec.

XXXIII.   *Stoppage of Machines*: 9 shots, 578 fr. (67,984–68,561), 32 sec.

XXXIV.   *Washing and Grooming*: 6 shots, 414 fr. (68,562–68,975), 23 sec.

XXXV.   *Recreation*: 24 shots, 2,667 fr. (68,976–71,642), 2 min. 28 sec.

XXXVI.   *Wall Newspaper*: 8 shots, 754 fr. (71,643–72,396), 42 sec.

XXXVII.   *Track and Field Events*: 37 shots, 3,236 fr. (72,397–75,632), 3 min.

XXXVIII.   *Swimming, Diving, and Gymnastics*: 14 shots, 1,279 fr. (75,633–76,911), 1 min. 12 sec.

XXXIX.   *Crowd on the Beach*: 24 shots, 2,323 fr. (76,912–79,234) 2 min. 9 sec.

XL.   *Magician*: 17 shots, 960 fr. (79,235–80,194), 53 sec.

XLI.   *Weight Reducing Exercises*: 18 shots, 1,488 fr. (80,195–81,682), 1 min. 23 sec.

XLII.   *Basketball*: 18 shots, 645 fr. (81,683–82,327), 36 sec.

XLIII.   *Soccer*: 30 shots, 1,402 fr. (82,328–83,729), 1 min. 18 sec.

XLIV.   *Motorcycle and Carousel*: 43 shots, 1,944 fr. (83,730–85,673), 1 min. 48 sec.

XLV.   *Green Manuela*: 3 shots, 648 fr. (85,674–86,321), 36 sec.

XLVI.   *Beerhall*: 16 shots, 1,391 fr. (86,322–87,712), 1 min. 15 sec.

XLVII.   *Lenin's Club – Playing Games*: 8 shots, 812 fr. (87,713–88,524), 45 sec.

XLVIII.   *Shooting Gallery*: 41 shots, 1,172 fr. (88,525–89,696), 1 min. 5 sec.

XLIX.   *Lenin's Club – Listening to the Radio*: 22 shots, 1,013 fr. (89,697–90,709), 56 sec.

L.   *Musical Performance with Spoons and Bottles*: 111 shots, 1,354 fr. (90,710–92,063) 1 min. 15 sec.

LI.   *Camera Moves on Tripod*: 21 shots, 1,519 fr. (92,064–93,582), 1 min. 24 sec.

EPILOGUE: 4 sequences, 271 shots, 8,722 fr. (93,583–102,304), 8 min. 5 sec.

LII.   *Spectators and the Screen*: 89 shots, 4,881 fr. (93,583–98,464), 4 min. 31 sec.

LIII.   *Moscow Bolshoi Theater*: 3 shots, 465 fr. (98,465–98,929), 26 sec.

LIV.   *Accelerated Motion*: 70 shots, 2,675 fr. (98,930–101,604), 2 min. 29 sec.

LV.   *Editor and the Film*: 108 shots, 699 fr. (101,605–102,304), 39 sec.

BLACK SCREEN WITH THE TITLE "END": 69 fr. (102,305–102,374)

TOTAL: 55 sequences, 1,682 shots, 100,523 frames, 93 min. 10 sec.

The Prologue begins symbolically with a shot of a tiny Cameraman climbing up a giant camera. This is followed by a series of shots of streets and a movie theater as the Cameraman and audience enter it. The projection booth and orchestra pit are prepared for the screening: medium shots and close-ups of the projectionist, the projector, and the reels precede the shots of the conductor, the musicians, their instruments, and the seated audience. From the outset, the notion of film-making, projection, and screening informs the audience that the "film-thing" they are going to see will involve both the medium of cinema as well as everyday life situations recorded by the camera.

Part One opens with a shot of the numeral "1" (numerals "2" and "3" do not appear – as one may expect – in the surviving prints*). The

* According to the 1935 shot list compiled by A. A. Fedorov and G. Averbakh (kept in the Dziga Vertov Archive, Moscow), in the original print of the film three additional numerals were included: the numeral "2" appeared after the "Arrested Movement" sequence (XVI), the numeral "3" after the "Fire Engine and Ambulance" sequence (XXIV), and the numeral "4" after the "Traffic Controller and Automobile Horn" sequence (XXXII). See Feldman, *Dziga Vertov*, pp. 98–110. However, the existing position of the numeral "1" does not stand at the end of the first reel, that is, after the "Washing and Blinking" sequence (IX), but after the "Performance" sequence (V). It is obviously placed there to introduce Part One, which clearly implies that Vertov used the numerals to divide different parts (segments) of his film on a structural/thematic level. Hence, my contention is that the original placement of the numerals appeared after the Prologue, Part One, Part Two, and before the Epilogue. Even the design of this numeral (which essentially differs from the conventional numbers used to mark the reels) indicates that its function was conceptual and not technical: it is simply composed as a vertical figure against a black background.

numeral "1" slowly rises toward the camera and is followed by several shots of empty streets at dawn as people awaken, wash, and prepare for work. Gradually, the traffic increases, and more people are seen walking the streets or riding in carriages, trains, and trolleys. The act of filmmaking is reemphasized by showing the Editor at work. At this point (in the sequences "Death, Marriage, and Birth" and "The Street and Eye") Vertov achieves cinematic abstraction by concentrating on formal compositional patterns prevailing in the shots and graphic designs of photographed objects and events. Part One concludes with a straightforward recording of an accident in the street: a man is hit by a car, an ambulance races across the screen in one direction and is repeatedly crosscut with a fire engine speeding away in another.

Part Two begins with several shots of the lens (in close-up) and the Cameraman (in medium shot) filming in the streets, power plants, factories, mines, workers' clubs, stores, amusement parks, beaches, sports stadiums, pubs, and theaters. After the day's work, workers prepare for their recreation; the central sequences show people playing games, listening to the radio in a workers' club, or attending a "concert" created by a man hitting ordinary objects with spoons. The Cameraman and the Editor are repeatedly shown involved in their everyday work on the film to be projected in the movie theater, and are both seen again in the Epilogue. At the end of Part Two, the camera assumes human characteristics: the tripod begins to move, and the audience, watching the film in the same movie theater introduced in the Prologue, laughs at it.

The Epilogue is comprised of shots of the audience in the movie theater intercut with shots of other people and objects moving in accelerated motion on the screen-within-the-screen. The closing sequence focuses on Svilova as she edits shots seen earlier in the film. The final shot – a close-up of the mirror image of the camera lens with a human eye superimposed on it – metaphorically concludes the film with the message that the "Film-Eye" method produces a "film-thing" in which reality is captured by the "Film-Truth" principle, which "observes and records life as it is, and only subsequently makes conclusions based on these observations."[10]

It is pertinent to note that The Man with the Movie Camera begins and ends with images related to the acts of filmmaking and film viewing: the camera and the Cameraman, the movie theater and the projector – all are associated with the spectators as they watch the screening accompanied by an orchestra. The central part of the film depicts various aspects of life in a Soviet city, intercut with images of the actual shooting, editing, and screening of the film. The closing segment summarizes the "film-thing" in a most dynamic visual manner: extremely brief shots – seen throughout the film – are repeated here, condensed into a symphonic crescendo cut off abruptly by the emblem of the "Film-Eye" method.

A "difficult" movie

Throughout the film, the process of filmmaking is presented as one of many working activities, with those involved in it shown as an integral part of a socialist environment. Following the constructivist tradition, Vertov acknowledges both the productive and creative aspects of cinema, believing that the masses will appreciate the *kinoks'* innovative approach to filmmaking. In his romantic revolutionary enthusiasm, however, Vertov overestimated his audience: not only common movie-goers but many of the avant-garde filmmakers, theorists, and critics were disappointed with the film. As already mentioned, Eisenstein accused Vertov of producing "trickery" and "unmotivated [formal] mischief,"[11] even though Vertov clearly stated that *The Man with the Movie Camera* was conceived and executed with one major intention: to rid the viewers of their conventional manner of watching movies. He maintained that the film's complex structure could be difficult in the same way "serious essays by Engels and Lenin are difficult."[12] Yet the critical attitude toward Vertov's work as being "difficult" and "inaccessible" has persisted over the last fifty years.

Only recently have some critics gone beyond regarding Vertov's film as a mere display of cinematic fireworks and instead have recognized its unique structural and cinematic importance.[13] Commenting on the structural difficulty of the film, Noel Burch writes:

This film is not made to be viewed only once. It is impossible for anyone to assimilate this work in a single viewing. Far more than any film by Eisenstein, *The Man with the Movie Camera* demands that the spectators take an active role as *decipherers* of its images. To refuse that role is to leave the theater or escape into revery.... One may safely say that there is not a single shot in this entire film whose place in the editing scheme is not overdetermined by a whole set of intertwined chains of signification, and that it is impossible to fully decipher the film's discourse until one has a completely topographical grasp of the film as a whole, in other words, after several viewings.[14]

If one wants to go beyond the "topographical grasp" of this film, it is necessary not only to see this film "several" times, but to examine each sequence and even individual shots on an analyst projector or editing table. The forthcoming analysis is based on such a close and rigorous "shot-by-shot" study of the film, including the segments that consist of only one or two frames and transparent or black leader.

This concentration on every aspect of the film's structure and its thematic function corresponds to the actual process by which *The Man with the Movie Camera* was made. Vertov and Svilova spent nights and days cutting out and adding in single frames of innumerable shots scattered throughout their workshop, arguing for hours whether a shot should be one frame longer or shorter. The analysis that follows parallels this working procedure, but *in reverse:* in order to determine the basic filmic units that generate thematic meaning, this analytical procedure deconstructs the film's montage framework, which consists of sequences, segments, shots, frames, and so-called subshots (montage units, which are not clearly demarcated).

The four parts of *The Man with the Movie Camera* (Prologue, Part One, Part Two, and Epilogue) build a circular structure that evokes the theme of Vertov's work — a Cameraman's daily activity in a Soviet city — reflecting the cyclic notion of cinematic creation. Continually reminding the viewers of the perceptual illusion of the projected image, Vertov demonstrates how "the film stock is transformed from the movie camera, through the laboratory and editing process, to the screen."[15] By disclosing the cinematic procedure, *The Man with the Movie Camera* confirms the educational function of the "Film-Eye" method; by focusing on ordinary people "caught unawares" in everyday situations, Vertov's film underlines the social aspect of the "Film-Truth" principle.

Because the film communicates through purely visual means, critics often highlight formal or technical aspects alone, instead of concentrating on the *role* technique plays in creating thematic meaning through intellectual associations. Once it becomes clear that this film has neither cogent narrative continuity nor developed dramatic characters, two choices remain: either reject Vertov's work as an "eccentric" display of optical tricks, or look for the meaning and interpretation in the structural relationship between form and content. This interaction can be fully understood only through a close scrutiny of the complex linkage between the representational aspect of each shot and the function of the cinematic devices employed in the process of shooting, editing, and laboratory development.

In film histories, Vertov's work is most often classified as a "city symphony" and is commonly compared to Walter Ruttmann's 1927 film, *Berlin: Symphony of a Great City*. This comparison, as Vertov himself notes, is "absurd," since Ruttmann's film, conceived within a traditional documentary framework, lacks genuine avant-garde characteristics. In his July 18, 1929, "Letter from Berlin," Vertov wrote: "Some Berlin critics — attempting to explain the cinematic features of the *Film-Eye* series — claim that my 'Film-Eye' method is merely a more 'fanatic' version of the concept Ruttmann used in *Berlin*. This half-statement, this half-truth is absurd."[16] Vertov's claim is even more pertinent to the innovative structure of *The Man with the Movie Camera*. The film does not merely depict a city but rather reflects life's dynamism – and its multifaceted contradictions – in Soviet society, developing a cinematic metaphor for human perception and the interdependence of life and technology. This metaphoric connotation is implicit in the film's diegetic structure, which follows the constructivist principle that the creative process is part of the work's meaning and aesthetic import. The constructivist preoccupation with the relationship between man and technology is also manifested in Vertov's title, *The Man with the Movie Camera*, as opposed to the title Keaton gave to his film with a similar thematic content, *The Cameraman* (1928).* Unlike Keaton's film, which implies a specific profession, Vertov's title suggests that his Cameraman is only an individual among numerous citizens-workers who participate in building a society using various tools – in this case, a camera. This idea permeates the entire movie by means of visual juxtapositions that create the analogy between the filmmaker and his camera, and the worker and his tools.

Thematically, one can discern five types of images in *The Man with the Movie Camera*: industrial construction, traffic, machinery, recreation, and citizen-workers' countenances. The construction shots are mostly stationary and of a broad scale, with either enhanced or curtailed perspective (depth of field). In the traffic shots, the camera, often with reduced cranking speed, catches glimpses of life. Machines are shown mostly in close-up, interrelated with workers' enthusiastic expressions and fervent movements. The images of citizens enjoying recreational sports and participating in various forms of entertainment are photographed in close-up or medium shot and are rhythmically juxtaposed to the shots depicting the sports competitions. The montage integration of these five types of images creates a "grand metaphor" about a society free of any capitalist exploitation of workers. At the same time, however, this cinematic trope discloses all the contradictions of an undeveloped and/or badly managed socialist state. The overall ideological message of the film is meant to work "at a distance," that is, it depends on the viewers' active mental participation during the screening, on their subsequent thoughts, repetitive viewing, and additional research. Isolated from this analytical framework, *The Man with the Movie Camera* is often dismissed as a "difficult" film

---

* Keaton's silent film *The Cameraman* (1928), directed by Edward Sedgwick, is considered a masterpiece; it includes several sequences that can be related to Vertov's film on a conceptual level (e.g., shooting a newsreel on the streets of New York, or accelerated motion to produce comic effects).

with an "obscure" meaning, "overloaded" with optical tricks. Only when seen within its structural context can this film reveal its full connotative potential and its ideological significance.

Reactions to the camera

The response of the people within the film to the act of shooting plays a substantial part in the film's self-referentiality. For the most part, the citizens, involved in their work, remain unaware of the camera and pay no attention to the shooting. However, there are several exceptions to this pattern, as in the shot of the poorly dressed woman who throws plaster on the wall and, unashamed of the dirty work she is engaged in, casts a flirting smile acknowledging the presence of the camera (Fig. 48). The majority of the workers in the factories do not pay attention to the Cameraman who perpetually runs around them, be it in the mine (Fig. 145), the factory (Fig. 147), or at the dam (Fig. 148). But when flames blast from furnaces (in front of which the Cameraman appears as a silhouette), a worker warns him to move away for his own protection (Fig. 146).

The female workers in the mill reveal rather indirectly their awareness – even pleasure – of being photographed: although they seem absorbed in their activity, their facial expressions and physical gestures acknowledge the presence of the camera. Similarly, the ladies on the beach subtly display their awareness of the camera as they coquettishly apply their lipstick (Fig. 162), cover themselves with mud (Fig. 161), or chat with one another (Fig. 163). The male workers seem to be more involved in their work, rarely paying any attention to the Cameraman, even when he shoots them from unusual positions (Figs. 56, 57). Kaufman and Svilova are equally immersed in their respective activities, with one possible exception: at the end of the first part of the film, Kaufman's assistant, while shooting from a moving fire engine, recognizes the presence of another camera (Fig. 120). Perhaps those most oblivious of the camera are the children (Fig. 165) watching the magician's tricks (Fig. 166), or both children and adults when involved in situations that capture their complete attention, as in riding a carousel (Fig. 174).

Those citizens who live in uncomfortable conditions exhibit a different attitude toward the camera's omnipresent eye: they consider it an intrusion upon their privacy and respond accordingly. For example, when the camera turns toward the young woman sleeping on the park bench and focuses on her legs, she indignantly jumps up and flees (Fig. 53). A milder reaction occurs in the shot of two ladies in a carriage: they amusingly respond to the Cameraman by mimicking the Cameraman's cranking of his camera, and then conceitedly gaze in the opposite direction (Fig. 69). Later in the same shot, a barefoot woman, absorbed by her duty of carrying the ladies' luggage, shows no awareness of the camera, while a boy on the sidewalk acknowledges the act of shooting with obvious amusement (Fig. 81). A young bum, ragged and lying on littered grounds, responds nonchalantly to the camera by making faces (Fig. 28). A woman, signing a divorce agreement in the Marriage Bureau, covers her face with a purse, as if to protect herself from being exposed to the camera, while her ex-husband laughs with overt contentment (Fig. 93). To emphasize the difference in the couple's reactions, the shot is cut at the point when the husband signs the paper with obvious satisfaction, as the wife dejectedly turns away and leaves. The intention is clear: the camera exposes "Life-As-It-Is," recognizing people's different reactions to being filmed. One might say that by so doing, Vertov, Kaufman, and Svilova violated one of the tenets of the "Film-Truth" principle, which states that the filmmaker must shoot people in such a way that his or her own work does not impede the work of others.[17] This may be only partially true because, although the camera "impedes" the communication between the bureau clerk and the couple, it functions as a "witness" to a "life-fact." By recording bureaucratic procedure, the camera captures the couple's individual responses toward the matter of divorce, and, in its own way, conveys the filmmaker's attitude with regard to the concept of marriage in a socialist country.

The citizens filmed on the street are engaged in their actions and respond to the camera only when it intrudes on their work or "threatens" them physically, as when the tracking camera makes its way through a crowd of startled pedestrians running on all sides (Fig. 110). Consequently, the audience is made "aware" of both the "life-fact" as it occurs in reality and of how such a "fact" is modified when the "subjects" become aware of the rolling camera. Nevertheless, the most common response to the camera is an unconcealed empathy toward the recording apparatus, a notion that contributes to the idea that filmmaking is like any other work, and that the Cameraman is in no way an exceptional citizen; rather, he is part of "a whirlpool of interactions, blows, embraces, games, accidents"[18] representing "Life-As-It-Is."

Self-referential associations

It is through associative editing and symbolic intercutting that Vertov conveys his commentary on the recorded "life-facts," especially when ordinary people are shown in conjunction with *quotidien* and yet connotative objects. There are numerous examples of this editing procedure. A shot of a young woman washing her face (Fig. 40) is followed by a shot of a sprinkler hosing down the street (Fig. 29); in the same vein, a shot of the young woman drying herself off with a towel (Fig. 40) is compared with a shot of another woman cleaning a window (Fig. 48). On a more self-referential level, the act of splicing film (Fig. 129) is associated with fingernail polishing (Fig. 128), stitching (Fig. 130), and sewing (Fig. 131). As a couple signs their marriage papers (Fig. 88), an insert of a manual traffic signal changing its position against the sky appears briefly (Fig. 33). When another couple is seen arguing over their divorce (Fig. 91), there suddenly appears on the screen a split image of two streets "falling" away from each other (Fig. 92). As the traffic fills the streets, a slapstick effect is created by accelerating the motion of the vehicles. After filming in a pub, the Cameraman is shown "drowning" in a magnified beer mug (Fig. 182), and the ensuing hand-held shots (of beer bottles carried on a tray) are unsteady (Fig. 183), as though photographed in an inebriated state. Similarly, a magician's performance is "outdone" by the camera's tricks, when frame-by-frame shooting produces the illusion that five sticks independently form a pyramid on the ground (Fig. 155). The magician himself "materializes" (through a dissolve) on the screen (Fig. 151), thereby implying that the camera is even more "magical" than the illusionist, or, on a more metaphorical level, that the Cameraman's work is not mechanical but creative.

At other points, the camera performs unexpected optical surprises by "catching" hurdling athletes in midair (Fig. 160) and freezing horses as they trot in a race or gallop through the street (Fig. 70). The prowess of a weight lifter is optically ridiculed: as he lifts weights, his legs and arms are severed and decomposed (Fig. 167). At the end of the film, the camera operates without the guidance of the Cameraman and attains human capabilities as it "walks" on its three "legs" and shoots independently, as indicated by the turning crank-handle (Fig. 197). This animated (through stop-trick) anthropomorphism (enhanced by the spectators' acceptance of the illusion) reinforces the already promulgated idea of the marriage of man and machine. The camera's "human behavior" is further emphasized when it is shown "standing" on its tripod as if on guard duty while the Cameraman, dressed in his bathing suit, takes a break and cools off in the shallow end of the beach (Fig. 164).

While the film's most humorous situations are created by unusual mise-en-scène, visual jokes are achieved through montage, by building an expectation in one shot and then disappointing the viewer with an improbable resolution of the situation in the following shot. For example, in the "Soccer" sequence (XLIII), shots of the soccer players are intercut with the shot of an athlete throwing a javelin (Fig. 170), followed by a slow motion shot of the goalkeeper catching a soccer ball coming from the same direction (Fig. 171). The most humorous effects, however, are achieved by the accelerated motion of the traffic and pedestrians (sometimes moving in reverse), which seems to ridicule the frantic tempo of urban life.

Within the context of the constructivist practice of "baring the device," the film repeatedly reveals the cinematic technique used in a given shot. In addition to enlightening the audience as to how the film was made, its self-referential aspects help the viewers to understand the process of human perception and its similarity to – and distinction from – the camera's "perception." Vertov's comments on various events are conveyed through particular cinematic devices: slow, accelerated, and reverse motion, superimposition, pixillation, overlapping, jump cuts, leitmotifs, and various other montage techniques. As will be demonstrated, these self-evident devices are always intrinsically related to the thematic aspect of the photographed object-event. Furthermore, in order to expand upon the notion of reflexivity, Vertov repeatedly points to the following: the motion picture as perceived by the viewer; the motion picture projected on the screen and simultaneously recorded by the camera (screen-within-the-screen); the "freeze-frame"; the film frames as part of the material (footage) handled by the Editor; the actual film moving through the editing table; and the film posters recorded by the movie camera and subsequently projected on the screen (like a slide). All these correspond to Vertov's directorial style, according to which the basic function of the "Film-Truth" principle is "not to rewrite life in terms of a literary script, but to observe and record 'Life-As-It-Is,'"[19] thus providing material (footage) for the construction of the film by the "Film-Eye" method.

Ideological implications

In *The Man with the Movie Camera,* parallel editing is intended to provoke the viewers to think about juxtaposed shots and to establish ideological connections between various events. For example, the shot of a nude woman on the beach covering her chest and neck with mud for salubrious purposes (Fig. 161) is followed by a shot of a woman (obviously belonging to the prerevolutionary bourgeoisie) in a fancy bathing suit and pearl necklace, applying heavy lipstick in an effort to make herself more attractive (Fig. 162). The similarity between the application of fingernail polish (Fig. 128), the act of splicing film (Fig. 129), and the act of stitching (Fig. 130) or sewing (Fig. 131) provides a basis for a metonymic comparison that works on both psychological and metaphorical levels: the parallelism between these procedures is essentially technical, but the implication subliminally alludes to the social differences between the activities of the bourgeoisie and those of the working class. Other shooting devices underscore the ideological distinction between the filmmaker's personal attitude toward the filmed events and things as they objectively exist in external reality. One of the most obvious examples is the split-screen view of the Bolshoi Theater: the classical columned façade of the old building suddenly breaks apart (Fig. 213), symbolizing Vertov's (and the constructivist's) break with bourgeois art and cultural tradition.

The interaction between montage pace and camera movement (panning, tracking, and tilting) reveals Vertov's attitude toward social changes occurring in postrevolutionary Russia. The "Lenin's Club – Playing Games" sequence (XLVII) consists of five shots (linked by invisible cuts) in which the camera glides in front of the religious store, tracks along a cobblestone street, tilts diagonally over the façades and church spires to refocus on the main entrance of one church where Lenin's portrait is exhibited above the door, then, with a swift pan, finally focuses on another church entrance bearing the inscription "Lenin's Club" (Fig. 184). These five shots are perceived as a continuous and fluid camera movement within a unified space that, through the relationship between the smooth cuts and the camera movement, provides a clear ideological message: on a cinematic level, the sensorial impact of the "swish" and "flick" pans "converts" the church environment into the workers' club, thus "sanctioning" the historical "life-fact" of the new social reality in which the religious stores and church buildings are turned into socially utilitarian environments. Due to the camera's fast panning of the sky and the buildings' façades, the transitions between the five shots are hardly perceptible; thematically, the ideological associations in this sequence are similar to the message conveyed by authentic footage showing people demolishing churches at the beginning of *Enthusiasm*.*

A close examination of this sequence's structure confirms that its ideological implication results from the integration of cinematic devices and the images' representational content. For example, the introductory shakey close-up of blurred beer bottles carried on a tray (by an invisible waiter) through a crowded beer hall (Fig. 183) in contrast to the closing shot of checkers and chess figures miraculously jumping into place on a board (Figs. 185, 186) humorously alludes to the roguish chaos of the beer hall as opposed to the orderliness of the workers' club. The two environments are connected by the camera's panning and tracking through space: camera movement selects "life-facts" from their respective milieux and prompts the viewer to syn-

---

* The introductory sequences in *Enthusiasm* include archival footage of the revolutionary masses knocking down the cross from the steeple and taking out icons from the church.

thesize ideologically the images of drunken people in a beer hall (Fig. 181), a religious store, and church buildings transformed into workers' clubs (Fig. 184) where the camera encounters only several workers relaxing (Fig. 187). These images are interrelated on a thematic level through crosscutting, thus creating a new cinematic whole with a message that metaphorically merges the two locations (beer hall–religious store) and two actions (demystification of churches–formation of the workers' clubs), suggesting that in the new society the pub and the church should be replaced by the cultural club, just as bottles have been replaced by the checker game, and church icons have been replaced by portraits of Marx and Lenin. At the same time, the sequence's ideological message reflects a paradoxical situation with ironic overtones: although the pub is filled with many customers, inside the workers' club there are only a few people, Vertov among them (Fig. 188). Obviously, the masses do not readily change their cultural and spiritual habits despite the revolution. Following the "Film-Truth" principle, Vertov refrains from misrepresenting that reality, let alone falsely embellishing it to satisfy propaganda. Instead, he acknowledges "life-facts" as they appear in front of the camera at a given moment, and only in the process of editing adds to them his personal comments.

Some of Vertov's allusions require that the viewers be acquainted with the specific contemporary circumstances, as in the shots, for example, depicting three film posters that, within the montage context, signify more than just a technical reference to the current movie repertory. One of the posters advertises a popular foreign film by depicting a young woman standing next to a man who holds his finger to his lips, as if warning her to keep silent (Fig. 26). This poster is shown in different scales, four times throughout the first part of the film, compelling the viewer to wonder why so much attention is focused on it. Was Vertov so fascinated by this poster's graphic execution that he wanted his audience to see it in various contexts? Or was the advertised film chosen for its particular content in order to discredit commercially oriented contemporary film production/distribution in the Soviet Union?

The poster is first seen (sequence VI) inserted between two closeups of a sleeping woman, thereby automatically suggesting "keep quiet – the woman is sleeping" (Fig. 25). On a strictly graphic level, its design can be related to postrevolutionary posters of the period that warned the Soviet citizens to remain vigilant and closelipped in fighting the "enemies" of socialism. It is not until "Street Traffic" (sequence X) that a shot appears in which the entire poster is revealed, advertising the popular German film *The Awakening of a Woman** (or

---

* *The Awakening of a Woman* or *The Awakened Sex* [*Probuzhdenie zhenshchini ili Pro-*

The Awakened Sex), launched at that time as "an artistic drama of passionate love" (Fig. 26). Familiar with this type of film, contemporary viewers were expected to make their own judgment of the sleeping young woman (obviously of bourgeois origin) and the bourgeois lady appearing in the German movie known for its trivial treatment of sex. The postponed revelation of the film's title on the poster, in conjunction with the sleeping young woman, suggests a humorous double entendre, especially for those spectators who are familiar with the German movie and know what kind of awakening is implied. In the second instance (sequence VII, 1), the close-up of the movie poster follows the shot in which Kaufman, toting his camera, leaves an apartment building (or the *kinoks*' workshop), gets into a car, and hurries off to work (Fig. 34). Again the difference between romanticized staged films (photo plays) and documentary cinema (newsreels) is brought to the fore: instead of going to a studio – where movies like *The Awakening of a Woman* are made – the Cameraman veers into everyday life, just as Vertov urged his *kinoks* to do.[20] In the third instance (sequence X, 8), there is a long shot of the same poster exhibited at the entrance of a movie theater, clearly a direct allusion to the current entertainment repertory promulgated by the New Economic Policy and the "Leninist Proportion." The viewers are enlightened as to the poster's actual scale because they see it in relation to the passing Cameraman (from right to left) who, carrying the camera on his shoulder, now looks relatively small (Fig. 55). The spatial relationship between the enormous advertisement and the tiny Cameraman running to his daily assignment suggests that the latter is engaged in shooting "Life-As-It-Is," as opposed to the dramatized situations exploited by entertainment movies. The graphic display implicit in the decorative style of the huge poster highlights the phenomenological disparity between the two worlds – one fabricated by a "dream factory," the other reflecting the real world from which the Cameraman selects significant "life-facts." The fictional cinema epitomized by the huge film poster and the newsreel represented by the tiny Cameraman are shown as opposite facets of the same environment in which *The Man with the Movie Camera* was made and shown. As Kaufman bustles in front of the fanciful poster without paying any attention to it, one realizes that the antithetical worlds of the *kinoks* and commercial cinema coexist indifferently. Yet, there is a practical interdependence between business and perception, as in the ensuing shot which focuses on an inscription, decoratively exhibited in the window of an optician's shop as the blinds are rolled up and reveal the words "GLASSES – PINCE NEZ" (Fig. 62).

buzhdennyi pol] are the Russian titles for the German film, *Das Erwachsen des Weibes* (1927), directed by Fred Sauer.

The final appearance of the poster (sequence XIII, 17) is a summation of all the contradictions. The poster, reflected in the revolving door of a movie theater, looks even more paradigmatic of the world it represents. As the door begins to rotate, the reflection of the poster slowly exits to the left of the frame and is gradually replaced by that of a distant city moving from right to left. This optical mutation, the transformation of one image (the fictionalized world of a photoplay) into the other ("Life-As-It-Is"), suggests a triumph of Vertov's "Film-Truth" principle over entertainment cinema. The optical blending of different images reflected in the window hypostatizes the self-referential aspect of the film while confirming the illusory nature of cinematic projection and the ambiguity of human perception. The shot is composed of four visual phases in which one composition replaces the other: (1) the movie poster, (2) the skyline of a distant city, (3) the Cameraman cranking his camera, and (4) the door frame obliterating the reflection. The fascinating metaphorical peak of the shot is reached when the mirror image of the Cameraman cranking his camera (in front of the rotating glass) gradually replaces the view of the city until the Cameraman himself is obliterated by the wooden frame of the door (Fig. 63). This shot, by contrasting the reflection of a fictional movie poster with that of the outside world in which the Cameraman captures "Life-As-It-Is," metaphorically confirms the "life-fact" that the screening of an entertainment film supercedes the screening of a documentary film and newsreel. Contemporary viewers could easily make such a conceptual connection because the film genre advertised on the poster represented ninety-five percent of the Soviet film repertory,* and it exemplified the distributor's commercial credo: "The more conventional – the better" [*chem shablonnee chem luchshe*].[21] Indeed, this was the attitude against which the *kinok*s had to struggle in order to establish a new revolutionary cinema, and to abolish the production of bourgeois photoplays, which, according to Mayakovsky, "have nothing in common with contemporary Soviet life."[†]

Another movie poster appears in the second half of the film, and depicts the citizens' recreation. The film's title, *Green Manuela* or *Where They Trade in Bodies and Souls*,[‡] refers to another German "adventure spectacle" from the early twenties. The first shot of the "Green Manuela" sequence (XLV) is a long shot of several trees in a park. The following shot (a long take) begins with a pan of the sky and then moves to the façade of a building on which the film poster is

---

* See Chapter I, note 49.
† See Chapter I, notes 80–2.
‡ *The Green Manuela or Where They Trade with Bodies and Souls* [*Zelenaia Manuela ili Gde torguiut telom i dushom*] are the Russian titles for the German film *Die Grüne Manuela* (1923), directed by E. A. Dupont.

exhibited; the pan continues diagonally over the sky and across several trees to the roof of a movie theater where a large horizontal panel, marked "Proletarian Movie Theater," is displayed; finally, the pan scans past several telephone poles and rests upon a cluster of trees (Fig. 179). The third shot is, actually, comprised (along the horizontal axis) of two images in which the Cameraman, kneeling beside his tripod, reloads his camera on the roof of a tall building towering over the city (Fig. 180). The subsequent shot, a close-up of the sign "Beerhall/ Bierhalle" (Fig. 154), introduces the "Beerhall" sequence (XLVI). The message cannot be more clear: thanks to the NEP policy, trivial melodramas have invaded the "proletarian" movie theater. By preserving the spatial connection between the two phenomena – in a concrete environment and at a specific historical moment – the camera movement *(trajectoir)* makes an ideological gesture-statement that cannot be conveyed by a cut. Resolute diagonal upward panning functions as a kinesthetic metaphor for the *kinoks'* cry against bourgeois photoplays, the main target of Vertov's struggle against traditional staged cinema.

Finally, there is an insertion of a third movie poster, this time advertising a Soviet contemporary film, *The Sold Appetite,** directed by Nikolai Okhlopkov in 1928, and based on a political pamphlet by Paul Lafargue. Promoted at the time as "a social satire on millionaires," this film was advertised by a poster depicting a group of elegant ladies and gentlemen set against the background of a modern city (Fig. 52). A medium shot of the poster is inserted within a segment depicting early traffic on Moscow streets (Fig. 54), and is followed by the shot of the young woman sleeping on a park bench (Fig. 53). This juxtaposition ideologically brings together the "life-facts" of (1) everyday events captured "unawares" (traffic, pedestrians), (2) historical documents (film posters), (3) social conditions (citizens sleeping on the streets), and (4) the technological device (the camera's lens). The phenomenological interaction of these elements is intended to confront

---

* *The Sold Appetite* [*Prodannyi appetit*], produced by VUFKU (Odessa) in 1928 and directed by Nikolai Okhlopkov, was based on a satirical pamphlet, *Un apetit vendy,* by Paul Lafargue. Some sequences of this dramatic film contain original archival footage of Lenin's funeral (January 24, 1924), intercut within the main story of the film. The action is situated in a "capitalist country." A multimillionaire suffers from a mysterious disease: his stomach cannot digest food. Doctors recommend that he replace his stomach and try to find someone who is willing to sell his own. A poor bus driver, pressed by his girlfriend, agrees to sell his stomach to the millionaire. The operation is performed, and the re-stomached millionaire begins to consume enormous quantities of food; in turn, however, the bus driver becomes weak, falls into depression, and attempts to commit suicide. His girlfriend tries to revive his interest in life, and slowly he recovers. He continues to drive the bus, but, after several attacks of depression, he drives into a wall on the street and kills himself; at the same time, the millionaire dies of obesity in his fancy home.

the viewers with the paradoxes of Soviet reality, just as, on the other hand, the necessity of cooperative relations between various industries is alluded to in the sequence "Power Plant and Machines" (XXX) through parallel montage: shots of factories in full production are juxtaposed to shots of the Cameraman shooting a dam (Fig. 148) that provides the power to drive the machines (Plate 1).

Through the careful selection and interaction of "life-facts" as found in everyday life, Vertov and Svilova use the "Kuleshov effect"* in a highly sophisticated manner to achieve more complex associations and ideological implications that, in most sequences of *The Man with the Movie Camera,* emerge not only from the Kuleshovian juxtaposition of different images but also from the ideological connotation intrinsic to the execution of the shot. For example, the famous split-screen shot of the Bolshoi Theater (Fig. 213) is associative in and of itself, that is, by its representation of a prerevolutionary architectural monument being "slashed into halves," and equally so by its position among other shots. The direct ideological implication emerges from the shot's composition and its optical distortion. Because the shot of the Bolshoi Theater already carries a particular cultural and ideological implication, when it is intercut between two close-ups of a big pendulum, its ideological connotation becomes multifaceted: it links the past with the present. In the first close-up, the pendulum swings at normal speed, as if to denote the regular passage of time (Fig. 212). After the split-screen shot of the theater, the same pendulum (by now a death knell for the Bolshoi and all traditional art) begins to swing faster, metaphorically signifying the dynamism of the new society in which classical art (symbolized by the decorative Bolshoi architecture) appears anachronistic and doomed to be replaced (even abolished) by new forms of art and communication. (A similar idea is conveyed in Vertov's *Enthusiasm* through the multiple exposure of the crucifix and church cupolas splitting apart in an optical distortion.) Finally, after the splitting of the Bolshoi Theater is completed, all shots of traffic and pedestrians are shown in accelerated motion, foreshadowing the end of the film and its dynamic montage sequence in which Svilova's eyes (Fig. 227) and repeated brief shots of the swinging pendulum (Fig. 231) are interspersed among numerous close-ups of the film spectators (Fig. 198) sitting in the movie theater (Fig. 204), apparently the same one seen at the film's beginning (Fig. 4). Thus, the notion of *temporal progression,* symbolizing the dynamism of the revolutionary era (as opposed to the stagnancy of bourgeois art), culminates in the

---

* The "Kuleshov effect" is based on the montage principle according to which the ultimate meaning of a shot is qualitatively affected by the preceding or following shot. See Lev Kuleshov, *Kuleshov on Film,* p. 200.

film's final montage crescendo where representational shots merge into a semiabstract kinesthetic and symphonic vision characteristic of pure cinema.

Negation of narrative

On the diegetic level, *The Man with the Movie Camera* defies the narrative as a means of drawing the viewer's attention to its meaning. Yet certain events are presented in a sequential order which fosters the expectation of linear development. However, each time such a narrative core becomes apparent, it is immediately thwarted. The initial shots of the Cameraman carrying his camera and entering the movie theater suggest that we are about to follow the film's "protagonist" throughout different stages of his daily work. After the shot of the camera (Fig. 1), the top of a tall building (Fig. 2), and a streetlight pole (Fig. 3), there appears the empty movie theater (Fig. 4), with its light fixtures (Fig. 5) and a cordon at its entrance (Fig. 6). The Cameraman enters the theater (Fig. 7); then the projector is seen (Fig. 8) and is prepared for the screening by the projectionist (Figs. 9–11). As the audience fills the auditorium (Figs. 12–14), the conductor and his orchestra get ready to accompany the film (Figs. 15–22). With this, the "mininarrative" is completed, and any further appearance of the Cameraman is related to situations that take place elsewhere. Actually, he does reappear in the movie theater at the end of the film, this time not among the spectators, but rather as the object of their perception – on the screen-within-the-screen (Figs. 217, 226).

The most evident example of the negated narrative core occurs in the "Awakening" sequence (VII) in which a young woman, upon awakening, washes and dresses herself as she prepares to leave her apartment. This diegetic embryo could be developed into a full narrative story, but the moment it reaches a thematic statement (in which the young woman's blinking is compared to the opening and closing of shutters), the "character" portrayed by the young woman no longer appears. However, other components of this sequence (e.g., the blurred shots of the speeding train, which illustrate the young woman's sleeping consciousness) reappear as associative inserts at the end of the film, contributing to the montage crescendo of the finale.

The first shot of the young woman shows her asleep in bed (Fig. 25); this and the following close-up are intentionally composed in a fashion that suppresses the "reading" of its representational content: the young woman's head is cut off by the upper line of the frame, and only after repeated intercutting of the same images does the viewer detect a female hand, chin, and neck under the sheets. The setting in which she sleeps is then compared – through parallel editing – to the dirty streets in which derelicts, a handicapped man, and a young woman sleep (Figs. 28, 53), alluding to the state's inability to provide shelter for all its citizens. The sleeping young woman is reintroduced after a shot in which the Cameraman leaves a building (possibly the *kinoks'* quarters) carrying a camera, and getting into a car (Fig. 34). On his way he crosses the railway tracks with his convertible (Fig. 43) and shoots the on-coming train from below by placing the camera alongside the tracks (Fig. 37). Completing his assignment, the Cameraman leaves the railroad (Fig. 42), and the sequence comes to a close with a long shot of the convertible speeding along a dusty road, telephone poles occupying the left side of the frame (Fig. 44). By means of crosscutting between the two places (exterior/railroad and interior/bedroom), the sleeping young woman is shown again, this time with her right hand resting on her head (Plate 5). Immediately thereafter, a series of brief shots of the young woman's head moving from left to right is juxtaposed to a set of brief shots of a speeding train (Fig. 38). The semiabstract composition of these shots, intensified by accelerated and reverse motion, parallels the woman's transitional phase of sleep prior to awakening. This oneiric mood is further enhanced by the flickering effect: as the young woman wipes her face with a washcloth and begins to blink (Fig. 49), an exchange between brief tracking shots of the railway tracks (Fig. 41) and black frames creates an optical pulsation akin to one's visual perception for the first few moments while emerging from sleep.

The "story" of the young woman continues to develop on a diegetic level: after she gets up from her bed, she moves around the room and prepares for work (Figs. 39, 40). Suddenly, there appears a close-up of the Cameraman's hand replacing the regular lens of his camera with a telescopic one (Fig. 45). Then, the camera swiftly turns toward the right side of the frame, and the subsequent shot reveals a derelict lying on a pile of garbage. The medium shot of the derelict is intercut by two close-ups of the camera being cranked, the second of which is seen upside down (Fig. 134), as the young man reacts to the act of filming by making faces, arranging his cap, and scratching his bare chest (Fig. 28). This uninhibited exchange between the derelict and the Cameraman informs the viewer about the candidness of the "Film-Truth" principle: the camera is neither avoiding nor covering up the unpleasant "life-facts," and the derelict − freed from moral or political restrictions − is not intimidated by the camera's presence. The derelict shots are then related to the shots of a female worker sweeping the streetcar tracks (Fig. 48) and another (older) bum (with an amputated leg) lying on a street bench (Fig. 28). While perceiving all these situations, the spectators are made aware of the Cameraman's being an eyewitness to these "life-facts," as he is reflected in the lens (Fig. 46).

The shots of the young woman blinking (Fig. 49), edited to produce the flickering effect, are compared to the shots of opening and closing venetian blinds (Fig. 50), while the shot of the contracting and expanding photographic iris (Fig. 47) is compared to the shot in which a blurred image of flowers gradually comes into focus. Both of these cinematic effects function self-referentially as they draw the viewer's attention to the nature of the film's projection. At the same time, the crosscutting between the contracting iris and blooming flowers points to the technical aspect of the cinematographic apparatus as well as the nature of human perception. Once again, the *kinoks*' idea of the merger between human being and machine is brought to the fore: the eye "armed" with the camera lens yields an "extracting" way of seeing, by which one can unearth the essence of the photographed objects.

The "Ladies in a Carriage" sequence (XV) is another example of a diegetic core that transforms into a cinematic metaphor devoid of linear development. First, by crosscutting a close-up of locomotive wheels and a medium tracking shot of a horse-drawn carriage, two means of transportation are related. At the outset of the sequence, the Cameraman is seen standing behind his camera mounted upon its tripod in a moving convertible (Fig. 65). But the Cameraman remains inactive as several horse-drawn carriages pass before him. Then a shot of three well-dressed ladies sitting in a stationary carriage (Fig. 66) is followed by a tracking shot of the Cameraman's convertible moving through traffic; this time, two ladies with an open parasol ride in front of him. In the ensuing shot, photographed from behind the convertible, the Cameraman stands poised but does not yet use his apparatus. Toward the end of this shot, the Cameraman takes his right hand off the camera in order to adjust his hat. At this point, a low-angle close-up of stationary locomotive wheels (Fig. 67) is inserted. The next shot is the second part of the previous shot in which the Cameraman and his assistant prepare to shoot. In another insert of the locomotive, the wheels finally begin to turn and, as if "triggered" by this movement, in the following shot, the Cameraman begins shooting: positioned behind the tripod, he cranks the camera and directs the lens at the ladies in the carriage riding parallel to his convertible (Fig. 65). The third insert of locomotive wheels shows the train picking up speed as white steam fills the right corner of the frame. The succeeding shot is a rear view of the Cameraman in the convertible, zealously cranking the camera as he films the ladies in the moving carriage (Fig. 66). A fourth insert of the locomotive — an extreme low-angle shot of railway tracks over which a dark train rushes from foreground to background as pedestrians move in accelerated motion on the right side of the moving train — concludes the sequence (Fig. 68). Because of the Cameraman's determined pursuit of the ladies, the viewer expects further development of their "story." However, after the ladies reach the apartment house where a barefoot maid waits to carry their luggage into the building, they no longer reappear.

On a thematic level, the intercutting of the locomotive wheels reiterates the theme of traffic and general transportation shown throughout the film. On a denotative level, the modern means of transportation, the locomotive – a symbol of the technological age – is contrasted to the outmoded form of the carriage which, with its (bourgeois) passengers, belongs to the prerevolutionary era. The juxtaposition of these two sets of images is repeated several times, as the initial stirring of the locomotive is compared with the starting of the camera, both products of modern technology. By associating the camera with a locomotive, Vertov creates another cinematic metaphor for his "Film-Eye" method influenced by the constructivist vision of the world and the futurist admiration for the technological age, suggesting that the machine should dominate all areas of human activity – transportation, industry, as well as cinema.*

In other instances, Vertov and Svilova use specific cinematic devices to emphasize the idea of technological revolution as an essential feature of the contemporary world. In the "Accident on the Street" sequence (XXIII), the image of a telephone (Fig. 114) becomes a decisive communication channel between the site of the accident (Fig. 118) and the approaching ambulance (Fig. 115). After a montage sequence (achieved by intercutting the eyeball and street traffic), the viewer's perception is "shaken" by an unexpected optical jolt: a close-up of the ambulance rushing toward and over the camera (Fig. 116) is inserted between two medium shots of the operator answering an emergency call (Fig. 113); this optical shock sensorially foreshadows the actual accident, which is not shown until later. The message (anticipating the accident) is conveyed in a purely visual manner: the order of the shots and the camera position create the illusion that the ambulance is running over the operator – and the spectator – who responds to the emergency call. This perceptual "warning" is followed by the shot of the Cameraman jumping into his convertible, his camera ready and mounted on its tripod (Fig. 117). The automobile exits frame left, while the operator's hand is shown hanging up the receiver (Fig. 114), confirming the emergency call and dispatching help. The apparent "story" related to the accident is underscored sensorially by the Cameraman's subjective point of view: a fast tracking shot (taken from the moving vehicle as it penetrates the crowd) forces several surprised and fright-

---

* About the futurists' adoration of machines and the technological age, as well as the constructivists' preoccupation with metallic structures, see Chapter I, "Futurist and formalist expression."

ened pedestrians to jump aside (Fig. 110). This is followed by a symbolic oblique shot of the traffic with pedestrians seen blurred in the
foreground (Fig. 111). The sequence ends with multiple crosscuts between the ambulance going in one direction and the fire engine speeding off in another (Fig. 119).

In response to the camera's physical movement (particularly its aggressiveness toward the pedestrians), the ensuing shot reveals a
wounded young man lying on the pavement, his bleeding head
wrapped in bandages (Fig. 118). This is an example of Vertov's metonymic "visual" syntax: the tracking camera is identified with the vehicle that "runs over" the pedestrians (Fig. 110) *before* the actual
accident is shown. The two additional shots, an oblique view of the
street "tilting" the moving cars (Fig. 111) and a shot of a trolley running over the camera (Fig. 112), enhance the meaning and sensorial
impact (the "danger") of the previous aggressive tracking shot. Together these three shots complement the function of the "Street and
Eye" sequence (XXII) which ends elliptically, by visually conceptualiz-
ing the tragic consequences of the accident (Fig. 118). The tension is
accordingly built by means of a genuine cinematic device (montage)
and resolved by a straightforward depiction of the accident, which
emotionally attracts the viewers' attention to the injured man. (A shot-
by-shot breakdown of this sequence is included in Chapter III.)

Disruptive–associative montage

The metaphorical implications of *The Man with the Movie Camera* result from the apposition of often unrelated and contradictory themes.
The emergence of new imagery at the end of a sequence invites the
viewer to establish an ideational connection between two topics, one
fully developed, another just emerging. Once introduced, the new
theme takes over in the forthcoming sequence, only to be replaced by
another subject as the sequence approaches its end. This editing procedure is based on "disruptive–associative" montage that develops
through several phases: a sequence establishes its initial topic and develops its full potential through an appropriate editing pace until a
seemingly incongruous shot (announcing a new topic) is intercut, foreshadowing another theme that, although disconcerting at first glance,
serves as a dialectical commentary on the previously recorded event.
The metaphorical linkage between the two disparate topics occurs
through an associative process that takes place in the viewer's mind.
Through such dialectical intercutting, the initially presented topic ac-
quires an additional meaning that complicates the already achieved
thematic integrity of the sequence. But this apparent complication is
only momentary: the instant the inserted "disruptive" shot is per-

ceived, it begins to function retroactively, providing more information about the surrounding shots than about itself. The "disruptive" shot(s) are repeated (often through different pictorial composition) until their content begins to dominate the screen, developing a new meaning that will then suffuse the ensuing sequence.

Disruptive–associative montage can be seen as a cinematic parallel to the "dialectical unity of opposites," which Friedrich Engels defines in the following way:

The two poles of an antithesis, like positive and negative, are just as inseparable from each other as they are opposed.... Despite all their opposition, they mutually penetrate each other.... Dialectics grasp things and their images, ideas, essentially in their interconnection, in their sequence, their movement, their birth and death.[22]

One of Vertov's most dialectical implementations of montage is based on Engels's belief of criticizing and challenging all things, including Marx's own teaching. Vertov and Svilova used this principle to confront the overt meaning of a sequence by inserting "subversive" shots that function as thematic antitheses which prompt a dialectical grasp of the sequence's message. Eisenstein also considered the dialectical thesis–antithesis conflict as part of his theory of intellectual montage. Drawing from Hegelian dialectics, Eisenstein developed his concept of dialectical montage to "resolve the conflict-juxtaposition of the psychological and intellectual overtones"[23] through "conflicting light vibrations" that affect the viewer on a physiological level and, at the same time, "reveal the dialectical process of the film's passage through the projector."[24] According to this definition, Eisenstein's dialectical conflict is more comparable to Vertov's "Theory of Intervals" (the dialectical juxtaposition of the various movements within the connected shots) than to his disruptive–associative montage (the dialectical function of a disruptive shot on a thematic level).

Unlike Eisenstein's concept of dialectical conflict that produces emotional/intellectual overtones due to the optical pulsation of images projected on the screen, Vertov's cinematic dialectics result from unexpected insertions of shots whose thematic connotation contradicts the already established meaning of the entire sequence. Vertov's disruptive-associative montage is best exemplified in the "Editing Room" sequence (XVII), the "Controlling Traffic" sequence (XVIII), the "Marriage and Divorce" sequence (XIX), and the "Death, Marriage, and Birth" sequence (XX). Altogether, these four sequences are made up of ninety-six shots, with a total duration of approximately four minutes. The shot scales vary as indicated in the shot-by-shot breakdown (below), which includes the following specifications: high angle (HA), low angle (LA), extreme close-up (ECU), close-up (CU), medium close-up (MCU), medium shot (MS), medium long shot (MLS), long shot (LS), and extreme long shot (ELS). At the end of each shot description, it is often noted that "the first frame is black," pointing to an optical "pulsation" within the sequence (discussed in Chapter III). The length of the shots, marked by the number of frames, indicates the montage pace of the sequence.

XVII *Editing Room:* 38 shots, 3,506 fr. (34,039–37,544), 3 min. 20 sec.

1. MS. Two shelves of film rolls, one above the other; their tails extend upward against a lit background so that the frames can be easily identified (128 fr.).
2. HAMS. Seven parallel shelves with rolls of labeled film; three signs in Cyrillic (*zavod* – plant; *mashiny* – machines; *bazar* – market) indicate that the rows are arranged thematically (71 fr.).
3. CU. Empty circular film plate rests on editing table (51 fr.).
4. ECU. A filmstrip with two frames of a peasant woman, head wrapped in white scarf; frames are positioned horizontally with image on its side (3 fr.).
5. CU (same as VII, 6). The film plate rotates with filmstrip winding around central spool rotating counterclockwise (77 fr.). Note: first frame black.
6. HAMS. Svilova, in profile, working at her editing table, examining a piece of filmstrip and watching it against the light table while cranking handle with her right hand (46 fr.).
7. HACU. A dark piece of filmstrip moving rapidly and diagonally from upper right to lower left against lit screen; the movement is reversed, and a bright piece of film strip (with image of an infant) moves from lower left to upper right; a silhouetted hand holding a pair of scissors enters from the right and cuts the strip where the light and dark segments join; hand withdraws frame right, leaving two pieces of film strip on the lit screen (143 fr.).
8. HAMS (same as XVII, 9). Svilova takes a roll of filmstrip from a plate on her right and labels it (63 fr.).
9. ECU (same as XVII, 7). The frame of the peasant woman in a white scarf is now seen right side up (74 fr.).
10. LAMS. Svilova in right foreground working at editing table; she puts a roll of film on the top shelf in front of her, below a hanging lamp, and then looks at the exposed frames lit from behind; the rest of the frame is in darkness (94 fr.).
11. CU (same as XVII, 7 and 12). The peasant woman in white scarf, smiling and moving her head to the right (94 fr.).
12. HAMS (same as XVII, 11). Svilova examines the filmstrip, looking at it against the lit screen (37 fr.).
13. ECU. A filmstrip with bands of perforation on both sides; one and a half frames of the face of a laughing boy with skull cap facing left and girl behind him (102 fr.).
14. HACU. The boy laughing, seen on the filmstrip in previous shot (102 fr.).

15. MS (same as XVII, 15). Svilova examines film, leaning over the lit screen (39 fr.).

16. ECU. Faces of two children, girl in center and boy at right of frame, with bands of transparent perforation on both sides (105 fr.).

17. CU. Faces of children from the filmstrip in previous shot, now seen directly on the screen (77 fr.).

18. HACU (same as XVI, 6; freeze-frame). An old peasant woman (50 fr.).

19. HALS (same as XVI, 5; freeze-frame). Street and square filled with people (31 fr.). Note: the first frame is black.

20. CU (same as XVII, 20). Two children's faces (29 fr.).

21. HALS (same as XVII, 22). Street filled with moving pedestrians (137 fr.).

22. HAMCU (same as XVII, 18). An old peasant woman arguing and moving forward and backward diagonally from lower left to upper right (106 fr.).

23. MS (same as XVII, 18). Svilova examining filmstrip on the light table (33 fr.). Note: the first frame is black.

24. CU (similar to XVII, 7). A strip of film moving diagonally from lower left to upper right across the light table; strip moves until it reveals a new shot with darker images (52 fr.).

25. HAMS (same as XVI, 2; freeze-frame; motion). Two ladies sharing parasol and man in straw hat; the shot is frozen, but after twenty-eight frames the freeze-frame turns into a motion picture, with pedestrians moving in the background (127 fr.). Note: the second part (i.e., motion picture) of the shot is composed slightly differently from the freeze-frame; it is a jump cut created by the exclusion of a few frames from the continuity of the action from freeze-frame to motion. (243 fr.). Note: the first frame is black.

26. CU (same as XVII, 2). Face of a middle-aged peasant woman laughing (53 fr.).

27. CU (similar to XVI, 1). The head of the dappled horse (seen earlier) in profile facing left as it pulls vehicle; houses, pedestrians, and trees in background (77 fr.).

28. MS (similar to XVI, 4). Two ladies in black hats in profile facing left in carriage as it moves from right to left (158 fr.). Note: the first frame is black.

29. CU. A filmstrip moving vertically across the light table from bottom to top, with hand silhouetted against light table (51 fr.).

30. HAMS. The back of the carriage driver in left foreground, as the lady in white dress pays him; the woman in the black hat and the maid in the background walk forward, while the boy in the left middle ground stares at the camera (95 fr.). Note: the first frame is black.

31. CU (same as XVII, 8). A small roll of film spinning on spindle in the center of the film plate (53 fr.). Note: the first frame is black.

32. HAMS (same as XVII, 30). Barefoot maid comes between the two women and accepts a big trunk from the carriage driver; the carriage occupies the left horizontal foreground; in middle ground the boy who was staring at the camera exits frame right; the maid puts the trunk on her left shoulder

and walks into the background, behind one of the women, while the other takes her coat from the carriage and walks toward the background (243 fr.).

33. HAMS (lateral tracking). With camera over his left shoulder the Cameraman walks toward the left, in shadows of buildings and trees; at intervals, vertical tree trunks appear in the foreground, creating the illusion of moving from left to right (68 fr.). Note: the first frame is black.

34. HAMS. The carriage with dappled horse in the left half of the frame; the carriage driver unloads suitcases and hands them to the two ladies and a child, one lady already carrying a small suitcase; they exit frame right (154 fr.).

35. LAMCU. Rotating upper edges of the panels of a revolving door moving clockwise, projecting shadows on the ceiling (80 fr.).

36. HALS. Street square and park; traffic moves from left to right in the middle ground, pedestrians mill in the background (159 fr.). Note: the first frame is black.

37. MS. The revolving door as silhouetted people pass through it and exit right foreground (151 fr.).

38. HALS. An intersection, traffic moving perpendicularly and passing each other, from upper right to lower left and middle left to lower right corner of the frame (162 fr.).

XVIII *Controlling Traffic.* 7 shots, 423 fr. (37,545–37,967), 24 sec.

1. HAMS. A woman sits at desk and picks up a telephone receiver from frame right (55 fr.).

2. MS. Lower segment of a traffic signal, with a car passing in background; two hands and a torso of a uniformed traffic policeman shown as he touches the control's handle (53 fr.).

3. MS (same as XVIII, 1). The woman on the phone takes notes (51 fr.).

4. LAMS (tilted). The traffic policeman, seen from chest up, blows his whistle; he then puts his left hand on the control lever and looks away (58 fr.).

5. HALS (same as XVII, 39). Square and traffic (99 fr.). Note: the first frame is black.

6. LACU (tilted). The traffic signal turns, silhouetted, against the gray sky, changing its diagonal position from lower left–upper right to upper left–lower right corners of the frame (52 fr.).

7. HALS. The camera with telescopic lens in right foreground tilts downward toward street and receding tall buildings and traffic (105 fr.).

XIX *Marriage and Divorce.* 35 shots. 7,726 fr. (37,968–45,693), 7 min. 9 sec.

1. MS. A man in dark suit at left and a woman in white blouse at right leaning over the counter in the middle ground; a clerk sits at left reading from a book; the man and woman are listening to him (156 fr.). Note: the first frame is black.

2. ECU. Marriage application, with typed and written words positioned diagonally (parts of words cut off); text is in Ukrainian and in Cyrillic: "Record of Marriage. Place – Veresna. Year – 1928" (80 fr.).

3. MS (same as XIX, 1). The couple converses with the clerk sitting in the foreground (87 fr.). Note: the first frame is black.

4. HALS (same as XVIII, 7). The camera slowly pans to right, revealing more of the street and traffic in the background (82 fr.).

5. MS (same as XIX, 3). The clerk in the foreground stands up and hands the couple the marriage certificate; the woman signs it (140 fr.).

6. HALS (same as XIX, 4). The camera continues panning to right (51 fr.).

7. MS (same as XIX, 4). The man signs the marriage certificate (65 fr.).

8. LACU (same as XVIII, 6; tilted). The traffic signal in its changed position, as the top of a trolley passes diagonally from lower right to upper left (42 fr.).

9. MS (same as XIX, 7). The man smiles and folds the certificate (95 fr.).

10. LACU (same as XIX, 8). The traffic signal returns to its original position (124 fr.). Note: the first frame is black.

11. MS (same as XIX, 9). The man and woman leave the room, while the clerk sits down and continues to work at his desk (63 fr.).

12. HACS (same as XIX, 6). The camera, facing toward the background, suddenly turns 180 degrees; the street and traffic are seen in background (58 fr.).

13. MS (closer view of XIX, 11). A couple, woman on left and man on right, with the clerk's head in the foreground; both look grimly at the clerk, who is looking down and apparently writing (74 fr.).

14. ECU. A divorce certificate with printed and written information in Ukrainian (78 fr.).

15. LAMCU. The woman in pearls and modern dress (seen in the shot before last) with right hand on her cheek looking down with a worried expression on her face (67 fr.).

16. LAMS (same as XIX, 13). The couple (woman on left, man on right) listen to the clerk (47 fr.).

17. LAMCU (same as XIX, 15). The woman moves her head to left (60 fr.). Note: the first frame is black.

18. MS (same as XIX, 16). The couple listens to the clerk reading (64 fr.).

19. LAMCU (same as XIX, 17). The woman with right hand on her cheek looks down (32 fr.). Note: the first frame is black.

20. LAMCU. The man talks while gesticulating with left hand in the foreground (28 fr.).

21. LAMCU (same as XIX, 19). The woman looks toward the man and speaks (44 fr.).

22. LAMCU (same as XIX, 20). The man speaks, gesticulating with left hand in the foreground (31 fr.).

23. LAMCU (same as XIX, 21). The woman with right hand on her cheek lifts her head (18 fr.).

24. LAMCU (same as XIX, 22). The man looks down, his hand in front of his mouth (20 fr.).

25. LAMCU (same as XIX, 21). The woman begins to speak; top of the clerk's head appears in left foreground (106 fr.).

26. LS (split screen; tracking). Two tilted views of street with traffic as the camera moves perpendicularly forward; produces feeling that the screen is falling apart with traffic going in opposite directions in either half (159 fr.).

27. MS. The woman, in profile, facing right, signs a document, leans forward and finally moves out of lower right frame to sign the paper (31 fr.).

28. LAMCU (same as XIX, 24). Man looks down while speaking (66 fr.). Note: the first frame is black.

29. MS (similar to XIX, 27). Woman receives a paper handed to her by the clerk below the frame; she reads it while the hands of her husband enter frame right (115 fr.).

30. HALS (similar to XXI, 5). Two trolleys passing each other in opposite directions (91 fr.).

31. MS (similar to XIX, 18). The man on left and the woman on right hiding her face with her left hand, while the clerk sitting in left foreground writes and talks; as the woman turns her head away from the camera, the man looks at the camera and smiles (82 fr.).

32. HAMS. In the center of the screen, a weeping woman wearing a dark scarf on her head, leans over a fence. In the background there is a tombstone revealing the family name "Brakhman" (103 fr.).

33. MS (same as XIX, 31). There is a man on the right and a woman in a white scarf with a purse over her face to hide herself while signing a document handed to her by the clerk. The man smiles and looks on as she signs (169 fr.).

34. HAMS. An old woman in white scarf weeping over a grave (131 fr.).

35. MS. The woman finishes signing certificate and leaves while the man signs it; a hand enters from frame right with a piece of paper and then retracts frame right (67 fr.). Note: the first frame is black.

XX *Death, Marriage, and Birth.* 16 shots, 1,890 fr. (45,694–47,583), 1 min. 45 sec.

1. HAMS (parallel tracking). A dead man in an open casket. In the foreground, strewn flowers are seen moving from left to right. People in the background move in the same direction (131 fr.).

2. MS (panning). A bride in white, carrying flowers in her left arm, is helped out of a carriage. A man and woman follow her (57 fr.).

3. HAMCU. The face of a woman screaming in pain; a hand enters frame right and arranges white towel on the woman's forehead. (200 fr.).

4. HAMLS (tracking). A limousine carrying a casket as people move toward the screen; the windshield of the car is seen in the foreground, the casket in the middle ground and the crowd in the background (152 fr.). Note: the first frame is black.

5. MS. The bride and groom get into a horse-drawn carriage; she is carrying

flowers and an icon; in the background peasants stand and watch; the driver sits in front (96 fr.). Note: the first frame is black.

6. HAMS (similar to XX, 3). The woman, lying in a bed, screaming in pain (94 fr.).

7. MS–LS. The bride and groom at left, sitting in the carriage; he carries an icon, she carries an icon and flowers; as the moving carriage exits frame right, there is a long shot of a road with peasants in the background (96 fr.).

8. HAMCU (same as XX, 3). A woman screaming because of intense pain (214 fr.).

9. LS. Two rows of cars on a street lined with dark trees silhouetted against clear sky. The vehicles move toward the foreground with the trees receding into the distance, and the sky in the middle (251 fr.).

10. MS. The woman's legs spread with open vagina from which a nurse receives newborn infant; she unwinds the umbilical cord from around the infant's neck (59 fr.).

11. LAMLS (split screen; tilted; superimposition). Two different buildings recede diagonally from lower right to upper left, forming a triangular strip with sky above; the two shots are joined along a diagonal line; in lower left corner the superimposed right hand of the Cameraman moves the camera toward upper right, then he looks through the lens and begins to crank (122 fr.).

12. HAMS. A nurse's hands are shown washing the infant in a tub. (119 fr.).

13. LAMLS (same as XX, 11). The Cameraman continues to crank his camera (36 fr.).

14. HAMS. Having given birth, the woman, covered with a white blanket, lies still in bed; the nurse enters from right with the infant wrapped in a labeled blanket; the mother reaches for the infant (105 fr.).

15. LAMLS (same as XX, 13). The Cameraman continues to crank his camera (54 fr.).

16. HAMCU. The mother, with the aid of the nurse, holds her infant in bed; she kisses it and laughs (104 fr.).

A close examination of these four sequences confirms that Vertov and Svilova used disruptive–associative montage to create metaphors about life, society, class distinction, and human behavior. In the "Editing Room" sequence (XVII), the idea of mechanical motion and the idea of a frantic urban tempo are expressed in a triple range of shots: a revolving glass door through which people continuously rush (Fig. 83), the ladies in a carriage arriving at their apartment (Fig. 81), a crowded square with traffic moving in various directions and pedestrians milling about (Fig. 84). The "Controlling Traffic" sequence (XVIII) begins with the operator picking up the receiver (Fig. 85) and continues with a shot of the policeman manipulating a mechanical traffic signal (Fig. 86). The juxtaposition of a telephone and a traffic signal emphasizes the common theme of communication (one aural, another visual). The symbolic link between street traffic and the city life's panopticum is visually enhanced by a split image in which two views of street traffic, each leaning toward the opposite side, are merged so that it looks as if the cars are falling apart (Fig. 92). Although organically belonging to the previous sequence, this shot reappears in the middle of the "Marriage and Divorce" sequence (XIX), functioning on a thematic level as a disruptive–associative image. Consequently, this shot can be read in two ways: as a reminder to the viewer that a different world exists outside the Marriage Bureau, and as a comment on the actual situation (divorce) shown in the previous shots. The most symbolic shot (no. 6) of the sequence is a low-angle close-up of the silhouetted traffic signal against the gray sky (Fig. 33). Graphically, this shot is abstracted to the extent that if it were to be shown isolated and severed from its diegetic context, identifying it as a traffic signal would be difficult if not impossible. As a metaphor of communication – both mechanical and human – the traffic signal is inserted (intercut) according to the disruptive–associative principle, and it assumes various connotations depending upon its position within the sequence's montage structure.

Another constructivist technique known as "baring the device" (revealing the respective creative process) is used to acquaint the viewers with the immediate creators of the film – the Cameraman and the Editor. The Cameraman is first seen (in the "Editing Room" sequence) walking along the street with the tripod over his shoulder (Fig. 82). Then, at the end of the "Controlling Traffic" sequence and in the middle of the "Marriage and Divorce" sequence, the camera alone is shown with its telescopic lens (Fig. 87), while in the following "Death, Marriage, and Birth" sequence, the Cameraman is superimposed over the compounded images of the buildings he photographs (Fig. 105). Consequently, the self-referential nature of the film manifests itself in different contexts: (1) the Cameraman performing his daily routine; (2) the omnipotent "eye" of the shooting apparatus ready to capture "life-unawares"; and (3) the magical capacity of cinema to capture "invisible" aspects of reality that are inaccessible to the naked eye.

The "Editing Room" sequence introduces several new topics: the montage process as part of filmmaking, the perceptual distinction between motion pictures and the freeze-frame, and urban activity as part of social stratification represented by the contrast between the peasant women and the bourgeois ladies. Near the end of the sequence, two additional inserts of the revolving door (Fig. 83) are associated with traffic and city commotion, creating a metaphor for the repetitiveness and limitation of life's circles. Similarly, in the "Controlling Traffic" sequence, the events on the street (traffic, pedestrians) are directly related to mechanical aspects of communication, as exemplified by the linkage of the operator answering the telephone (Fig. 85)

and the policeman handling traffic (Fig. 86). In this context, the operator functions as a liaison between the accident on the street and the
ambulance, while the sequence ends with a self-referential shot of the
camera, armed with a telescopic lens ready to catch "life-unawares"
from a distance (Fig. 87). Though invisible, the Cameraman's presence
is evident as the camera swings around to capture something on the
other side of the shooting axis that has obviously drawn his interest —
the Marriage Bureau.

Once the physical relationship between the camera and the environment is established, the "Marriage and Divorce" sequence begins with
a seemingly narrative event. A young couple stands in front of a desk
while being interviewed by a Marriage Bureau clerk (Fig. 88). The next
shot is a close-up of a white piece of paper bearing the inscription
"Marriage Certificate" (Fig. 89), followed by the same medium shot of
the couple conversing with the clerk (Fig. 88). Then comes the shot
already seen at the end of the previous "Controlling Traffic" sequence
(XVIII), that of the camera panning to the right and overlooking the
street from a high angle (Fig. 87). This shot is inserted within the
shots of the couple signing the marriage certificate (Fig. 88), thus pre-
paring the viewer for the symbolic shot of the traffic signal (Fig. 33)
already seen in close-up in the previous sequence (XVIII, 6). In this
context, the traffic signal connotes the marriage approval. The bride-
groom smiles and folds the certificate as, in the ensuing shot, the
traffic signal returns to the "go" position, humorously implying that
the road to life is open for the new couple! The comic overtone of the
situation has already been anticipated by the shot of the camera
equipped with a telescopic lens that abruptly turns to the street as if
to catch up with the outside world (Fig. 87): as soon as the couple
leaves the bureau, the camera hastily turns forward (as if "facing" the
audience), and the ensuing shot reveals the second couple standing in
the same spot while listening to the clerk as he reads a divorce certificate (Fig. 90). The next ten shots of the couple arguing are edited on
the shot–countershot principle (Fig. 91), culminating with a notable
metaphorical image (split-screen) composed of two tracking shots of
the street, each half tilted to the opposite side (Fig. 92). The alternate
movement of the traffic adds to the graphic symbolism of this shot by
creating the impression that the screen is being rent. The visual metaphor (implying a broken marriage) is intensified on the level of mise-
en-scène in the following shot depicting the depressed wife signing
the paper, the husband arguing with her, and the woman receiving the
divorce certificate (Fig. 91). Finally, the communicative aspect of
traffic is reintroduced to create a pun on the speed and facility with
which a divorce can be obtained in the Soviet Union: the marriage's
instant termination is indicated by a series of shots depicting the third

couple (Fig. 93) and an insert of two trolleys passing each other in opposite directions (Fig. 94). But the camera does not merely focus on the bureaucratic procedure; it is particularly engaged in recording the human condition, as in the shots of the spouse who hides from the camera while the husband appears pleased with the outcome of the case (Fig. 93). Near the end of the sequence, an unexpected disruptive–associative shot is inserted: an old woman stands weeping over a tombstone (Fig. 95). The final shot returns to the divorce procedure: as the wife signs the certificate, she covers her face with her purse (Fig. 93). Then an additional disruptive–associative insert of another old woman crying over a grave (Fig. 96) foreshadows the next sequence, which begins with a public funeral (Fig. 97).

The "Death, Marriage, and Birth" sequence (XX) opens with a shot of a public open-casket funeral (Fig. 97), followed by a shot of a bride in white (Fig. 98), a shot of a woman in labor (Fig. 99), another shot (a frontal view) of a limousine bearing the casket (Fig. 100), a shot of the bride and groom climbing into a horse-drawn carriage (Fig. 101), another shot of the woman in labor (Fig. 99), a shot of the bride and groom holding religious icons (Fig. 102), and the closing long shot of the cars in the funeral procession (Fig. 103). The sequence culminates with a shot of the woman giving birth to a child (Fig. 104), generally considered the most provocative image in the entire film. In the next compound shot, the figure of the Cameraman cranking his camera is superimposed over two tall buildings (their positions askew), presumably the hospital (Fig. 105). This shot is repetitively inserted among the shots of the woman giving birth (Fig. 104), of two hands washing the infant in a tub (Fig. 106), of the mother lying in bed and reaching for the baby (Fig. 107), and of her kissing her child (Fig. 108). The "Film-Eye" is alert at all times: while the midwife assists the woman in her delivery, the Cameraman is involved in recording "life-facts," without closing his eyes even in front of the most "shocking" occurrences. But the "Film-Eye" uses this event as an opportunity not to develop a plot, but rather to document "Life-As-It-Is."

On the structural level, these four sequences support the ideological implications initiated throughout Part One: the interrelationship between various aspects of "Life-As-It-Is" and the unique power of technology to expand human experience and perception. The "Editing Room" sequence (XVII) develops the theme of people (mostly in close-ups) and traffic (mostly in long shots) as the two most dynamic aspects of urban life, a milieu to which the Cameraman, Editor, and Filmmaker belong. In the "Controlling Traffic" sequence (XVIII), the traffic signal becomes a symbol of a more personal human relationship. Inserted frequently in the "Marriage and Divorce" sequence (XIX), the signal parallels the second couple's conflict. As the sequence reaches its thematic peak, the characteristic gestures and expressions of the divorcing couple are alternated in ten shots, while the ironic comment on the divorce procedure is rendered by the insertion of a compound shot of two streetcars passing in opposite directions. Then a third couple appears in front of the Marriage Bureau clerk, and it is at this point that a disruptive–associative shot of an old woman crying over a gravestone is inserted. To emphasize this parallelism, after the couple signs the divorce papers, another shot of the old woman crying in the graveyard is inserted to complete the "Marriage and Divorce" sequence. Although the ensuing sequence, "Death, Marriage, and Birth" (XX), begins with the shot of a corpse in an open coffin carried in a limousine, the marriage shots dominate by a ratio of seven to three; and even though the death theme prevails emotionally and visually in the tracking shots of the funeral, the sequence ends with a celebration of life through a series of shots in which the happy mother cuddles and kisses her newborn baby.

Other examples of disruptive–associative montage in *The Man with the Movie Camera* (based on a similar principle of intercutting shots seen earlier in the film) prod the viewer to search for the images' metaphoric meaning within the context of the respective sequence. For example, the shots of machines and gears are inserted in sequences completely unrelated to industrial production; in this associative context, they are meant to symbolize the movement and progress of a new society. Similarly, the shots of a train, first inserted at the beginning of the "Awakening" sequence (VII), reappear in "Travelers and Pedestrians" (XII), "Ladies in a Carriage" (XV), and "Spectators and the Screen" (LII). Distinct types of labor, shown in the "Various Kinds of Work" sequence (XXV), are reinserted in "Working Hands" (XXVII), "Traffic Controller and Automobile Horn" (XXXII), and in "Washing and Grooming" (XXXIV). "Disruptive" inserts appear among the sports events to disrupt the montage flow of the games; for example, the shot of a somersaulting athlete (Fig. 172) is inserted at the beginning of the "Motorcycle and Carousel" sequence (XLIV), between a shot of a ball in flight (Fig. 169) and the shot of cyclists on the motorcycle track (Fig. 173). The same insert appears among other shots of the racing motorcyclists; the third time, however, the somersaulting athlete is shown jumping backwards, associatively alluding to the danger of motor racing. Similarly, an insert of a female athlete doing the high jump (Fig. 159) appears among the shots of the rotating carousel. In the same vein, several blurred shots of the speeding train (Fig. 38) introduced in the "Awakening" sequence (VII), reflect the sleeping young woman's consciousness and appear within the "Vehicles and Pedestrian" sequence (XIV) to emphasize the hectic tempo of city life. Finally, in the "Spectators and the Screen" sequence (LII), the same blurred shots of the passing train (photographed from an extreme low angle) are inserted among images projected on the screen-within-the-screen, just as the shot of the young sleeping woman is inserted among the shots of the "Morning" sequence (VI) to illustrate this sequence's main theme (the dawn) and to anticipate the next sequence's theme (awakening). In general, the "disruptive" shots – whose associative meanings depend upon the diegetic context of each separate sequence – contribute to the film's rhythmic pulsation, stimulating the viewer to think about montage as *the* determinator of thematic meaning.

Vertov and Svilova build a dialectical unity of thematic opposites on the structural basis of disruptive–associative montage, as the selected "life-facts" are related to each other not through narrative continuity but through an ideological juxtaposition of presented events. Because the connection between the inserted shots and the main thematic blocks depends upon the viewer's capacity and willingness to search for and establish the ideological implication of the montage concatenation, the sequences based on disruptive–associative montage pose a substantial demand on the viewer both during and after screening *The Man with the Movie Camera.*

Social and political commentary

Social criticism in *The Man with the Movie Camera* can easily be overlooked or misread. Due to the metaphorical function of disruptive–associative montage, the full ideological meaning of the intercut images emerges only retroactively. Note, for example, the shot of a giant bottle dominating the park landscape (Fig. 27) preceding the shot of a derelict asleep on a park bench surrounded by rubbish (Fig. 28). By virtue of instant association, the shot of the giant bottle (shaped like a common wine container) implies that it contains alcohol. At the same time, the composition of the shot with the decorative bottle in the center of a park connotes abundance, leisure, or pleasure, and as such, it is in ideological conflict with the derelict's living conditions (dirty streets). Obviously, Vertov expected his audience to ask questions pertinent to the social circumstances that surround and identify these two environments.

More relevant social criticism is generated by relating shots of sweating workers carrying ore in primitive carts (Fig. 56) and shots of activity in a dirty factory yard (Fig. 57) to those of well-dressed women strolling down the street and riding the trolley (Fig. 209), alongside poorly made horse carts in the middle of a public square (Fig. 64). Different social strata – the working class and the bourgeoisie, the poor and the well-to-do – are juxtaposed, alluding to the contradictions in their coexistence within the new socialist regime. A similar ideological implication is conveyed by juxtaposing images of a rich display of various (some of them quite luxurious) consumer products in city store windows (Fig. 31) with images of poorly dressed female workers engaged in heavy physical labor (Fig. 48), or juxtaposing well-to-do ladies being made up in the beauty salon (Fig. 121) with the haggard faces of peasant women at the market and on the street (Figs. 59, 71). A less ideological, more thematic association is achieved by crosscutting the shot of women doing laundry (Fig. 122) with the shots of women having their hair shampooed and dried (Fig. 121).

At some key junctures, entire sequences are juxtaposed for social purposes. The sequence in which a group of citizens is shown drinking beer in a *crowded* pub (Fig. 181) precedes the sequence of a workers' club dedicated to "V. I. Ulyanov – Lenin" (Fig. 195), where only a *few* individuals-workers are shown reading papers, playing checkers and chess (Fig. 187). In other sequences, Vertov's social criticism is more satirical, assuming the form of a political joke. The shaving of a man's face (Fig. 123) is humorously associated with the sharpening of a razor (Fig. 124), which in turn is juxtaposed to the sharpening of an ax on a large grindstone (Fig. 125). This triple comparison, in addition to its thematic meaning, implies the shortage of high-quality razors and the general lack of consumer goods in the postrevolutionary period.

Montage juxtaposition sometimes lends itself to a direct political comment which stems from Vertov's statement that "either one serves the members of the new bourgeoisie, or one works to eliminate them."[25] This belief shines through poignantly in another juxtaposition of the bourgeois ladies enjoying the attention lavished upon them in a beauty parlor (Fig. 121) with the close-up of the ax being sharpened (Fig. 125). Moreover, in the latter shot, the worker's hand is missing the middle and index fingers, as opposed to the beautifully manicured hands of the bourgeois ladies (Fig. 128). Other shots make their sociopolitical statements through a more direct contrast, as, for example, when a traditional peasant wedding, with a horse and buggy carrying the formally dressed bride and the groom holding religious icons (Fig. 102) is juxtaposed with the bureaucratic and businesslike nature of a civil wedding hastily performed and, with even greater expedience, later invalidated in the Marriage–Divorce Bureau, a grim place devoid of any ritualistic or ceremonial atmosphere (Fig. 88). Vertov compares these two "life-facts" without explicitly conveying his personal opinion, allowing the viewers to make their own judgments according to their socioreligious inclinations.

Perhaps the most blatant social criticism is made by the shot depicting elegant bourgeois ladies arriving at their apartment building in a carriage, while a barefoot and shabbily dressed maid obediently waits out on the street to carry their heavy suitcases on her shoulders (Fig. 81). The characteristic reactions of the individuals in this shot reveal their different socioeconomic backgrounds and attitudes. The maid, earnestly involved in her work (carrying the burden), does not pay any attention to the camera, while the well-dressed ladies either flirt with the camera or disdainfully pretend to be uninterested. To emphasize the spatial aspect of the situation, Kaufman found the optimal position for his camera: he photographed the ladies sitting comfortably in the carriage from a high angle so that they appear in the foreground of the shot, while beneath them the barefoot maid moves deferentially in the background. The inquisitive boy (standing on the side) is positioned in the middle ground facing the camera, and the coachman (who places the suitcases on the maid's shoulders) fills the upper left foreground. As the ladies and the maid withdraw into the background, the driver pulls out of the left foreground, and the boy exits to the right, leaving the shot composition "open," in contrast to its being "closed" at the beginning. The integration of the camera angle, mise-en-scène, depth of field, and the spontaneous reaction of the people points to class distinction in the Soviet Union, a contrived irony revealed by the "Film-Truth" principle. Although it is not explicitly stated whether the ladies belong to the old bourgeoisie or represent the "new class" emerging from the growing socialist bureaucracy, it is obvious that Vertov disapproves of one group of people exploiting another. This is corroborated in a humorous way by the next (and last) shot of the sequence, in which the Cameraman is shown walking along the street with the tripod and camera over his shoulder (Fig. 82), unequivocally allying himself with the barefoot maid carrying the suitcase.

In the early 1920s, most of the truly revolutionary Soviet artists were profoundly disappointed with the consumer mentality of the NEP era that perpetuated a bourgeois worldview. Vertov, Kaufman, and Svilova responded to such a mentality by recording "life-facts" from this period while identifying themselves with ordinary citizens and workers who suffered because of the economic situation. Vertov compares the Cameraman cranking his camera (Fig. 134) to the shoeshiner brushing shoes (Fig. 127), and shows Kaufman reflected in the mirror on which a shoeshine sign is painted (Fig. 126), visually elaborating his claim that the kinoks should be proud of equating themselves with the "shoemakers of cinema," rather than the fictional film directors, whom Vertov labeled as "film-mensheviks," "directors of enchantment," "priests-directors," and "grandiose directors."* Reacting against all these, Vertov and his kinoks sided with ordinary working people as opposed to the old bourgeoisie and the "new class."

* These terms can be found throughout Vertov's *Articles,* as, for example, "shoemaker of cinema" [*sapozhnik kinematografii*], p. 71; "film-mensheviks" [*kinomen' sheviki*], p. 79; "director-enchanter" [*volshebnik-rezhiser*], p. 92; "director-priest" [*zhrets-rezhiser*], p. 96; "grandiose directors" [*grandioznye kinorezhisery*], p. 99.

The nature of the film image

Vertov's ideological allusions are further enhanced by cinematic techniques that call into question the ontological authenticity of the motion picture image. Particularly, the appearance of freeze-frames within the motion pictures emphasizes the perceptual distinction between still and motion photography. The perceptual "clash" created by juxtaposing freeze-frames and motion pictures projected consecutively on the screen points to the fact that the cinematic vision can be expanded by modern technology in order to provide a deeper insight into the external world. On the other hand, by pinpointing the perceptual distinctions among still photography, freeze-frames, and motion pictures, Vertov acknowledges his commitment to "cinema of fact," inviting his audience to experience "Life-As-It-Is" from the standpoint of the "Film-Truth" principle and "Film-Eye" method, which can achieve, as no other medium, "condensed time" (accelerated motion), a "negative of time" (reverse motion), "paralyzed time" (freeze-frame), "fractured time" (stop-trick), and a "close-up of time" (slow motion).*

Trick processing is also used in the film's introductory shot of the tiny Cameraman who, carrying his camera on a tripod, appears on the top of the giant camera – a metaphor which, at the very outset, generates a surreal image, even though composed of authentic "life-facts." The same effect of compounding two images is accomplished in the shot of the Cameraman looming over the city and loading his camera on a building's roof (Fig. 180). Some of the most pictorially attractive compound shots, dissolves, and multiple exposures of the city traffic and factory scenes are achieved by complex trick effects (Plates 1–4).

Stop-trick (frame-by-frame shooting) is extensively used in the "Shooting Gallery" sequence (XLVIII) to promulgate another political statement: the young woman (Fig. 189) repeatedly shoots (aims the gun at) the swastika, the symbol of nazism (Fig. 190). The political innuendo becomes clear at the moment the bullet hits the swastika on the figure's hat: the target flips over, and on its rear side there is the inscription "Death to Fascism!" (Fig. 191). Later in the same sequence, Vertov uses this technique to draw an ideological association by cross-cutting between another young woman shooting (Fig. 192) and a set of bottles arranged in a wooden box (Fig. 193). As the young woman fires, the bottles disappear one after another, creating the illusion that the bullets are hitting their "target" (Fig. 193); it becomes obvious that the young woman is "shooting" alcoholism.

Vertov does not only distinguish between the image and the written word but also delineates specific techniques of projecting images. The

---

* "Close-up of time" is, actually, the term introduced by Vsevolod Pudovkin. See also notes 27 and 28.

phenomenological difference between the (static) freeze-frame and (dynamic) motion pictures is fully demonstrated near the end of the film in several shots that combine – by means of matched frames – the motion picture screen-within-the-screen and the frozen and moving images of the theater. In the first shot, both segments move, as the audience watches the abstract rotating spool of wire on the screen-within-the-screen (Fig. 201). In the next four shots, the audience is seen "frozen," while the images on the screen-within-the-screen (planes, the Cameraman shooting from the motorcycle, a train) are moving (Figs. 216, 224). In the last two shots of the auditorium, again both segments of the image move (Fig. 226). The third combination, however – the "live" audience and the "frozen" screen-within-the-screen – never takes place, which may symbolically imply that, for the *kinoks*, the *cinematic illusion* cannot be destroyed. The "Film-Eye" never sleeps, the "Film-Eye" is always active, shaking the audience to life! This message is reiterated in the shot where a locomotive runs directly over the "petrified" audience in the movie theater (Fig. 208). To transmit the feeling of being awakened from mental and perceptive inactivity, Vertov uses the same shot of the rushing locomotive, this time over the real screen (Figs. 207, 223), perceived by the contemporary viewers (Fig. 198). Symbolically, the ensuing shots of the milling pedestrians and the traffic on the street are shown in extremely accelerated motion, as if in reaction to the lifelessness of the audience sitting in front of the screen-within-the-screen. Then the Cameraman, zealously cranking his camera in the speeding convertible, appears on the screen-within-the-screen. After several additional shots of the street crowd in accelerated motion, the shot of Svilova editing the footage marks the beginning of the montage crescendo that will end the film.

Reduced to a small rectangle within the real screen, the moving image on the screen-within-the-screen looks like the theater's "window" facing reality; although it is not always possible to identify what is projected on the screen-within-the-screen (e.g., the ambiguous shot associated with the rotating spool of wire, whirling strips of light, or spinning cones on wheels), the images on the screen-within-the-screen clearly represent the external world. In the "Spectators and the Screen" sequence (LII), two "realities" interact, producing an exciting cinematic experience through the amalgamation of images projected on the real screen with those appearing on the screen-within-the-screen. In this context, the three shots of the rotating spool of wire are extremely significant. First, we see an abstract close-up of a rotating structure (a spool of wire) on the real screen (Fig. 200). The shot is positioned between the "Camera Moves on Tripod" sequence (LI) and the "Spectators and the Screen" sequence (LII), thus marking the "border" between Part Two and the Epilogue. Then there appears the same rotating structure projected on the screen-within-the-screen in front of the seated audience (Fig. 201). Finally, the previous abstract close-up of the rotating spool reappears on the real screen and is followed by a high-angle shot of the sparse audience conversing and ignoring the screen (Fig. 202). In contrast, after the next two shots (composed like a typical constructivist collage) which depict dancers performing to piano accompaniment (Fig. 203), the audience's interest is recaptured, and its attention is redirected toward the screen (Fig. 204). Comparing these two sets of shots – one abstract and the other representational – Vertov reveals the variety of responses elicited by the cinematic image, demonstrating at the same time the distinction between (1) the film image as part of the diegetic world and (2) the film image as a graphic structure with purely abstract/kinesthetic significance/impact.

In accordance with his decision to make a film "without the aid of intertitles," Vertov uses verbal inscriptions only when they function as organic parts of the image, as, for example, in the shots of the "Beer-hall/Bierhalle" (Fig. 154); the Cameraman's reflection in the mirror with the sign "Shoemaker" (Fig. 126); the inscription on the optician's store, "Pince-nez" (Fig. 62); the "Proletarian Movie Theater" (Fig. 179); the target in the shooting gallery, "Death to Fascism" (Fig. 191); the workers' club, "V. I. Ulyanov" (Fig. 195); the mailbox (Plate 2); the marriage and divorce certificates (Fig. 91); the ambulance (Fig. 115); the film posters (Figs. 26, 52, 179); the street banner announcing the anniversary edition of Maxim Gorky's collected works (Fig. 32); and the religious store (Fig. 184). In the "Wall Newspaper" sequence (XXXVI), the written text is used as a thematic "bridge" between two different topics within the segment which shows a worker arranging hand-printed articles, drawings, and photographs on a board known as "wall newspapers" (Fig. 156), widely used in the Soviet Union at the time of the paper shortage and reduction of the official newspaper's circulation. The last shot of this segment is a close-up of an article's hand-written title that reads "About Sports," followed by the introductory shot of the sequence depicting various sports activities (Figs. 157–9).

The variety of perceptual experiences in *The Man with the Movie Camera* is summarized in the finale, which points to the various natures of the projected images, to the distinct methods of subverting the illusion of reality on the screen, to the technical aspect of cinematic creation *before, during,* and *after* shooting, and to the multiple levels of visual interpretation inherent in the cinematic process. Through the interaction of these four aspects of the film medium, Vertov invites his viewers to reconsider their perception of both cinema and reality or, as he put it, to "clarify their vision" in order to see the world from a fresh perspective that will then allow "the proletariat of the entire world to determine their position in relation to the circumstances which surround them."[26]

Cinematic illusion

Perhaps the most important feature of Vertov's method is that it scrupulously examines the ambiguity between the objective and subjective aspects of human perception. This is most evident in the shot of the Cameraman standing on the ground floor while being photographed by another camera from inside an ascending/descending elevator. As the elevator rises, the Cameraman slowly disappears beneath the bottom edge of the frame (Fig. 109). This deceptive "motion" produces perceptual ambiguity due to the illusion that the Cameraman – who in reality remains stationary – has been moving! More precisely, as a result of the eye's natural tendency to accept every movement on the screen as a faithful record of external reality, the viewers are under the impression that the Cameraman and camera are "descending." Due to this optical illusion, the shot calls the viewer's attention to the unseen cameraman (Vertov?) located in the moving elevator. This deceptive effect unsettles the viewer's common perception of movement: as the abrupt plummeting creates a kinesthetic shock, the elevator shaft momentarily plunges the entire screen into darkness, suspending every illusion and revealing only the black screen (as shown on the final frame enlargement in Fig. 109).

Other shooting strategies in *The Man with the Movie Camera* subvert the conventional perception of space and time, and challenge the locus of movement as it is experienced in external reality. The viewers often cannot be sure of what is actually moving on the screen, and their capacity to discern where the "real" motion occurs and at what point their eyes are deceiving them is thwarted. Part One ends with several lengthy shots filmed by the omniscient camera tracking along a moving fire engine on which the Cameraman and his assistant operate their apparatus (Fig. 120). The two parallel movements create the impression that the Cameraman and his assistant, carried by the fire engine, appear stationary in contrast to the rapid movement of pedestrians, traffic, and the apparent movement of building façades "rushing" in opposite directions behind them. Again the attention of the viewer is shifted to the invisible camera which the assistant acknowledges; consequently, the lengthy tracking shot is cut off by the insertion of a static close-up of the camera lens, this time without the superimposition of a human eye or the reflection of the Cameraman on it (Fig. 47). Such subversion of the spatiotemporal continuity and expansion of the diegetic space established by the wide tracking shot intercut with the stationary close-up (the lens) has a structural function: it punctuates the screen both symbolically and graphically at the border between the two parts of the film, one dealing mostly with working activities, the other with recreation.

In the second portion of the "Motorcycle and Carousel" sequence (XLIV), another enigmatic shot (no. 42) disrupts both the action and the illusion of reality on the screen. After the shot of the Cameraman riding a motorcycle with his camera mounted on the handlebars (Fig. 175), and after the shot of the rotating carousel (Fig. 176), there appears a shot of dark and white waves photographed from a moving boat, with a metal railing occupying the lower left corner of the frame (Fig. 177). Unexpectedly the shot "freezes," as if the projector has suddenly stopped! A close examination of the frames reveals that they contain identical halves of two "frozen" frames combined into one horizontally split image. Both segments of the frame represent a more detailed view of the previous shot – the water – seen only in the lower right segment of the frame, while the rest of both segments remains transparent (Fig. 178). This freeze-frame is mechanically reproduced fifty-four times (lasting about three seconds when projected at eighteen frames per second) before the tracking shot of the water continues to move, as if the projector or the camera – after malfunctioning for a while and tearing the film stock – continues to run again. It seems legitimate to ask whether this "torn" piece of film is a mistake created during shooting or processing. The print that is preserved in the Moscow State Film Archive contains the identical shot, as do those distributed in other countries. But since the original negative of *The Man with the Movie Camera* no longer exists, there is no evidence that this camera "mischief" is deliberate or that it occurred after the final printing of the positive.* Intentional or unintentional, the impact of this insert is shocking: it "lays bare" the technological aspects of filmmaking (shooting, projection, film stock, movie screen) while subverting the illusion of reality by abruptly replacing the image of moving water with a piece of fractured film. In addition, it makes the viewer aware of the

---

* In the course of my research on *The Man with the Movie Camera* at the Museum of Modern Art (New York), I suggested that the Film Study Center compare the print kept in its collection with the original print held in the Moscow State Film Archive. As a result of this enquiry, the following letter arrived (dated March 26, 1976), addressed to Eileen Bowser (then Associate Curator) from the director of Goskfilmfond, with the following information: "The print of Dziga Vertov's *The Man with the Movie Camera* which we hold in Gosfilmfond fully corresponds to the copy you have in your archive. The number 'one' appears on the screen after the introduction just as it does in yours, i.e., without, however, any other number appearing before the following sequences. The repetition of the frozen shot (of the torn film) also takes place in our copy. Unfortunately it would be impossible now to establish whether these two details existed in the original negative, since unluckily the original negative has not been preserved."

physical existence of the projection beam thrown on the bare screen, and points to the distinction between projected slides and motion pictures.

The "overlapping effect" is used sparingly in *The Man with the Movie Camera*. It appears for the first time in the sequence showing a young woman in a white dress as she opens wooden blinds seen from outside of the building. The shots of the shutters being opened are repeated five times, each time photographed from different angles, and connected by four slow dissolves that further underscore the temporal duration of the action (Fig. 61). This extended duration is appropriate to the theme of the forthcoming sequences which depict the solitude of city streets at dawn (Fig. 32) and the awakening of the young woman (Figs. 39, 40).

Overlapping is used again in the "Basketball" (XLII) and "Soccer" (XLIII) sequences, where fragments of the players' moving bodies – especially their arms – are repeated to create kinesthetic tension. In this case, the overlapping works against the basic tempo already established by editing because it slows down the actual movement of the soccer players and creates the illusion that they are dancing (Fig. 168) or that the ball is "flying" in the air (Fig. 169). As a result, the movements of the players become "balletic" and are intended to glorify – in a kinesthetic way – the physical nature of sports. In other instances, overlapping is used within otherwise "logically" edited shots, as, for example, in the sequence where the Cameraman walks toward the workers' club ("V. I. Ulyanov"). In the first shot, the Cameraman is seen moving toward the club's entrance; the shot is cut at the point where he reaches the bottom of the building's stairs; the next shot repeats the second portion of the Cameraman's walk, but on a smaller scale (Fig. 194). One can speculate as to the meaning of this spatiotemporal inconsistency, together with its facetious tone, which could be read as the evolutionary "distance" between the overcrowded pub seen earlier and the solitary workers' club. Yet it seems its primary function is to enhance the mise-en-scène visually through the repetition of portions of the same movement (action).

There are several explanations for Vertov's tempered use of the overlapping effect. He probably considered overlapping too contrived a rhetorical device that did not suit the nature of "life caught unawares," particularly at the time when Eisenstein used it extensively in his silent films, repeating many times over the closing segments of the same action to create a metaphor for extended temporal duration of a dramatic event (e.g., the endless opening of the draw bridge in *October*, ordered by the tsarist officer to prevent the demonstrators from entering the city). Or perhaps it was Svilova who did not appreciate this type of editing, which is dependent upon the available footage, especially if combined with a dissolve (achieved, at that time, by rewinding the filmstrip in the camera).

The dissolve is most successfully employed in so-called optical metamorphoses where the subjects of the camera are transformed. For example, the magician "materializes" in front of a cluster of trees before he himself makes things disappear (Fig. 151); a group of exercising women suddenly appears on an empty concrete platform (Fig. 150); swimmers "emerge" on the water's surface (Fig. 152); the covered carousel is magically unveiled so that the wooden horses are seen on their platform (Fig. 153); and the Russian title *"Pivnaia"* turns into the German *"Bierhalle"* (Fig. 154). In another instance, the stop-trick is used to provide the illusion of physical transformation, as, for example, with the disappearance, one by one, of beer bottles (Fig. 193) shot at in a target range by a young woman (Fig. 192). The same technique achieves the effect of the camera "walking" on its tripod (Fig. 197), and the sticks moving and forming themselves into a pyramid (Fig. 155).

The illusion of slow or accelerated motion (produced by cranking the camera faster or slower than sixteen or eighteen frames per second) in *The Man with the Movie Camera* is mostly associated with sporting events or traffic movement, in order to express the elegance of the athletes' motion or to intensify the hectic tempo of urban life. This technique is essential to Vertov's "Film-Eye" method, as it makes the viewer aware of the fact that the human eye, as opposed to the mechanical "eye," cannot halt ongoing motion in reality. The same holds for freeze-frames: the moment a horse, an athlete, a soccer player, or a human face appears frozen on the screen, action is isolated from the temporal flow of its natural movement, which shifts the cinematic illusion into the realm of still photography. These stationary images (equivalent to slides) are graphically relegated to the foreground (thus giving the impression of pictorial flatness), and contrast with the moving images that surround them. At the same time, freeze-frames permit a close view of the presented events or objects, revealing those visual features that are otherwise imperceptible when shown in tiny fractions of time. By their immobility, freeze-frames add to the self-referential aspect of the film by reminding the viewer of the illusionistic nature of motion pictures and their technological context. In contrast to the freeze-frame, slow motion functions as a "close-up of time," in Pudovkin's words,[27] or, as Vertov described it in his article "The Birth of the 'Film-Eye,'" slow motion is the "microscope and telescope of time, the negative of time, [thus providing] an opportunity to see things without limits and without spatial distance."[28]

Accelerated motion is used most often in the traffic sequences, particularly near the finale, which reinforces the montage pace of the symphonic coda of the film. In the last two sequences, "Accelerated Motion" (LIV) and "Editor and the Film" (LV), Vertov and Svilova insert numerous accelerated shots seen earlier in the film so that the viewers can immediately identify them and be fully immersed in the kinesthetic experience afforded by the optical beat of a montage cadence. The ontological authenticity of the accelerated final shots is considerably undermined through montage as their spatiotemporal condensation approaches cinematic abstraction. Consequently, in the closing portion of the film, the accelerated shots attain a level of "estrangement" [ostranenie] by "making it difficult" [zatrudnenie]* to discern what is actually moving on the screen. However, it is perfectly clear that the movement reflects "Life-As-It-Is" transformed into a "film-thing" by means of the "Film-Eye" method – the cinematic rebuilding of everyday reality.

Reverse motion is employed several times in *The Man with the Movie Camera*. At the beginning, through cinematic technique, a surreal mood is produced by the shots of pigeons flying backwards onto a roof (Fig. 36). Then, even a more surreal situation is achieved when checkers and chess figures arrange themselves on two playing boards (Figs. 185, 186); and, although barely visible during screening, the reverse motion is utilized in the two shots of the runner who is seen, though only for an instant, somersaulting both forward and backwards (Fig. 172). In this last case, the technique acts as a perceptual accent within the montage juxtaposition of various track and field events ending with a speeding motorcycle (Fig. 173) and a rotating carousel (Fig. 174). Lastly, reverse motion is employed in the finale of the film, which shows people walking backwards on the street (LV, 49; LV, 57). Combined with accelerated motion, reverse motion adds to the frenetic dynamism of city life. In particular, by deviating from the phenomenological norm of movement in reality, reverse motion exemplifies Vertov's belief that the "cinematic way of seeing" penetrates beneath the actual appearance of external reality, and conveys the filmmaker's personal attitude toward "life-facts."

At this point it would seem appropriate to discuss Vertov's and Svilova's use of jump-cuts, but since *The Man with the Movie Camera* is structurally based on the subversion of narrative linearity, jump-cuts appear almost at every instant of its diegetic development, contributing to the overall dialectical deconstruction of the film's spatiotemporal unity.

The Man with the Movie Camera also subverts the continuity of space and time by the use of pixillation, the blurring of images,

* See footnote on p. 11.

and the stroboscopic flickering effect. Of all these devices, the flickering effect is most apparent, since it is achieved by an abrupt exchange of bright and dark impulses on the screen (produced by intercutting black frames within a shot). For example, in the "Awakening" sequence (VII), the shot of the railway tracks (with the camera running over them) is interspersed with dark glimmerings (at the rate of two to four frames each time) that disrupt the natural flow of perception while assuming a metaphor for cinematographic projection and its intrinsically stroboscopic nature (Fig. 41). Likewise, in the "Accelerated Motion" sequence (LIV), the shot of two women and a man in a white suit being driven in a carriage (Fig. 214) is cut off by twenty black segments (each segment two or three frames long) as the actual movement of the carriage is gradually accelerated, thereby intensifying the deconstruction of the action's diegetic spatio-temporal continuity. Naturally, the viewers are inclined toward the representational continuity of the photographed event (the undisturbed motion of the carriage on the street), but as the recurrent flickering effect attains a disturbing level of intensification, the exchange of light and darkness on the screen assumes a hypnotic function that parallels the whirling of city traffic – the representational content of the sequence.

Finally, there are hundreds of dark frames, appearing mostly at the beginning of shots, produced by a delayed opening of either the shutter or the iris when the cranking begins. The "optical interference" of these frames is visually exciting as it intensifies the stroboscopic pulsation of the projected image. The function of the dark frames becomes obvious when an almost equal number of semidark frames at the very end of the shots draw attention to themselves and disrupt the illusion of spatiotemporal continuity on the screen. Less frequently, the last frame of the shot is lightened to the point of transparency, thus further contributing to the overall optical pulsation of the film. From a perceptual standpoint, the entire film can be seen as a challenge to the illusion of real time and space, both of which are taken for granted in conventional films. Vertov "warns" the viewers to question ceaselessly their perception of reality in general and as it is experienced in the movie theater. In this respect, *The Man with the Movie Camera* is, indeed, a dialectical negation of its own "being" since it deconstructs the very base of its existence – the "Film-Truth" principle. Consequently, the perception of reality is questionable per se: it consists not only of what one is accustomed to seeing but also of subliminal data that modify our cognitive grasp of the visible world and intensify our emotional response. Vertov demonstrates that these invisible components of perception exist in the materialistic sense (as one-frame shots) and that they considerably affect our understanding of reality in an unconscious way, creating a new vision of and attitude toward "Life-As-It-Is," not "Life-As-It-Appears."

Because the ontological authenticity of *The Man with the Movie Camera* is preserved in individual shots, even the most deconstructed sequences are not divorced from reality. The viewers are constantly reminded of the actual existence of events within an environmental context, even though the nonlinear progression of these events forces the spectators to establish for themselves a new spatiotemporal relationship among the objects and characters. On a psychological level, this self-referential aspect of the film generates a feeling of "estrangement" (defamiliarization) by showing everyday objects and events from unusual perspectives, thereby making the viewers more consciously aware of them. This is in harmony with the futurist attitude that encourages the audience to assume a critical position toward the art work: the disclosure of various techniques of filmmaking expands the viewers' awareness of the creative process, which is as important as the product itself. From such a duality of the presented images, there emerges a dialectical collision between the illusion of reality depicted on the screen and the "laying bare [of] the device" [*obnazhenie priema*]* that makes the projected illusion possible. This perceptual collision, initiated at the film's beginning and reiterated throughout, culminates in the finale as the montage pace becomes extremely aggressive. Kinesthetically compressed, the finale turns into a metaphor of the "Film-Eye" method: Svilova's eyes (Fig. 227) and the projection beam (Fig. 228) fuse with numerous shots retrieved from earlier parts of the film, as the film closes with the emblem of the "Film-Eye" method, exemplified by the image of the camera and the Cameraman's eye superimposed over the lens. The final image – just like the opening one – relates to the cinematic process: as the iris slowly closes, the superimposed eye continues to stare at the viewer (Fig. 233), perceptually ready to "arm" itself with the camera lens and capture "life-unawares."

Point of view

In a narrative film, the viewer is usually informed about the source of the camera's point of view, as each shot represents either a third-person's (the storyteller's) standpoint or a character's (actor's) view. In a traditional documentary film, point of view almost always resides in the third person, be it the filmmaker or the cameraman. *The Man with the Movie Camera* incorporates various perspectives, as it basically shifts between the third-person (author's) point of view and the subjective (Cameraman's) point of view.

* See footnote on p. 45.

The first five shots of the film clearly imply that matching points of view, typical of traditional cinema, will not be observed. The point of view of the opening shot, that is, the tiny Cameraman carrying the tripod and camera over his shoulder as he climbs a giant camera (Fig. 1), provides the audience with the instant expectation that the next shot will represent either the giant camera's point of view or that of the Cameraman's own tiny camera. Instead, what follows is a shot photographed from an extreme low-angle showing the top floors and the decorative façade of a tall building with the gray sky above (Fig. 2). The third-person point of view in the third shot is identical to the first one: the Cameraman toting the tiny camera over his shoulder descends from the giant camera that continues to "gaze" at the spectator (Fig. 1). The fourth shot is a low-angle view of a street light with clouds swiftly drifting behind it (Fig. 3). These four shots forewarn the viewer that there will be no diegetic continuity between angles of observation, and they anticipate the unorthodox cinematic structure of the entire film. Once it becomes obvious that the point of view cannot be justified by a conventionally valid logic, the connotative link between shots assumes a metaphorical signification, as the various points of view demonstrate the filmmaker's personal attitude toward reality and comment upon the nonnarrative relationships between the photographed objects.

From time to time, the isolated narrative cores in *The Man with the Movie Camera* provide the basis for a diegetic interpretation of the point of view in the sequences they occupy. However, each interpretation is unique to its corresponding sequence and cannot be applied to the following one, even if it deals with the same event or involves characters and locations seen in previous sequences. The relationship between the Cameraman's position and the photographed object is the sole basis on which the viewer establishes his comprehension of the (cinematic) world shown on the screen. With this in mind, one can distinguish six points of view, on the basis of (1) objective, narrative continuity; (2) the "protagonist's" vision of reality; (3) the position of the cinematic apparatus; (4) the relationship of the *montageur* with the film footage; (5) the interaction between people and objects or events; and (6) images that can be attributed to neither representational denotation nor diegetic connotation:

1. The third-person (author's) point of view
2. The Cameraman's point of view
3. The diegetic camera's point of view
4. The Editor's point of view
5. The character's point of view
6. The ambiguous point of view

The film begins with the third-person (author's) point of view of the Cameraman as he shoots with his camera positioned on a giant camera, and ends with an amalgamation of the Cameraman's and camera's points of view as conceived by the "Film-Eye" method – the human eye superimposed over the camera's lens. But it is the third-person point of view that dominates throughout the Prologue and 120 shots of Part One.

In Part One, two objective shots of the Cameraman – first, a full shot of him as he kneels on the railway track and positions himself to shoot the approaching train by placing the camera between the two tracks (Fig. 37); then, a close-up of his face in profile as the train speeds by – precede the Cameraman's direct point of view of the side of the blurred train. One would expect that, rather than this objective close-up, the next shot would be a subjective view of the oncoming train. Any such narrative development, however, is subverted by this and the succeeding objective close-up of the Cameraman seen again in profile, this time facing to the right as the train rushes behind him. The subjective shot of the train running over the camera (Fig. 68) does not appear until right before the second shot of the sleeping young woman moving restlessly in her bed (Fig. 25). A variation of this subjective shot reappears in the final sequence, "Editor and the Film" (LV), both on the real screen and the screen-within-the screen (Figs. 223, 224). On a psychological level, the abrupt intercutting of these objective shots (the Cameraman as he sets up his shot, as the train passes behind him, as he gets his foot caught in the track) with subjective ones (the blurred train seen both from the side at an oblique angle and directly oncoming) relate not only to the state of mind of the Cameraman – his fear of the approaching train – but also to the hypnagogic state of mind of the sleeping young woman introduced at the beginning of the "Awakening" sequence (VII), and shown throughout (see graphic display of shots in "Oneiric Impact of Intervals," in Chapter III).

The first time the Cameraman's and the camera's points of view are shown together is in sequence VIII ("Vagrants in the Street"), in which the Cameraman's hand and the camera, with its telescopic lens, rotate ninety degrees and face forward (Fig. 45). The ensuing high-angle medium shot shows vagrants reacting (Fig. 28) to the camera seen in the previous shot. Throughout this sequence, the Cameraman himself is not exposed, although the shot–countershot of the vagrant and the cranking camera is repeated several times, as the camera's point of view is enhanced by the extreme close-up of the lens in which the camera and the Cameraman's hand are reflected (Fig. 46). Symbolically representing the camera's point of view, this shot is highly self-referential: it informs the viewer about the act of shooting, and simultaneously reveals both the technological means of cinema and the object that has been "captured" on the camera lens.

In the "Washing and Blinking" sequence (IX), a character's (subjective) point of view is introduced more emphatically than in any other shot in the film. After the shots of the young woman awakening and getting out of bed, putting on her stockings, dressing, washing, drying herself off with a towel (Figs. 39, 40), and blinking (Fig. 49), a series of shots are inserted of venetian blinds opening and closing (Fig. 50), followed by a close-up of the camera lens contracting its iris (Fig. 47). Here two points of view are interrelated: the one directly associated with the young woman, the other metaphorically linked with the camera. Then a close-up of the young woman (as she begins to blink) is repeatedly intercut among a series of medium shots of the blinds alternately opening and closing. This intercutting compares the mechanism of the human eye with that of the camera lens. The parallelism is underscored by an inserted compound shot in which the cranking camera and the lens itself are reflected in a close-up of another lens with a superimposed close-up of a human eye (Fig. 46), serving as the emblem of the "Film-Eye" method. This compound shot is preceded by a shot of a rather well-dressed woman lying on a bench in the middle of a city square (Fig. 53) and is followed by a close-up of the same woman's legs. Another compound shot of the "Film-Eye" emblem reappears after this close-up, whimsically implying the camera's point of view and humorously alluding to the Cameraman's interest in women. Similarly, in the "Awakening" sequence (VII), when the young woman gets up from her bed, the Cameraman conspicuously focuses on her legs also. On an ideological level, the juxtaposition of the shots of one woman sleeping on a comfortable bed and another on a street bench confirms Vertov's critical attitude toward the inequality in living conditions. In reaction to the camera's intrusion of the citizen's private life, the young woman lying on the park bench – antagonized by the act of shooting – makes a discontented gesture and leaves (Fig. 53). On a more metaphorical level, the Cameraman hastily acknowledges his having overstepped the bounds of "life caught unawares," as the ensuing shots revert to the depiction of street traffic.

In the "Factory and Workers" sequence (XI), the Cameraman's point of view is indicated by a very low-angle view of the yard as the workers pull their carts over the (invisible) camera (Fig. 56). This point of view is subsequently corroborated by the succeeding high-angle (third-person) point of view that discloses Kaufman cranking his camera on the ground as a worker pulls his cart over the Cameraman (Fig. 57). Of course, the camera's point of view would be recognized even without the subsequent shot that uncovers the actual position of the camera; but, by underscoring the high angle, Vertov and Svilova make a clear distinction between the two points of view (the third person and the Cameraman's). In another case, the Cameraman's point of view is implied not by an exaggerated angle but by the camera's unsteady movements through space. For example, a street shot is executed with the hand-held camera that follows two peasant women walking along the street (Fig. 59). The vibration of the image instantly suggests that the camera is carried by the Cameraman as he walks, a notion already descriptively conveyed by the previous shot of the Cameraman holding his camera as he passes over an elaborate steel bridge (Fig. 58), and especially by the shot in which the Cameraman, with the camera over his shoulder, makes his way through the crowd (Fig. 60). Consequently, all the hand-held tracking shots are associated with the Cameraman's point of view, while also demonstrating his physical exertion and his active participation in everyday life.

The most equivocal sequence concerning point of view is the one in which ladies are driven in a moving carriage while the Cameraman photographs them from a speeding convertible (Fig. 65). In one of the shots, the lady in the striped blouse looks directly into the lens and moves her hand in a circle to imitate the cranking of the camera (Fig. 69). This self-referential gesture provokes the viewer's awareness of the cinematic process, as the ensuing shots turn into freeze-frames of horses, ladies in the carriage, traffic, the crowd on the street, and children (Fig. 71), drawing a phenomenological distinction between motion pictures and still photography. Freeze-frames, by their nature, can be considered neither the Cameraman's nor the motion picture camera's point of view. It is also obvious that these are not stationary stills photographed by the motion picture camera, but rather produced in the lab. As such, they inform the viewer about yet another phase of the cinematic process – that of laboratory printing. Because of these features, freeze-frames do not belong to any of the basic points of view; they stand instead outside of the film's diegetic structure, thereby implying an ambiguous point of view.

The self-referential notion is further enhanced by the inclusion of perforations on both sides of the filmstrip handled by Svilova in her editing room. The image on the filmstrip represents a little girl attentively looking ahead (Fig. 72); this shot is succeeded by a shot of numerous reels of film arranged on shelves (Fig. 73). Another set of shots reiterates the ambiguous point of view, some showing classified film reels (Fig. 74), others depicting an empty plate on Svilova's editing table (Fig. 75). Partially third-person and partially self-referential, these shots prepare the spectator for a new point of view, that of Svilova (the Editor) working at the editing table (Fig. 80). Since she looks at the filmstrips from above, all the shots of the editing table match the Editor's (high-angle) point of view: the film plate (Fig. 75), filmstrips (Fig. 76), scissors (Fig. 77), the lighting board (Fig. 78), and Svilova's hand as she writes numbers on index cards (Fig. 79). The

Editor's point of view is conceptually reinforced near the end of the film by a close-up of Svilova's eyes intercut among numerous brief and accelerated shots of traffic, pedestrians, pendulums, and the screening in the movie theater, metaphorically reflecting her creative vision.

In the puzzling elevator shot, the movement of the elevator confuses the viewer as to whether or not the Cameraman (standing behind the camera in the hall) is actually moving (Fig. 109). The point of view in this shot is equally perplexing: first it appears to be a shot taken by a stationary camera, but in fact it is the *omniscient* camera that is moving, not the object being shot (the Cameraman standing behind his tripod and camera). This perceptually deceptive point of view (trompe l'oeil) is displaced by the next shot in which the camera tracks along the street as pedestrians get out of its (or the vehicle's) way (Fig. 110). There is no doubt that in this shot the camera is physically moving and that the people are reacting to it. In contrast, the illusory movement of the ascending/descending Cameraman/elevator creates an impression similar to the experience of a traveler watching a moving train from his or her stationary position within another train.

In the "Street and Eye" sequence (XXII), a stationary close-up of a blinking eye (Plate 6) crosscut with the blurred swish-pan of a street photographed from an oblique angle (Fig. 111) generates a "psychological" point of view associated with the "frustrated" perception of pedestrians caught within hectic traffic. The dialectical clash between the contrasting graphic forms (circular/diagonal/horizontal/vertical), for the most part appearing superimposed one over the other, is reinforced by the vibrating camera movement (often blurring the image) and a frenetic montage pace (approaching the threshold of imperceptibility). The tumultuous tempo of this sequence contributes to the disturbing impact of the "life-fact" presented in the next sequence, in which the actual "victim" of the frantic traffic is shown lying injured on the street (Fig. 118).

In Part Two, the emphasis on the Camerman's or character's point of view is not as strong as it is in Part One. Instead, the physical dynamics of the photographed events (such as recreation and various sports) determine the montage pace, while the use of different photographic devices, including extremely oblique angles, supplies the sequence with optical expressivity rather than signifying a particular point of view. Only after more than 400 shots can one discern a character's point of view in the "Track and Field Events" sequence (XXXVII). Numerous shots of sports fans (Fig. 158) are matched by point-of-view shots related to the spectators' field of vision – the sports events themselves (Fig. 159). Similarly, in the "Magician" sequence (XL), close-ups of the children's astonished faces (Fig. 165) are matched by the shot of the magician performing his tricks (Fig. 166). This sequence begins with a close-up of a boy looking down to the right, followed by a high-angle medium close-up of the magician, the latter shot clearly implying the boy's subjective point of view. In this segment, point-of-view interaction creates a geographical ambiguity: by establishing a *spatial* relationship between shots obviously photographed in *different* locations,* Vertov and Svilova create the impression that people are looking at one another (according to the "Kuleshov effect"). In the "Basketball" (XLII) and "Soccer" (XLIII) sequences, the Cameraman's point of view is reinforced by the panning and tracking after the "flying" soccer ball photographed by a hand-held camera, which constantly changes its position, angle, and speed of movement through space (Fig. 169). Here the camera's point of view and motion are identified with that of the "dancing" soccer players (Fig. 168); the hand-held camera movement contributes to the viewer's motor-sensory experience of the event.

Both objective and subjective shots in the "Motorcycle and Carousel" sequence (XLIV) are sensorially exciting, as the viewer experiences the parallel circular motions (the rotating of the carousel and the movement of the motorcycles as they arc around a track) from a variety of angles. Shots of children and adults enjoying their ride on wooden horses (Fig. 174) represent the third-person point of view, as do the shots of the Cameraman shooting while on the carousel (Fig. 176) or while riding a motorcycle himself, his camera mounted on the handlebars (Fig. 175). The blurred images of spectators around the carousel (Fig. 174) obviously represent the subjective points of view of the Cameraman and the other riders. In addition, a male athlete turning a somersault (shown previously and here both forward and in reverse) and a female doing the high jump are intercut within a series of objective shots of the racing motorcycles and rotating carousel as they turn in opposite directions, apparently comparing the speed and movements of the carousel and motorcycles to physical human feats. The sequence ends with a low-angle view of the Cameraman as he rides his motorcycle and hits the objective camera. As if in response to this aggressive action, a brief semiabstract shot of water is quickly succeeded by a shot of torn film (Fig. 178), indicating in an unusual manner that an "accident" has taken place, both on the race track and in the projection booth – a self-referential shot that can be read as the ambiguous point of view and/or the point of view of the film's spectators.

In the "Shooting Gallery" sequence (XLVIII), the young women's points of view (Figs. 189, 192) correspond to the close-ups of the targets they aim at (Figs. 190, 193). In the "Musical Performance with Spoons and Bottles" sequence (L), the characters' points of view are underscored by montage, as close-ups of people looking at and listening to the musician as he performs are alternately exchanged (Plate 9).

---

* A close examination of the shots reveal that their backgrounds do not match.

The fact that the characters' points of view are inconsistent (since the listeners look in various directions) contributes to the emotional impact of this sequence, which achieves an abstract musical rhythm. The character's point of view prevails again toward the end of the film, in the "Spectators and the Screen" sequence (LII), which shows spectators attending the screening in the movie theater. The notion of film spectatorship is already touched upon in the previous sequence, the "Camera Moves on Tripod" (LI), which makes it clear that the people laughing at the animated tripod and camera (Fig. 197) are, in fact, the same spectators attending the screening of *The Man with the Movie Camera* in the movie theater (Figs. 198, 199), apparently the same one shown in the introductory sequence of the film (Figs. 13, 14).

There are ninety shots of the "Spectators and the Screen" sequence (LII) interspersed with arrhythmic insertions of the spectators (in close-up) engaged in watching the film projected on the screen-within-the-screen. At the beginning of the sequence, the movie audience watches (on the screen-within-the-screen) two ladies and the man in a white suit in a moving carriage (Fig. 215). Then the carriage is shown on the real screen (Fig. 214) in a shot that represents the third-person point of view, reiterated by the next shot of the Cameraman on a motorcycle, appearing on the miniature screen-within-the-screen (Fig. 217), and followed by a shot of him as he shoots from the convertible now seen on the real screen (Fig. 225). At this point, the existence of a diegetic point of view (related to the real screen) and a self-referential one (related to the screen-within-the-screen) is evident. After a series of crosscuts between these two shots, the shot of the two women and the man in a white suit reappears on the real screen: this can be read both as the Cameraman's point of view and the movie audience's point of view. The actual spatial relationship as well as the geographic connection between the Cameraman and the ladies in the carriage is specified by the earlier sequence (XV) in which several shots of the Cameraman (driven in a convertible in the foreground as he shoots the ladies driven in a carriage in the background) realistically depict the situation as it occurs in external reality (Fig. 65). All these conflicting points of view inform the viewer about the two levels of perception in cinema: one associated with the film's various themes, the other related to the filmmaking process. V. V. Ivanov refers to this collision of different points of view in Vertov's film as the "reverse connection" between the movie audience and the real audience, both engaged in watching images recording "life caught unawares," later to be restructured by means of montage into a "film-thing" from which selected shots are subsequently extrapolated and shown on the screen-within-the-screen. Ivanov particularly emphasizes the relationship between the shots that are part of the film's diegetic structure and these same shots that appear on the screen-within-the-screen – a "reverse connection" that contributes to the "the perceptual tension between the cinematic illusion and the audience's critical judgement."*

The Editor's point of view within the montage structure saturates the film's last two sequences (LIV and LV). After twenty-four shots of the Cameraman and street traffic in full commotion, a close-up of Svilova at work appears on the screen; the Editor's point of view prevails because of the repeated close-up of her eyes (Fig. 227) as she looks down at the editing table. During the central portions of the final sequence (shots 50–126), Svilova's close-up (composed of only two or three frames) recurs among equally brief shots of pedestrians and traffic, underscoring the notion that all these shots *conceptually* imply her editorial vision. As the frames whisk in front of her eyes, the phi-effect (illusion of double exposure of Svilova's eyes and various views of traffic) takes over, reflecting the Editor's ideational point of view, as well as the filmmaker's creative fantasy at work and the suprematist concept of film as a complex structure.

The Epilogue reintroduces the "Film-Eye" emblem – a fusion between the human and mechanical eye (Fig. 233) – signifying Vertov's method and exemplifying the *kinoks*' relationship to the camera: "I am eye.... I am a mechanical eye.... I, machine, show you the world."[29] The film's end recapitulates the interaction between machine, traffic/communication, and the cinematographic apparatus with the following shots: a traffic signal (Fig. 229), an automobile mounted on the railway tracks and running over the camera (Fig. 230), swinging pendulums (Fig. 231), a streetcar running over the camera (Fig. 232), ten black frames, and, finally, the superimposition of the eyeball and the gradually closing iris over the lens (Fig. 233). The eyeball remains visible throughout the iris's contraction, which lasts for eighty-six frames. The film ends as it begins – with the camera – but the final point of view is attributed to the human eye, which continues to stare at the viewer, even after the iris completes its contraction.

Taken in its entirety, *The Man with the Movie Camera* contains nearly an equal number of shots implying the Cameraman's and the Editor's points of view. Added together, these approximate the number of shots representing the third-person point of view, which provides the viewer with a balanced proportion of opposing perspectives, simultaneously confirming and challenging the objectivity of human perception. The lesser number of shots relates to the character's (subjective)

* V. V. Ivanov, "The Categories and Functions of Film Language" [*Funktsii i kategorii yazyka kino*], *Trudy po znakovym sistemam,* no. 7 (1975), pp. 170–92 (unpublished translation by Roberta Reeder). Analyzing the relationship between the two different points of view at the end of Vertov's film (i.e., real audience versus the audience seen on the screen), Ivanov writes: "Vertov uses extensively what could be termed a 'reverse connection' with the auditorium. In several sequences, the auditorium appears together with the screen-within-the-screen on which there is the same image seen earlier in the film, hence indicating a 'reverse connection' " (p. 3).

point of view, as in the shot where we see the object at which a young woman aims her rifle – the fascist symbol (connoting a political message); the shots following the young woman's blinking eyes (illustrating human perception); the shots following the close-ups of sports spectators (revealing the source of their excitement); and the shots appearing on the real screen directly after the close-up shots of the audience looking at the screen-within-the-screen (establishing the viewers' points of view in the auditorium).

Point of view is an essential structural component in *The Man with the Movie Camera:* it acknowledges the extent to which Vertov's film departs from traditional filmmaking as well as from conventional documentary film. The interaction of the three self-referential points of view (the camera's, Cameraman's, and Editor's) with those of the third person and of various "characters" generates a unique distancing effect sustained throughout the film. At the same time, this causes a shift of the viewer's perception from objective to subjective, with recurrent emphasis on the cinematographic creative process. Underscoring the perceptual distinction between reality as it appears in the exterior world and as it is presented on the screen, *The Man with the Movie Camera* proposes a unification of the human eye with the "Machine-Eye," in order to create a more substantial, more dynamic, and more revealing vision of reality. As Vertov astutely claimed: "If an artificial apple and a real apple are photographed in such a way that one cannot distinguish between them, this demonstrates not the skill of shooting but rather the lack of it."[30]

Glorifying technology's capacity to aid the naked eye, examining the nature of human perception, presenting reality with a critical attitude, *The Man with the Movie Camera* does not limit itself to one particular point of view. Rather, it affords the viewer with the privilege of having looked at life from all possible perspectives through dynamic cinematic means – a vision that is the ultimate goal of the "Film-Eye" method: not only to view life differently but above all to provide a more profound vision of reality than conventional observation can allow.

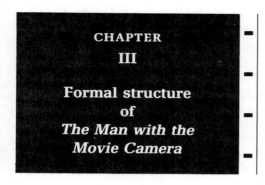

CHAPTER

III

Formal structure
of
*The Man with the
Movie Camera*

A mathematics of facts

The cinematic complexity and unorthodox structure of *The Man with the Movie Camera* prevented most critics of the period (including some of the avant-garde filmmakers) from recognizing the significance of the formal execution in the film's aesthetic impact. While most Soviet critics attacked Vertov's film for being "formalistic" and "inaccessible" to the masses, American critics by and large found it confusing and superficial, as exemplified by Raymond Ganly's 1929 review, which stated that *The Man with the Movie Camera* was "a hodge-podge . . . just a titleless newsreel embellished with trick photography."* Even a sophisticated critic such as Dwight Macdonald ridiculed "Vertov's extremist school," which "believes that it is possible to make a movie out of any shots that happen to be lying around the laboratory."[†] This attitude still prevails among traditional American film critics and historians, including Arthur Knight who, demonstrating his inability to perceive the cinematic features and aesthetic values of Vertov's work, continues to claim that Vertov's film is "increasingly mechanical and trick-filled."[1]

A close analysis of the film's montage structure reveals that *The Man with the Movie Camera* is far from being a "trick-filled" "hodge-podge," and that the film's unique value lies in the integration of its filmic devices (particularly its shot composition and montage) with all other elements

---

* Raymond Ganly, "Man with a Camera," *The Motion Picture News* (October 26, 1929), p. 2. The film was premiered in New York, September 16, 1929, and in San Francisco at the beginning of October, i.e., only five months after the Moscow opening (April 9, 1929).
[†] Dwight Macdonald, "Eisenstein and Pudovkin in the Twenties," *The Miscellany*, no. 6, March 1931, p. 24. This is the second part of the original article, which is – symptomatically – omitted from the book *Macdonald on Movies* (New Jersey: Prentice Hall, 1969). At the Film Conference held at the City University of New York (July 1975), Macdonald reconfirmed his misunderstanding of Vertov's film: at the panel discussion on Vertov, he stated that *The Man with the Movie Camera* "is but a small film about a photographer who runs around a city" (the quotation is taken from my personal notes kept during the conference).

to form a self-contained cinematic whole. Vertov emphasized that his film is not a mere demonstration of cinematographic technique or the craft of editing, but an attempt to create a "film-thing" that will convey a particular meaning and generate enough kinesthetic energy to affect the viewer's consciousness. He disregarded not only those reviewers who attacked the film as a "formalist attraction," but also those critics who discussed the film's montage structure from a journalistic perspective calling it a "mesmerizing visual concert." Vertov proposed instead that *The Man with the Movie Camera* be analyzed in concrete cinematic terms without the mystification characteristic of pretentious abstract theorizing. He insisted that his film be seen as neither a merely "fascinating collection" of "life-facts," nor just a "symphonic interaction" of shots, but as an integration of both:

The film is the sum of events recorded on the film stock, not merely a summation of facts. It is a higher mathematics of facts. Visual documents are combined with the intention to preserve the unity of conceptually linked pieces which concur with the concatenation of images and coincide with visual linkages, dependent not on intertitles but, ultimately, on the overall synthesis of these linkages in order to create an indissoluble organic whole.[2]

Earlier in this essay Vertov refers to his film as "a theoretical declaration on the screen," and emphasizes his concern with the interaction between the formal aspect of montage ("visual linkages") and the thematic meaning of juxtaposed shots ("conceptually linked pieces") in order to reach an ultimate cinematic integration ("overall synthesis of shot juxtapositions"). This implies that in order to grasp the full and appropriate meaning of *The Man with the Movie Camera,* it is necessary to undertake an in-depth analysis of the film's formal structure and its relationship to the content of each shot.

Adhering to the constructivist principle that a work of art is like a "building" unified by the cinematic integration of its numerous components, Vertov regarded every aspect of his film as inherently significant because each part would (1) affect the viewer by its own force and (2) acquire its proper meaning through its interaction with other elements and their combined or total relation to the photographed event. Thus, the shot's formal (pictorial) outlook becomes the "aesthetic fact" contributing to the diegetic meaning of the film's "indissoluble organic whole," its overall montage structure, which integrates its thematic/ideological meaning and its formal/cinematic execution.

Shot composition and visual design

Since shot composition is the basic perceptual unit of cinematic structure, we shall begin our analysis by examining the pictorial execution of the shots in *The Man with the Movie Camera.* There are three major characteristics of Vertov's and Kaufman's pictorial treatment of individual shots: (1) the black and white contrast of the image, (2) the graphic pattern dominating the frame, and (3) the abstract or semi-abstract outlook of the shot.

The black and white contrast is underscored mostly in wide-angle shots depicting factory machines, moving vehicles, traffic, mine shafts, bridges, and other metal constructions. This is most visible in the shots of the steel foundry, where the Cameraman and his camera appear silhouetted against the glowing light of the furnace or in those shots that depict bridges and trains photographed against the sky (Plate 1). Sometimes the distribution of black and white within the frame is carefully balanced, but for the most part it changes throughout the duration of the shot. Usually, early on in the shot, the composition depicts representationally various objects and events with a depth of field created by natural lighting; then, gradually, a sharp black and white contrast overcomes the screen, reducing the perspective and making the shot look "flattened." This is achieved either by changing the position of the camera while it continues to shoot against the light coming from behind the object (hence producing high contrast) or by narrowing the aperture so that less light is permitted to expose the film. Without depth of field, the photographed objects assume a symbolic meaning; deprived of detailed representational features, the shots subvert their own diegetic world. This shooting procedure is exemplified in the shot of the Cameraman climbing up a metal construction and looking much like an acrobat or a tightrope walker with the camera as his "balancing pole" (Plate 3). Similar visual symbolism is achieved with other silhouetted objects, such as the traffic signal photographed in various positions against a gray sky (Fig. 33) or the lower body of the train's wagon rushing over the camera and filling the foreground as it seems to "seal" the Cameraman back into the underground hole from which he is shooting (Fig. 68). The tilted angle of these shots (indicating the Cameraman's point of view) simultaneously enhances the thematic meaning (traffic's dynamism) and functions self-referentially. Numerous other shots taken from unusual and exaggerated angles are also associated with the Cameraman's activity or with the camera and its lens. These are mostly high-contrast shots (Plate 3), which invite comparison with Rodchenko's photographs; because of their pronounced graphic symbolism, these shots were often reproduced on the posters, programs, and leaflets promoting the film.*

The pictorial composition of split-screen images, double exposures, dissolves, and compound shots is particularly significant in that it illustrates Vertov's decision to use tricks not merely as attractive optical effects or picturesque images but as cinematic devices capable of con-

---

* See also p. 11.

veying messages through the very technique by which they are produced. The manner in which the Bolshoi Theater "falls apart" on the screen reveals the idea of "opening a new road" – the narrow black pathway that leads toward deep perspective – beneath the two parts of the severed building (Fig. 213). Compared to the shot of the same building that appears at the beginning of the film (Fig. 30), with its solid imperial façade, its classic columns, and decorative pediment photographed from a frontal low angle, this split-screen image of the Bolshoi Theater reinforces the ideological meaning implied by the special effect. The famous double exposure of the spinning wheel and the female worker's face is visually and metaphorically expressive because of the graphic balance of the head's position within the spinning wheel, both in its relation to the circular (or, to be more precise, oval) shape of the wheel and to its rotating movement (in opposition to the movement of the head), as white threads spread like sun rays from the center of the woman's forehead, connoting workers' enthusiasm (Fig. 206).

Dissolves, in general, are executed by the juxtaposition of similar graphic forms. The best example of this is the photographic presentation of Vertov's "Film-Eye" method: the interrelationship of two circular forms, the eye and lens (Figs. 46, 233). In contrast to this, the idea of "Radio-Ear" is conveyed through the juxtaposition of the circular form of a loudspeaker and the various forms of the ear, mouth, accordion, and piano keyboard (Fig. 196).

Perhaps the most fascinating compound shots are those of traffic, which combine two or more images of vehicles moving in various directions (Plate 2). This is most evident in the shots of streetcars as they move perpendicularly in different spatial zones, so that the combination of the vehicles' movements and their positions within the frame produces a surreal vision. Vertov and Kaufman executed these shots with a remarkable sense for merging the medium's tendency toward the ontological authenticity of the photographed object and its unique capacity to create fantastic situations by optical means. The composition of the compound shots usually begins as a faithful presentation of a street scene; then – although hardly perceptible – the positions of vehicles change, and one suddenly realizes the improbability of the newly developed situation. To achieve such deceptive and visually complex imagery, Vertov and Kaufman made sure that the "seams" between the compounded and/or superimposed shots would remain invisible: only after meticulous examination of these shots can one discover that the various vehicles are both compounded *and* superimposed. Even without such detailed scrutiny, the common viewer subliminally experiences the optical transformation of the shot – from a naturalistic presentation of "Life-As-It-Is" to a graphic abstraction – which immediately calls attention to cinematic technique.

The majority of compound shots depicting street crowds forces the viewer's perception to fluctuate. For a moment, the viewer has the impression of watching a large group of people teeming around a spacious square; then, a streetcar appears (from the left or right side of the frame) and penetrates the crowd, cutting it horizontally into two distinct segments. At this point, the viewer realizes the shot's collage structure – a self-referential act in itself – and begins to *examine* the shot as a pictorial composition rather than simply perceive it as a visual recording of a "life-fact." At other times, a shot's compounded composition is indicated by purely photographic means: as the area between two assembled images gradually turns darker or transparent, the border connecting the two shots gradually reveals itself on the screen. For example, the compound shot of the working typists is initially perceived as a long shot of numerous typists seated in several rows of desks (Fig. 221); as the shot continues, the flatness of the image becomes apparent, clearly indicating that the shot combines several images of typists lined up horizontally (this composition is irresistibly reminiscent of modern photographic collages).

One of the many shots depicting switchboard operators particularly manifests Vertov's and Kaufman's photographic technique. Upon seeing this shot for the first time, it looks as if the two groups of operators are sitting at parallel desks; but the moment one of the operators extends her hand and "plugs" a line "into" the neck of a fellow worker sitting in front of her, the representational illusion instantly vanishes (Fig. 222). A similar effect is repeated in numerous traffic shots (almost always taken from a high angle) where people and vehicles move in various directions. The viewer is often uncertain whether a street is actually oblique/curved and traffic chaotic, or, instead, photographically distorted by the compounding of two angles (views) of the same street and/or several images in which trolleys and cars run against and over each other (Plate 2). It is these semiabstract shots particularly that confuse and disturb common audiences as well as conventional critics who still refer to the film as "trick-filled" and "visually excessive." To serious theorists, however, these same shots confirm the sophistication of their creators, inspired by constructivist photographs that represent life situations in a slightly surreal manner, yet never completely cut from their organic ties with reality.

The plates "Factories and Machines" (1), "Traffic and Means of Communication" (2), "Graphic Shot Composition" (3), and "Visual Abstraction" (4) illustrate Vertov's and Kaufman's cinematic treatment of their subjects. Many of the visually exciting shots depicting the industrial environment are backlit, so that only silhouetted workers can be seen, thus unifying the human figures with the surrounding steel constructions. Shots of traffic are often either compounded or taken from high and/or oblique angles, which reveal the photographers' ideological and emotional attitudes toward their subjects. Industrial equipment and consumer goods are usually shot in close-up, with emphasis on their (horizontal, vertical, circular, square, rectangular, and triangular) shapes. In general, visually abstracted shots are executed in two ways: through the distortion of the representational depiction of the object by the proximity of the camera to the photographed surface, and through the meaningful graphic interaction of superimposed images.

The film's overall visual design is generated by three basic graphic patterns that dominate the entire film: the circle and vertical and horizontal lines. The circular form is most notable because of its natural association with the human eye and the camera lens, whereas the vertical and horizontal forms are generally related to industrial constructions, traffic, and communication. All three graphic forms are present in the very first shot of the film: the circular lens occupies the center of the frame, the horizontal position of the large camera (box) dominates the frame, and the vertical figure of the Cameraman carrying his tripod (which changes its position and becomes diagonal) appears on top of the large camera (Fig. 1). The viewer's attention is promptly drawn to the circular form of the lens by the mirror image of the camera manufacturer's logo "Le Parvo" ("Le Parvo") reflected in the lens' rim, forcing the viewer to read the words counterclockwise. The same circular form is reiterated in the closing shot of the film, showing a round camera lens with a human eye superimposed over it (Fig. 233). Between these two paradigmatic shot compositions, all other shapes and designs develop and change throughout the film according to their *visual* association with the respective themes and ideas prevailing in a given sequence.

After the first shot, the circle reappears in different contexts and with specific graphic variations. Initially associated with the camera's lens (shown in close-up), it is subsequently related to the actual screening of the film. In the projection booth, the emphasis is on close views of the circular film cores, cans, and projector reels (Figs. 8–11), whereas in the movie theater, the circular form is discerned in the various orchestra instruments (e.g., French horn) that accompany the screening (Fig. 17). As the film progresses, the circular form is underscored in traffic (wheels, headlights), in typewriter keys, in factories (gears, metal hoops, spindles, valve controls), in recreation (the wheels of bicycles, carriages, cars, a carousel), in sports (balls, ball and chain, motorcycles), in specific detailed areas of the locomotive, in the radio loudspeaker, in the pendulum, in the magician's hoops, in various targets at the shooting gallery, in the cranking of the camera, in the stacked reels of unedited film, and in the rotating plates on Svilova's editing table (Figs. 75, 80). It is important to note that the emphasis on the circular form is achieved not only by the careful selection of objects but also by photographing them in close-up (thus extracting the circular shape) and by contrasting them with different designs.

The vertical pattern (including squares and upright rectangles) appears in most of the shots depicting architectural constructions, buildings, scaffoldings, windows, machines, posters, mailboxes, checker boards, newspapers, street carts, and cigarette packets, as well as in those shots depicting the auditorium screen, the cable car moving across the dam, and the camera body. Verticality is most notable in the smokestacks, telephone poles, columns, bottles, pedestrians, and street lights. The horizontal pattern is associated with stretches of landscapes and sky (in the long shots), bridges, railroad tracks, trolleys and trains moving horizontally, as well as the filmstrip laid out across the editing table (Fig. 78). These three graphic forms often merge at climactic points into a pictorial composition of multiple crossing patterns without any single form being dominant. This is most evident in the superimposed shots of the sequence "Musical Performance with Spoons and Bottles" (L), which merges different forms, such as hands, keyboards, spoons, dancers, plates, and feet (Plate 9), or in the shots that reinforce one particular pattern by presenting variations of the same form, as in the superimposition of the woman's round face positioned in the center of threads moving around a spinning wheel (Fig. 206). In contrast, the "Street and Eye" sequence (XXII) merges two different forms through the "phi-effect," which juxtaposes a close-up of an eye (circle) with the sharp horizontal, diagonal, and vertical movements of the camera and street traffic (Plate 3). The "phi-effect" is also used in the "Cameraman and Machines" sequence (XXXI), where the juxtaposition of the image of the Cameraman (who appears basically as a vertical shape) with the circular designs of machines and wheels creates the illusion of superimposition, although none of the shots contains two images overlaying each other (Plate 8).

The semiabstract design of shots in *The Man with the Movie Camera* commonly serves as the transition from one shot composition to another. At these junctions, the fluctuating graphic and pictorial transformations in a particular shot turn each and every aspect of the "mise-en-scène" (the arrangement of elements in front of the camera) into the "mise-en-shot" (interaction of the camera movement with the mise-en-scène), eliminating any trace of the stationary composition characteristic of a still photograph. Periodically, and then only briefly, these transitional and transformational graphic patterns become highly kinesthetic moments that, while affecting the viewer on a subliminal level, can be examined only with the aid of an analyst projector. Such is the nature of the famous "enigmatic shot," composed of rotating horizontal and curved lines that form zigzag patterns projected on the screen-within-the-screen (Fig. 201); it is impossible to figure out the representational signification of this shot even after repeated screenings. Only when examined frame by frame does it become clear that the photographed object is a rotating spool of wire (Figs. 200, 201). Vertov obviously does not want the viewers to be able to identify immediately the object on the screen; rather, he wants to challenge the viewers to "decipher" the representational denotation of the shot positioned at the "border" between the two sections of the film (the end of Part Two and the beginning of the Epilogue). Similarly, the shot composed of a myriad undulating lines (or rays) crisscrossing the screen (Fig. 205) looks like a semiabstract luminogravure with shining threads diagonally intertwining all over the screen. And only by examining the shot frame by frame does one realize that it is composed of multiple superimpositions of glowing silken strands on a spinning loom that form a starlike composition.

Graphic abstraction in *The Man with the Movie Camera* occurs most often when objects or persons are positioned very close to the lens so that their representational appearance is either blurred or lacks sufficiently recognizable features for the entire object to be identified. For example, in the "Recreation" sequence (XXXV), a gray surface fills the entire frame and forms a triangular shadow in the upper right side of the screen with a slightly tilted line toward the lower part of the screen. The shot is instantly perceived as an "abstract tableau" reminiscent of a Malevich painting, until it dissolves into a gray concrete platform with bathers exercising in front of an instructor positioned in the lower part of the frame (Fig. 150). In the same sequence, the shot of the swimming pool opens as an abstract undulating composition before the swimmers gradually appear (through a dissolve) on the water's surface and swim in a geometrically arranged pattern (Fig. 152). In other shots, the representational composition appears first, and then gradually evolves into an abstract design, as in the "Shooting Gallery" sequence (XLVIII), in which a carton of beer bottles is slowly emptied (through stop-trick) so that the white box with square compartments (photographed against a black background) becomes a semiabstract composition reminiscent of constructivist paintings often reduced to simple geometric lines which interact with the rectangular shape of the frame (Fig. 193).

This manner of pictorial abstraction should be credited to Kaufman's meticulous use of the camera and its various – especially wide

– lenses, as in the "Swimming, Diving, and Gymnastics" sequence (XXXVIII). For example, one of the shots opens with two blurred vertical forms separated by a gray strip appearing at the right side of the screen, while the rest of the frame is black; as the form moves away from the camera, it becomes clear that it is a tripod carried by the Cameraman (Fig. 164). In other instances, soft focus blurs the physical appearance of the object on the screen, as in the "Spectators and the Screen" sequence (LII), in which the side of passing trolleys is constantly blurred and decomposed so that the white lines on them appear as parallel horizontal stripes vibrating on a black background; as the trolleys withdraw from the foreground, the semiabstract composition of the shot becomes a representational image clearly depicting the passing vehicles (Fig. 210). However, most often the representationally identifiable parts of objects are intentionally excluded from the frame, as in the "Crowd on the Beach" sequence (XXXIX). The shot, composed of a white surface with dark spots on the lower left and right sides of the screen, is equally reminiscent of a Malevich abstract painting, until hands enter the frame and smear mud on what becomes recognizable as a woman's back (Fig. 161). Finally, the deconstruction of the object's representational appearance in *The Man with the Movie Camera* is achieved by the rapid operation of machines, as in the "Cameraman and Machines" sequence (XXXI), where the shots of a rotating flywheel, photographed in extreme close-up, reach the point of abstraction and produce an intense interplay between diagonal and star-shaped graphic patterns (Plate 3).

The variety of graphic patterns, visual designs, and, especially, their kinesthetic interaction ought to be credited not only to Kaufman, who photographed most of the film's footage, but also to Svilova, who edited the shots in such a way that their formal features are instantly perceptible either by the contrast or similarity between the juxtaposed images. But it was Vertov who conceived the overall formal structure of the film, with the ultimate goal of demonstrating the medium's unique visual capacity. The coexistence of different visual designs is conceptually foreshadowed in the first shot of the film (the tiny Cameraman standing on the giant camera), and is restated in the final shot of the film (a close-up of the camera's lens). Of course, many of the shots' formal elements affect the viewer on a subliminal level; these abstract shot compositions constitute an "absolutely visual" and "universally accessible" means of communication, to use Vertov's terminology, and convey messages in purely cinematic terms. As explained in Chapter I, this concept is homologous to the structure of futurist poetry. Emphasizing the shots' visual design and creating kinesthetic links between them on the principle of "intervals," Vertov "destroys both the conventional semantics of the shots (by means of unusual frame compositions and camera angles) and the conventional syntag-matic relationship that would advance a narrative (by means of a striking use of montage)."[3] By considering the shot as a "montage phrase," Vertov creates a "film poem" in which "shots-phrases rhyme with one another,[4] attesting to the influence of Mayakovsky on Vertov's film method.

Following both the futurist's and constructivist's concepts of "art of fact," Vertov urged his *kinoks* to "observe people and objects in mo-tion" and to achieve the "condensation and deconstruction of time" through a "concentrated way of seeing."[5] In many of his theoretical es-says written during the making of *The Man with the Movie Camera,* Vertov defines his cinematic tactics as being primarily concerned with the correlation of planes, shot scales, foreshortenings (by choice of an-gles and lenses), movements within the frame, light (reflections, shades), and speed (both of the events photographed and of the cam-era). His preoccupation with the formal aspects of filmmaking is evi-dent in his manifestos, which describe cinema as "an art of organizing the various movements of objects in space,"[6] and which hail "dynamic geometry, the race of points, lines, and volumes."[7] Perhaps the most important claim in Vertov's declarations is his contention that "the material and elements of the art of cinematic movement are the *inter-vals* (transitions from one movement to the next), and by no means the movements themselves," that is, the optical clash occurring at the juncture where one movement "touches" another, and thus "pushes the movement toward a kinetic resolution."[8] Obviously, Vertov had in mind here the *kinesthetic* impact of a film, although he used the term "kinetic" (more appropriate for mobile sculptures). To demonstrate his concept of kinesthetic orchestration (which he also called "organized fantasy of movement" and "geometric extraction of movement"[9]), Ver-tov decided to produce a film whose structure would generate a thun-dering impact on the viewer. The result of this experimentation with a "dynamic geometry" of recorded and consequently rearranged "life-facts" is *The Man with the Movie Camera.*

Vertov's "Theory of Intervals" is fundamental to the understanding of the formal aspect of his film. Theoretically, it can be related to Ei-senstein's "Montage of Conflicts," which juxtaposes the shots according to the direction of movement within the frame, its scale, volume, depth, graphic design, and its contrast of dark and light.[10] In his es-says, Eisenstein attributes his use of the same term, "interval," to mu-sic's influence on his theory, but fails to mention that it was Vertov who first applied it to cinema. Eisenstein's contention was that "the quan-tity of intervals determines the pressure of the tension,"[11] especially the perceptual stimulation of the viewers. Depending on the se-quence's thematic meaning, Eisenstein used "intervals" to *intensify* montage structure, whereas Vertov considered them the "elements of the art of movement" that contribute to the "poetic impact of the sequence," provided that the intervals are conceived as a "geometrical extraction of movement through the exchange of images."[12] Such an attitude is purely constructivist in its recognition of the physiological impact of the cinematic image, as will be shown in the analysis of those sequences whose montage structure is based on a "geometric" interaction of shots. Vertov's constructivist attitude is reflected in his claim that "the film's goal was not to *conceal* cinematic rhetoric but to *acquaint* the viewers with the grammar of cinema's expressive means."[13] It is of no surprise then that such an attitude was proclaimed "formalistic," and that the majority of viewers proved insensitive to the latent signification of the film's formal structure.

Phi-effect and kinesthesia

Vertov's interest in the theory of perception is evident in his use of the phi-effect* to achieve a highly kinesthetic impact on the viewer. Due to the fact that our eyes retain a perceived image on the retina for one one-hundredth of a second *after* an actual perception is completed (i.e., persistence of vision), the viewer experiences an illusion of double exposure (through a coalescence of two or more images on the same screen). As a result, the impression of a previous image merges with the perception of the succeeding image, and if the sequence contains a series of different images (shots) following one another in rapid succession, the film viewer will experience the stroboscopic illusion of these images being superimposed. Yet it is essential to note that this optical deception differs substantially from the mechanical superimposition of two shots (i.e., the *simultaneous* appearance of the two images on the same screen). While the mechanical superimposition – whether produced by the camera or through a laboratory process – affects the viewer's perception on a purely optical level, the phi-effect generates a stroboscopic pulsation that has a hypnotic impact on the viewer. Instead of perceiving an actual combination of two (or more) objects projected on the screen, the viewer sensorially experiences "intervals," which pulsate between the exchanging shots. In the former case, the impact is *soothing* and optically *impressive,* while in the latter it is *irritating* and optically *aggressive.* One can understand

---

* The phi-effect is determined by the stroboscopic nature of the cinematic projection. If two objects or graphic forms are projected alternately on the same screen, the viewer will have the illusion that one form is transformed into another, and/or that they exist simultaneously (which is a different effect from superimposition). Correspondingly, if the image of the same object is projected alternately on different areas of the same screen, the viewer will have the illusion that the object is jumping back and forth.

why Vertov opted for the latter: it conformed to his concept of revolutionary cinema as a way of "reshaping" the viewers' perception and forcing them to participate in exploring the external world through the "penetration" of its internal structure.

The following diagrams indicate the collision of intervals in the "Street and Eye" sequence (XXII), which generates the phi-effect in order to enhance the viewer's sensorial experience of the traffic accident. The diagrams include the scale, duration, content (objects, events), and the direction of movement in each shot. Assisted by frame enlargements (Plate 6), the reader can figure out how, through a "battle of movements," kinesthetic energy is built up in this sequence, and to what extent the impact of intervals is "geometrically" increased by gradually reducing the shots' duration. The graphic scheme of the basic movements in the alternating shots explains the "orchestration of the movements" in this sequence:

1.	CU:	5 fr.:	EYE:	
2.	ML:	25 fr.:	STREET:	
3.	CU:	6 fr.:	EYE:	
4.	ML:	22 fr.:	STREET:	
5.	CU:	6 fr.:	EYE:	
6.	ML:	17 fr.:	STREET:	
7.	CU:	5 fr.:	EYE:	
8.	ML:	19 fr.:	STREET:	
9.	CU:	4 fr.:	EYE:	
10.	ML:	23 fr.:	STREET:	
11.	CU:	4 fr.:	EYE:	
12.	ML:	27 fr.:	STREET:	
13.	CU:	6 fr.:	EYE:	
14.	ML:	19 fr.:	STREET:	

15. CU: 5 fr.:   EYE:

16. ML: 19 fr.:   STREET:

17. CU: 7 fr.:   EYE:

18. ML: 17 fr.:   STREET:

19. CU: 4 fr.:   EYE:

20. ML: 21 fr.:   STREET:

21. CU: 5 fr.:   EYE:

22. ML: 21 fr.:   STREET:

23. CU: 6 fr.:   EYE:

24. ML: 11 fr.:   STREET:

25. CU: 5 fr.:   EYE:

26. ML: 11 fr.:   STREET:

27. CU: 6 fr.:   EYE:

28. ML: 16 fr.:   STREET:

29. CU: 6 fr.:   EYE:

30. ML: 8 fr.:   STREET:

31. CU: 6 fr.:   EYE:

32. ML: 7 fr.:   STREET:

33. CU: 5 fr.:   EYE:

34. ML: 8 fr.:   STREET:

35. CU: 5 fr.:   EYE:

36. ML: 7 fr.:   STREET:

37. CU: 4 fr.:   EYE:

38. ML: 6 fr.: STREET:

39. CU: 2 fr.:   EYE:

40. ML: 6 fr.: STREET:

41. CU: 3 fr.:   EYE:

42. ML: 5 fr.: STREET:

43. CU: 3 fr.:   EYE:

44. ML: 4 fr.: STREET:

45. CU: 2 fr.:   EYE:

46. ML: 4 fr.: STREET:

47. CU: 2 fr.:   EYE:

48. ML: 3 fr.: STREET:

49. CU: 2 fr.:   EYE:

50. ML: 3 fr.: STREET:

51. CU: 2 fr.:   EYE:

52. ML: 3 fr.: STREET:

53. CU: 2 fr.:   EYE:

54. ML: 3 fr.: STREET:

55. CU: 2 fr.:   EYE:

56. ML: 3 fr.: STREET:

57. CU: 2 fr.:   EYE:

58. ML: 3 fr.: STREET:

59. CU:	1 fr.:	EYE:	
60. ML:	2 fr.:	STREET:	
61. CU:	1 fr.:	EYE:	
62. ML:	2 fr.:	STREET:	
63. CU:	1 fr.:	EYE:	
64. ML:	2 fr.:	STREET:	
65. CU:	1 fr.:	EYE:	
66. ML:	2 fr.:	STREET:	
67. CU:	1 fr.:	EYE:	
68. ML:	2 fr.:	STREET:	
69. CU:	1 fr.:	EYE:	
70. ML:	2 fr.:	STREET:	
71. CU:	1 fr.:	EYE:	
72. ML:	2 fr.:	STREET:	
73. CU:	1 fr.:	EYE:	
74. ML:	2 fr.:	STREET:	
75. CU:	1 fr.:	EYE:	
76. ML:	2 fr.:	STREET:	
77. CU:	1 fr.:	EYE:	

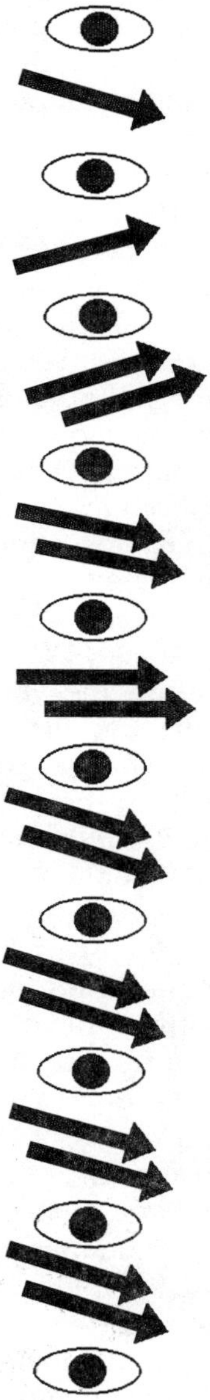

Characteristically, the first shot of the ensuing "Accident on the Street" sequence (XXIII) is entirely representational: it shows an operator talking on the phone, apparently responding to an emergency call (Fig. 113). As such, this shot has a transitional function, providing the necessary explanation for the unusual montage tension built up by the previous sequence. The kinesthetic energy released in the "Street and

Eye" sequence represents a cinematic equivalent of the subsequent street accident whose tragic aftermath is shown *consecutively* on the screen in straight newsreel manner (the arrival of an ambulance and treatment of the victim).

The phi-effect is used here to "shock" the viewers perceptually and to warn them *sensorially* of the approaching danger. In addition, this sensorial stimulation is prefigured by the three closing shots of the previous "Traffic, Elevators, and Cameraman" sequence (XXI). The first of these shots is a long, shaky traveling take in which the camera penetrates through the street as pedestrians scatter in all directions to avoid being run over by the vehicle on which the camera is placed. The spatial dynamism, sensorial impact, and the fluctuating pictorial composition of this lengthy tracking shot is reinforced by the aggressive perpendicular movement of the camera through the street (Fig. 110). At the same time, this shot's impact differs from the notion of "kinesthesia"* created later by the "Street and Eye" sequence (XXII) because the camera's tracking *through space,* in the "Traffic, Elevators, and Cameraman" sequence (XXI), preserves the spatial unity of the environment, thus affecting the viewer's sensory-motor centers. On the other hand, the phi-effect of the street and eye oscillation generates a stroboscopic pulsation (flashes) that excites the viewer's retina on a purely perceptual level. In the second shot, the street is photographed from an extremely tilted angle so that the trolleys and buses appear to move in opposite (diagonal) directions across the screen, while the blurred pedestrians obstruct the foreground (Fig. 111). The third and final shot of this introductory segment is an extremely low-angle (stationary) view of a trolley running over the camera and, presumably, the Cameraman shooting from a manhole (Fig. 112). This shot opens with the sky occupying the center of the frame and trees on either side receding into the background (twenty-five frames long); a trolley appears from the bottom center of the frame and moves aggressively forward (completely obstructing the view) until it disappears, revealing again the sky and trees (for only five frames). In addition to its sensorial impact, this shot functions as an overture to the "Traffic, Elevators, and Cameraman" sequence (XXI). In contrast, the introductory shot of the "Street and Eye" sequence (XXII) is perceptually unaggressive: it depicts an eyeball looking downward, and it appears on the screen for only an instant (five frames). Thus, at the very transition between the circular composition of the shot with the eyeball (occupying the greater portion of the frame) and the shot of the oncoming trolley, which then darkens the entire frame, an interval is created that pro-

---

* See footnote on p. 27.

duces a perceptual stimulus and acts as an overture to the succeeding "Accident on the Street" sequence (XXIII).

The "Accident on the Street" sequence, with its apparent narrative implication, has a thematic function: after a cinematic "announcement" of a disaster (in the "Street and Eye" sequence), an authentic "life-fact" is shown directly – undisturbed by montage. The thematic link between the two sequences is reiterated by the shot of the operator as she receives an emergency call that, naturally, causes the viewer to question what has happened at the end of the "Street and Eye" sequence. The answer is gradually revealed. First, the ambulance and the Cameraman's convertible, photographed from above and obviously heading toward the site of the accident, are shown speeding through crowded streets (Fig. 117). The expectation is cinematically intensified and only subsequently presented in narrative terms: the viewers are initially stimulated on a sensory-motor level and – once charged with the kinesthetic tension – they perceive the event as it occurs in external reality. The viewers' direct experience of the "life-fact" is preceded by a sensorial frustration created by the "Film-Eye" method. All key montage sequences in *The Man with the Movie Camera* can be read as cinematic "transpositions" of the previous or succeeding segments, which depict events in a direct documentary manner. They comment both ideologically and emotionally on "life caught unawares," by employing particular shooting techniques that "decode" the visible world and "extract" a deeper meaning from it.

The "Street and Eye" sequence (XXII) consists of "intervals" that collide through different shot compositions and durations (e.g., the eyeball moving in various directions and the camera panning and drifting over the street). The motion of the eyeball occurs from right to left (or vice versa) and up and down (or vice versa), whereas the camera movement mostly slants sideways and jumps diagonally. The chaotic confrontation of divergent movements is intensified by the variable and ever-increasing editing pace, so that near the end of the sequence the kinesthetic tension becomes perceptually aggressive, as the length of each shot is consecutively shortened until the image of the street (with its horizontal and diagonal lines) is seen "superimposed" over the eye, cutting across its circular shape. Probably more than in any other case, the formal structure of this sequence is the actual source of its conceptual meaning which transcends a mere illustrative depiction of the hectic traffic. At its perceptual and kinesthetic culmination, the sequence reaches a point of cinematic abstraction composed of the two basic graphic patterns: a circle and a line, the former representing the act of seeing, the latter the act of physical movement (traffic).

At first, the image of the eyeball is kept on the screen long enough (between five and six frames) to be perceived as a real human eye engaged in watching something (the street traffic). Gradually, the shots of the eye become shorter, until near the end of the sequence when the shot duration does not exceed more than one or two frames, thereby achieving the phi-effect. Although the eye is wide open throughout the sequence, in the final close-up the eye is almost totally closed, so that the eyeball, clearly visible in all preceding shots, can no longer be seen. Metonymically and symbolically, the sequence ends with a "closed eye," implying "nonseeing," a rejection of the foreshadowed disaster (accident), as the complete impression of the "superimposition" of the two forms takes place in the final forty shots (out of a total of seventy-seven shots). This kinesthetic buildup is unexpectedly halted by a stationary shot of a nurse answering the telephone; consequently, the following shots depict an ambulance rushing through the streets to rescue a young man hit by a car, the Cameraman (with his camera) participating also in that "rescue chase."

On an interpretive level, the development of the "Street and Eye" sequence (with several surrounding shots) can be described in the following way:

1. Urban streets filled with traffic.
2. Hectic and confused vehicular movement.
3. The camera penetrates the street.
4. A trolley runs over the camera (and spectators).
5. A human eye gazes restlessly (at street activity).
6. Traffic becomes frantic and accelerated.
7. Various movements (camera's, traffic's and eye's) collide.
8. Traffic (horizontal lines) "severs" the human eye.
9. A nurse answers the emergency call.
10. An ambulance races to the scene of the accident.
11. The Cameraman follows the ambulance.
12. The injured young man lies unconscious on the pavement.

These twelve events can be seen as part of a latent "story" expressed through visual symbolism and brought to a climax by means of a specific cinematic device (the phi-effect). Vertov's idea of developing "an ultimate international language" is thus conveyed via pure cinematic means generating an impact that no other medium can achieve.

There can be other ways of interpreting the formal structure of the "Street and Eye" sequence, but the attempt to associate the shot of the "severed" eye with the "slicing" of the eye in Buñuel's and Dali's *Un Chien Andalou* (1928) seems farfetched. The purpose of Buñuel's razor *physically* slashing the eyeball is to produce an "eccentric shock" (in a common dadaist/surrealist manner), while it may also be graphically associated with the preceding shot of a thin cloud passing across a full moon in a dark sky. Contrary to this, the viewer of Vertov's film gets the impression that the street traffic *deconstructs* the eyeball,

which has an ideological implication both within the context of the ensuing sequence (the actual accident on the street) and in relation to
other sequences which depict hectic traffic. It is important, therefore,
to note that the "severance" of the eye in Vertov's film is *built into* the
sequence's kinesthetic montage structure, and not presented merely as
a flash of only one representational shot (as in Buñuel's film). On a
structural level, this sequence yields multifaceted meaning: not only
does it foreshadow the actual accident but its climactic portion also
contributes to the sensorial experience of an urban environment with
all its inherent contradictions. But above all, this segment is "a complex experiment" that sharply contraposes "Life-As-It-Is" seen "from
the point of view of the human eye armed with the camera's eye"
("Film-Eye") and "Life-As-It-Is" seen "from the point of view of the un-
aided human eye."[14]

Vertov obviously desired maximum control over the viewer's conscious and unconscious perception of the projected images. In order to
achieve this goal, he chose two basic graphic patterns – the circle and
the line – associated with two objects (the eye and the street). It is
probable that Vertov was acquainted with the phenomenon of the
fovea, "a sphere smaller than a pinhead near the center of the eye's
retina which appears to be the major source of consciously induced
visual information."[15] The fovea permits only a small portion of visual
data to be filtered into awareness, whereas the greatest amount of the
picture's detail – especially areas on the periphery of vision – is routed
to the unconscious. Most of the meaning generated by the brain, however, is based on *both* conscious and unconscious data, although
modern psychology claims that "greater significance and meaning are
derived, apparently, from the unconscious, i.e., from the enormous
quantity of subliminal information."[16] This is especially pertinent for
artistic perception. The manner in which Vertov edits this sequence indicates that he was particularly interested in the subliminal impact of
shots whose duration approaches the awareness threshold.

Vertov's "Theory of Intervals" is based on the subliminal effect of
the instantaneous conflict between two opposing movements. In the
"Street and Eye" sequence, the same concept is applied to the conflict
between different graphic shot compositions and light distributions.
The brief close-ups of the eye show the eyeball's extremely subtle motions (micromovements) in a series. These conflicts cannot be perceived
directly because they are registered on a subliminal level and, as such,
stimulate sensory-motor activity in the viewer. The variety of movements and their repetitive patterns generate a kinesthetic power that
has a great psychological impact with emotional overtones. In his
work entitled *Subliminal Perception,* N. F. Dixon acknowledges that
"there are enough scientific studies which have successfully employed

psychological concomitance of emotion as indicators of subliminal effect."[17] Careful analysis of the key sequences in *The Man with the Movie Camera* supports the claim that Vertov was aware of the possibility of producing such an effect through subliminal montage: with it, he could arouse fear in the audience *before* the street accident actually occurs in the film or compel the viewers to empathize with the Cameraman when he "floats" in the "Cameraman and Machines" sequence (analyzed later in this chapter).

Intervals of movement

Although Vertov saw a great cinematic potential in the merger of "the eye plus the camera lens," he allowed the eye to be "severed" by the camera's tracking through space. As previously elaborated, the illusion of that severance is created by a "battle" of intervals from which the kinesthetic power of the "Film-Eye" method stems. In other instances, the interaction of intervals functions on either an ideological level, as in the "Working Hands" sequence (XXVII), or a poetical one, as in the "Cameraman and Machines" sequence (XXXI).

Both sequences are photographed with an emphasis on motion within the frame and are edited with maximum attention to the linkage of opposing movements (intervals). Yet, at the same time, the representational aspect of the photographed subject is preserved, while the intervals accumulate great kinesthetic energy that has a metaphorical implication: the "Working Hands" sequence symbolizes human work in general, and the "Cameraman and Machines" sequence presents the filmmaker as an integral part of the workers' society. In spite of the optical subversion of reality (through rapid editing, lens distortion, accelerated or decelerated motion, reverse screening, overlapping, split-screen, multiple exposure, camera movement, flickering, pixillation, and other filmic devices), both sequences retain a phenomenological semblance of photographed objects and events; their cinematic abstraction, however, begins at the point where the intervals approach the awareness threshold, creating an oneiric vision that makes an impossible situation probable.

The "Working Hands" sequence (XXVII) is positioned in the film's structural center, between two other sequences that depict various working activities: it is preceded by "Manufacturing Process" (XXVI) and succeeded by "Mine Workers" (XXVIII). The former is introduced by the Editor, shown arranging shots on the editing table; also in this sequence, other working activities are added to illustrate different aspects of human labor, represented by a steel worker, engineer, miner, shoeshiner, hairdresser, magician, entertainer, dancer, musician, driver, trolley conductor, waiter, athlete, traffic controller, barber, operator, and film editor. Thus the "Manufacturing Process" sequence (XXVI) functions as a thematic introduction to the "grand metaphor" built up cinematically in the "Working Hands" sequence (XXVII).

The "Working Hands" sequence (XXVII) is composed of seventy-three shots that accomplish maximum optical condensation during twenty-three shots (shots 47–69), focusing on hands engaged in various jobs. The sequence begins with a series of rhythmically arranged shots (mostly two or three frames long) depicting a woman's hands packing cigarettes in a factory (Fig. 132). These twenty-eight brief shots are followed by a stationary close-up of a typist's hands flying across the keyboard (Fig. 133) and a close-up of the Cameraman's hand cranking the camera (Fig. 134). Once the gestural similarity among these three activities is established, the next segment introduces the following shots depicting various manual activities: applying mascara (Fig. 135), calculating on an abacus (Fig. 136), putting on lipstick (Fig. 137), and operating a cash register (Fig. 138). Unexpectedly, there appears a close-up of a pistol being loaded (Fig. 139), followed by a close-up of a hand plugging in an electric cord (Fig. 140), a close-up of a hand pressing the buzzer next to a wall telephone (Fig. 141), a close-up of an operator's hands hanging up the receiver (Fig. 142), the operators' hands at work on a switchboard (Fig. 143), and the playing of the piano (Fig. 144). All these brief shots continue the sequence's thematic preparation for its climactic segment composed of twenty-six shots (47–73), which are juxtaposed on the principle of intervals, as described in the following shot-by-shot breakdown:

1. HACU. Hand enters from right and picks up the receiver from an ornate telephone (16 fr.).
2. CU. Cameraman's left hand cranks the camera clockwise (9 fr.).
3. HACU. Pair of hands playing piano on a diagonally positioned keyboard (13 fr.).
4. HACU. Pair of hands in lower frame typing on a Cyrillic typewriter in upper frame (9 fr.).
5. HAM (same as XXVII, 49). Hands play on piano keyboard (13 fr.).
6. HACU (same as XXVII, 50). Hands continue to type (10 fr.).
7. HAM (same as XXVII, 51). Hands continue to play on keyboard (11 fr.).
8. HACU. Razor being sharpened on leather strap positioned diagonally lower right to upper left (9 fr.).
9. CU. Gloved hands reach up vertically in the center of the frame for a cord and pull it down against a dark background (10 fr.).
10. HACU. Ax being sharpened, held by two workers' hands, index finger missing on right hand; the ax is sharpened horizontally on a grinding wheel (9 fr.).
11. MS. Lateral view of a group of silhouetted workers standing face right and pulling rods to the left; right side of frame in darkness (8 fr.).

12. LAMCU. Lateral view of woman's right arm operating the wheel on the right side of a sewing machine; the arm moves diagonally from upper right to lower left against a dark background (10 fr.).

13. CU (same as XXVII, 55). Gloved hand continues to pull cord down vertically against a dark background (7 fr.).

14. CU (same as XXVII, 35). Two female hands packing cigarettes seen horizontally from middle left to middle right against a white background (9 fr.).

15. MS (similar to XXVII, 57). Silhouetted workers push rods to the right against a dark background (10 fr.).

16. LAMCU (same as XXVII, 58). Woman's right arm seen diagonally against a dark background and turning the wheel of a sewing machine (6 fr.).

17. MS (similar to XXVII, 61). Workers push rods horizontally to the right against a dark background (11 fr.).

18. LAMCU (same as XXVII, 62). Woman's right arm moves diagonally, first to upper right, then to lower left against a dark background (6 fr.).

19. CU. Two blurred hands moving a flat chisel back and forth against a white background (11 fr.).

20. LAMCU (same as XXVII, 64). Woman's right arm moves diagonally from upper right to lower left against a dark background (8 fr.).

21. CU (same as XXVII, 65). Two blurred hands move chisel horizontally back and forth against a white background (11 fr.).

22. CU. Machine bar moves downward in center foreground; hand-held oil can stands behind it against a dark background (11 fr.).

23. CU (same as XXVII, 67). Two blurred hands move the chisel back and forth against a white background (10 fr.).

24. CU (similar to XXVII, 68). A closer view of metal bar moving up and down on left edge of the frame, with a worker's torso in the middle ground, and the right half of the frame dark (42 fr.).

25. HAMS (same as XVII, 2). Seven parallel shelves with rolls of labeled film; three signs (plant, machines, market) in Cyrillic indicate the rows are classified thematically; Svilova enters frame right and puts labeled reels on the upper shelves (85 fr.).

26. CU. Svilova's right hand places a reel of film on an upper shelf in the center of the frame; then her hand exits lower left; her hand reappears from below, placing another labeled reel on the left side of the shelf (49 fr.).

27. HAMS (same as XXVII, 71). After placing reels on upper shelves, Svilova exits to the right, leaving the horizontal shelves with classified and labeled reels of film (31 fr.).

Reduced to their basic graphic schemes and subordinated to the dominant montage beat, the first twenty-two shots are compressed through the reduction of their temporal duration, thus creating a symphony of optical movements (Plate 7). This kinesthetic orchestration illustrates what Vertov terms "a superior way of organizing documentary material, a method by which shots organically interact, enriching each other and unifying their forces to form a collective body." Vertov particularly emphasized that this method "is by no means formalistic but something completely different, an inevitable development that must not be avoided in the process of montage experimentation."[18]

The actual temporal duration (i.e., metric length) of these twenty-three shots is meant not only to produce the phi-effect but also to fuse optically different images of working hands by interrelating their gestures. The first four shots and the last four shots are of longer duration and thus function as frameworks for the symphonic interaction of intervals. In this interaction, two visual components — the pictorial composition of the shot and the hands' movements — collide with each other, thereby producing a sensorial as well as emotional impact that heightens the poetic meaning of the entire sequence.

Although there is great thematic variety in the chosen professional activities — ranging from heavy physical work in the steel foundry, through skilled labor (such as sewing, carpentry, and packing), to the kind of work involved in typing and playing the piano — it is the pictorial composition, graphic form, and direction of movement within each shot that make the sequence cinematically exciting. The shapes of the photographed objects are continuously underscored by their movement (e.g., the diagonal motion of a razor being sharpened or the horizontal glide of wood planing), often contrasted by an opposite movement (e.g., the circular gesture of the hand in contrast to the horizontal position of the sewing machine or the perpendicular position of the pianist's hands against the keyboard displayed diagonally). By building the sequence on the intervals of mechanical and gestural movements that complement or contradict each other, Vertov and Svilova achieve a fascinating choreography of physical activities, juxtaposing various forms and shapes characteristic of the nature of each respective activity. As a result, the kinesthetic orchestration produces a perceptual impact simultaneously disturbing and pleasing to the viewer, while never obscuring the thematic meaning of the sequence — the human hand at work.

The structural framework of the sequence enhances its ideological implication: the first shot is a close-up of the switchboard operator's hand hanging up the receiver (Fig. 142); the last two shots are a close-up of Svilova as she places a reel of film on a shelf (Fig. 73), followed by another medium shot of her arranging reels on the shelves in preparation for final editing (Fig. 74). These two functions of the hand (the operator's and the Editor's) are associated with two aspects of communication: one conveys messages verbally (by answering the telephone), another visually (by relating shots as image-signs). Activities not related directly to the hand are chosen rather arbitrarily, yet always with a distinct emphasis on the ritualistic nature of the work, as well as the movements characteristic of an industrial environment. Vertov's principle of choosing and juxtaposing "life-facts" is radically different from the one Walter Ruttmann demonstrated in his film *Melody of the World* (1929), in which he provides a topical survey of similar working activities occurring all over the world and at the same time of day, linking the shots either through thematic associations or through contrast, but with only marginal – if any at all – emphasis on the formal interaction between the movements (intervals) and graphic similarities/distinctions within the connected shots.*

In the climactic segment of the "Working Hands" sequence, the prevailing shot movement varies from horizontal (typing, sharpening an ax, planing a board with a chisel) to vertical (pulling a wire, lifting steel) to diagonal (playing a piano, sharpening a razor) to circular (sewing at a machine, cranking a camera). All these movements are interrelated on the graphic level as well, so that their juxtaposition (as demonstrated in Plate 7) produces a montage dynamism governed not only by the intervals' beats but also by the optical transformation of moving shapes. Pictorially, each shot incorporates both a graphic design intrinsic to the nature of the work activity shown and elements of a graphic design prefiguring the shape of the ensuing shot. For example, the cranking of the camera is basically circular except for the element of vertical design established by the square shape of the camera itself. And the operator's hand reaching for the telephone's base begins as a diagonal movement which terminates vertically, but also contains elements of horizontal design due to the position and shape of the receiver.

The beginning of this sequence is conceived in a semiabstract manner, as the viewer is aware only of the movement per se, with very little if any revelation of its actual purpose. As the sequence evolves, the precise function of the movements is emphasized rhythmically by the intervals' beats. Yet in spite of this substantiation of movements, the kinesthetic abstraction of the sequence is not weakened; rather, it becomes even more powerful as the graphic variations of different movements are persistently tied to the notion of the specific work the hand performs. Consequently, the sequence assumes a symphonic structure, developing into a "cinematic ode" to the *hand that produces*, as illustrated by the following diagrams:

---

* Although Ruttmann produced his two major films, *Berlin, Symphony of a Great City* [*Berlin, die Symphonie einer Grossstadt,* 1927] and *Melody of the World* [*Die Melodie der Welt,* 1929], before *The Man with the Movie Camera,* Vertov had not seen these two films before he completed his. Actually, Ruttmann was influenced by Vertov's early work, particularly the *Film-Eye* and *Film-Truth* series. In his *Weekend* [*Wochende,* 1929], a "sound film without images," Ruttmann follows directly Vertov's concept of "Radio-Ear" and his principle of radiophonic montage.

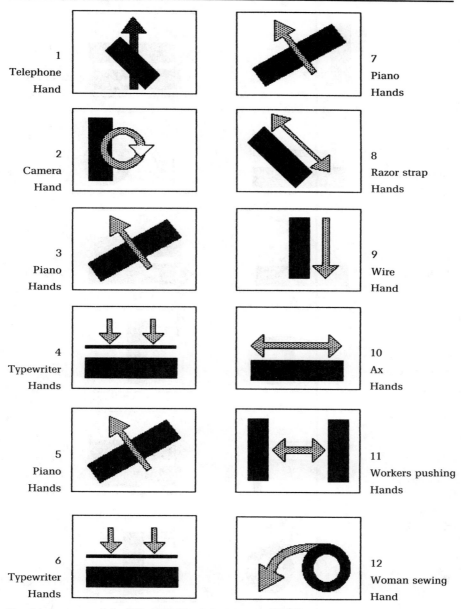

Graphic patterns of the "Working Hands" sequence (XXVII)

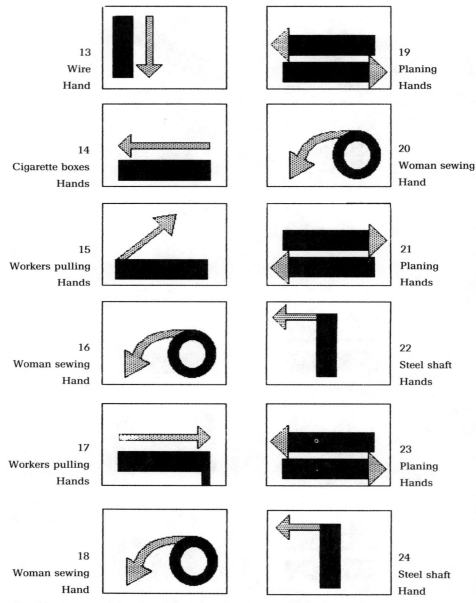

13
Wire
Hand

19
Planing
Hands

14
Cigarette boxes
Hands

20
Woman sewing
Hand

15
Workers pulling
Hands

21
Planing
Hands

16
Woman sewing
Hand

22
Steel shaft
Hands

17
Workers pulling
Hands

23
Planing
Hands

18
Woman sewing
Hand

24
Steel shaft
Hand

Graphic patterns of the "Cameraman and Machines" sequence (XXXI)

The position of this sequence within the film's structure justifies its semiabstract outlook: it is the second sequence in Part Two, following the "Manufacturing Process" sequence (XXVI) and preceding the "Mine Workers" sequence (XXVIII), two relatively descriptive segments of the film. Symbolically, the latter sequence concludes with Svilova as a worker-editor, with the focus on her right hand placing a small reel on a shelf (Fig. 73). Within such a structural framework, the "Working Hands" sequence functions as one of the major poetic, emotional, and ideological points of the entire film. In the broader context of international avant-garde experimentation, it is necessary to note a surprising correspondence between Vertov and the American filmmaker Maya Deren. In her theoretical pronouncements about cinema, Deren compared the function of "poetic illuminations" in film to that of dramatic monologue:

Every once in a while, the filmmaker arrives at a point of action where he wants to illuminate the meaning of *this* moment of drama, and at that moment he builds a pyramid or investigates it "vertically," if you will, so that you have a "horizontal" development with periodic "vertical" investigations, which are the poems, which are monologues.[19]

Deren's concept of "vertical" investigation/penetration seems relevant to the intervals of movement in Vertov's film. Like Maya Deren, Vertov and Svilova "vertically" investigate the phenomenological substance of a specific event and "poetically" intensify the ideological implications of its kinesthetic dynamism. The "Working Hands" sequence is one such "vertical" investigation, based on Vertov's "Theory of Intervals" and fully imbued with the ideological meanings that the film's middle section conveys, with neither explanatory intertitles nor explicit political allusion.

Subliminal propulsion

The "Working Hands" sequence (XXVII) is succeeded by three relatively brief sequences (composed of 9, 16, and 23 shots) that depict miners (XXVIII), steel workers (XXIX), and a power plant (XXX). In each of them, the Cameraman shoots as he runs tirelessly through mine shafts and factories. At the power plant he films the dam from a cable car as he hangs over the sloping water (Fig. 148). Then, an unexpected and "disruptive" split-screen image of traffic and pedestrians (Plate 2) introduces the "Cameraman and Machines" sequence (XXXI). The "Cameraman and Machines" sequence contains 152 shots and lasts less than fifty seconds, achieving another kinesthetic condensation of repeated visual data that turns into a cinematic metaphor about the Cameraman and the productive labor process of which he is a part. Numerous shots of machines are compiled from various factories (just as the traffic shots are photographed in different cities within the Soviet Union), so that their fusion (on the screen) assumes a broader environmental connotation related to the industrial environment essential for the building of a socialist society.

The interaction among shots in the "Cameraman and Machines" sequence is based on movement that occurs at two levels: the representational (the Cameraman's body moving in a semicircle) and the more abstract (visually distorted wheels and gears rotating in various directions). The juxtaposed shots include the three basic directions of motion – circular, vertical, and, most frequently, horizontal – supported by the complementary movement (of the tripod) progressing along the diagonal of the frame. Some shots of the machines are composed with the clear intention to underscore their linear design (bars and shafts), others their circular construction (wheels and gears). In the climactic portion, eighty-nine shots with linear composition are progressively "bombarded" by sixty-three medium shots of the moving Cameraman and the tripod placed diagonally over his shoulder. Here Vertov and Svilova create what may be termed "subliminal propulsion" of movements and shapes by intercutting discordant mechanical locomotion with the Cameraman's smooth and ethereal movement. The machines and wheels turn from left to right (clockwise), whereas the Cameraman and his tripod revolve incrementally in a diagonal from the upper right toward the upper left corner of the frame, forming a counterclockwise arc and creating a resplendant counterpoint of spiral movements that suffuse the entire frame with a kinesthetic syncopation.

The sequence begins with ten close-ups of rotating wheels, gears, and the cranking camera, establishing a pattern of repeated circular motion. Then a large factory chute (with black smoke billowing downward) suddenly breaks the circular pattern, followed by another vertical composition of two tall smokestacks. These inserts reinforce the vertical pattern that is subsequently superseded by the diagonal pattern of the shots with the Cameraman: seventy-six one-, two-, or three-frame shots of smokestacks, gears, wheels, and valves intercut with sixty-one shots (of the same duration) of the Cameraman. The differing pictorial composition of these two sets of shots is manifested not only through their graphic design but even more so by means of lighting, as can be seen in the frame enlargements (Plate 8). The shots are predominantly dark with bright contrasting accents created by the Cameraman's hand and tripod or bright reflections produced by the metallic surface of pistons and gears.

The entire sequence consists of 152 shots (lasting only 49 seconds), with the climactic segment containing only 55 shots that create an intense kinesthetic pulsation due to the frequency of cuts. The first 10 shots are relatively lengthy (ranging from 15 or 17 frames, to 52 and up to 108 frames), representing various parts of machines, with an emphasis on the triangular rods moving up and down (nos. 4, 6, 8, and 10). Inserted among these images are three shots of a lateral view of the camera, with the Cameraman's hand cranking it. The next three shots are: (no. 11) the vertical composition of the factory chutes (15 fr.); (no. 12) the triangular composition of the rods (2 fr.); and (no. 13) the lateral view of the Cameraman with tripod and camera over his shoulder (1 fr.). Then a strongly vertical composition reintroduces the dominant graphic pattern against which the diagonal composition of the Cameraman is juxtaposed. The climactic section of this sequence can be divided into three parts, based on the physical position of the Cameraman and the graphic design of machines within the frame. The first part contains twenty shots (14–33), as can be seen in the following shot-by-shot breakdown:

1. LS. Two tall, vertical smokestacks silhouetted against white smoke and gray clouds; other silhouetted factory constructions appear in the lower foreground; the upper and right side of the frame is dark (1 fr.).

2. LAMS. Diagonal (upper right to lower left) view of the Cameraman, against a dark background, with tripod and camera over his left shoulder (1 fr.).

3. LS. Vertical smokestacks (2 fr.).

4. LAMS. Diagonal position of Cameraman (1 fr.).

5. LS. Vertical smokestacks (2 fr.).

6. LAMS. Diagonal position of Cameraman (1 fr.).

7. LS. Vertical smokestacks (2 fr.).

8. LAMS. Diagonal position of Cameraman (1 fr.).

9. LS. Vertical smokestacks (2 fr.).

10. LAMS. Diagonal position of Cameraman (1 fr.).

11. LS. Vertical smokestacks (2 fr.).

12. LAMS. Diagonal position of Cameraman (1 fr.).

13. LS. Vertical smokestacks (2 fr.).

14. LAMS. Diagonal position of Cameraman (1 fr.).

15. LS. Vertical smokestacks (2 fr.).

16. LAMS. Diagonal position of Cameraman (1 fr.).

17. LS. Vertical smokestacks (2 fr.).

18. LAMS. Diagonal position of Cameraman (1 fr.).

19. LS. Vertical smokestacks (2 fr.).

20. LAMS. Diagonal position of Cameraman (1 fr.).

It is important to note that Vertov and Svilova chose two compositionally distinct shots, one with a stable vertical structure (smokestacks) and another slowly moving, diagonal composition (the Cameraman) to mark the first climax of the kinesthetic progression. The second part of the sequence's climax contains twenty-two shots. It begins with a medium shot of five steam valves moving against a black background; this shot is then juxtaposed to the shot of the Cameraman (shots 34–55), as specified in the following breakdown:

1. MS. Five vertical steam valves on black background, two in left foreground, three in right middle ground, moving rapidly against the dark background (2 fr.).
2. LAMS. Diagonal position of Cameraman (1 fr.).
3. MS. Vertical steam valves (2 fr.).
4. LAMS. Diagonal position of Cameraman (1 fr.).
5. MS. Vertical steam valves (2 fr.).
6. LAMS. Diagonal position of Cameraman (1 fr.).
7. MS. Vertical steam valves (2 fr.).
8. LAMS. Diagonal position of Cameraman (1 fr.).
9. MS. Vertical steam valves (2 fr.).
10. LAMS. Diagonal position of Cameraman (1 fr.).
11. MS. Vertical steam valves (2 fr.).
12. LAMS. Diagonal position of Cameraman (1 fr.).
13. MS. Vertical steam valves (2 fr.).
14. LAMS. Diagonal position of Cameraman (1 fr.).
15. MS. Vertical steam valves (2 fr.).
16. LAMS. Diagonal position of Cameraman (1 fr.).
17. MS. Vertical steam valves (2 fr.).
18. LAMS. Diagonal position of Cameraman (1 fr.).
19. MS. Vertical steam valves (2 fr.).
20. LAMS. Diagonal position of Cameraman (1 fr.).
21. MS. Vertical steam valves (2 fr.).
22. LAMS. Diagonal position of Cameraman (2 fr.).

In the next part, the image of the Cameraman is overpowered quantitatively by the image of technology – namely, steam valves – in the ratio of 2:1 (the image of technology occupies twice as many frames as the image of the Cameraman). A certain compositional balance is achieved on a purely photographic level: the shots of valves are photographed through diffusion, whereas the shots of the two prominently positioned vertical smokestacks (seen in the first part of the segment) are composed sharply against a dark background with pulsating bright spots.

The third part of the segment first alternates a three-frame shot of machine rods and gears moving up and down with a two-frame shot of the upright Cameraman. The world of machines is represented through various details: after ten close-ups of rods and a gear, other elements of machinery gradually take over. Two of them are particularly notable: horizontally rotating spindles and a blurred spinning wheel. They are intercut with shots of the Cameraman at a rate of three frames (of spindles and wheel) to two frames (of the Cameraman). After sixty-five shots, the Cameraman (who maintains a more or less stable diagonal position in the shot) begins to move slowly – at first counterclockwise and then in various directions, sometimes jumping from one position to another. The second section of this third part contains twenty-four shots (from 129 to 152) and brings the intervals' beats to the height of optical propulsion by maximally reducing the shot duration (one frame equals one shot).

As in the "Street and Eye" sequence, this segment of the film demonstrates Vertov's awareness of the fovea phenomenon.* The function of one-frame shots is to filter minimal visual data to the viewer's consciousness, simultaneously emphasizing the specific pictorial design of each shot by focusing on details that subliminally stimulate the viewers in a particular way. For example, the curved, spiral, and diagonal motions of the Cameraman's body are intended to incite the viewer's emotional identification with the "floating" Cameraman, as one can see from Plate 8 and the following shot-by-shot breakdown:

1. LAMS (double exposure). Cameraman with goggles (1 fr.).
2. HAECU. Rods and wheels spinning (1 fr.).
3. LAMS. Cameraman with goggles facing left (1 fr.).
4. CU. Spindles on a rotating wheel (1 fr.).
5. LAMS. Cameraman with goggles (1 fr.).
6. CU. Machine positioned diagonally (from lower right to upper left) with wheel turning at right and valves rotating in upper background (1 fr.).
7. LAMS (double exposure). Cameraman with goggles (1 fr.).
8. CU. Blurred wheel spinning (1 fr.).
9. LAMS (double exposure). Cameraman with goggles (2 fr.).
10. HAECU. Rods and wheels spinning (1 fr.).
11. CU. Spindles on rotating wheel (1 fr.).
12. HAECU. Rods and wheels spinning (1 fr.).
13. CU. Blurred wheel spinning (1 fr.).
14. CU. Spindles on rotating wheel (1 fr.).
15. CU. Blurred wheel spinning (1 fr.).
16. CU. Spindles on rotating wheel (1 fr.).
17. CU. Blurred wheel spinning (1 fr.).
18. CU. Spindles on rotating wheel (1 fr.).
19. CU. Blurred wheel spinning (1 fr.).
20. CU. Spindles on rotating wheel (1 fr.).
21. CU. Blurred wheel spinning (1 fr.).
22. CU. Spindles on rotating wheel (1 fr.).

* See also p. 147.

23. CU. Blurred wheel spinning (1 fr.).

24. CU. Spindles on rotating wheel (1 fr.).

XXXII. *Traffic Controller and Automobile Horn.* 28 shots, 989 fr., 55 sec.

1. ECU. The mirror image of the camera and the Cameraman reflected in the lens (1 fr.). Note: this shot is the same as shot 43 in the "Various Kinds of Work" sequence (XXV).

The montage crescendo of the final part of the "Cameraman and Machines" (XXXI) sequence is composed of twenty-four one-frame alternating shots of the Cameraman and rotating spindles. The two-frame duration of the shot of the Cameraman with goggles (no. 9) is arbitrary; it cannot be explained by any structural principle. There is no substantial reason for this unexpected disruption of an otherwise consistent pattern of shot duration, unless the single two-frame shot is seen as a reinforcement of the fovea phenomenon with regard to the Cameraman's vertical position versus the amorphous background formed by wheels and gears.

The emphasis on the graphic pattern of the movement within the shots creates a kinesthetic abstraction subliminally perceived by the viewer as a progressive spiral rotation. Thematically, this upward movement is associated with the representational aspect of the shots (the Cameraman, wheels, cylinders, spools, dynamos). Subliminally, the denotative meaning of the photographed subjects is linked with the kinesthetic experience of the physical transformations undergone by the Cameraman and tripod on the screen. Thus, when the Cameraman appears to float over the machines, the viewer's sensorial experience reaches a peak. As a result of this thematic/formal interaction, the vision of an elevated human body unified with the working machines can be interpreted as Vertov's celebration of the technological power controlled by the workers.

The collision of two directions of movement in this sequence provides a unique kinesthetic experience stimulated by the intervals as constructed by Vertov and Svilova. The rotating wheel introduces circular and elliptical patterns to the vertical and diagonal formations, as illustrated in the diagrams on p. 161.

The juxtaposition of circular–elliptical and vertical–diagonal patterns creates – through their continuous rotation – a surreal ambiance in which the Cameraman appears to be flying among and over machines. Gradually, the Cameraman's "flight" transforms his body's vertical position into a rotating circular structure similar to the structure of rotating machines. The abrupt "stop" to this kinesthetic choreography is produced by a one-frame close-up of the camera with the Cameraman reflected in its lens, an image that marks the beginning of the next sequence, "Traffic Controller and Automobile Horn" (XXXII).

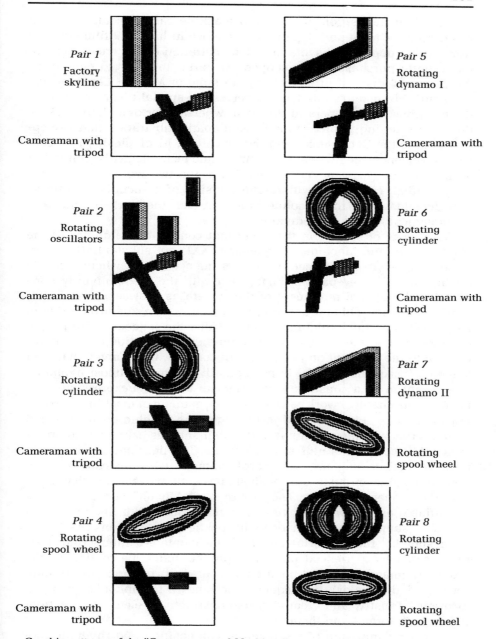

Pair 1
Factory
skyline

Cameraman with
tripod

Pair 2
Rotating
oscillators

Cameraman with
tripod

Pair 3
Rotating
cylinder

Cameraman with
tripod

Pair 4
Rotating
spool wheel

Cameraman with
tripod

Pair 5
Rotating
dynamo I

Cameraman with
tripod

Pair 6
Rotating
cylinder

Cameraman with
tripod

Pair 7
Rotating
dynamo II

Rotating
spool wheel

Pair 8
Rotating
cylinder

Rotating
spool wheel

Graphic patterns of the "Cameraman and Machines" sequence (XXXI)

Vertov's juxtaposition of man and machine can be compared with Eisenstein's "Cream and Separator" sequence in his 1929 film *Old and New,* which depicts peasants at a demonstration of the cream separator recently purchased by a cooperative farm. In order to emphasize the peasants' distrust of technology (in spite of Marpha Lapkina's excitement), Eisenstein's montage preserves the spatial distance between the machines and farmers in the barn, whereas Vertov's shots exclude the factory setting in order to achieve a spatial abstration that perceptually fuses the Cameraman and the machines. Ideologically, in Eisenstein's sequence, the two worlds – human and technological – contradict each other, whereas in Vertov's sequence, the two worlds are organically unified, complying with Vertov's vision of a socialist enterprise that depends upon the absolute unity between the workers and their technological means of production.

The variety of shapes in the shots that constitute the climax of the "Cameraman and Machines" sequence (XXXI) are substantially different from those in the "Street and Eye" sequence (XXII), where a steady circular form (an eyeball) is juxtaposed with the predominantly horizontal and diagonal movement of the camera as it sweeps over buildings and streets. This sequence is perceptually more disturbing due to its phi-effect and its structural position (after the sequence with people drinking beer in the pub), as well as its diegetic function (as an introduction to the accident on the street). In contrast, the "Cameraman and Machines" sequence (XXXI) is perceptually soothing, almost hypnotic; it is meant to be a constructivist statement about the expressivity and beauty of mechanical work as well as the dynamism of machines, reflecting the *kinoks'* admiration of technology. The graphic design created by the forms and movements in individual shots is extremely compact, although it consists of numerous elements. The light patterns continue to be vertical or diagonal and sharply angular, with unsteady and undistinguishable circular–elliptical shapes and movements that overtake the sequence's finale. The fact that the "flying" human being is identifiable as *the Cameraman* – a worker armed with his own set of "tools" – supplies this sequence with poetic reverberations. As Eisenstein stated,[20] the sensorial effect of the montage's interacting overtones can be experienced only through the actual perception of the projected images. Integrating all basic graphic patterns (horizontal, vertical, and circular), the sequence becomes a metaphor for communication, industry, and creativity, its constructivist elements functioning on both formal and thematic levels.

A close examination of the pictorial composition and rhythmic progression of the shots in the "Cameraman and Machines" sequence reveals the particular attention that Vertov and Svilova paid to the formal aspect of the shots. One should keep in mind that the technology of editing at the time was undeveloped and even primitive, particularly in the Soviet Union where a limited number of archaic editing tables existed. However, Svilova managed to splice numerous one- or two-frame shots in order to achieve a subliminal propulsion on the screen, producing the illusion that the Cameraman is superimposed over the rotating machines. The photographic execution of these shots is equally sophisticated: the vertical position of Kaufman's body within the frame consistently matches the diagonal position of his camera, so that the tripod appears as an extension of the Cameraman's body – a mechanical tool inseparable from the worker who uses it.

The first shot of the Cameraman in the sequence is a lateral view of his left profile with the tripod extended behind his back in the center of the frame; then, he appears on the right with a bright triangle of smoke from burning steel rising in the background. Wearing goggles like the other factory workers, the Cameraman moves further to the left (almost exiting the frame), as a sudden burst of bright smoke appears in the upper right corner over the camera. These eighteen one-frame shots form a flickering effect, introducing a bright accent to the predominantly dark image. Unlike the shots of machines, wheels, and gears photographed in a more abstract fashion, the shots of the Cameraman never lose their representational configuration. The accelerated movement of gears and wheels produces yet another blurring effect that enhances the graphic pattern of white lines within circular and diagonal movements. Integrated with the balletic motion of the Cameraman's body and his tripod, through a rhythmic alternation of images, these shots create the illusion of the Cameraman "floating" through and among the machines. An integral part of the technological environment, he is identified with the workers engaged in building the new society.

The last shot of the "Cameraman and Machines" sequence (XXXI) is a close-up of a circular spindle, followed by the close-up of the camera lens reflecting the camera. The ensuing "Traffic Controller and Automobile Horn" sequence (XXXII) begins with a tracking shot of the street and traffic signal. In the third shot of this sequence, the Cameraman is seen shooting as he sits on the cobblestone street amid milling pedestrians and cars (Fig. 147). With their relatively long duration (128 and 147 frames), these two shots structurally "break" the accelerated montage tempo (reached at the end of the "Cameraman and Machine" sequence), which is now replaced by the camera's own physical exploration of space. Consequently, the viewer's attention shifts from the stroboscopic "pulsation" of the subliminal montage to a sensorial experience of the film image as a reflection of the external world.

The kinesthetic choreography of the "Cameraman and Machines" sequence builds a metaphor of the Cameraman as a worker and an indispensable part of the industrial world. Overtaken by the mighty whirl of machines, the Cameraman appears free from the pressure of gravity as he floats in the factory milieu, dancing and hovering with his camera as a balancing pole. Gradually losing his earthbound identity, he becomes a "superman," a truly omnipotent "cinematic magician." Due to the hypnotic effect of the stroboscopic pulsation, the Cameraman's figure appears flat, therefore contributing to the oneiric effect of the entire sequence. The transition to the following sequence is abrupt, as if one had suddenly awakened from a vivid dream. As reality intercedes, the Cameraman is again seen performing the routine duties of his occupation, busily running along the streets as he "veers into the tempestuous ocean of life" from which he extracts details to build a new, more significant vision of the external world.

The dreamlike setting within which Mikhail Kaufman is presented in the "Cameraman and Machines" sequence (XXXI) can be interpreted as a futuristic poetic vision of the ultimate unification of the workers and their productive means. The fact that the Cameraman (wearing the proper protective gear and the worker's cap) is identified with the factory worker extends the cinematic metaphor further, in that it complies with Vertov's alliance of the *kinoks* with workers and engineers trained to use modern technology (the camera) in order to contribute to the building of a socialist country. The kinesthetic impact of the concentrated intervals is employed here to substantiate – in a poetic way – the filmmaker's ideological position in relation to technology, whereas, in other instances, the intervals' impact has a more direct oneiric implication (as in the "Awakening" sequence).

Oneiric impact of intervals

In addition to the kinesthetic and hypnotic power of the intervals (as demonstrated in the "Street and Eye" and the "Cameraman and Machines" sequences), Vertov and Svilova also employ the principle of cutting on intervals to parallel an anxious consciousness (the Cameraman's) and a sleeping consciousness (the young woman's).

The "Awakening" sequence (VII) is intended to induce a hypnopompic sensation* in the viewer by the inclusion of representationally am-

* There are two transitional states of consciousness: one preceding and the other succeeding the four stages of dreaming. Charles Tart describes them in the following way: "When we lie down to sleep at night, there is a period of time in which it would be difficult to say with any certainty whether we are awake or asleep. This borderline pe-

biguous shots that become clarified only within the context of their surrounding shots. The sequence begins with two such shots of the sleeping young woman reduced to semiabstract imagery that is difficult to identify because the shots include only the woman's neck and a fragment of the bed in which she sleeps (Fig. 25). The third shot is a long shot of a sunny terrace lined with trees and tables against an undefined horizon in the background (Fig. 27); the fourth shot is a long shot of the Cameraman placing his camera between the tracks as a train emerges from deep perspective (Fig. 37). After this introduction, the conflict of intervals begins. By intercutting shots of the sleeping woman among shots of a speeding train, a preawakening tension is generated, which at the same time matches the Cameraman's nervous tension. The following schematic presentation of the sequence illustrates the principle of editing on intervals. It also reveals Vertov's concern for diverse directions of movement within the same shot. (Compare the schematic drawings of these shots with the actual frame enlargements in Plate 5.)

1. HACU. A woman's chin and neck under sheets. A stationary shot forming a semiabstract composition in which the white area prevails (40 fr.). Note: The difficulty of recognizing what the photographed object represents intensifies the viewer's desire to find out what is excluded from the frame.

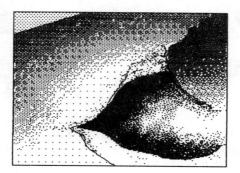

2. MLS. Part of a terrace with empty tables and two trees in the foreground, silhouetted against empty sky; branches of trees move slightly in the wind

riod has been termed the 'hypnagogic' period. The transitional state that occurs when we awake from sleep is called the 'hypnopompic' period." See Charles Tart, "Between Waking and Sleeping: The Hypnagogic State," *Altered States of Consciousness* (New York: Anchor Books, 1972), p. 75. In film theory, however, the term "hypnagogic" is used as a general term to indicate both borderline periods. Also, some contemporary film theorists use this term to describe the oneiric aspect of nonnarrative films, or to single out a specific movement in avant-garde cinema, such as "hypnagogic films" made by certain new American filmmakers.

(79 fr.). Note: The brightness of the composition and tranquility of the environment create a dreamy mood.

3. LS–MS. Railroad tracks with a train approaching from deep background and steadily moving toward the foreground; the Cameraman, kneeling on the tracks in the right foreground, prepares his camera (200 fr.). Note: The position of the camera in relation to the approaching train enhances the threatening situation.

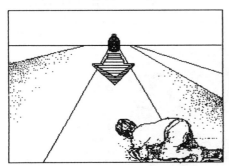 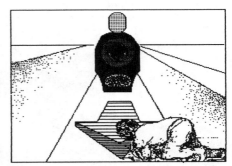

4. CU. The Cameraman's head in lower right portion of the frame, with tracks in the background; the turning wheels are blurred (7 fr.). Note: The optical shock produced by a jump cut (the position of the Cameraman's head does not match his position in the previous shot) marks the beginning of the oneiric part of the segment.

5. LACU. One side of the speeding train, as the windows move from upper right to lower left (22 fr.). Note: The camera's tilting and panning contribute to the semiabstract appearance of the speeding train.

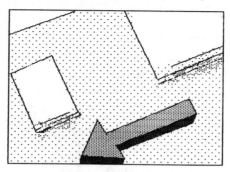

6. CU. The Cameraman's head in lower left portion of the frame, with tracks in the background and the wheels in blurred motion (5 fr.). Note: Another optical shock is produced by the reverse position of the Cameraman's head – identical but opposite to shot 4 (the flipped shot).

7. MCU. Train cars with windows move diagonally across the frame from the upper right to lower left corner; image is blurred due to the speed of the movement (22 fr.). Note: Simultaneous movement of the camera (panning and tilting) and the speeding train generate a kinesthetic impact on the viewer.

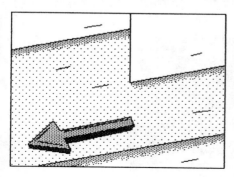

8. CU. The Cameraman's foot caught on a railroad track (13 fr.). Note: As in shot one, the unusual composition of this shot enhances the viewer's desire to see the excluded part of the photographed object (the Cameraman's body). The tension is considerably heightened by the viewer's awareness of the approaching train and the position of the railway tracks within the frame, emphasizing the Cameraman's perilous position.

9. MS. Low angle (from beneath the train); the locomotive rapidly approaches the camera (and the spectators) and runs over it (40 fr.). Note: This is the most aggressive optical shock, intensified by the exclusion of frames (pixillation) which mechanically increases the train's advance.

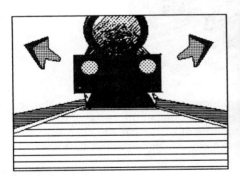 

10. HACU. The woman's hair and forehead moving slowly from left to right, revealing the entire arm of the sleeping person (24 fr.). Note: This shot provides necessary information for a contextual denotation of shot 1. The head's movement anticipates a semiabstract appearance of the train in the following shot.

 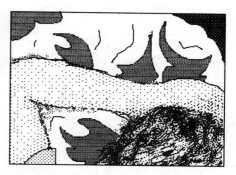

11. MS–LACU. The train at full speed moving diagonally from center background toward left of the frame, as the camera pans to the left, focusing on the windows, which first move diagonally, then horizontally, and again diagonally from upper right to lower left (26 fr.). Note: As in shot 5, the camera's tilting and panning intersperse with the movement of the speeding train and produce an even more abstract pattern on the screen.

 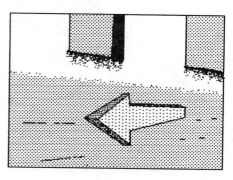

12. LAMS–CU. Blurred windows moving in different directions, constantly changing the composition and graphic patterns of the shot (68 fr.). Note: This is a central shot that achieves the greatest oneiric impact through its ten conflicting semiabstract and abstract movements/shapes, so that both the representational and spatial aspects of the photographed object are subverted and deconstructed.

 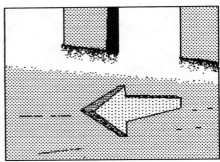

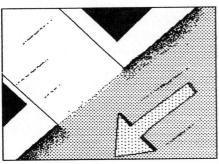 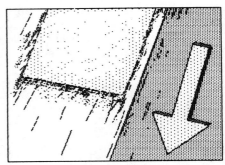

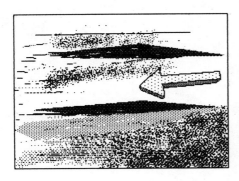 

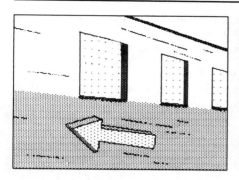 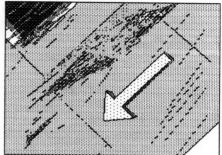

 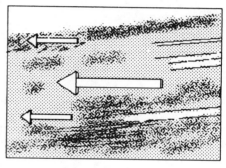

13. CU. The woman's head with her hair visible in the lower right corner;
slowly, her arm extends horizontally to the left as her head makes a horizontal movement from right to left; in the upper part of the frame, decorative patterns of the bed sheet are prominent (18 fr.). Note: Perceptually,
this shot "halts" the movement dominating previous shots and redirects
the viewer's attention to the thematic aspect of the sequence (sleeping).

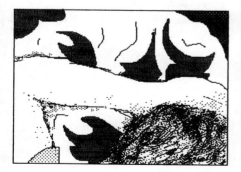 

14. LACU–MS. Blurred windows of the train moving from upper right to lower left; the caboose becomes clear as it moves from a tilted to a horizontal position and then tilts again as the now silhouetted train disappears into the lower left corner; in the frame a clear sky and a telephone pole occupy lower right center (28 fr.). Note: With its changing graphic pattern, this shot visually unifies the abstract and the representational aspects of the sequence. It clearly implies the end of an optical dynamism, a sense of disappearance and departure.

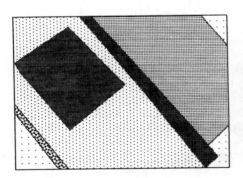
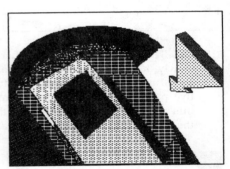

15. HAMCU. The arm and torso of the woman as she sits up in the bed; gradually her lower body and legs are seen as she gets out of the bed (57 fr.). Note: The clear representational outlook of this shot brings the thematic aspect of the sequence into full focus (wakening).

16. MCU. High angle of railroad tracks beneath the camera, which moves over them (168 fr.). Note: Although objectively the camera moves forward, it appears as if the tracks move in the opposite direction. A flickering effect is created by alternating black frames with the images of the tracks, according to the following scheme:

1. 28 fr. of track	9. 14 fr. of track	17. 5 fr. of track
2. 2 fr. of black	10. 2 fr. of black	18. 2 fr. of black
3. 25 fr. of track	11. 9 fr. of track	19. 5 fr. of track
4. 4 fr. of black	12. 2 fr. of black	20. 2 fr. of black
5. 19 fr. of track	13. 7 fr. of track	21. 4 fr. of track
6. 2 fr. of black	14. 2 fr. of black	22. 2 fr. of black
7. 17 fr. of track	15. 5 fr. of track	23. 4 fr. of track
8. 2 fr. of black	16. 2 fr. of black	24. 2 fr. of black

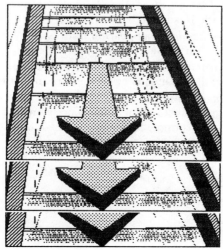

STRUCTURAL RECAPITULATION OF THE ONEIRIC SIGNIFICANCE OF THE "AWAKENING SEQUENCE"

1. *Semiabstract image: sleeping young woman*
   Function: introduction of oneiric state
   (ambiguous shot composition)

2. *Representational image: terrace with trees*
   Function: juxtaposition of exterior
   (reference to reality)

3. *Representational image: Cameraman and approaching train*
   Function: introduction to simultaneous event

4. *Representational image: Cameraman's head and turning wheels*
   Function: further amplification of dramatic tension

5. *Semiabstract image: speeding train*
   Function: extension of expectation – danger

6. *Representational image: Cameraman's head and turning wheels*
   Function: further amplification of dramatic tension – danger

7. *Semiabstract image: train moving diagonally*
   Function: further extension of expectation – danger

8. *Representational image: Cameraman's foot caught on railroad track*
   Function: peak of dramatic tension

9. *Representational image: approaching train*
   Function: visual aggression – strong motor-sensory impact

10. *Representational image: sleeping young woman*
    Function: linkage to oneiric state

11. *Semiabstract image: train moving diagonally*
    Function: intensification of oneiric effect

12. *Abstract image: train moving in various directions*
    Function: peak of oneiric effect – strong kinesthetic impact

13. *Representational image: sleeping young woman*
    Function: thematic linkage to oneiric state

14. *Representational image: disappearing train*
    Function: conclusion of oneiric state

15. *Representational image: young woman getting out of bed*
    Function: end of simultaneous event – return to reality

16. *Semiabstract image: railroad tracks*
    Function: cinematic abstraction of sequence's oneiric signification
    (tracking shot – flickering effect)

As one can see, at the beginning of this segment, Vertov relates the sleeping young woman's hypnopompic state of mind to the instinctive reaction of the Cameraman, who avoids the train by abruptly jerking his head. In fact, it is the Cameraman's response that triggers a series of semiabstract shots of the speeding train, which are then associated with the sleeping young woman. In turn, the slow-moving gestures of the young woman's head are contrasted to the abrupt jerking of the Cameraman's head. At the same time, her slow gestures are juxtaposed with the reckless movements of the train whose representational appearance is reduced to a few horizontal, diagonal, and square patterns. In shots 12 and 14, the pictorial compositions change rapidly, due to the camera's tilting and panning, or because of the variation in angle and scale of the shot. Although these two shots are relatively brief (sixty-seven and twenty-eight frames) and are without clear representational meaning, they consist of numerous visual elements, each introducing a new direction of movement and different composition. For example, in shot 12 one can discern ten different "subshots," each consisting of a particular graphic design. It is, of course, questionable whether these conflicting patterns and movements are produced by cuts (in the editing room) or during shooting. What is important here is the fact that on the screen they appear as separate pictorial units (subshots). It is through the interaction of these ten conflicting patterns and corresponding movements that optical tension ultimately affects the viewer on a subliminal level, thus intensifying the oneiric impact of the entire sequence. After shot 14 (which contains six subshots), the young woman gets out of bed as if "awakened" by this kinesthetic shock! Again, the duration of the patterns and movements in these subshots is irregular (the length of the juxtaposed pieces is not arithmetically determined), paralleling the uncomfortable feeling one customarily experiences upon awakening.

In a visual analogy to the sleeper's gradual emergence from the dream state, the young woman is not shown in full (through a long shot) as she gets up from bed, but rather in fragments. First, we see her legs slowly moving out of the bed and touching the floor (Fig. 39); then the diegetic progression of the action taking place in the bedroom is broken by an exterior shot that can be related to the earlier shot of the Cameraman shooting the train (Fig. 37). This disruptive shot is, actually, the concatenation (through montage) of twenty-four pieces (subshots) of railroad tracks (Fig. 41) crosscut with frames of black leader. The swift and optically irritating exchange of bright and dark surfaces flashing on the screen is spontaneously linked with the somnolent state of the young woman's consciousness as she awakes. With its stroboscopic pulsation, this shot (perhaps it is more legitimate to call it an optical effect) represents another example of a cinematic "illumination" of the human psyche. A more obvious connection between this nondiegetic shot (especially its perceptual impact) and the narrative core of the sequence is established later, when the young woman is shown in close-up, blinking her eyes as she dries her face (Fig. 49). This action is subsequently compared to the opening and closing of venetian blinds (Fig. 50), and also is related to the contraction of the camera's iris (Fig. 47). Once again, the eye's function is equated with the function of the cinematographic apparatus (the Camera-Eye).

Optical music

Many avant-garde filmmakers of the silent era were preoccupied with the idea of creating musical sensations by purely visual means. The French *cinéastes* of the twenties extensively experimented with cinematic images as components of musical structure. In an attempt to relate cinema to music, they introduced various metaphorical terms, such as *"la musique de la lumière"* (Ricciotto Canudo), *"l'inscription de rhythme"* (Leon Moussinac), or *"symphonie optique et visuelle"* (Germaine Dulac). Inspired by this concept, René Clair and Fernand Leger created two "musical" silent films, *Entr'acte* (Clair, 1924) and *Le Ballet mécanique* (Leger, 1924), in which shots interact – through editing – like notes in a musical composition.* Upon seeing another of Clair's experimental films, *Paris qui dort* (1923), Vertov explained that he had always wanted to experiment along these lines, particularly with accelerated and decelerated motion, but had been unable to pursue his vision.†

As a student, Vertov's interest in auditory perception and its mechanical recording stemmed from his experiments in the "Laboratory of Hearing" where he explored the "possibilities for making documentary recordings of the world of sounds through montage."[21] While

---

* In spite of many similarities in the use of specific cinematic devices to create visual abstraction on the screen, there is no evidence that Vertov actually saw *Entr'acte* or *Le Ballet mécanique* (both 1924) during his visit to Paris.

† Vertov, "Notebooks" (April 12, 1926), *Articles,* p. 161. The entry reads: "I saw the film *Paris qui dort* in the Art Theater. It upset me. Two years ago I had designed an identical project in which I wanted to use the same technical devices that have been employed in this film. All the time I have been searching for a chance to realize it. But that opportunity has never been given to me. And now, they have made it abroad. Film-Eye missed another position for attack. It is such a long road from the idea, conception, plan to its final realization. Unless we are given the opportunity to realize our innovative projects in the course of their actual execution, there will always be a danger that we shall never materialize our inventions." See also Annette Michelson, "Dr. Craze and Mr. Clair," *October,* no. 11, Winter 1979, pp. 31–53. Michelson infers that "Clair's ironic gloss upon the dynamics of alienation finds its extension in Vertov's systematic use of reverse motion ('negative of time') in the visual trope of hysteron proteron [which] thus becomes the pivotal element in the elaboration of his [Vertov's] Marxist propadeutic (p. 52), which is a less apprehensible and more convoluted explanation about the ideological significance of Vertov's cinematic execution than he himself could ever have intended.

working on his early *Film-Truth* and *Film-Eye* series, Vertov often drew the viewers' attention to the sensation of sound by including shots that triggered aural associations. In *The Man with the Movie Camera*, the most evident example of this editing principle can be found in the "Traffic Controller and Automobile Horn" sequence (XXXII), in which a close-up of a horn (Fig. 149) is inserted twelve times among long shots of traffic and medium shots of the Cameraman shooting traffic on the street (Fig. 147). The idea of sound is alluded to earlier in the film (at the end of the Prologue) through the depiction of the conductor and the orchestra as they accompany the film screening (Figs. 15–22). The rhythmic exchange between various instruments and the conductor's gestures creates the illusion of a musical orchestration. A more kinesthetic representation of sound appears in the "Awakening" sequence (VII), through the intercutting of numerous blurred shots (of the speeding train) with close-ups of the sleeping young woman. The optical pulsation of these blurred shots functions as an equivalent to sound waves and, as if in response to them, the sleeping woman wakes up (as analyzed previously in this chapter).

But the most "auditory" sequence is "Musical Performance with Spoons and Bottles" (L), near the end of Part Two, with its 111 shots that build to a montage climax paralleling the structure of a musical score and its orchestration (Plate 9). At the end of the previous sequence, sound is denoted rather illustratively, that is, by a close-up of a radio with a large circular loudspeaker that fills the entire frame. The notion of sound is enhanced through multiple double exposures of details (implying sound) within the loudspeaker's circle: (1) a human ear, (2) two hands playing on a keyboard, and (3) a singing mouth (Fig. 196). These symbolic images replace one another by superimposition, slowly moving within the stationary circular loudspeaker attached to the radio, next to the drawing of a tsarist officer on horseback (in the left portion of the frame). Then follows the first shot of the musician's hands playing with spoons on a table, on top of which a cup, a plate, a tray, an ashtray, a washboard, and seven bottles are displayed. As soon as the musician begins to hit the "instruments" with two spoons, a "higher mathematics of facts" takes over, interrelating 111 shots of the "musical performance" and its listeners. Their order and duration, as shown in the following shot-by-shot breakdown, provide an idea of Vertov's and Svilova's strategy in building a montage glissando to stimulate auditory sensation through visual associations.

L. *Musical Performance with Spoons and Bottles.* 111 shots, 1,354 fr., 1 min. 15 sec.

1. HAMCU. Row of seven dark bottles with white labels arranged diago-

nally from lower left foreground toward upper right background, ending with a jar, and wood and metal scrubboard on dark table; behind is a row consisting of a light pot lid, six spoons, an overturned metal tray; from upper left corner two white hands with a spoon in either hand, blurred, move around, hitting various objects, lifting and banging pot lid on its surface (97 fr.).

2. LACU. Woman on left with white scarf looking down and laughing; then she turns to right and begins to move out of frame against wooden door. She is identified as Woman 1 (54 fr.).

3. HACU (similar to L, 1). Musician's two hands hitting objects with two spoons (57 fr.).

4. LACU. Profile of woman with long dark hair, her face in shadow, facing left, laughing; then she turns forward and laughs, turns back to left, becoming silhouetted against white sky. She is identified as Woman 2 (57 fr.).

5. HACU (same as L, 3). Hands hit objects with spoons (41 fr.).

6. CU. Woman with short hair on left, face brightly lit, facing right; then she turns left, moves back, then looks forward and laughs; she is against dark background. She is identified as Woman 3 (50 fr.).

7. HACU. Hands with spoons, tilted to the right against a dark background, tap on washboard (43 fr.).

8. CU. Two women, one facing the camera, the other with head turned in the opposite direction. Their foreheads meet (81 fr.).

9. HACU (same as L, 5). Hands gather up spoons and throw them on the table; hands then hit the tray with a spoon (43 fr.).

10. CU. Profile of unshaven man smoking, facing left; right side of his face highlighted, the rest in shadow against dark background (27 fr.).

11. HACU (same as L, 9). Hands throw the spoons on surface, then pick them up (15 fr.).

12. MCU. Several workers with caps; laughing worker in center and part of face of another worker on left also laughing and looking down toward right (15 fr.).

13. HACU (same as L, 11). Hands hit metal tray with spoons (14 fr.).

14. LACU. Three-quarter view of Woman 3 looking left; her face in shadow against light sky in background (15 fr.).

15. HACU (same as L, 13). Hands continue to hit metal tray with spoons (15 fr.).

16. LACU (same as L, 4). Woman 2, laughing in shadow, looks left against light background (10 fr.).

17. HACU (same as L, 15). Hands hitting objects with spoons (15 fr.).

18. CU (same as L, 14). Against dark background, Woman 3 with brightly lit smile; she is at frame left and looks down (10 fr.).

19. HACU (sames as L, 17). Hands hit objects with spoons (15 fr.).

20. LACU. Face of Woman 1 on left in white scarf, laughing and looking to lower right (9 fr.).

21. HACU (same as L, 19). Hands hit objects with spoons (11 fr.).
22. CU (same as L, 10). Profile of man facing and looking down left; he laughs and smiles; right part of his face highlighted, rest of his face in shadow, against dark background (8 fr.).
23. HACU (same as L, 21). Hands hit objects with spoons (12 fr.).
24. MCU (same as L, 12). Several workers laughing and looking down to right (8 fr.).
25. HACU (same as L, 23) Hands hit objects with spoons (10 fr.).
26. LACU (same as L, 18). Woman 3 faces left (7 fr.).
27. HACU (same as L, 25). Hands hit objects with spoons (9 fr.).
28. LACU (same as L, 16). Woman 2 with face in shadow, laughing, looking left, against light background (7 fr.).
29. HACU (same as L, 27). Hands hit objects with spoons (8 fr.).
30. CU (same as L, 26). Woman 3 on left, smiling and looking down (6 fr.).
31. HACU (same as L, 29). Hands hit objects with spoons (8 fr.).
32. LACU (same as L, 20). Face of Woman 1 on left in white scarf looking to right and sticking out tongue (6 fr.).
33. HACU (same as L, 31). Hands hit objects with spoons (8 fr.).
34. CU (same as L, 22). Profile of man facing left, right part of his face highlighted, rest of his face in shadow against dark background (66 fr.).
35. HACU (same as L, 33). Hands hit objects with spoons (8 fr.).
36. MCU (same as L, 24). Workers laughing and looking down to right (5 fr.).
37. HACU (same as L, 35). Hands hit objects with spoons (6 fr.).
38. LACU (same as L, 26). Woman 3 in shadow looking left against light background (4 fr.).
39. HACU (same as L, 37). Hands hit objects with spoons (6 fr.).
40. LACU (same as L, 28). Woman 2, laughing in shadow, looking left against light background (4 fr.).
41. HACU (same as L, 39). Hands hit washboard with spoons (6 fr.).
42. CU (same as L, 30). Woman 3 on left looking down, then raising head and turning right against dark background (4 fr.).
43. HACU (same as L, 41). Hands hit washboard with spoons (6 fr.).
44. LACU (same as L, 32). Woman 1 on left in white scarf laughing and looking right against dark background (3 fr.).
45. HACU (same as L, 43). Hands hit washboard with spoons (4 fr.).
46. CU (same as L, 34). Profile of man smiling and looking left, right part of his face highlighted, rest of his face in shadow against dark background (3 fr.).
47. HACU (same as L, 45). Hands hit washboard with spoons (4 fr.).
48. MCU (same as L, 36). Worker in center, his right profile in shadow, leans back and raises right hand (3 fr.).
49. HACU (same as L, 47). Hands hit washboard with spoons (4 fr.).

50. LACU (same as L, 38). Woman 3 in shadow facing left against light background (2 fr.).

51. HACU (same as L, 49). Hands hit washboard with spoons (3 fr.).

52. LACU (same as L, 40). Woman 2, face in shadow, laughing and looking left against light background, then turns her head slightly down (2 fr.).

53. HACU (same as L, 51). Hands hit washboard with spoons (3 fr.).

54. CU (same as L, 42). Woman 3 on left looking to right with open mouth against dark background (2 fr.).

55. HACU (same as L, 53). Hands hit washboard with spoons (3 fr.).

56. LACU (same as L, 44). Face of Woman 1 on left in white scarf laughing and looking right against dark background (2 fr.).

57. HACU (same as L, 55). Hands hit washboard with spoons (3 fr.).

58. CU (same as L, 46). Left profile of smiling man, right part of his face highlighted, rest of his face in shadow against dark background (2 fr.).

59. HACU (same as L, 57). Hands hit washboard with spoons (3 fr.).

60. LACU (same as L, 50). Woman 3 in shadow facing left against a light background (2 fr.).

61. HACU (same as L, 59). Hands hit washboard with spoons (3 fr.).

62. LACU (same as L, 52). Woman 2 with face in shadow against light background looks left (2 fr.).

63. HACU (same as L, 61). Hands hit washboard with spoons (3 fr.).

64. LACU (same as L, 62). Woman 2 with face in shadow against light background looks left, face turned more toward camera (1 fr.).

65. HACU (same as L, 63). Hands hit washboard with spoons (3 fr.).

66. LACU (same as L, 64). Woman 2 with face in shadow against light background looks left; face turned to right (1 fr.).

67. HACU (same as L, 66). Hands hit bottles with spoons (3 fr.).

68. LACU (same as L, 66). Woman 2 with face in shadow against light background looks left (1 fr.).

69. HACU (same as L, 67). Hands hit bottles with spoon (3 fr.).

70. LACU (same as L, 68). Woman 2 with face in shadow against light background looks left (1 fr.).

71. HACU (same as L, 69). Hands hit objects with spoon (3 fr.).

72. LACU (same as L, 70). Woman 2 with face in shadow against light background looks left (1 fr.).

73. HACU (same as L, 71). Hands hit objects with spoon (3 fr.).

74. LACU (same as L, 72). Woman 2 with face in shadow against light background looks left (1 fr.).

75. HACU (same as L, 73). Hands hit objects with spoon (2 fr.).

76. LACU (same as L, 74). Woman 2 with face in shadow against light background looks left (1 fr.).

77. HACU (same as L, 75). Hands hit objects with spoon (2 fr.).

78. LACU (same as L, 76). Woman 2 with face in shadow against light background looks left (1 fr.).

79. HACU (same as L, 77). Hands hit objects with spoon (2 fr.).

80. LACU (same as L, 78). Hands hit objects with spoon (1 fr.).

81. HACU (same as L, 79). Hands hit objects with spoon (2 fr.).

82. LACU (same as L, 80). Woman 2 with face in shadow against light background looks left (1 fr.).

83. HACU (same as L, 81). Hands hit spoons with spoons (2 fr.).

84. LACU (same as L, 82). Woman 2 with face in shadow against light background looks left (1 fr.).

85. HACU (same as L, 83). Hands hit spoons with spoons (2 fr.).

86. LACU (same as L, 84). Woman 2 with face in shadow looks left against light background (1 fr.).

87. HACU (same as L, 85). Hands hit objects with spoons (2 fr.).

88. LACU (same as L, 86). Woman 2 with face in shadow against light background looks left (1 fr.).

89. HACU (same as L, 87). Hands hit objects with spoons (2 fr.).

90. LACU (same as L, 88). Woman 2 with face in shadow against light background looks left (1 fr.).

91. HACU (same as L, 89). Hands hit objects with spoons (2 fr.).

92. LACU (same as L, 90). Woman 2 with face in shadow against light background looks left (1 fr.).

93. HACU (same as L, 91). Hands hit objects with spoons (2 fr.).

94. LACU (same as L, 92). Woman 2 with face in shadow against light background looks left (1 fr.).

95. HACU (same as L, 93). Hands hit objects with spoons (2 fr.).

96. LACU (same as L, 94). Woman 2 with face in shadow against light background looks left; she moves her head back and laughs (4 fr.).

97. HACU (multiple exposure, superimposition). With two spoons, the two blurred hands hit six spoons placed on table; after three frames, shoes appear tapping on floor with bottom of striped pants visible in the center, while the hands move back and forth in upper right; on lower edge of screen is lateral view of arm and snapping fingers (74 fr.).

98. LACU (same as L, 96). Woman 2, with face in shadow against a light background, laughs and looks left (4 fr.).

99. HACU (similar to L, 97; multiple exposure, superimposition). With two spoons, the two blurred hands hit six spoons on table; three piano pedals appear, then right foot steps on right pedal; keyboard appears in upper center extending toward upper diagonal right; left foot steps on left pedal (35 fr.).

100. LACU (same as L, 98). Woman 2 with face in shadow against light background looks and turns left (3 fr.).

101. HACU (same as L, 99; multiple exposure, superimposition). Keyboard ex-

tends diagonally from lower left to upper right across entire frame, while two hands with spoons move in various directions (30 fr.).

102. LACU (same as L, 100). Woman 2 turns more to left (3 fr.).

103. HACU (same as L, 101; multiple exposure, superimposition). Another keyboard superimposed horizontally, cutting the frame into two parts, as hands move in all directions; feet and pedals gradually disappear (68 fr.).

104. LACU (same as L, 102). Woman 2 turns left (3 fr.).

105. HACU (same as L, 103; multiple exposure, superimposition). Continuation of L, 103 (13 fr.).

106. LACU (same as L, 104). Woman 2's left profile; she turns to right (2 fr.).

107. HACU (same as L, 105; multiple exposure, superimposition). Diagonal keyboard repeatedly alternated between being lit and being in shadow; snapping fingers appear in center (92 fr.).

108. LACU (Same as L, 106). Woman 2 turns to right (2 fr.).

109. HACU (same as L, 107; multiple exposure, superimposition). Six spoons and a white lid are exposed against a dark background and positioned in the lower part of the screen (10 fr.).

110. LACU (same as L, 108). Woman 2 looking at camera (2 fr.).

111. HACU (same as L, 109; multiple exposure, superimposition). After twenty frames, two hands grab the spoons, lift them up and throw them down; two other hands on large keyboard are more visible (59 fr.).

This sequence of 111 shots (all close-ups) lasts just a little over a minute and is one of the most dynamic and visually expressive sequences in the film. It perfectly demonstrates Vertov's concept of organizing film-pieces into a film-thing, where the duration of the shot progressively decreases in established increments. While the decimal alternation of shots and the repetition of specific scales or lengths contribute to auditory sensation, the divergent, often totally opposed, movements within individual shots and their literal superimposition through multiple exposure produce an optical glissando associated with the musical performance. Here, Vertov created a *cinematic* variation of music, even though he believed that shots – however abstract – cannot replace notes, "just as literary descriptions of Scriabin compositions cannot express the true sensation of his music."[22]

The eight introductory shots of this sequence are relatively lengthy and stationary, with little perceptible movement of the women's heads. The cuts between close-ups of the listeners' heads and the medium shots of the musician's hands occur when each listener's movement becomes perceptible, and often just before the head leaves the frame (by "cutting on movement"). As the shots' lengths decrease, the physical movement of the head is considerably reduced, so much so that the viewer perceives the close-ups of the three young women – each with different facial features – as dominant circular shapes juxtaposed against the rectangular shape of the table with diagonally arranged bottles and the musician's hands playing the spoons. The medium shots of spoons and bottles are in fact segments of a continuous take broken up into separate shots and intercut among close-ups of the womens' heads; it is because of their strong representational outlook that these segments are perceived as a continuous action, in spite of the fact that the original take is broken up by the intercutting.

The musical overtones of this sequence are generated by the arrhythmic – or rather syncopated – reduction of the length of the shots that depict listening to the performance. If one traces the number of frames in shots 50–95, it becomes clear that Vertov and Svilova followed a specific arithmetic pattern: the women's heads in close-up are held for one to three frames, while the spoons and bottles are held for two or three frames. The overall montage pace of this segment is determined by: (1) duration of shots, (2) their scale, (3) their pictorial composition, (4) the conflict of divergent movements between the shots (intervals), and (5) the tension between the continuity of the physical action (musical performance) shown on the screen and its "metric" breakdown into montage units (individual shots). The connotation of musical sound arises from medium shots of spoons and bottles as they are intercut with close-ups of women "listening to the music," while the rapid alternation of the two sets of shot compositions (circular versus horizontal; vertical versus diagonal) reflects, in visual terms, the structure of a musical score.

Vertov's application of "metric editing" to intervals in order to create the notion of music is unique in the theory of silent cinema. He uses the same device in *The Eleventh Year* (1928), "linking montage with sound" by intercutting details of machines, hammers, axes, and saws on a "metric principle," thus achieving a musical "mechanical heart beat."[23] At the time when Eisenstein, Pudovkin, and Alexandrov launched their "Statement"[24] calling for the contrapuntal use of sound, Vertov was experimenting with his own concept of "visually conveyed sound," which, according to him, was an expansion of his "Film-Eye" method into the "Radio-Eye" method. Had Vertov realized his intention to "construct" an accompanying musical score for *The Man with the Movie Camera*, this sequence would probably be based on sight and sound counterpoint.* Soon after the completion of the film, Vertov wrote the essay "From 'Film-Eye' to 'Radio Eye,'" explaining that his film was conceived as a transition from "Film-Eye" to "Film-Radio-Eye."[25] In this respect, *The Man with the Movie Camera* can be seen as

---

* See Chapter I, note 149. Vertov's sound score for *The Man with the Movie Camera* would probably consist of ordinary sounds (recorded in reality) and musical inserts from various compositions and songs (mixage).

Vertov's conceptual exploration of the relationship between montage and sound, an idea fully realized in his next work, *Enthusiasm* (1930), the first avant-garde Soviet sound film.

To demonstrate the difference between the illusion of double exposure (created by the phi-effect) and the real superimposition (produced by the camera or in the laboratory) of two or more images that appear simultaneously on the screen, Vertov includes two sets of mechanical superimpositions in the "Musical Performance with Spoons and Bottles" sequence (Plate 9). One is composed of the two hands playing with spoons and snapping fingers, the other of a Jew's harp and dancing legs seen "through" keyboards. Placed next to each other, these superimpositions point to the difference between the phi-effect and mechanical double exposure, the latter lacking genuine kinesthetic energy, however visually attractive. This difference is even more perceptible in the multiple exposure of these and other objects, which appear in the sequence eight times (shots 97, 99, 101, 103, 105, 107, 109, 111). Shots 103–11 incorporate the additional image of two piano keyboards diagonally crossing each other and piano pedals with feet on them. Functioning as a "visual dominant" within the montage structure, the repetition of the multiple exposure (lasting ten to ninety-two frames) is disrupted by seven close-ups of Woman 2 (only two to four frames long) perceived as optical flashes that appear at various intervals. The smooth flow of these multiple exposures is rhythmically "bombarded" by close-ups of the woman's head as she listens to the performance, thus creating an arrhythmic beat of alternating compositions and durations: one contains numerous visual motifs and various designs perceived for a relatively long period of time (multishaped superimpositions); the other contains only one visual motif, the woman's head (the circle) pulsating on the screen. With its pronounced "musical" beat achieved through "metric editing," the "Musical Performance with Spoons and Bottles" sequence (L) foreshadows the symphonic finale of *The Man with the Movie Camera*, culminating with the "Editor and the Film" sequence (LV).

Movement versus stasis

In the "Musical Performance with Spoons and Bottles" sequence (L), kinesthetic tension is built up by juxtaposing stationary close-ups of the listeners with dynamically composed and superimposed shots of a "musical performance." In the "Spectators and the Screen" sequence (LII), even greater kinesthetic tension is created by juxtaposing similar close-ups of the movie audience, photographed by a stationary camera, with medium and long shots of various moving events photographed by a tracking camera.

In this sequence, the spectators in close-up watch the trolleys, cars, and pedestrians moving before their eyes on the screen-within-the-screen. A similar kinesthetic effect is achieved in the "Basketball" (XLII), "Track and Field Events" (XXXVII), and "Soccer" (XLIII) sequences whenever athletes' movements are "halted" by stationary close-ups of spectators or fixed objects. In all these sequences, the interaction between movement and stasis is repeatedly related to the photographed object's particular direction of movement. Movement versus stasis in the basketball shots is predominantly vertical (due to the players' jumping). In the soccer shots, it is mostly horizontal; in the track and field shots, the direction of the movement varies depending upon the sport. In the street shots, horizontal and curved movements interfuse, creating a perceptual obstruction that subverts the representational aspect of the juxtaposed images (vehicles and pedestrians).

The most kinesthetic interaction between movement and stasis is produced in the "Spectators and the Screen" sequence (LII) through the collision between the motionless audience and the moving vehicles captured by the camera as it pans from left to right. The camera then moves further to the right, revealing a deep perspective of the street (Fig. 210). In turn, the photographed objects are first perceived as representative images, then as semiabstract (blurred) silhouetted close-ups, which move further to the right as the camera follows them (at comparable speed and without adjusted focal lengths), so that near the end of the shot the back of one moving vehicle is clearly seen in long shot at the right middle ground, with traffic and buildings on the left side. These shots last only between forty and sixty frames (two to four seconds) and are repeated ten times in the same segment, continuously interrupted by close-ups or medium shots (twelve in all, each ten to fifteen frames long) of pedestrians' heads, which pop into the shot to occupy the entire frame. The result of this clash between the camera motion (panning) and the stationary shots (close-ups) produces a unique perceptual conflict that affects the viewers sensorially. Although this principle is used throughout the film, it is most apparent in the sequences that show spatial interaction between people and objects. It can also be detected – although to a lesser degree – in all the phi-effects, as, for example, in the "clash" between tracking shots of objects or buildings and relatively stationary close-ups of the eyeball in the "Street and Eye" sequence (XXII).

Static versus dynamic tension suffuses the entire structure of *The Man with the Movie Camera.* In a broader sense, the film begins with stationary images (the camera does not move throughout the entire Prologue). The first tracking shot, in which the camera moves perpendicularly toward a closed window, does not appear until the beginning of Part One. The numerical relationship between stationary and moving shots varies, depending upon the theme of the sequence. For example, all sequences of factories and machines consist of stationary shots juxtaposed to each other graphically, whereas in the sequences dealing with traffic and sports events, the majority of shots are photographed with the camera gliding through space or circulating around people and objects. Symbolically, the film begins with *stasis* and ends with intense *kinesis,* corresponding to the cycle of a working day, which starts slowly after wakening and then gradually increases its tempo through various urban activities that reach an explosive finale. As one might expect from Vertov, his film does not close with relaxation and composure, but rather with an ever-increasing montage crescendo that ends not with a "whimper," but with a "bang"!

Movement versus stasis is particularly emphasized after the "Musical Performance with Spoons and Bottles" sequence (L), which is built on the conflict between stationary close-ups of listeners and dynamic shots incorporating various objects. In the "Camera Moves on Tripod" sequence (LI), the first apparent juxtaposition of movement versus stasis is achieved through the apposition of static close-ups of faces — later recognized as the audience — and medium shots of the animated tripod and camera (Fig. 197). Once it becomes clear that the faces watching the camera "walking" on its three "legs" are the seated viewers in the movie theater, the movement versus stasis conflict is enhanced by freeze-frames of the auditorium (photographed from a high angle), incorporating the screen-within-the-screen on which the abstract image of the rotating spool of wire is projected (Fig. 201). This conflict is continued by alternating medium shots of the viewers (Fig. 204) with composite images of ballet dancers and double exposures that merge various entertainers and a piano keyboard (Fig. 203). Then, after a shot of the spectators seen from above (Fig. 199), there are shots of the Cameraman shooting planes (Fig. 219) with a telescopic lens (Fig. 218), followed by several composite shots of traffic (Fig. 220) and a compound shot of numerous diligent typists (Fig. 221); this segment ends with the abstract shot of the glittering spinning loom (Fig. 205) and the shot designed in a markedly constructivist manner — the superimposition of a rotating wheel carrying spools of thread and a close-up of a smiling female worker (Fig. 206).

The climax of the motion versus stasis conflict begins, in the "Spectators and the Screen" sequence (LII), with the juxtaposition of freeze-frames of the auditorium and a tracking shot of the Cameraman as he shoots from a motorcycle speeding toward the audience. This shot alternately appears on both the screen-within-the-screen (Fig. 217) and the real screen (Fig. 216). Then, a speeding locomotive (shot with the camera attached to its side) appears on the screen-within-the-screen (Fig. 208), followed by a composite shot of the Cameraman superim-

posed above the milling crowd (Fig. 211). The climax is further intensified by yet a greater perceptual separation of moving and stationary
shots. This distinction is achieved by an arithmetic exchange of stationary close-ups of the film spectators with moving objects photographed by a panning camera, while the editing pattern is established
by a progressive reduction in the number of alternating groups of
shots, in the following manner:

Four close-ups of the spectators versus a carriage moving in front of the
camera

Seven close-ups of the spectators versus a trolley moving in front of the
camera

Four close-ups of the spectators versus a woman getting out of a trolley and
moving in front of the camera

Three close-ups of the spectators versus a bicyclist passing in front of the
camera

One close-up of a spectator versus two female pedestrians walking in front of
the camera

Two close-ups of the spectators versus one pedestrian (the lady with a white
hat) moving in front of the camera

Two close-ups of the spectators versus a car speeding in front of the camera

One close-up of a spectator versus a motorcycle driven in front of the camera

One close-up of a spectator versus a cabriolet speeding in front of the camera

One close-up of a spectator versus the front upper part of a trolley moving in
front of the camera

One close-up of a spectator versus rear upper part of a trolley moving in front
of the camera

One close-up of a spectator versus a carriage with women and children moving
in front of the camera

The pattern is broken by the inclusion of a single medium shot of
pedestrians (two ladies) walking in front of the camera from left to
right, followed by one close-up of a spectator juxtaposed to a shot in
which a speeding train moves laterally from right to left. This right–
left movement of the train is then repeated four times on the screen-
within-the-screen. The disruption of the montage pattern is therefore
heightened by a reversed direction of movement: while all the previous
movements occur from left to right (forming a curve that approaches
the camera and obscures the lens' view as it pans in the direction of
movement), the train moves from right to left as it crosses the screen-
within-the-screen, first horizontally, then diagonally. The auditorium is
reintroduced, this time with the spectators fidgeting in their seats,
while the motion picture images projected on the screen-within-the-
screen show the Cameraman shooting from a moving convertible (Fig.
226), which later appears on the real screen (Fig. 225); a carriage with

two ladies and a man in a white suit, on both screens (Figs. 214, 215); and numerous shots of the traffic. A long shot of the Cameraman superimposed over a milling crowd (Fig. 211), a split image of the Bolshoi Theater (Fig. 213), and a close-up of a swinging pendulum (Fig. 212) introduce the "Editor and the Film" sequence (LV).

Structurally, the film builds step by step, from an apparently linear presentation of events (preparation for a film show, with the audience filling the auditorium and an orchestra beginning to play for the screening) toward a montage condensation of innumerable visual components, creating a kinesthetic abstraction of "Life-As-It-Is" that is more powerful – and more meaningful – than the representational content of each individual shot. The opening of the film is explanatory, as it provides the audience with basic information about cinema as a means of communication, while the end reaffirms cinema as a means of artistic expression, a unique medium capable of constructing its own time–space integrity.

The Man with the Movie Camera ends majestically, like the final chord of a great symphony. Its abrupt ending indicates that the true concern of its creators lay not so much in the mechanical recording of reality as with its cinematic transposition. Obviously, they chose to leave the viewer not with a thematic – nor even an ideological – statement about the concrete environment (a Soviet city) but with an exciting emotional experience that acknowledges cinema as a unique means of *aesthetic* construction. The "Film-Truth" principle of observing and recording the external world is thus integrated with the "Film-Eye" method used by the *kinoks*-engineers to deconstruct the recorded images and reveal the substantial truth about everyday reality, about "Life-As-It-Is," about those who produce the "film-thing," and about those who perceive it in the movie theater – both the real one and the one within the film.

Structural recapitulation

The "Camera Moves on Tripod" sequence (LI) serves as a preparation for the Epilogue, in which the audience attends a film screening. The first shots of this sequence are close-ups of men and women responding to the camera as it "walks" on its "legs"; hence the impression that they are amused by an "animated fact" incompatible with reality – an illusion further enhanced by the placement of the "walking" camera in an exterior. Suddenly, among the close-ups of the same people, there are inserted long shots of the audience sitting in front of the screen-within-the-screen on which appear various moving images of real events. These shots, marking the transition to the "Spectators and the Screen" sequence (LII), employ the composite image technique whenever both the audience and the screen-within-the-screen are seen simultaneously. The images on the screen-within-the-screen, in these composite shots, are always in motion, while the audience in front of it is sometimes "alive" and sometimes "frozen," thus further obscuring the border between reality and cinematic illusion.

The "Editor and the Film" sequence (LV) concludes the film by reemphasizing – both thematically and cinematically – the prominent role of montage in filmmaking. This sequence contains 108 shots in accelerated forward and reverse motion. The first shot of a dark film-strip moving diagonally over the brightly lit lighting board (Fig. 78) is followed by a close-up of Svilova as she looks downward (Fig. 80). These two shots are intercut four times before a close-up of Svilova's eyes appears on the screen, marking the beginning of the climactic part of the sequence (Fig. 227). Throughout the segment, the close-up of Svilova's eyes is repeated thirty-eight times with a progressive re-duction of frames. Toward the end, brief shots of her eyes are con-trasted with longer shots depicting traffic on the street; sporadically inserted, they produce another subliminal effect associated with the light pulsation of the film projection. The initial duration of the eye shots is between two and three frames (as, e.g., in nos. 20–45); however, the en-suing close-up of a moving trolley (no. 46) is twelve frames long, and the medium shot of the crowded theater (no. 47) is only eight frames long. The climax of the segment is composed of fifty-five shots, all of which belong to one of two groups: shots of two or three frames (close-ups of Svilova's eye) and shots of six or seven frames (traffic, pedestrians, the projector beam in the auditorium, a traffic signal, and a pendulum). Of all these flash shots, the projector beam (Fig. 228), the traffic signal (Fig. 229), and the pendulums – both the large one, which makes min-ute movements (Fig. 212), and the smaller one, which sweeps rapidly from side to side (Fig. 231) – carry the greatest weight in the montage rhythm. After the nine-frame shot of a speeding train photographed from below (no. 54), the duration of the shots alternates at a rate of three frames (Svilova's eyes) to six frames (trolley, traffic, auditorium). This geometric reduction of the shot length creates a visual abstrac-tion that is abruptly terminated by the penultimate twenty-frame shot of the trolley running over the camera (Fig. 232) and a seventy-four-frame closing shot of the camera lens with the human eye superimposed over it (no. 108), functioning as a symbolic conclusion to the entire film (Fig. 233).

The montage structure of the "Editor and the Film" sequence (LV) is based on the juxtaposition of two different graphic forms: close-ups of Svilova's eyes (perceived as circles) intercut with close-ups of a pen-dulum (perceived as an unstable circular design) variously scaled shots of trolleys, the projector beam and the auditorium, a traffic sig-nal, and a busy intersection – all of which fill the frame with vertical

190

or diagonal patterns (shots 55–91). In this introductory section, the close-ups of the traffic signal (silhouetted against the gray sky) and the medium long shots of the projector beam (horizontally piercing the dark auditorium) contrast sharply with the circular forms of Svilova's eyes. In the closing section, Svilova's eyes are excluded, and the film ends with eighteen flash shots of the traffic signal, pendulum, auditorium, city market, railway cars, railroad tracks, trolleys, and the camera lens (shots 92–108).

What follows is a shot-by-shot breakdown of the last sequence of the film, its final 108 shots (out of a total of 1,682 shots in the film). From the specification of each shot's duration (given in frames) and the cranking speed (acceleration/deceleration), one can sense the fervent pace that distinguishes the film's finale:

LV. *Editor and the Film:* 108 shots, 699 fr. 39 sec.

1. HACU (similar to XXV, 50; accelerated motion). Dark filmstrip on light table moving from lower left to upper right (13 fr.).
2. LACU (similar to XVI, 11; accelerated). Right profile of Svilova looking down, face lit from below against dark background (15 fr.).
3. HACU (same as LV, 1; accelerated). Filmstrip continues to move diagonally from lower left to upper right (10 fr.).
4. LACU (same as LV, 2; accelerated). Svilova looks down (10 fr.).
5. HACU (same as LV, 3; accelerated). Filmstrip moves diagonally (5 fr.).
6. LACU (same as LV, 4; accelerated). Svilova looks down (4 fr.).
7. LAMLS–MS (similar to LIV, 4; tilted frame, accelerated). Dark strip of railway track extends from middle left to lower right with telephone poles silhouetted against gray sky and receding into distance; dark locomotive appears passing to right through foreground so that only lower part of coaches are seen; train moves quickly over the camera positioned below the track (28 fr.).
8. HAMLS (accelerated). Crowd milling about a market and filling the screen; in the lower right corner of the frame are brightly lit rectangular booth tops (55 fr.).
9. LAMLS (same as LIV, 64; accelerated). Train moves from background to foreground with landscape of a hill on either side. There is a shack on the left and a few trees silhouetted against the sky. As the train moves forward it fills the screen with its dark shape (10 fr.).
10. ECU (accelerated). Svilova's eyes and nose lit from below; the eye on the left is cut in half by the frame line; the eye on the right looks to the left, down center, then left, then center again (9 fr.).
11. LAMS (similar to LV, 7; accelerated). Dark train coaches pass over the camera positioned below the tracks; they are moving toward the audience; hill, trees, and sky are seen in upper right (9 fr.).
12. ECU (same as LV, 10; accelerated). Svilova's eyes move down center, then left, and back to center (6 fr.).

13. LAMS (same as LV, 11; accelerated). Dark train coaches move forward over the camera (6 fr.).

14. ECU (same as LV, 12; accelerated). Svilova's eyes move down center, left, then close and open again (5 fr.).

15. LAMS (same as LV, 11; accelerated). Dark train coaches move over the camera (9 fr.).

16. ECU (same as LV, 14; accelerated). Svilova's eyes move left, then center and down (4 fr.).

17. LAMS (same as LV, 15; accelerated). Dark train coaches move forward over camera (7 fr.).

18. ECU (same as LV, 16; accelerated). Svilova's eyes move down center, then left (3 fr.).

19. LAMS (same as LV, 17; accelerated). Dark train coaches move forward over the camera and pass it, then exit, revealing track and landscape with a hill on either side and a few trees silhouetted against sky (8 fr.).

20. HACU (same as LV, 1; accelerated). Dark filmstrip on the light table moving from lower left to upper right (5 fr.).

21. ECU (same as LV, 18; accelerated). Svilova's eyes look down center (2 fr.). Note: light from below is stronger than in previous shot.

22. HACU (same as LV, 20; accelerated). Filmstrip continues to move diagonally (4 fr.).

23. ECU (same as LV, 21; accelerated). Svilova's eyes look down center, then right (3 fr.).

24. HACU (same as LV, 22; accelerated). Filmstrip continues to move diagonally (5 fr.).

25. ECU (same as LV, 23; accelerated). Svilova's eyes look right, then move left (3 fr.).

26. LACU (similar to XVIII, 10; accelerated). Traffic signal, silhouetted against gray sky, rotates from right to left, changing diagonal position from lower left–upper right to upper left–lower right (65 fr.).

27. MLS. Trolley stands in center of screen; "No. 25–Saratovo-Leningrad-skaya" is written on top of it, with blurred pedestrians crossing from left to right in foreground; part of trolley on right seen moving toward background with buildings on left (7 fr.).

28. ECU (same as LV, 25; accelerated). Svilova's eyes look down, in center (2 fr.).

29. MLS (accelerated). Pedestrians passing in front of moving trolley in right foreground (7 fr.).

30. ECU (same as LV, 28; accelerated). Svilova's eyes look down, then move left (2 fr.).

31. MLS (accelerated). Pedestrians pass in front of moving trolley in right foreground (6 fr.).

32. ECU (same as LV, 30; accelerated). Svilova's eyes move from right to left (2 fr.).

33. MLS (same as LV, 31; accelerated). A few pedestrians obstruct background as they pass from left to right, extreme foreground; trolley moves forward (6 fr.).

34. ECU (same as LV, 32; accelerated). Svilova's eyes look right (2 fr.).

35. MLS (same as LV, 33; accelerated). One person, passing from left to right extreme foreground, obstructs background; trolley moves forward (5 fr.).

36. ECU (same as LV, 34; accelerated). Svilova's eyes look left (2 fr.).

37. MLS (same as LV, 35; accelerated). Person obstructs background while passing from right to left, extreme foreground; trolley moves forward (6 fr.).

38. ECU (same as LV, 36; accelerated). Svilova's eyes look right (2 fr.).

39. MLS (same as LV, 37; accelerated). Person obstructs background while passing from right to left, extreme foreground; trolley moves forward (6 fr.).

40. ECU (same as LV, 38; accelerated). Svilova's eyes look left (2 fr.).

41. MLS (same as LV, 39; accelerated). Person obstructs background while passing from right to left, extreme foreground; trolley moves forward (6 fr.).

42. ECU (same as LV, 40). Svilova's eyes look down right (2 fr.).

43. ECU–MS (accelerated). Dark blurred side of trolley in extreme foreground moves right and reveals tall buildings in left background; pedestrians and another trolley (No. 25) in center middle ground moving forward (6 fr.).

44. MLS (accelerated). Projector beam coming from small square aperture in upper left corner and extending diagonally toward center right against completely dark background; a thick black strip breaks the beam near the aperture, and another thin white vertical strip breaks it in the center; the intensity of the beam is diffused in the right; it dims for a moment, then reappears (6 fr.).

45. MLS (accelerated). Trolley in center moves forward as blurred pedestrians pass to right in foreground (2 fr.).

46. ECU–MLS (accelerated). Side of trolley in extreme foreground moves left, revealing trolley in center, part of trolley on right, and buildings and sky in distant background (12 fr.).

47. HAMLS (accelerated). Dark theater auditorium with audience facing left; pulsating projector beam positioned from upper center background toward upper left foreground (8 fr.).

48. ECU–MLS (same as LV, 43; accelerated). Dark blurred side of trolley in extreme foreground moves right, revealing tall buildings in left background and another trolley (No. 18) in center middle ground; pedestrians milling about (6 fr.).

49. ECU (same as LV, 42; accelerated). Svilova's eyes look down, then move left (2 fr.).

50. MLS (same as LV, 27; accelerated). A few pedestrians pass to right foreground in front of standing trolley (5 fr.).

51. ECU (same as LV, 49; accelerated). Svilova's eyes look left, then move right (3 fr.).

52. HALS (same as LII, 89; accelerated). Street filled with crowd moving in various directions and occupying lower part of the screen; dark landscape and gray sky above in background; on right, shadowed row of telephone poles receding from foreground to center background; dark trolley moving from left foreground to center background (6 fr.).

53. ECU (same as LV, 51; accelerated). Svilova's eyes look down, then move left (3 fr.).

54. LAMCU (similar to LII, 87; accelerated). Bottom of train car moving diagonally from middle right to lower left with blurred vertical white stripes flashing in the foreground (9 fr.).

55. ECU (same as LV, 53; accelerated). Svilova's eyes look down, then move right (3 fr.).

56. HALS (same as LV, 52; accelerated). Trolley continues to move toward center background in the midst of a crowd (6 fr.).

57. ECU (same as LV, 55; accelerated). Svilova's eyes look down (3 fr.).

58. HAMLS (same as LVI, 46; accelerated). Dark theater auditorium with audience facing left; pulsating projection beam positioned from upper center foreground to upper left foreground (6 fr.).

59. ECU (same as LV, 57; accelerated). Svilova's eyes look down (3 fr.).

60. HALS (same as LV, 56; accelerated). Trolley moves further into background (6 fr.).

61. ECU (same as LV, 59; accelerated). Svilova's eyes look right and open wide (3 fr.).

62. ECU (same as LV, 2; accelerated). Round brightly lit pendulum swings back and forth against dark background (6 fr.).

63. ECU (same as LV, 61; accelerated). Svilova's eyes look down, then she tilts face to left (3 fr.).

64. HALS (same as LV, 60; accelerated). One trolley disappears while another trolley enters blurred, left foreground (6 fr.).

65. ECU (same as LV, 63; accelerated). Svilova's eyes look down center (2 fr.).

66. LACU (same as LV, 26; accelerated). Traffic signal, diagonally positioned (from upper left to lower right) and silhouetted against gray sky rotates to right and comes into a vertical position, with black wire on left (5 fr.).

67. ECU (same as LV, 65; accelerated). Svilova's eyes look left, then move down (2 fr.).

68. HALS (same as LV, 64; accelerated). Trolley in left foreground continues to move right, obstructing the background; through the windows of the trolley one sees pedestrians on the other side of the street (6 fr.).

69. ECU (same as LV, 67; accelerated). Svilova's eyes look down center (2 fr.).

70. LAMCU (same as LV, 54; accelerated; panning, tilted frame). Blurred side of train moves upper right to lower left; as shot moves left, more windows and a strip of sky are revealed (6 fr.).

71. ECU (same as LV, 69; accelerated). Svilova's eyes look left (2 fr.).

72. HALS (same as LV, 68; accelerated). Trolley in foreground moves further to right, revealing milling crowd in background (6 fr.).

73. ECU (same as LV, 71; accelerated). Svilova's eyes look down, then move right (2 fr.).

74. HAMLS (same as LVII, 58; accelerated). Dark theater auditorium with audience facing left; pulsating projector beam positioned from upper center foreground to upper left foreground (6 fr.).

75. ECU (same as LV, 73; accelerated). Svilova's eyes look down (2 fr.).

76. HALS (same as LV, 72; accelerated). Crowd milling in street, no trolley (6 fr.).

77. ECU (same as LV, 75; accelerated). Svilova's eyes look down (2 fr.).

78. ECU (same as LV, 62; accelerated). Pendulum moves back and forth against dark background (6 fr.).

79. ECU (same as LV, 77; accelerated). Svilova's eyes look down (2 fr.).

80. HAELS (same as XVI, 38; accelerated). Dark shot of city intersection with lit building; in upper left pedestrians and traffic move through the streets (6 fr.).

81. ECU (same as LV, 79; accelerated). Svilova's eyes look down (2 fr.).

82. LACU (same as LV, 66; accelerated). Traffic signal silhouetted against sky rotates right, coming into diagonal position, upper left to lower right (4 fr.).

83. ECU (same as LV, 81; accelerated). Svilova's eyes look down, then left, and open wide (2 fr.).

84. HAELS (same as LV, 80; accelerated). Traffic continues to move at intersection (6 fr.).

85. ECU (same as LV, 83; accelerated). Svilova's eyes look left, then right (2 fr.).

86. LAMLS (similar to LV, 54; accelerated). Train moves from right foreground diagonally to lower left background against a light sky (6 fr.).

87. ECU (same as LV, 85; accelerated). Svilova's eyes look right (2 fr.).

88. HAELS (same as LV, 84; accelerated). Traffic continues to move at intersection (5 fr.).

89. ECU (same as LV, 87; accelerated). Svilova's eyes look left (2 fr.).

90. MLS (same as LV, 44). Diagonal projector beam pulsates, with an additional spot of light in upper right just above the beam (9 fr.).

91. ECU (same as LV, 89; accelerated). Svilova's eyes look left, then right (2 fr.).

92. LAMLS–MS (similar to LVI, 54; accelerated). Blurred windows of train moving diagonally from upper right to lower left (6 fr.).

93. LACU (same as LV, 82; accelerated). Traffic signal, silhouetted against

gray sky, rotates from diagonal position on upper right to vertical position on lower left (3 fr.).

94. CU (same as LIV, 2). Blurred small circular pendulum of clock with quatrefoil frame moving back and forth against black background (2 fr.).

95. HAMLS (same as LV, 74; accelerated). Dark auditorium with audience facing left; pulsating projector beam positioned from upper center foreground to upper left foreground; one person is at lower brightly lit left corner (7 fr.).

96. LACU (same as LV, 93; accelerated). Traffic signal silhouetted against gray sky rotates from diagonal position on upper left to lower right, then reenters upper right to lower left with wire on left (5 fr.).

97. HAMLS (same as LV, 8; accelerated). Market, crowd milling about and filling entire frame; four brightly lit rectangles formed by tops of roofs (6 fr.).

98. CU (same as LV, 94; accelerated). Pendulum moves back and forth (5 fr.).

99. LACU (same as LV, 96; accelerated). Traffic signal silhouetted against gray sky rotates clockwise from a vertical to a diagonal position, then from an upper right to a lower left position (4 fr.).

100. HAMS (same as LV, 59; accelerated). Crowded market with people dressed in dark and light clothes move quickly in all directions; trolley wires intersect on left (6 fr.).

101. CU (same as LV, 98; accelerated). Pendulum moves back and forth (5 fr.).

102. LAMLS (similar to LV, 19; accelerated). Railroad ties in center receding toward background; small hills on left and right; sky filling upper part of frame; silhouetted coach appears in the foreground, moves over camera toward background (6 fr.).

103. HALS (same as LIV, 69; accelerated). Street with buildings and shadow upper left; light building in upper center and gray building in upper right; crowd moves quickly in all directions (6 fr.).

104. LACU (same as LV, 100; accelerated). Traffic signal silhouetted against gray sky rotates counterclockwise from an upper right to a lower left position, then from upper left to lower right (4 fr.).

105. LAMLS (similar to LV, 103; accelerated). Railroad ties in center receding toward background, with V-shaped telephone poles on right; railway coach silhouetted against light sky moves toward foreground over camera, revealing horizontal strip of brightly lit sky near top; rest of frame dark (6 fr.).

106. CU (same as LV, 102). Pendulum moves back and forth (2 fr.).

107. LAMLS–MS–CU (same as XXI, 18). Front of trolley with bright sky above and dark trees on both sides; trolley moves forward, then passes over camera, filling entire screen with darkness (frames 12–18); trolley exits, revealing horizontal strip of light with sky and trees at bottom of frame. "No. 812" at bottom of trolley, "No. 7" on top (20 fr.).

108. ECU. Camera lens with human eye superimposed over it, both reflected in a mirror; after twenty frames, the iris begins to close over the staring eye (74 fr.).

Black screen with title "Konets" ("The End") in white Cyrillic letters that slowly fade away (69 fr.).

Structurally, the closing sequence produces a vigorous montage outburst in which the optical beat is conceived as the finale of a symphonic score. The "auditory" overtones triggered in the "Musical Performance with Spoons and Bottles" sequence (L) are replaced here by the optical sensation achieved through a dynamic exchange of shots figuratively connoting the "dissonance" of city life and paralleling the "musical" dynamism of human work (including film editing).

The kinesthetic orchestration of shots in this climactic section is achieved by the juxtaposition of different shot compositions, directions of movement, scales, and durations of shots. Once again, the idea of editing is brought to the fore: the close-ups of Svilova's eyes are so brief that, at the sequence's peak, the eyes are perceived merely as two circular shapes punctuating the series of different graphic patterns. With all its abstraction, the musical connotation of this closing section does not destroy the thematic denotation of shots depicting (1) traffic (trolley, cars); (2) time (the pendulum); (3) people in everyday life (market and street); (4) machines (the train, tracks); (5) film projection (pulsating beam in the movie theater); and, in the closing image, (6) the camera lens and human eye. All thematic and formal aspects of the film are reintegrated by way of its most potent means – montage – which builds the ending into a powerful symphonic structure whose kinesthetic intervals overcome the viewers on both perceptual and sensorial levels.

Ideology of graphic patterns

Formal examination of key sequences in *The Man with the Movie Camera* leads to further interpretation of Vertov's and Svilova's selection of graphic patterns and their interaction. All matching or juxtaposing of shot compositions is intentional and executed with precision, especially in the pivotal sequences wherein the montage beat is a dominant aspect of the sequence's structure and an essential source of its kinesthetic impact. By grouping the graphic patterns according to their pictorial components, one can discern appropriate meaning for each of the three basic shot compositions as they appear on the screen in clusters and different contexts.

The most dominant pattern in both shape and movement is *horizontal,* appearing in numerous shots that depict streets, traffic, trains, cars, pedestrians, country landscapes, workers in action, and athletes exercising. The next prevailing pattern is *vertical,* expressed most dramatically in wide-angle views of factories, smokestacks, chimneys, steel constructions, elevators, cranes, street lights, and tall buildings in the urban environment. The third is *circular,* a pattern that tends to envelop all forms and shapes by virtue of its visually prominent aestheticism. The circular pattern also appears to be significant on the thematic level, and is underscored throughout the film by close-ups of the camera lens, film reels, human faces and eyes, factory wheels and gears, radio loudspeakers, and steel construction equipment. Symbolically, *film stock as material for filmmaking* appears on the screen in all three forms: horizontally (and diagonally), as strips of film (footage) displayed by Svilova on her editing table; vertically, as the classified and selected piece of film footage hung on the shelves in the editing room; circularly, as round film cans ready for shipment, as strips of film being wound into cores, and as 35mm metal reels used for projection in the movie theater.

The repetition of the three basic graphic patterns in *The Man with the Movie Camera* assumes a broad metaphorical implication, associated with the particular thematic representation of each shot. As part of a cognitive system, the three basic patterns can be related to the film's thematic meaning in the following way:

Pattern	Content	Theme
Horizonal	Cars, trains	Communication
Vertical	Smokestacks, cranes	Industry
Circular	The eye, the lens	Creativity

The ideological implication of these patterns depends upon and varies according to the content of the shot. If one analytically focuses on the specific pattern, it turns out that its recurrent association with the respective diegetic connotation tends to develop into an ideological metaphor. For example, the vertical design of factories, tall buildings, and constructions – especially when reenforced by the low camera angle – parallels industrial construction in the new society. The horizontal movement of traffic (trolleys and trains) is naturally linked with the expansive development of the urban environment in postrevolutionary Russia. Of course, horizontal movement is often combined with topics of opposite significance (e.g., bourgeois women driven in a carriage) and can be read as a dialectical unity of opposites achieved through the disruptive–associative montage principle.

An outstanding example of such a dialectical contradiction of movements is demonstrated at the end of the "Death, Marriage, and Birth" sequence (XX), generating a philosophical association with the photographed event — the funeral procession shown only in three shots. In the first shot, the camera shoots from a high angle as it moves parallel to the limousine, which carries an open casket and is progressing *laterally* (Fig. 97). The two parallel movements neutralize the hearse's progression by focusing on the dead man's face in the open casket — the stasis of death. After two disruptive inserts, the stationary shots of a bride (Fig. 98) and a woman experiencing the pain of child labor (Fig. 99), there is another tracking shot of the same funeral procession, this time photographed by the camera withdrawing directly in front of the limousine carrying the open casket (Fig. 100). The position of the camera and its movement in this shot contribute to the viewer's (sensory and emotional) participation in the funeral procession.

In the sequences of street traffic, the lateral movement of the trolleys and pedestrians crossing from left to right or from right to left either obliterates actual physical movement, implying dislocation, or pokes fun (through split-screen, multiple exposure, oblique angles, acceleration) at the hectic tempo of a great city. The positioning of the camera on trains, convertibles, fire engines, motorcycles, carousels, carriages, or simply held by the Cameraman, emphasizes the dynamism of movement through space.

The dislocation of movement that results from the "battle" between different graphic patterns implants itself in the viewer's consciousness, especially when it occurs in composite shots, as in those with flocks of pedestrians moving in various directions and graphically "colliding" with each other within the same frame (Plate 3). Generally, the crowd's movement is perceived as horizontal, whereas the composite shots combine the horizontal movement of the trolleys and pedestrians with the vertical rectangular forms of different vehicles as seen from the rear. In addition, the horizontal traffic movement is counteracted by vertical telephone and electric poles, traffic signs, tall buildings, and the Cameraman himself as he stands above and superimposed over the crowded streets (Fig. 211).

There are also other graphic patterns — diagonal, elliptical, amorphous, zigzag, intercrossing, and disconnected lines — all of which are incorporated within the three basic patterns and movements. The accumulation of particular shapes and movements prompts the viewer to link graphic repetitions with their ideological meanings and thereby arrive at a broader metaphoric reading of the sequences in which the specific pattern dominates. Furthermore, various complementary optical changes on the level of lighting and tonality set off the basic graphic configurations underscored by the dominant patterns in each shot.

The consistent repetition of various graphic patterns as well as their optical integration creates a visual metaphor that comments on the three major themes of *The Man with the Movie Camera:* communication, industry, and the creative process (filmmaking). The three basic graphic patterns are always related to the actual objects and movements occurring in the concrete environment: the sequential progression of the traffic, the verticality of the industrial constructions, and the concentric and/or circular motion of human work/creation. Through their optical mutation, these three graphic patterns generate abstract imagery with symbolic implication:

Graphic pattern	Metaphorical implication
Horizontal (sequential movement)	Environmental progress (traffic)
Vertical (upward development)	Industrial construction (technology)
Circular (concentrated activity)	Human work (creativity)

In the climactic moments of the major sequences, the interaction of the three basic graphic patterns produces a unique "overtonal impact" that, according to Eisenstein, provides the most powerful and uniquely cinematic experience.[26] After an in-depth analysis of the film's structure and repeated viewing of the film, one begins to perceive Vertov's intervals as overtones that kinesthetically fuse the horizontal, vertical, and circular movements perceived in the juxtaposed shots. The metaphorical significance of these overtones exceeds the representational denotation of the photographed objects, and reaches a point where the recorded "life-facts" are not merely "the sum of the facts," but "a higher mathematics"[27] of the recorded, deconstructed, and reconstructed events.

A cornerstone of world cinema

The Man with the Movie Camera demonstrates more than any other film of its time the uniqueness of cinematic language. With its complex formal structure and many levels of thematic meaning, it is Vertov's "theoretical declaration on the screen" of his "Film-Eye" method and the "Film-Truth" principle. It is the outcome of his belief that the "human eye armed with a camera" can reveal the true social reality, the essence of "Life-As-It-Is."[28]

The final shot of *The Man with the Movie Camera* fuses the photographic lens with the eye, reiterating the unification of human perception and technology. As in many other instances, the metaphorical meaning of this merger transcends its obvious signification: it functions as a proposal to the viewer to look at life in a new way, to perceive more than the "naked human eye" can detect, to think not only about what appears right before us but also about what is hidden beneath the surface of reality. That was the *kinoks'* chief objective as Vertov defined it in his early proclamations, following constructivist, futurist, and formalist tenets.[29]

In discussing Mayakovsky, Vertov referred to the poet's work as "a lighthouse"[30] in the world of poetry. The same metaphor can be applied to *The Man with the Movie Camera:* it was, it is, and will continue to be a lighthouse illuminating the path that leads cinema toward a revolutionary art form. As a reaction against fictional (staged) as well as conventional documentary films, produced during a period of intensified political suppression of avant-garde movements and "ideologically inappropriate" experimentation, misunderstood by its contemporaries, proclaimed "inaccessible" to the masses, ideologically attacked from both left and right, rejected by domestic and foreign critics as a "formalist visual attraction," Vertov's film has at last received the recognition it deserves as the most innovative achievement in the silent era. Moreover, it has become increasingly evident that *The Man with the Movie Camera* marks a cornerstone in the entire history of world cinema; as such, it can also be viewed as a monument to the freedom of artistic expression, a tribute to the necessity of personal creativity and the right to experiment in any art or medium. Like an underground current, persistent though inconspicuous, it has paved the path all true artists should take in their struggle against the commercial and political exploitation of any art, cinema in particular.

THE CREDITS

<u>The Man</u>
<u>with the Movie Camera</u>

A Record on Celluloid
IN 6 REELS
Produced by VUFKU
1929

(An Excerpt from the Diary
of a Cameraman)

(365 fr.)

ATTENTION

VIEWERS:

THIS FILM
Represents in Itself
AN EXPERIMENT
IN THE CINEMATIC COMMUNICATION

Of Visible Events

(629 fr.)

WITHOUT THE AID OF
INTERTITLES

(A Film Without Intertitles)

(765 fr.)

WITHOUT THE AID OF
A S C E N A R I O
(A Film Without a Script)

(901 fr.)

WITHOUT THE AID OF
T H E A T E R
(A Film Without Sets,
Actors, etc.)

(1,061 fr.)

THIS EXPERIMENTAL
WORK WAS MADE WITH THE INTENTION OF
CREATING A TRULY
INTERNATIONAL
ULTIMATE LANGUAGE OF
CINEMA ON THE BASIS OF ITS
T O T A L S E P A R A T I O N
FROM THE LANGUAGE OF THEATER
A N D L I T E R A T U R E

(1,476 fr.)

Author-Supervisor of
the Experiment
Dziga VERTOV

(1,580 fr.)

Chief Cinematographer
M. KAUFMAN

(1,660 fr.)

Assisting Editor
E. SVILOVA

(1,776 fr.)

Since the sources of information for this bibliography were often secondary, the original dates of publication as well as pagination are not always included. When not indicated, the place of publication is Moscow. Complete citations for Vertov's unpublished articles can be found in Seth Feldman's *Dziga Vertov: A Guide to References and Resources*, pp. 183–220.

1922

"We. A Variant of a Manifesto" [*My. Variant manifesta*]. *Kinofot,* no. 1 (August 25–31), 11–12.

The first published theoretical statement in which Vertov outlines his concept of the newsreel and documentary cinema, emphasizing his directorial method, "Film-Eye," his principle of shooting, "Film-Truth," and his concept of presenting material on the screen, "Life-As-It-Is." According to Vertov, the first variant of this manifesto was written in 1919 under the title "A Manifesto About the Disarmament of Theatrical Cinema" [*Manifest o razoruzhenii teatral'noi kinematografii*].

"He and I" [*On i ia*]. *Kinofot* (September), 9–10.

A sequel to the first statement. It reviews the first nine issues of the *Film-Truth* series, emphasizing the distinction between the *kinoks*' montage style of presenting everyday events and the theatrical style and content of films produced in America.

"The Fifth Number of Film-Truth" [*Piatyi nomer "kinopravdy"*]. *Teatral'naya Moskva,* no. 50.

An analysis of *Film-Truth No. 5,* emphasizing Vertov's concept of abstracting events (often geographically unrelated) by means of montage.

1923

"Kinoks. Revolution" [*Kinoki. Perevorot*]. *LEF,* no. 3 (June–July), 135–43.

A manifesto about the new concept of "unstaged" documentary film, its aesthetic and social function. The text includes a brief introduction written earlier

(January 1923) and signed by the "Council of Three" (Vertov, Kaufman, Svilova).

"Commemorating the Anniversary of Film-Truth" [*K godovshchine "Kinopravdy"*]. *Kino,* nos. 3–7.

In an interview, Vertov surveys the first sixteen issues of the *Film-Truth* series, the material that was chosen to be filmed, as well as the montage structure, and the use of intertitles.

"A Project for Reorganizing Film-Truth" [*Proekt reorganizatsii "Kinopravdy"*]. *Kino,* nos. 3–7.

Vertov's report to Goskino on the first Experimental Unit of newsreel production, suggesting its reorganization into a "Documentary Experimental Station" within Goskino production.

"Film-Truth" [*Kinopravda*]. *Kinofot,* no. 6, 13.

Vertov characterizes the *Film-Truth* series as the most popular "cinema-newspaper" in Russia and outlines the need for the state support of its further development.

"A New Current in Cinema" [*Novoe techenie v kinematografii*]. *Pravda* (July 15), 7.

Vertov summarizes the *kinoks*' declaration that unstaged cinema is the only appropriate response to the commercial photoplay and announces the *kinoks*' plan to produce a "Radio Newsreel."

1924

"Directors on Themselves" [*Rezhissery o sebe*]. *Kino* (March 4).

Vertov answers several questions about his work, emphasizing the unique social function of documentary film.

" 'Film-Eye': A Newsreel in Six Issues" [*Kinoglaz: kinokhronika v 6 seriyakh*]. *Pravda* (July 19), 6.

Vertov summarizes the principles to be applied in shooting the six issues of the *Film-Eye* series. Only the first part, also known as "Life Caught Unawares" [*Zhizn' vrasplokh*], was realized.

"An Answer to Five Questions" [*Otvet na piat' voprosov*]. *Kino,* no. 43 (October 21).

Vertov presents the theoretical platform of the *kinoks*, followed by a critical evaluation of the first issue of *Film-Eye*. It also contains Vertov's critical comments on Gan's film *The Island of the Young Pioneers* [*Ostrov pionerov*] (1924).

1925

"The Basics of Film-Eye" [*Osnovnoe "Kinoglaza"*]. *Kino,* no. 6 (Feb. 3).

Vertov discusses the "Film-Eye" method as the most appropriate means of presenting "Life-As-It-Is," proclaiming it the only way for cinema to "march toward October."

" 'Film-Eye' about 'Strike' " [*"Kinoglaz" o "Stachke"*]. *Kino* (March 24), Kharkov.

Vertov analyzes Eisenstein's *Strike,* characterizing it as the first attempt to apply the "Film-Eye" method and the "Film-Truth" principle to staged (acted) cinema.

" 'Film-Truth' and 'Radio-Truth' " [*"Kinopravda" i "radiopravda"*]. *Pravda* (July 16), 8.

Vertov discusses the possibility of "campaigning with facts," not only in the sphere of viewing ("Film-Truth" and "Film-Eye") but also in the realm of listening ("Radio-Eye"). This article also calls for the application of the "Leninist Proportion" to film production, that is, the balance between the distribution of entertainment movies and the documentary film and newsreel.

"For the Film Newsreel!" [*Za kinokhroniku!*]. *Kino* (December 25).

Vertov delimits the role of the newsreel within "agit-prop" activity as defined in the party's proclamation "About Political Activity in the Villages."

1926

"The Factory of Facts" [*Fabrika faktov*]. *Pravda* (July 24), 6.

Vertov discusses the success of the "Film-Eye" method in documentary films and its influence on staged (acted) films, among which are Eisenstein's *Strike* and *Battleship Potemkin*.

" 'Film-Eye' and the Battle for the Film Newsreel: Three Stages of the Battle" [*"Kinoglaz" i bor'ba za kinokhroniku: tri etapa bor'by*]. *Sovetskii ekran*, no. 15.

Vertov identifies *Film-Weekly*, *Film-Truth*, and *Film-Eye* as three stages in the process of establishing the creative and ideological platform of the *kinoks*.

"One Sixth of the World" [*Shestaia chast' mira*]. *Kino* (August 17).

In an interview, Vertov describes his film *One Sixth of the World* as the victory of the "Film-Eye" method over the methods used in staged films with actors, sets, and literary plots.

"The Fight Continues" [*Srazhenie prodolzhaetsia*]. *Kino* (October 30).

In a sequel to the previous interview, Vertov discusses the organizational problems faced by the *kinoks* in completing *One Sixth of the World*.

"Film-Eye" [*Kinoglaz*]. In *On the Paths of Art* [*Na putiakh iskusstva*], a collection of articles published by Proletkult, pp. 210–29.

Vertov analyzes the first issue of the *Film-Eye* series; his analysis is followed by a description of the *kinoks'* future projects and of their struggle against staged cinema.

1927

"Dziga Vertov Refutes" [*Dziga Vertov opovergaet*]. *Nasha gazeta* (Jan. 19).

Vertov replies to the Sovkino criticism, explaining the "ideological motives" upon which his theoretical concepts are based. After this article, Vertov was dismissed from Sovkino.

"Letter to the Editor" [*Pis'mo v redaktsiiu*]. *Kinofront*, no. 4.

Vertov replies to the review of *One Sixth of the World* by Ippolit Sokolov printed earlier in the same periodical (no. 2), refuting Sokolov's remark that the film suffers from the inclusion of too many facts and too broad a perspective for the subject.

1928

"Film-Eye and The Eleventh Year" [*"Kino-oko" i 11–i*]. In *The Eleventh Anniversary* [*Odinnadtsatyi*], a collection of articles in Ukrainian, published by VUFKU (Kiev), pp. 17–18.

Vertov characterizes his film *The Eleventh Year* as an experiment in the expression of ideas in "pure film language."

"Film Has Begun to Shout. Our Filmmakers for Sound Film" [*Kino zakrichalo. Nashi fil'mari pro tonfil'm*]. *Kino*, no. 12 (Kiev).

In Ukrainian. Vertov makes a statement on the specific nature and future development of sound film, characterizing it as a new step in the history of cinema.

"The Eleventh Year – Excerpts from the Shooting Diary" [*Odinadtsatyi – Otryvki iz s'emochnogo dnevnika*]. *Sovetskii ekran*, no. 9.

Illustrating five sequences from the script, Vertov comments on the process of shooting the film.

"The First Soviet Film Without Words" [*Pervaia sovetskaia fil'm bez slov*]. *Pravda* (December 1), 7.

Vertov's brief statement describes the structure and goals of the film *The Man with the Movie Camera*, which was then in production.

1929

"Film Is Threatened by Danger" [*Fil'me grozit opasnost'*]. *Novyi zritel'*, no. 5.

In an interview, Dziga Vertov assesses *The Man with the Movie Camera* in the context of the general tendencies of Soviet film production and characterizes it as a "theoretical *exposé* expressed in cinematic terms."

"The Man with the Movie Camera - Ultimate Film-Writing and Radio-Eye" [*"Liudina z kinoaparotom" – Absolutnii kinopis i radio-oko*]. *Nova generatsiia*, no. 1 (Kharkov). In Ukrainian.

Vertov's second and major commentary on his last silent film. This statement, part of which was distributed to the audience during openings in Kiev and Moscow, was published in its entirety only posthumously in Drobashenko's collection of Vertov's articles, *Articles. Diaries. Projects* (1966). The Russian title of the statement reads "The Man with the Movie Camera – A Visual Symphony" [*Chelovek s kinoapparatom – zritel'naia symfoniia*].

"A Letter to the Editor" [*Pis'mo v redaktsiiu*]. *Kino* (March 19).

Vertov expresses his indignation at the inappropriate distribution of *The Man with the Movie Camera* in Soviet commercial theaters.

"Watching and Understanding Life" [*Bachiti i chuti zhittia*]. *Kino* (Oct. 1), Kiev. In Ukrainian.

A theoretical discussion of the function of sound in documentary film is related to Vertov's forthcoming project, the production of the first Soviet sound film *Enthusiasm, or Symphony of the Don Basin* (1930).

1930

"The March of Radio-Eye" [*Mart radioglaza*]. *Kino i zhizn'*, no. 20 (June), 14.

Vertov presents his ideas on using sound in cinema and its relationship to the image in his film *Enthusiasm (Symphony of the Don Basin)*.

"The Paths of Documentary Film" [*Puti dokumental'noi fil'my*]. *Kinofront* (May 11).

Vertov replies to the questions formulated by the editors of *Kinofront*. Summarizing his theoretical and artistic goals, he emphasizes the differences between "staged" and "unstaged" cinema, the function of sound in film, and the experimental concept of *The Man with the Movie Camera*.

"Radio-Film-Eye" [*Radio-kino-oko*]. *Vechirnia robitnitsa gazeta* (June 17), Kiev. In Ukrainian.

In an interview, Dziga Vertov outlines the concepts and problems related to the realization of his film *Enthusiasm (Symphony of the Don Basin)*.

"Agitational-Propaganda, Scientific-Educational, Instructional Film and the Film-Newsreel" [*Agitatsionno-propagandistskyi, nauchno-uchebnyi, instruktivnyi fil'm i fil'm-khronika*]. In *For Film in the Reconstruction Period*, Moscow, pp. 107–11.

In his statement presented at the First Moscow Conference on nonfeature film, Vertov proposes the formation of a special "film factory" dedicated to the exploration of documentary film and the expansion of the newsreel.

1931

"Film-Eye, Radio-Eye, and So-called 'Documentarism' " [*Kinoglaz, radioglaz i tak nazyvaemyi "dokumentalizm"*]. *Proletarskoe kino*, no. 4.

Vertov contrasts the creative principles of the kinoks to the conventional documentary film, presenting a brief survey of the evolution of "Film-Eye" as a new method for capturing reality with a movie camera.

"Let's Discuss the First Sound Film of Ukrainfil'm, *Symphony of the Don Basin*" [*Obsuzhdaem pervuiu zvukovuiu fil'mu Ukrainfil'm, "Simfoniia Donbassa"*]. *Sovetskoe iskusstvo* (Feb. 27).

Vertov explicates the audiovisual structure of his first sound film.

"Whom Does Proletarian Cinema Need?" [*Kto nuzhen proletarskomu kino?*]. *Kino* (March 8).

Vertov replies to questions, asked by editors of the journal, concerning the education of young filmmakers in the areas of documentary and newsreels.

"The First Steps" [*Pervye shagi*]. *Kino* (April 16).

Vertov further elaborates the sight-and-sound counterpoint used throughout *Enthusiasm (Symphony of the Don Basin)*.

"In Lieu of a Reply to the Critics" [*Vmesto otveta kritikam*]. *Kino* (June 16).

Vertov defends the ideological meaning and cinematic significance of his film *Enthusiasm*, criticizing the official distributors who insisted on a montage revision of the film for foreign markets.

"Libretto for *Enthusiasm*" [*Libretto za Entuziazm*]. Vertov's statement about sound film has been published only in English in *The Film Society Programme*, performance No. 49 (Nov. 15). Translated by Thorold Dickinson.

Summarizes the three "movements" of the film and characterizes it as the "ice-breaker-in-chief" of the sound newsreel. The original version exists only in manuscript form and is kept in the Dziga Vertov Archive.

1932

"Charlie Chaplin, the Workers of Hamburg, and a Review of Dr. Wirth" [*Charlie Chaplin, gamburgskie rabochie i prikaz doktora Virta*]. *Proletarskoe kino*, no. 3.

Vertov reports on the success of *Enthusiasm* in Germany, expressing his fascination with various aspects of life abroad, concluding with favorable responses from René Clair, Moholy-Nagy, Charlie Chaplin, and the German critic, Wirth.

"Once Again about So-called 'Documentarism'" [*Eshcho o tak nazyvaemom "dokumentalizme"*]. *Proletarskoe kino*, no. 3.

Vertov criticizes "documentarism" as the mechanical application of the "Film-Eye" method to staged films.

"Approaching the Second Five-Year Plan" [*Na podstupakh k vtoroi piatiletka*]. *Proletarskoe kino*, no. 4 (April 19), 5–6.

In reply to the periodical's questionnaire, Vertov outlines his plans for filmmaking over the next five years.

"The Complete Capitulation of Nikolai Lebedev" [*Polnaia kapituliatsiia Nikolaia Lebedeva*]. *Proletarskoe kino*, no. 5 (May), 12–18.

Vertov's rebuttal to Lebedev's criticism of Vertov's "formalism" and "eccentricity" in *The Man with the Movie Camera*, presented in his article "For Proletarian Film Journalism" [*Za proletarskuiu kinopublitsistiku*] published in the journal *Literatura i iskusstvo*, no. 9–10 (Nov. 1931). Vertov condemns Lebedev's orthodox view of art, especially his contention that socialist realism must be applied to, or rather imposed upon, cinema.

"Creative Growth" [*Tvorcheskii pod'em*]. *Kino* (May 24).

Vertov suggests the reorganization of Soviet film production in light of the decree "On the Reorganization of Literary-Artistic Institutions" [*O perestroike literarno-khudozhestvennykh organizatsii*] issued by the Central Committee of the Communist Party.

"In the Front Ranks" [*V pervuiu sherengu*]. *Kino* (Sept. 6).

Vertov's report (which he gave as the representative of Mezhrabpomfil'm Production Company to the International Anti-War Congress in Amsterdam) proposes that cinema be used against warmongers.

1934

"How We Made a Film about Lenin" [*Kak my delali fil'm o Lenine*]. *Izvestiya* (May 24), 6.

Vertov discusses the production of *Three Songs about Lenin,* revealing that during his research, several unknown shots of Lenin were discovered.

"Without Words" [*Bez slov*]. *Rotfil'm* (August 15).

Vertov explains the visual structure of the film *Three Songs about Lenin,* and the difficulties he encountered in the process of shooting.

"Three Songs about Lenin" [*Tri pesni o Lenine*]. *Kommuna* (Nov. 2), Voronezh.

A revised version of the article published in *Rotfil'm.*

"Three Songs about Lenin" [*Tri pesni o Lenine*]. *Sovkhoznaia gazeta* (Nov. 7).

In an interview, Vertov explains that his goal in the film was to emphasize the human aspect of Lenin's character.

"How I Worked on the Film 'Three Songs about Lenin' " [*Kak ia rabotal nad fil'mom "Tri pesni o Lenine"*]. *Proletarskaia pravda* (Nov. 7), Kalinin.

In an interview conducted by the chief editor of the newspaper, Vertov emphasizes the structural nature of the sound track in the film.

"My Report" [*Moi raport*]. *Izvestiya* (Dec. 15), 4.

Vertov gives a short summary of his creative evolution, issued in connection with the fifteenth anniversary of Soviet cinema. It also mentions the success of *Three Songs about Lenin* in New York.

"Three Songs about Lenin" [*Tri pesni o Lenine*]. *Ogonek,* no. 17–18.

Vertov briefly explains the thematic composition and the ideological message of the film.

"Film-Truth" [*Kinopravda*]. *Sovetskoe kino,* no. 11–12, 155–64.

This article was issued in connection with the fifteenth anniversary of Soviet cinema. Vertov elaborates extensively on his creative ideas, emphasizing the fact that *Three Songs about Lenin* expands his "Film-Eye" method and the "Film-Truth" principle.

1935

"Creative Report" [*Tvorcheskii raport*]. *Rabochaia Moskva* (Jan. 5).

Vertov's assessment of his own contribution to cinema. This article was issued in connection with the fifteenth anniversary of Soviet cinema.

"The Last Experiment" [*Poslednii opyt*]. *Literaturnaia gazeta* (Jan. 18).

Vertov explains the making of *Three Songs about Lenin* and its relation to his earlier films.

"Three Songs about Lenin" [*Tri pesni o Lenine*]. *Vechernaia Moskva* (Jan. 21).

Three sequences from the literary script of the film.

"Soviet Directors Speak" [*Govoriat Sovetskie rezhisery*]. *Kino* (March 1).

Vertov gives his impressions of the First International Film Festival in Moscow.

"We Must Arm Ourselves" [*Nado vooruzhat'sia*]. *Sovetskoe kino,* no. 4, 30.

Vertov outlines his ideas on future technical and organizational improvements in Soviet cinema.

"Dziga Vertov on Kino-Eye" and **"Dziga Vertov on Film Technique."** *Filmfront,* no. 2 (Jan. 7), 6–8 and *Filmfront,* no. 3 (Jan. 28), 7–9.

Partial translation from the French (by Samuel Brody) of Vertov's speech delivered during his visit in Paris (January 1929). The original Russian text, under the title "From 'Film-Eye' toward 'Radio-Eye': from the Alphabet of *Kinoks*" [*Ot 'kinoglaza' k radioglazu': iz Azbuki kinokov*], in four parts, containing an explanation of Vertov's "Theory of Intervals," was printed in *Iskusstvo kino,* no. 6 (June), 95–9.

1936

"Lenin in Film" [*Lenin v kino*]. *Sovetskoe iskusstvo* (Jan. 22), no. 22.

Vertov comments on his film dedicated to Lenin and recounts Lenin's remarks made after he saw *Film-Truth No. 13,* entitled *Yesterday, Today, Tomorrow* (1923).

"The Truth about the Struggle of Heroes" [*Pravda o bor'be geroev*]. *Kino* (Nov. 7).

Vertov surveys the first eight issues of the newsreel *On Events in Spain* [*K sobytiiam v Ispanii*], directed by Vladimir Makasseev and Roman Karmen. The same material was used by Esther Shub in her compilation film *Spain* [*Ispaniia,* 1936–1937].

"Song about a Woman" [*Pesnia o zhenshchine*]. *Krest'ianskaia gazeta,* no. 88.

In an interview, Vertov describes preparations for his new project, later to become the sound film *Lullaby* (1937).

1937

"First Encounter" [*Pervaia vstrecha*]. *Krokodil,* no. 29–30.

Vertov's reminiscences of the history and function of the first "campaign-train" *(agit-poezd),* named after M. I. Kalinin and used during the Russian Civil War period.

"Beautiful Life in the Soviet Land" [*Prekrasnaia zhizn' v sovetskoi strane*]. *Kino* (Oct. 12).

Vertov wrote this impressionistic political pamphlet for an occasion – the elections for the Supreme Soviet of the USSR. It also contains a brief reference to the film *Lullaby* (1937).

1938

"Woman in Defense of the Country" [*Zhenshchina v oborone strany*]. *Kurortnaia gazeta* (June 14), Sochi.

Vertov explains his new (unrealized) project with a short summary of a script-in-progress dealing with female Soviet soldiers.

1940

"From the History of the Newsreel" [*Iz istorii kinokhroniki*]. *Kino* (May 5).

Vertov recollects his earliest cinematic experience, focusing on *Film-Weekly* (1919), *Anniversary of the Revolution* (1919), *History of the Civil War* (1922), and *Film-Truth* (1922–5). This is the last article Vertov published before his death in February, 1954.

1957

"From the Working Notebooks of Dziga Vertov" [*Iz rabochikh tetradei Dzigi Vertova*]. *Iskusstvo kino*, no. 4, 112–26.

A lengthy selection of Vertov's writings, all later reprinted in the book *Articles, Diaries, Projects.*

1958

"About the Love for a Real Person" [*O livbvi k zhivomu cheloveku*]. *Iskusstvo kino*, no. 6 (June), 95–9. A draft of this article was written in 1940.

An essay written in the form of an imaginary discussion between Vertov and a film critic on the question of documentary film, emphasizing the "Film-Truth" principle as being the most appropriate means by which documentary cinema can achieve its goals "within the full spectrum of cinematic possibilities."

1959

"Autobiography" [*Avtobiografiia*]. *From the History of Film: Materials and Documents* [*Iz istorii kino: materialy i dokumenty*], II (Moscow: Akademiia nauk SSSR), pp. 29–31.

Dated May 1949. A brief resumé of Vertov's life and achievements.

"Recollections of Filming V. I. Lenin" [*Vospominanie o s'emkakh V. I. Lenina*]. *From the History of Film*, II, pp. 32–5.

Vertov's recollections about filming Lenin and several of Lenin's collaborators.

"The Creative Activity of G. M. Boltyansky" [*Tvorcheskaia deiatel'nost' G. M. Boltyanskogo*]. *From the History of Film*, II, pp. 63–7.

Vertov's eulogy on the work of Boltyansky, an established documentary filmmaker, delivered on March 3, 1945.

1960

"The Song of Two Hundred Million" [*Pesn' dvukhsot millionov*]. *Komsomol'skaia pravda* (March 22).

Vertov's comments on the composition of the film *Three Songs about Lenin*, briefly citing several sequences from the original script.

"Three Songs about Lenin – The Last Experiment" [*Tri pesni o Lenine – poslednii opyt*]. *Sovetskii ekran*, no. 8.

A reprint of the 1935 article "The Last Experiment."

1966

Articles, Diaries, Projects [*Statii, dnevniki, zamysly*], ed. S. Drobashenko. Moscow: Iskusstvo, 1966.

A collection of Vertov's major writings, accompanied by a critical introduction with explanatory comments, sources, and notes.

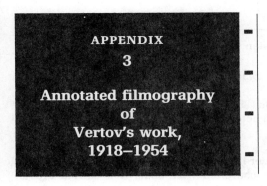

Duration of films is marked according to the original prints produced in 35mm.

Film Weekly [*Kinonedelia*] 1918–19
A newsreel series each consisting of one reel (12 min. each)
Produced by the Moscow Film Committee of Narkompros (Ministry of Culture)
Director: Dziga Vertov and Mikhail Koltsov
Camera: staff of M.F.C.
The forty-five segments of the series appeared weekly.

The Exhumation of the Remains of Sergei of Radonezh [*Vskrytie moschei Sergeia Radonezheskogo*] 1919
An antireligious agit-film in two reels (25 min)
Produced by the M.F.C.
Author-director and supervisor: Dziga Vertov
Camera: staff of M.F.C.
St. Sergei is one of Russia's most important saints. In the fifteenth century he founded the Trinity-Sergei Monastery in Zagorsk (near Moscow). It became a major center of religious life and still functions today in the Soviet Union.

Anniversary of the Revolution [*Godovshchina revolutsii*] 1919
Compilation film made from *Film-Weekly* material, in twelve reels (150 min.)
Produced by the M.F.C.
Director: Dziga Vertov

Battle of Tsaritsyn [*Boi pod Tsaritsynom*] 1920
Compiled documentary in three reels (40 min.)
Produced by "Revvoensovet" [Revolutionary Military Soviet] and the M.F.C.
Author-director: Dziga Vertov
Camera: staff of M.F.C.
This newsreel covers the famous Soviet offensive against General Anton Denikin and his White Army at Tsaritsyn (December 1919).

The Trial of Mironov [*Protsess Mironova*] 1920
Political newsreel in one reel (12 min.)
Produced by "Revvoensovet" and the M.F.C.
Author-director: Dziga Vertov
Camera: staff of M.F.C.
Filipp Mironov (1872–1921) was a Cossack commander who fought on the

side of the Soviets during the Russian Civil War against generals Krasnov and Wrangel.

Instructional Steamer "The Red Star" [*Instruktorskii parokhod "Krasnaia zvezda"*] 1920
A propaganda newsreel in two reels (25 min.)
Produced by VOFKO [All-Russian Photo-Cinema Department in the Ministry of Culture]
Director: Dziga Vertov
Camera: Alexandr Lemberg and Peter Ermolov
The "instructional steamers" were converted river boats that carried artists, Soviet officials, and other propaganda workers down the Volga to spread culture and propaganda among the workers, peasants, and citizens immediately after the revolution.

The All-Russian Elder Kalinin [*Vserosiiskii starosta Kalinin*] 1920
A documentary in two reels (25 min.)
Produced by the M.F.C.
Director: Dziga Vertov
Camera: staff of the M.F.C.
M. I. Kalinin, Soviet president between 1938–46, is shown visiting the agit-train "October Revolution" in early 1920. The agit-trains were sent all over the Soviet Union with propaganda workers who distributed posters, showed films, and performed agit-plays [*agitki*].

The Agit-Train VTSIK [*Agit-poezd VTSIK*] 1921
A travelogue in one reel (12 min.)
Produced by VTSIK [All-Russian Central Executive Committee] and the M.F.C.
Author-director: Dziga Vertov

Commander of the XIII Army, Comrade Kozhevnikov [*Komanduiushchii XIII armiei Tv. Kozhevnikov*] 1921
A compilation film in one reel (12 min.)
Produced by the M.F.C.
Director: Dziga Vertov. Editor: Elizaveta Svilova
Camera: Petr Ermolov
Kozhevnikov was a Soviet general who fought against the White Army at Tsaritsyn. The film compiles footage from various issues of *Film-Weekly* and *Battle of Tsaritsyn*.

History of the Civil War [*Istoriia grazhdanskoi voiny*] 1921
A newsreel in thirteen reels (175 min.)
Produced by VFKO [Central State Film Committee]
Author-director: Dziga Vertov
Camera: staff of VFKO

The Trial of the S.R.s [*Protsess Eserov*] 1922
A political newsreel in three reels (40 min.)
Produced by VFKO
Author-director: Dziga Vertov
Camera: staff of VFKO
The Social Revolutionary Party ("Eser") began in 1901 and was concerned with the interests of the peasants, while the Social Democrats advanced the cause

of the workers in the city. The members of S.R. committed a series of terrorist acts, and one member killed Grand Duke Sergei, uncle of the Tsar and governor-general of Moscow, in 1905. They became the largest political party in Russia. After the October Revolution in 1917, the Bolshevik party and the Social Democrats, suppressed the S.R.s. In Russia, a member of the S.R.s is referred to as an "eser."

Department Store [*Univermag*] 1922
An advertising film, a "film sketch" in two reels (25 min.)
Produced by VOFKO
Director: Dziga Vertov
Camera: staff of VOFKO
"Univermag" stands for *"universal'nyi magazin"* (universal store); one such store, called GUM (State Department Store), had opened in Moscow in Red Square.

Film-Truth [*Kinopravda*] 1922–5
Newsreel series (12 min. each)
Produced by Goskino
Supervisor, author of intertitles: Dziga Vertov
Editor: Elizaveta Svilova
Camera: staff of Goskino
Twenty-three segments were distributed under the general title *Film-Truth*, except for the following segments carrying their own titles:

Yesterday, Today, Tomorrow [*Vchera, segodnia, zavtra*] 1923
    A cinematic poem dedicated to the heroic events of October.
    (*Film-Truth*, no. 13) in three reels (35 min.)
Spring Film-Truth [*Vesennaia Kinopravda*] 1923
    A lyrical newsreel about everyday events (*Film-Truth*, no. 16) in three reels
    (40 min.)
Black Sea–Arctic Ocean–Moscow [*Chernoe more–Ledovityi okean–Moskva*]
1924
    A cinematic visit to a youth camp (*Film-Truth*, no. 20) in one reel (12 min.)
    Camera: Mikhail Kaufman
Leninist Film-Truth [*Leninskaia kinopravda*] February 6, 1924
    A cinematic poem about Lenin (*Film-Truth*, no. 21), in three reels (35 min.)
    Camera: G. Giber, A. Levitsky, A. Lemberg, N. Novitsky, M. Kaufman, E.
    Tisse, and others.
In the Heart of the Peasant Lenin Is Alive [*V serdtse krest'yanina Lenin zhiv*]
March 13, 1925
    A cinematic tale (*Film-Truth*, no. 22) in two reels (25 min.)
    Camera: M. Kaufman, A. Lemberg, and I. Beliakov
Radio Film-Truth [*Radio-Kinopravda*] 1925
    A special experimental newsreel about radio (*Film-Truth*, no. 23), in one
    reel (12 min.)
    Camera: M. Kaufman, I. Beliakov, and A. Bushkin
Five Years of Struggle and Victory [*Piat' let bor'by i pobedy*] 1923
A compilation film in six reels (75 min.)
Produced by VOFKO

Director: Dziga Vertov
Camera: staff of VOFKO
The film was dedicated to the fifth anniversary of the Red Army.

Today [*Segodnia*] 1923
An animated short in one reel (8 min.)
Produced by Goskino
Author-supervisor: Dziga Vertov
Animation: Ivan Beliakov and Boris Volkov
Camera: Mikhail Kaufman
The film depicts in graphic symbols the struggle between the emerging fascist forces and the communists. This is considered the first example of Soviet animation, although Vertov included animated segments earlier in some of his *Film-Truth* series.

Calendar of Goskino Film [*Goskinokalendar'*] 1923–5
A newsreel appearing weekly (12 min.)
Produced by Goskino [State Film Enterprise] and Kult'kino [Cultural Film]
Author-director: Dziga Vertov
To distinguish it from *Film-Weekly,* Vertov called this series "Newsreel-Lightning" [*Khronika-molniia*]. Kult'kino was the newly formed documentary section of Goskino, headed by Vertov.

Soviet Toys [*Sovetskie igrushki*] 1924
An animated political satire in one reel (12 min.)
Produced by Kul'tkino
Author-supervisor: Dziga Vertov
Animation: Ivan Beliakov, Alexandr Ivanov, and Alexandr Bushkin
Camera: Alexandr Dorn
The film was commissioned by the State Bank and drew upon the styles of both political newspaper cartoons and ROSTA posters, ridiculing the "Nepman" (speculator taking advantage of the NEP's economic policies).

Humoresques [*Iumoreski*] 1924
An animated propaganda film in one segment (3 min.)
Produced by Kul'tkino
Author-director: Dziga Vertov
Art director: Alexandr Bushkin
Animation: B. Volkov and B. Egerev
Camera: Ivan Beliakov
The film consists of three brief sections, each dealing with the current political and economic situation in the Soviet Union and abroad.

You Have Given Us the Air [*Daesh' vozdukh*] 1924
A special issue of the Calendar in one reel (12 min.)
Produced by Goskino
Author-director: Dziga Vertov
Camera: Mikhail Kaufman
An educational film about aviation.

Film-Eye – Life Caught Unawares [*Kinoglaz – Zhizn' vrasplokh*] 1924
First issue in six reels (82 min.)
Produced by Goskino

Director: Dziga Vertov
Editor: Elizaveta Svilova
Camera: Mikhail Kaufman
The other five issues planned were never produced. The original credits list Vertov as a "Cinema Scout," an allusion to the Soviet youth organization called "Pioneers."

The Foreign Cruise of the Ship of the Baltic Fleet, the Cruiser "Aurora," and the Training Ship "Komsomolets" [*Zagranichnyi pokhod sudov Baltiiskogo flota kreisera "Avroara" i uchebnogo sudna "Komsomolets"*] 1925
A newsreel in one reel (12 min.)
Director: Dziga Vertov
Camera: M. Pertsovich and A. Andiukhin
This is one of the first Soviet films in which footage of foreign countries was shot by Soviet cameramen.

Forward March, Soviet! – The Moscow Soviet in the Present, Past, and Future [*Shagai, Sovet! – Mossovet v nastoiashchem, proshlom i budushchem*] 1926
A film newsreel in seven reels (83 min.)
Produced by Sovkino (formerly Goskino)
Supervisor: Dziga Vertov
Assistant director: Elizaveta Svilova
Camera: Ivan Beliakov
The final intertitle of the film reads: "Socialist Russia will emerge from the Russia of the NEP."

One Sixth of the World – Export and Import of "Gostorg" in the U.S.S.R. – A Race of Film-Eye Around the U.S.S.R. [*Shestaia chast' mira – Eksport i import Gostorga SSSR – Probeg "kinoglaza" po SSSR*] 1926
A cinematic poem in six reels (77 min.)
Produced by Sovkino
Author-supervisor: Dziga Vertov
Assistant: Elizaveta Svilova
Chief cameraman: Mikhail Kaufman
Cameramen: I. Baliakov, S. Bendersky, P. Zotov, N. Konstantinov, A. Lemberg, N. Strukov, and Ia. Tolchen
Film Scouts: A. Kagarlitsky, I. Kopalin, and N. Kudinov
The final title reads: "Into the Current – Of the Common – Socialist – Economy." "Gostorg" stands for the Ministry of Trade.

The Eleventh Year [*Odinnatsatyi*] 1928
An anniversary newsreel in six reels (80 min.)
Produced by VUFKU (All Ukrainian Photo and Film Committee) in Kiev
Author-supervisor: Dziga Vertov
Assistant: Elizaveta Svilova
Camera: Mikhail Kaufman

The Man with the Movie Camera [*Chelovek s kinoapparatom*] 1929
A visual symphony in six reels (95 min.)
Produced by VUFKU
Author-supervisor of the experiment: Dziga Vertov
Montage editor: Elizaveta Svilova
Chief cameraman: Mikhail Kaufman

This is Vertov's last silent film. In his "Summary: Creative Autobiography" [*Konspekt: Tvorcheskaia autobiografiia*], written in 1934 but unpublished, Vertov mentions an earlier version of the film. Seth Feldman, in *Dziga Vertov: A Guide to References and Resources* (p. 110) states that there is no evidence of such a version and that it was not distributed.

Enthusiasm – Symphony of the Don Basin [*Entuziazm – Simfoniia Donbassa*] 1930
A documentary in six reels (96 min.)
Produced by Ukrainfilm VUFKU
Author-director: Dziga Vertov
Assistant: Elizaveta Svilova
Camera: B. Tzeitlin and K. Kuialev
Sound Engineer: Petr Shtro
Music: Timofeyev ("The Don Basin March") and Shostakovich ("The First of May Symphony")
This is Vertov's first sound film. The opening intertitle reads: "The shooting of the audio-visual material has been accomplished by means of the Shorin Recording System on location in mines, factories, etc."

Three Songs about Lenin [*Tri pesni o Lenine*] 1934
A documentary in six reels (70 min.)
Produced by Mezhrabpomfilm (International Workers' Film Enterprise)
Author-director: Dziga Vertov
Assistant: Elizaveta Svilova
Camera: D. Surensky, M. Magidson, and B. Monastirsky
Sound Engineer: P. Shtro
Composer: Yuri Shaporin
In the Vertov Archive in Moscow, there is a montage list and a detailed description of a silent variant of this film. However, Feldman (p. 103) states that there is no evidence of such a version and that it was not distributed. The existing version of the film is approximately sixty minutes long, as restored by Gosfil'mfond in 1970.

Lullaby [*Kolybel'naia*] 1937
A song to the liberated Soviet woman (60 min.)
Produced by Soiuzkinokhronika (Soviet Film Newsreel Production Company)
Author-director: Dziga Vertov
Codirector: Elizaveta Svilova
Camera: Dimitri Surensky and Staff of Soiuzkinokhronika
Composers: Dimitri and Daniil Pokrass
Sound Engineer: I. Renkov
Text of songs: V. Lebedev-Kumach
Commentary: Dziga Vertov

In Memory of Sergo Ordzhonikidze [*Pamiati Sergo Ordzhonikidze*] 1937
A compilation film in two reels (24 min.)
Produced by Soiuzkinokhronika
Directed and edited by Dziga Vertov and Elizaveta Svilova
Camera: Staff of Soiuzkinokhronika
Sergo Ordzhonikidze was commander of the Soviet batallion that routed Denikin's troops in the Ukraine.

Sergo Ordzhonikidze [*Sergo Ordzhonikidze*] 1937
A compilation film in five reels (60 min.)
Produced by Soiuzkinokhronika
Directors: Dziga Vertov, Iakov Bliokh, and Elizaveta Svilova
Camera: M. Oshurkov, I. Beliakov, V. Dobronitsky, Solovev, Adzhibeliashvili
Composer: I. Duanevsky
Sound Engineer: I. Renkov, Semenov
Note: In his "Diaries" (May 1945), Vertov stated that the completed version of
this film was subsequently "changed against my will" (*Articles*, p. 263).
The existing version of this film is, actually, an expansion of the newsreel *In
Memory of Sergo Ordzhonikidze,* made a few months earlier.

Glory to Soviet Heroines [*Slava sovetskim georiniam*] 1938
A documentary report in one reel (15 min.)
Produced by Soiuzkinokhronika
Author-director: Dziga Vertov
Codirector: Elizaveta Svilova
Camera: staff of Soiuzkinokhronika

Three Heroines [*Tri geroini*] 1938
A documentary portrait in seven reels (90 min.)
Produced by Soyuzkinokhronika
Script: Dziga Vertov and Elizaveta Svilova
Director: Dziga Vertov
Asst. Director: S. Somov
Chief cameraman: S. Semenov
Cameramen: Moskovskoi, Khabarovsky, and staff of the Documentary Studio
in Novosibirsk
Cameraman in the train: M. Troyanovsky
Composers: Dimitri and Daniil Pokrass
Sound Engineers: A. Kamponsky, Fomin, Korotkevich
The film depicts the activities of Marina Raskova (a military officer), Valentina
Grizodubova (an engineer) and Polina Osipenko (a pilot). Although completed,
the film was never released.

In the Region of Peak A [*V raione vysoty A*] 1941
A film chronicle from the front during World War II (known as the War for the
Fatherland in Russia), 15 min.
Produced by the Central Studio of the Army Film Chronicle
Director: Dziga Vertov
Camera: T. Buminovich and P. Kasatkin
Part of the regular Army Film Newsreel, no. 87.

***Blood for Blood – Death for Death – Crimes of the German Fascist Invaders
on the Territory of the U.S.S.R.*** [*Krov' za krov', smert' za smert' – Zlodeianiia
nemetskofashistkikh zakhvatchikov na territorii S.S.S.R*] 1941
A compilation film newsreel (15 min.)
Produced by the Central Studio of the Army Film Newsreel
Author-director: Dziga Vertov
Camera: staff of the Central Studio
A propaganda newsreel.

In the Line of Fire – Newsreel Cameramen [*Na linii ognia – Operatory kino-khroniki*] 1941
A report from the front during World War II, in one reel (12 min.)
Produced by the Central Studio of the Army Film Newsreel
Director: Dziga Vertov
Asst. Director and Editor: Elizaveta Svilova
Aerial shots: N. Vikhirev
Part of the regular "Soiuzkinozhurnal," no. 77.

To You, Front – Kazakhstan's Tribute to the Front [*Tebe, front – Kazakhstan frontu*] 1942
Documentary in five reels (60 min.)
Produced by the Alma-Ata Film Studio
Author-director: Dziga Vertov
Codirector and Editor: Elizaveta Svilova
Camera: K. Pumpiansky
Composers: G. Popov and V. Velikanov
Sound Engineer: K. Bakk
Text of poems: V. Lugovsky
A dramatized documentary with the well-known folksinger Nurpeis Baiganin, who tells the story of a Kazakhstan soldier fighting against the Germans.

In the Mountains of Ala-Tau [*V gorakh Ala-Tau*] 1942
Documentary in two reels (25 min.)
Produced by Alma-Ata Film Studio
Author-director: Dziga Vertov
Codirector and Editor: Elizaveta Svilova
Camera: B. Pumpiansky

The Oath of Youth [*Kliatva molodykh*] 1944
Documentary in three reels (40 min.)
Produced by the Central Studio of the Army Film Newsreel
Directors and Editors: Dziga Vertov and Elizaveta Svilova
Camera: I. Beliakov, G. Amirov, B. Borkovsky, B. Dementev, S. Semenov, V. Kositsyn, and E. Stankevich
The film deals with the activities of the Komsomol during World War II.

News of the Day [*Novosti dnia*] 1944–54
Daily film newsreel (12 min. each)
Produced by the Central Studio of the Army Documentary Film
Dziga Vertov supervised the following issues:
1944: no. 18
1945: nos. 4, 8, 12, 15, 20
1946: nos. 2, 8, 18, 24, 34, 42, 67, 77
1947: nos. 6, 13, 21, 30, 37, 48, 51, 65, 71
1948: nos. 8, 19, 23, 29, 34, 39, 44, 50
1949: nos. 27, 43, 45, 51, 55
1950: nos. 7, 58
1951: nos. 15, 33, 43, 56
1952: nos. 9, 15, 31, 43, 54
1953: nos. 18, 27, 35, 55
1954: nos. 31, 46, 60

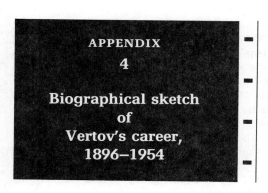

This chronology includes the facts important to Vertov's career, with emphasis on those cultural and sociopolitical events that, directly or indirectly, affected his work.

1896	Jan. 2	Denis Arkadievich Kaufman is born in the town of Bialystok, which belonged to the Russian Empire until 1918, and now is part of Poland. His father was a book-dealer and bibliophile.
1905		Writes a poem, "Masha," dedicated to his aunt, a school teacher with liberal views.
1912–1914		Attends high school [*realnoe uchilishche*] and music school (studying piano and violin) in Bialystok. Reads novels by James Fenimore Cooper, Jack London, and Arthur Conan Doyle.
1915	Spring	Moves with his family to Moscow.
1916	Spring	Moves to Petrograd and enrolls in the Psychoneurological Institute (special interest in human perception). Writes a pamphlet against the monarchist ideology promoted by the Russian government.
	Summer	Organizes the "Laboratory of Hearing," in which he performs experiments with sound recording. Writes a novel, *The Iron Hand* [*Zheleznaya ruka*], which has been lost.
1917	Fall	Returns to Moscow.
	Winter	Meets Alexandr Lemberg, a cameraman who introduces him to cinema, in the "Poets' Cafe" [*Kafè poetov*], the famous meeting place of Moscow artists.
1918	Spring	Meets Mikhail Kol'tsov, a writer who works on the Moscow Film Committee and who gives Vertov a job with the committee (Kol'tsov was also born in Bialystok).
	Summer	Becomes the secretary of the Newsreel Section of the Film Committee (also known as the All-Russian Photo-Film Department). Takes the pseudonym Dziga Vertov (which has been interpreted in many ways, including

"Spinning Top," "Spinning Gypsy," and "Rotating Film Reel," but the closest translation would be "Spinning Top That is Turning").

1918   Summer   Develops his "Film-Eye" method, a unification of the camera and the filmmaker's eye. First experiment: he photographs in slow motion his jump from the second floor of the Moscow Film Committee.

        June   First appearance of the *Film-Weekly* [*Kino-nedelia*] series.

1919   Spring   Formation of the *kinoks* group (also known as "*kinoglazovtsy*").

        Summer   Completes his first manifesto, "About the Disarmament of Theatrical Cinema," later expanded into "We. A Variant of a Manifesto."

        Oct. 20   Appointed as the director of the Film Section of the Revolutionary Military Service for the South-Eastern Front.

        Nov.   Release of *The Battle of Tsaritsyn*.

1919   Dec. 5   Supervises the shooting of the Seventh Congress of the Soviets in which Lenin also participated.

                  Reads the famous collection of film essays *Cinematography* [*Kinematograf*], focusing on the article "The Social Struggle and the Screen" [*Sotsialnaia bor'ba i ekran*] by Platon Kerezhentsev.

1920   Travels across the country in the agit-train "VTSIK."

                  Writes "A Synopsis for a Film About an Agit-Train Passing Through the Soviet Caucasus" (unrealized project).

1921   Summer   Release of *The Agit-Train VTSIK*.

        Fall   Release of *The History of the Civil War*.

                  Submits a report on the work of the Film Section (led by Vertov) to Alexandr Lemberg, Chief of the Agitational-Instructional Agit-Train project.

1922   April   Begins to work on the first issue of *Film-Truth* [*Kinopravda*].

        August   Publishes "We. A Variant of a Manifesto."

        Nov. 28   Koltsov's article "On the Screen" [*U èkrana*] published in *Pravda*. Koltsov praises Vertov's method used in the *Film-Truth* series.

        Dec. 8   Publishes the article "The Fifth Number of *Film-Truth*," in which he disagrees with Kol'tsov about the language of cinema as defined in Kol'tsov's article "The Alphabet" [*Azbuka*].

1923   Polemicizes with Aleksei Gan, a leading Soviet Constructivist theorist and the editor of *Kinofot*.

        Feb.   Completes a report to the directorial board of Goskino Film Company, "About the Significance of the Newsreel," later revised and published as "A Project for the Reorganization of the 'Council of Three.'" Vertov,

		Kaufman, and Svilova form the "triumvirate" that runs the *kinok*s workshop.
	Spring	Completes the synopsis of "The Adventures of the Delegates Arriving in Moscow to Attend the Comintern Meeting" (unrealized project).
	July 15	Vertov's first article published in *Pravda*, "A New Current in Cinema." The editor's note states that the article "is printed with the preservation of the author's style."
	Summer	Publishes the manifesto "*Kinoks*. Revolution," initially planned to be the introduction to an unpublished book.
1924	Jan.	Writes a synopsis of the article "The Birth of Film-Eye," later revised and published as " 'Film-Eye': A Newsreel in Six Issues."
	Jan. 21	Supervises the shooting of Lenin's funeral.
	Feb. 6	Release of *Lenin's Burial*, a newsreel edited by Vertov.
	April 9	Presents the paper "Film-Eye" at the *kinok*s' annual meeting.
	Summer	Eisenstein attacks Vertov's method of montage as "impressionistic" and "primitively provocative" in his article "On the Question of a Materialist Approach to Form."
	July 15	Completes the paper "Concerning the Artistic Dramatic Performance and Film-Eye."
	Fall	Release of *Film-Eye – Life Caught Unawares*, the only issue produced out of the projected six series.
1925	Jan.	Participates in the meeting "Left Front," and along with Aleksei Gan defends unstaged cinema and newsreels.
	Jan. 21	Release of *Leninist Film-Truth*, dedicated to the memory of Lenin.
	Feb. 3	*Kinok*s discuss the article "The Basics of Film-Eye" as the creative program of their workshop.
	March	Publishes the article " 'Film-Eye' about *Strike*," which initiates a lengthy controversy between Vertov and Eisenstein.
	March 13	Release of *In the Heart of a Peasant, Lenin is Alive*, which in addition to *Leninist Film-Truth*, commemorates the first anniversary of Lenin's death.
	July 16	Publishes the article "Film-Truth and Radio-Truth" in which the concept of the "Leninist proportion" is discussed.
1926	Jan.	Completes the article "Film-Eye" [*Kinoglaz*], which reiterates his theoretical ideas.
	April	Release of *Forward March, Soviet!*
	Summer	Vertov's ideological conflict with Nikolai Lebedev: he flatly rejects all critical remarks by this staunch defender of socialist realism.
		Completes a proposal for reorganization of the *kinok*s' productions according to the "Film-Eye" method.

	July 24	Publishes the article "The Factory of Facts," in which Vertov claims that Eisenstein used the "Film-Eye" method in his *Battleship Potemkin*.
	Oct.	The release of *One Sixth of the World*. Receives a prize for this film at the World Exposition in Paris.
	Nov.	Completes the script for *Ten Years of October* (unrealized project).
	Fall	The pressure against Vertov in Sovkino increases. His colleagues write a letter to *Pravda*, claiming that the current criticism of Vertov and his *kinok*s is an attack on the entire Soviet documentary film and newsreels.
1927	Jan.	Vertov is dismissed from Sovkino.
	Spring	Vertov accepts an invitation to work for VUFKU, Kiev.
	Dec.	A discussion organized by *Novyi LEF* entitled "*LEF* and Film" declares Vertov's and Shub's concepts of filmmaking identical to what the *LEF* group considered to be a "cinema of facts."
1928	Feb.	Release of *The Eleventh Year*.
	Feb. 16	Public discussion and acclaim of the film *The Eleventh Year*.
	Feb. 20	Writes the first version of his statement on *The Man with the Movie Camera* (published after his death).
	March 19	Writes the second version of his statement "*The Man with the Movie Camera*" (later published in Ukrainian).
	April	Panel discussion entitled "The *LEF* Ring" (organized by *Novyi LEF*) proclaims Vertov's film *The Eleventh Year* "superior" to Eisenstein's *October*.
	Summer	Writes the article "To All Workers of Unstaged Film" in which he criticizes both Eisenstein for making "mediated films" [*promezhutochnyi fil'm*] and Esther Shub for making "imitative films" [*podrazhatel'nyi fil'm*] (published posthumously).
	Fall	Publishes the article "Film Has Begun to Shout," which discusses the inclusion of sound in film as a progressive step in the evolution of the medium.
	Sept.	Previews of *The Man with the Movie Camera* in Kiev and Moscow.
	Nov. 8	Sends a letter to Aleksandr Fevralsky (the editor of *Pravda*), asking him to publish in *Pravda* the declaration "*The Man with the Movie Camera* – The Ultimate Film Writing and 'Radio-Eye.' " The text was rejected.
	Nov. 18	Issues the short statement "The First Soviet Film Without Words," published in *Pravda* (December 1), also known as "The First Statement on *The Man with the Movie Camera*."
1929	Jan. 8	Release of *The Man with the Movie Camera* in Kiev.

Feb.	Travels to Paris to show a selection from the *Film-Eye* series and deliver a lecture on sound film, the coming of television, and his directorial method.
Feb.	Attends the International Exhibition "Film and Photography" in Stuttgart. The Soviet section of the exhibition was organized by El Lissitzky and his wife, Sofia Lissitzka-Kupper. Gives a series of lectures on documentary film in Germany (Berlin, Dessau, and Essen).
	Publishes the Russian version of his Paris lecture "From 'Film-Eye' to 'Radio-Eye': From the Alphabet of *Kinok*s," in which his "Theory of Intervals" is elaborated.
	Publishes the second version of his statement, "*The Man with the Movie Camera* – The Ultimate Film Writing and 'Radio-Eye' " in Ukrainian (published only posthumously in Russian). Also known as "The Second Statement."
Feb.	Writes a series of drafts for statements explaining the montage structure of *The Man with the Movie Camera*. Only one of them is published at this time (in Kharkov), while others, including "*The Man with the Movie Camera* – A Visual Symphony," are published posthumously.
March 19	Writes a letter to the editor of *Kino* protesting the unsatisfactory distribution of *The Man with the Movie Camera*.
June	Refuses to participate in the conference on so-called documentarism, organized by the Moscow Association of Film Workers.
Fall	Participates in the International Anti-War Congress in Amsterdam, representing Mezhrabpomfil'm Company.
1931 Nov. 17	Meets Charles Chaplin (in London), who praises *Enthusiasm* as "one of the most exciting symphonies I've ever heard."
1933 March	Writes the synopses of "She" and "Night of Miniatures" (unrealized projects).
Summer–Fall	Travels to Northern Russia, the Caucasus, the Ukraine, and Central Asia.
	Undertakes research for the film *Three Songs about Lenin*; looks for documents, records, popular songs, and collects footage of related events.
1934 Spring–Summer	Writes a series of articles explaining the process of shooting and producing *Three Songs about Lenin*; in most of them Vertov emphasizes his intention to expand the *kinok*s' early concepts of nonstaged cinema.
Oct. 27	A series of discussions concerning *Three Songs about Lenin*, with Vertov's participation, following the film's preview organized by the Moscow Association of Film Workers.

	Nov. 1	Release of *Three Songs about Lenin* in Moscow; masses go to the theater carrying flags with the slogan "We Are Going to See *Three Songs about Lenin*."
	Nov.	Writes several articles on Mayakovsky, emphasizing the relationship between the "Film-Eye" method and Mayakovsky's poetry (published posthumously).
	Nov.–Dec.	Acclamation of *Three Songs about Lenin* in America and various countries in Europe.
	Dec. 15	Publishes the article "Film-Truth," summarizing his creative experience from 1918 up until this point.
1935	Jan. 11	Receives the order of "The Red Star" for his artistic achievements in cinema.
	Jan. 18	Publishes the article "The Last Experiment," which explains the meaning and structure of *Three Songs about Lenin*.
1936	Jan. 22	Publishes the article "Lenin in Film" which discusses the use of sound in *Three Songs about Lenin*.
	Oct. 2	Completes the article "About the Organization of a Creative Laboratory," never published in its original form; the revised parts of the text are later incorporated into different articles.
	Nov.	Plans to make a monumental compilation film about the Spanish Civil War.
1937	Nov.	Release of *Lullaby* in Moscow, in honor of the Twentieth Anniversary of the October Revolution.
1938	Fall	Completes the synopses of "When You Will Go To War" and "Women in Defense of the Country" (unrealized projects).
1939	Feb.	Delivers the paper "In Defense of the Newsreel" at the Symposium Dedicated to Twenty Years of Soviet Cinema.
	April 15	Completes the synopsis of "Gallery of Soviet Women" (unrealized project).
	April 17	Completes the synopsis of "Farmers in Kandybina Kolkhoz" (unrealized project).
	Sept. 19	Completes the synopsis of "Mama, Mama is Falling from the Sky" (unrealized project).
	Sept. 21	Completes the synopsis of "Ukrainian Village" (unrealized project).
	Oct. 4	Completes the synopsis of "A Girl Plays the Piano" (unrealized project).
	Dec. 21	Completes the synopsis of "Outside the Program" (unrealized project).
	Dec. 23	Completes the synopsis of "In My Hometown" (unrealized project).
1940	April 17	Completes the script "Tale About a Giant," written in collaboration with Elena Segal and M. Il'ina (unrealized project).

	June 15	Drafts the article "About the Love for A Real Person," which contains information on the difficulties Vertov encountered in completing his projects. Published posthumously in 1958.
	Summer	Release of the documentary "Our Cinema," directed by Fedor Kiselev, in which Vertov and his work are not mentioned.
1941	Feb.	Completes the synopsis of "Flying Man" (unrealized project).
	April 23	Completes the synopsis of "Meadowlands" (unrealized project). Coauthors the synopsis of "Elizaveta Svilova – Editor."
	July 12	Completes the synopsis of "Film Correspondent" (unrealized project).
	July 15	Completes the synopsis of "The Letter From a Girl Tractor Operator" (unrealized project).
	August	Completes the synopsis of "About Wounded Heroes and Their Friends" (unrealized project).
	Sept.	Evacuates to Alma-Ata (Kazakhstan), together with other Soviet artists, after Moscow has been threatened by the advancing German army.
1942	Spring	Works on the script "To You, Front."
	Summer	Works on the realization of the film *To You, Front*.
	Fall	Completes the synopsis of "The New Year's Present" (unrealized project).
	Winter	Organizes a series of screenings of *To You, Front* for the soldiers on the battle lines.
1943	Spring–Summer	Works on an army newsreel series in the Alma-Ata Film Studio.
	Aug. 25	Writes the synopsis of "Gallery of Film Portraits" (unrealized series of documentary films).
	Sept. 4	Writes the synopsis of "The Love for a Real Person" (unrealized project).
	Sept. 8	Writes the synopsis of "Little Anna" (unrealized project).
	Sept. 15	Writes the synopsis of "Germany," a compilation film (unrealized project).
	Oct. 10	Writes the synopsis of "Forward, Only Forward," a short film about a young female pig-herder from the Volga, Alexandra Lyskova (unrealized project).
	Nov.	Returns to Moscow from Alma-Ata.
1944–5		Works on "News of the Day" [*Novosti dnia*], a newsreel produced by the Central Studio of Documentary Film. Continues to work for the Central Studio, completing fifty-four newsreels, with his function defined in the credits as "Author-Director."
	Spring	Prepares a book on his artistic work. The unfinished manuscript consists of fifty-seven pages of notes, enti-

		tled "About the Creative Path" (published posthumously).
1946	Summer	Writes the synopsis of "The Honest Fool" (unrealized project).
	Fall	Delivers a speech during the meeting of the Documentary Section of the Home of Film in Moscow.
1949	Spring	Works on his autobiography; the unfinished manuscript consists of thirty-three pages of notes and recollections covering the period 1917–49.
	March 15	Delivers a speech at the opening of the party meeting discussing the creative aspects of documentary filmmaking.
1952	Spring	Delivers the speech "About Scripts in Documentary Film" during the meeting of the Conference of Cameramen in Moscow.
1954	Feb. 12	Dies in Moscow.
1956	July 15	An evening dedicated to the memory of Vertov in the Film Section of the Academy of Sciences, Moscow.
1959	March 27	An evening dedicated to screenings of Vertov's films in the Central Palace of Film, Moscow.
1966		Publication of the book *Dziga Vertov: Articles, Diaries, Projects*, edited and with an introduction by Sergei Drobashenko.
1967	April	Release of *Life Without Game* [*Zhizn' bez igry*], a documentary about Vertov and his work. Script by Sergei Drobashenko. Directed by Leonid Makhnach.
1974	Summer	Peter Konlechner, director of the Austrian Film Museum, compiles a 60-minute film, *Dziga Vertov*, which includes footage of Elizaveta Svilova commenting on the excerpts from Vertov's films and their cooperation.
1975	Nov. 12	Elizaveta Svilova Ignat'evna dies in Moscow (born September 5, 1900, in Moscow).
1976		Publication of the book *Dziga Vertov in the Reminiscences of His Contemporaries*, edited and with an introduction by Elizaveta Vertova-Svilova and Anna Vinogradova.
1980	March 21	Mikhail Kaufman dies in Moscow (born September 5, 1897, in Bialystok).
	June 24	Boris Kaufman, Vertov's youngest brother, dies in New York (born March 11, 1904, in Bialystok).

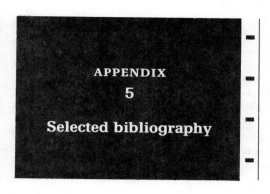

APPENDIX
5

Selected bibliography

Books and studies

Abramov, Nikolai. *Dziga Vertov* (Moscow: Akademiia Nauk, 1962), 165 pp.
Monograph with a thematic interpretation of Vertov's work.

Dobin, E.S., ed. *Razmyshleniia u ekrana* [Reflections on the Screen] (Leningrad: Iskusstvo, 1966), 367 pp.
The chapter entitled "Nasledie Dzigi Vertova i iskaniia 'cinéma-vérité' " [The Heritage of Dziga Vertov and the Aspirations of "Cinéma-Vérité"] by Tamara Selezneva (pp. 337–67) critically compares Vertov's work and method with that of Rouch, Leacock, and Pennebaker.

Drobashenko, Sergei. *Fenomen dostovernosti* [Phenomenon of Authenticity] (Moscow: Akademiia Nauk, 1972), 184 pp.
A theoretical study with a chapter dedicated to Vertov's theory of documentary film.

Feldman, Seth. *Evolution of Style in the Early Work of Dziga Vertov* (New York: Arno Press, 1977), 233 pp.
A facsimile reprint of the author's Ph.D. dissertation dedicated to Vertov's artistic development.

—*Dziga Vertov. A Guide to References and Resources* (Boston: G.K. Hall, 1979), 232 pp.
A chronological survey of Vertov's career with annotated filmography and bibliography.

Freeman, Joseph. *Voices of October: Art and Literature in Soviet Russia,* edited by Joseph Freeman, Joshua Kunitz, and Louis Lozowick (New York: Vanguard Press, 1930), 317 pp.
The chapter entitled "The Soviet Cinema" (pp. 217–64) focuses on Vertov's work on *One Sixth of the World.*

Gan, Aleksei. *Da zdravstvuet demonstratsiia byta!* [Long Live the Demonstration of Everyday Life] (Moscow: Goskino, 1923), 16 pp.
An ideological pamphlet emphasizing the political significance of Vertov's *Film-Truth* series.

Ginzburg, Sergei, ed. *Iz istorii kino: materialy i dokumenty* [From the History of Film: Materials and Documents], Vol. 2 (Moscow: Akademiia Nauk SSSR, 1959), 191 pp.

The chapter entitled "Montazhnye listy filmov Vertova" [Montage Lists of Vertov's Films] by Sergei Ginzburg discusses Vertov's early work, with particular attention to his development of the use of title cards (pp. 35–62). The chapter called "Arkhiv Dzigi Vertova" [Dziga Vertov's Archive] by L. M. Listov and Elizaveta I. Vertova-Svilova describes the material contained in Vertov's Archive in Moscow (pp. 132–55).

Herlinghaus, Hermann. *Dziga Wertow: Publizist und Poet des Dokumentarfilms* [Dziga Vertov: Journalist and Poet of the Documentary Films] (Berlin: Club der Filmshaffender der DDR und Deutsche Zentralstelle fur Filmforschung, 1960), 72 pp.

A historical/thematic survey of Vertov's work.

Marshall, Herbert. *Masters of the Soviet Cinema: Crippled Creative Biographies* (Boston: Routledge & Kegan Paul, 1983), 252 pp.

The chapter entitled "Dziga Vertov" (pp. 61–97) is dedicated to Vertov's career and his major films.

Marsollais, Gilles. *L'Aventure du Cinema Direct* [The Adventure of the Direct Cinema] (Paris: Seghers, 1974), 495 pp.

The essay called "Dziga Vertov" (pp. 31–9) discusses the relationship between Vertov and the modern documentary filmmakers.

Montani, Pierro. *Dziga Vertov* (Florence: La Nuova Italia, 1975), 139 pp.

A monograph on Vertov's life and work.

Pisarevskii, D., ed. *Iskusstvo millionov: Sovetskoe kino, 1917–1937* [The Art of Millions: Soviet Cinema, 1917–1937] (Moscow: Iskusstvo, 1958), 624 pp.

The chapter entitled "Fil'my Dzigi Vertova" [The Films of Dziga Vertov] by Il'ya Kopalin examines Vertov's early achievements.

Roshal', Lev. *Dziga Vertov* (Moscow: Iskusstvo, 1982), 264 pp., illust.

A critical survey of Vertov's work with emphasis on the thematic aspects.

Sadoul, Georges. *Dziga Vertov,* edited by Bernard Eisenschitz (Paris: Editions champs libre, 1971), 171 pp.

A critical study of Vertov, with a preface by Jean Rouch entitled "Cinq regards sur Vertov" (pp. 11–14).

Schnitzer, Luda and Jean. *Vertov* (Paris: Avant Scene du Cinema, 1968), 47 pp.

An essay on the ideological significance of Vertov's work.

Selezneva, Tamara. *Kinomysl' 1920'kh godov* [Film Thought of the 1920s] (Leningrad: Iskusstvo, 1972), 184 pp.

In the chapter called "Neigrovaia" [The Unstaged Film], Selezneva discusses Vertov's concept of nonfiction cinema.

Shklovskii, Viktor. *Ikh nastoiaschee* [Their Genuineness] (Leningrad: RSFSR Kinopechat, 1927), 85 pp.

The chapter called "Dziga Vertov" (pp. 61–7), which analyzes Vertov's cinematic concepts in the context of the early Soviet film, is translated in German in *Schriften zum Film* (Frankfurt am Main: Suhrkamp, 1968), pp. 63–8.

Vertova-Svilova, Elizaveta and Anna L. Vinogradova, comps. *Dziga Vertov v vospominaniiakh sovremennikov* [Dziga Vertov as Remembered by His Contemporaries] (Moscow: Iskusstvo, 1976), 277 pp.

A collection of articles dedicated to various aspects of Vertov's career and work.

Articles and essays

Abbott, Jere. "Notes on Movies," *Hound and Horn*, no. 2 (December 1928), pp. 159–62.

Abramov, Nikolai P. "Chelovek v dokumental'nom fil'me" [The Man in the Documentary Film], *Voprosi kino iskusstva*, no. 10 (Summer 1967), pp. 173–89.

—"Dziga Vertov: Poet and Writer of the Revolution," *Soviet Film*, no. 11 (1968), p. 11.

—"Dziga Vertov és a dokumentumfilm müvészete" [Dziga Vertov as a Documentary Filmdirector], *Filmkultura*, no. 5 (Budapest: January 1960), pp. 3–24.

—"Dziga Vertov i iskusstvo dokumental'nogo filma" [Dziga Vertov and the Art of the Documentary Film], *Voprosy kino iskusstva*, no. 4 (1960), pp. 276–308.

Amengual, Barthemlemy. "Vertov et Eisenstein: deux conceptions du cinéma politique" [Vertov and Eisenstein: Two Concepts of the Political Film], *Jeune Cinéma*, no. 93 (March 1976), pp. 10–19.

Anoshchenko, A. "Kinokoki" [A verbal parody of the word *kinok*s], *Kinonedelia* (February 19, 1924), p. 2.

Apon, A. and G. Verhage. "Sergei Eisenstein versus Dziga Vertov," *Skrien* (ed., Apon), 33 (March–April 1973), pp. 3–4.

Aristarco, Guido. "Le fonti di due 'Novatori,' Dziga Vertov e Lev Kuleshov," [The sources of two "Innovators," Dziga Vertov and Lev Kuleshov] *Cinema Nuovo*, no. 137 (Turin: January–February 1959), pp. 31–7.

Armes, Roy. "Vertov and Soviet Cinema," *Film and Reality* (London: Harmondsworth: Penguin Books, 1975), pp. 38–43.

Barrot, Billard, Brunelin, Decaudin, Delmas, Michel, Wyn, and Vrillac. "Le debat est ouvert sur 'L'Homme a la camera'" [Debate on "The Man with the Movie Camera" has opened], *Cahiers du Cinéma*, no. 22 (April, 1953), pp. 36–40 (a transcript of "Tribune de la F.F.C.C.")

Boltianskii, Grigorii M. "Teoriya i praktika kinokov" [Theory and Practice of the *Kinok*s], *Sovetskoe kino*, no. 415 (1926), pp. 10–11.

Bordwell, David. "Dziga Vertov: An Introduction," *Film Comment*, VIII/1 (Spring 1972), pp. 38–45.

Brik, Osip, Viktor Shklovskii, Esther Shub, and Serqei Tretiakov. "LEF i kino" [LEF and Cinema], *Novyi LEF*, nos. 11–12 (November–December 1927), pp. 5–70; English translation in *Screen*, no. 4 (Winter 1971–2), pp. 83–4.

Britton, Lionel. "Kino-Eye: Vertoff and the Newest Film Spirit of Russia," *The Realist*, no. 2 (October–December 1929), pp. 126–38.

Brunius, Jacques Bernard. "Le ciné-art et le ciné-oeil" [The Film-Art and the Film-Eye], *Le Revue de Cinéma*, no. 4 (October 15, 1929), pp. 75–6.

Burch, Noel. "Film's Institutional Mode of Representation and the Soviet Response," *October*, no. 11 (Winter 1979), p. 94.

Casaus, Victor. "Dziga Vertov: Notas sobre su Actualidad" [Notes on Reality], *Cine Cubano*, no. 76–77 (1972), pp. 106–11.

Cornand, J. "Sur deux films de Dziga Vertov 'Kino glaz' and 'L'homme a la camera" [About Two of Vertov's Films, "Film-Eye" and "The Man with the Movie Camera"], *Image et Son*, no. 207 (Paris: June–July 1975), pp. 55–62.

Croft, Stephen and Olivia Rose. "An Essay Toward *Man with the Movie Camera*," *Screen*, no. 1 (1977), p. 19.

Denkin, Harvey. "Linguistic Models in Early Soviet Cinema," *Cinema Journal*, no. 1 (Fall 1977), pp. 1–13.

Dickinson, Thorold. *"Enthusiasm*, or *The Symphony of the Don Basin*," *The Film Society Programme* (London: November 15, 1931), unpaginated.

Drobashenko, Sergei. ". . . und eines Tages flog er durch die Luft" [. . . One Day He Flew Through the Air], *Film und Fernsehen* (Berlin, DDR), no. 2 (February 1974), pp. 36–8 (interview with Svilova).

Durgnat, Raymond. *"Man With a Movie Camera*," *American Film*, no. 1 (1984), pp. 78–9, 88–9.

Durus. "Der Mann Mit Der Kamera," [*The Man with the Movie Camera*], Die Rote Fahne, no. 116 (July 5, 1929), unpaginated.

Eisenschitz, Bernard. "Mayakovski, Vertov." *Cahiers du Cinéma*, nos. 220–1 (May–June, 1970), pp. 26–8.

Enzensberger, Marsha. "Dziga Vertov," *Screen*, XIII/4 (Winter 1972–3), pp. 90–107.

Fargier, Jean-Paul, Claude Menard, Alain Leger, Simon Luciani, and Jean-Louis Perrier. " 'Ne copiez pas sur les yeux' disait Vertov" ["Do not Copy with the Eyes," said Vertov], *Cinéthique*, no. 15 (Spring 1973), pp. 55–92.

Feldman, Konstantin. "V sporakh o Vertove" [Disputes about Vertov], *Kino i kultura*, no. 5–6 (1929), pp. 12–13.

Feldman, Seth. "Cinema Weekly and Cinema Truth: Dziga Vertov and the Leninist Proportion," *Sight and Sound*, XLIII/1 (Winter 1973–4), pp. 34–7.

Ferguson, Otis. "Artists Among the Flickers," *The New Republic*, no. 1044 (December 5, 1934), pp. 103–4.

Fevral'skii, Aleksandr V. "Tendentsii iskusstva i 'Radio Glaz' " [Artistic Tendencies in the "Radio-Eye"], *Molodaia gvardiia*, no. 7 (July 1925), p. 167.

—"Tri pesni o Lenine" [*Three Songs about Lenin*], Literaturnaia gazeta (July 16, 1934) (review).

—"Dziga Vertov i 'Pravdisti' " [Dziga Vertov and "Pravdists"], *Iskusstvo kino*, no. 13 (December 1965); French translation "Dziga Vertov et les Pravdisty" in *Cahiers du Cinéma*, no. 229 (May 1971), pp. 27–32.

Fisher, Lucy. *"Enthusiasm:* From Kino-Eye to Radio-Eye," *Film Quarterly*, no. 2 (Winter 1977), pp. 25–34.

Ganly, Raymond. *"Man with a Movie Camera*," *The Motion Picture News* (October 26, 1929), p. 2.

Gansera, Rainer. "Dziga Wertow," *Filmkritik*, no. 11–12 (Munich 1972), p. 567.

Giercke, Christoph. "Dziga Vertov," *Afterimage*, no. 1 (April 1970), p. 6.

Gorenko, O. "Maister kino-ob'ektiv" [*The Master of the Film Lens*], *Kino*, no. 54 (Kharkov: March 1929), p. 10.

Gusman, Boris. "O kino-glaze" [About Film-Eye], *Pravda* (October 15, 1924), p. 7.

—"Kino-pravda" [Film-Truth], *Pravda* (February 9, 1923), p. 5.

Hall, Mordaunt. "Floating Glimpses of Russia," *The New York Times* (September 17, 1929), p. 36.

Hamilton, James Shelley. "*Three Songs about Lenin*," *National Board of Review Magazine*, no. 9 (December 14, 1934), p. 8.

Helman, A. "Dziga Wiertow albo wszechobecnosc kamery. Nasz Iluzjon" [Dziga Vertov, or the Omnipresence of the Camera. Our Illusion], (Poland) *Kino*, VIII/5 (May 1973), pp. 62–4.

Herlinghaus, Hermann. "Wertow-Mayakowski – Futurismus; eine Praemisse Georges Sadouls" [Vertov-Mayakovsky – Futurism; One Premise of George Sadoul], *Filmwissenschaftliche Beitraege*, No. 14 (Berlin, D.D.R., 1963), pp. 154–71.

Herlinghaus, Ruth. "Dsiga Wertow" [Dziga Vertov], *Film*, no. 1 (D.D.R. 1964), pp. 220–30.

Herring, Robert. "Enthusiasm?" *Close Up*, no. 1 (March 1932), pp. 20–4.

—"*Three Songs about Lenin*," *Life and Letters Today*, no. 13 (December 1935), p. 188.

Hill, Steven P. "*The Man with the Movie Camera*," *Film Society Review*, (September 1967), pp. 28–31.

Hughes, J. Pennethorne. "Vertov ad Absurdum," *Close Up*, no. 3 (September 1932), pp. 174–6.

Ivanov, V. V. "Funktsii i kategorii iazyka kino" [The Categories and Functions of Film Language], *Trudy po znakovym sistemam*, no. 7 (1975), pp. 170–92.

Kaufman, Mikhail. "Cine analysis," *Experimental Cinema*, no. 4, pp. 21–3.

—"Le troisieme frere" [The Third Brother], *Cinéma 68*, no. 123 (February 1968), pp. 33–5 (interview with Marcel Matthieu).

—"Vertov tam zhe" [Vertov Is There], *Sovetskii ekran*, no. 45 (1928), p. 15.

—"An Interview," (with Annette Michelson and Naum Kleiman), *October*, no. 11 (Winter 1979), pp. 55–76.

Kaufman, Mikhail, and Elizaveta Vertova-Svilova. "U kinokov" [With the Kinoks], *LEF*, no. 4 (August 1924), pp. 220–1.

Khersonskii, Kh. "U istokov" [At the Source], *Sovetskii ekran*, no. 4 (1962), p. 9.

Kol'tsov, Mikhail. "U ekrana" [On the Screen], *Pravda* (November 28, 1922), p. 1.

Kopalin, Il'ia P. "A Life Illuminated by the Revolution," *Soviet Film*, no. 1 (1971), pp. 13–17.

Koster, Simon. "Dziga Vertoff," *Experimental Cinema*, no. 5 (1934), pp. 27–8.

Kracauer, Siegfried. "*Der Man Mit Dem Kinoapparat*," *Frankfurter Zeitung* (May 19, 1929), p. 2.

Krautz, A. "Chaplin: Die Professoren sollten von ihm lernen" [Chaplin: The Professors Should Learn from Him], *Film und Fernsehen*, II/2 (February 1974), pp. 41–2.

Kubelka, Peter. "Restoring 'Enthusiasm,'" *Film Quarterly*, no. 2 (Winter 1977), pp. 35–6.

"LEF i kino" [LEF and Film], *Novyi LEF,* no. 11–12 (1927), pp. 50–70; also in *Screen,* no. 4 (Winter 1971–2), pp. 74–80.

Lawton, Anna. "Dziga Vertov: A Futurist with a Movie Camera," *Film Studies Annual,* Part 1 (West Lafayette: Purdue University, 1977), pp. 65–73.

—"Rhythmic Montage in the Films of Dziga Vertov: A Poetic Use of the Language of Cinema," *Pacific Coast Philology,* Vol. XIII (October 1978), pp. 44–50.

Lebedev, Nikolai. "Za proleterskuiu kinopublitsistiku" [For the Proletarian Cinema Journalism], *Literatura i iskusstvo,* no. 9–10 (1931), pp. 3–47.

Lenauer, Jean. "Vertoff, His Work and His Future," *Close Up,* Vol. V, no. 6 (December 1929), pp. 446–68.

Leyda, Jay. *"Three Songs about Lenin,"* The Film Society Programme (London: October 27, 1935), unpaginated; reprinted in *The Film Society Programmes 1925–1939* (New York: Arno Press, 1972), pp. 331–4.

Listov, Viktor. "Na puti k 'Kinopravdy'" [On the Road to "Film-Truth"], *Iskusstvo kino,* no. 2 (1971), pp. 112–19.

—"Kak nachinalas' 'kino-pravda'?" [How Did "Film-Truth" Begin?], *Iskusstvo kino,* no. 7 (July 1972), pp. 96–106.

—"O pis'me iz Petrograda, 'Avtokino' i Vertove" [About a Letter from Petrograd, "Autocinema" and Vertov], *Iskusstvo kino,* no. 1 (January 1975), pp. 109–18.

Macdonald, Dwight. "Eisenstein and Pudovkin in the Twenties," *The Miscellany,* no. 6 (March 1931), p. 24.

Malevich, Kazimir. "I likuiut liki na ekrane" [And Images Triumph on the Screen], *Kunozhurnal ARK,* no. 10 (1925), pp. 7–9; also in *Essays on Art, 1915–1928,* edited by Troels Andersen and translated by Xenia Glowacky-Prus, Vol. 1 (Copenhagen: Bongen 1971), pp. 226–32.

Malcovati, F., ed. "Nikolai Abramov su Vertov" [Nikolai Abramov on Vertov], *Bianco e Nero,* nos. 1–2 (January–February 1973), pp. 65–6 (interview).

— ed. "Cinque domande a Naum Klejman" [Five Questions to Naum Klejman], *Bianco e Nero,* nos. 1–2 (January–February 1973), pp. 63–5 (interview).

Mayne, Judith. "Kino-Truth and Kino-Praxis: Vertov's *Man with a Movie Camera,"* Cine-Tracts, no. 2 (Summer 1977), pp. 81–91.

Michelson, Annette. *"The Man with the Movie Camera:* From Magician to Epistemologist," *Art Forum,* no. 7 (March 1972), pp. 60–72.

—"Dr. Craze and Mr. Clair," *October,* no. 11 (Winter 1979), pp. 31–53.

Moussinac, Leon. "Dziga Vertov et le Kino Pravda" [Dziga Vertov and the Film-Truth], *Miroir du Cinéma,* no. 3 (Paris, October 1962), pp. 38–41.

—"Dziga Vertov on Film Technique," *Filmfront,* no. 3 (January 28, 1935), pp. 7–9.

Oille, Jennifer, " 'Konstruktivizm' and 'Kinematografiya'," *Artforum,* no. 9 (May 1978), pp. 44–9.

Pertsov, Viktor. "Igra i demonstratsiia" [Play and Demonstration], *Novyi LEF,* nos. 11–12 (November–December 1928), pp. 33–44.

Petrić, Vlada. "Dziga Vertov and the Soviet Avant-garde of the 20's," *Soviet Union/Union Sovietique*, 10, Part 1 (1983), pp. 1–58.

—"Dziga Vertov as Theorist," *Cinema Journal*, no. 1 (Fall 1978), pp. 29–44.

—"The Difficult Years of Dziga Vertov: Excerpts From His Diaries," *Quarterly Review of Film Studies*, no. 6 (Winter 1982), pp. 7–21.

Pleynet, Marcellin. "Sur les avant-garde revolutionaires" [About the Revolutionary Avant-Garde], *Cahiers du Cinéma*, nos. 226–7 (January-February 1971), pp. 6–13.

Richter, Erica. "Dsiga Wertow: Publizist und Poet des Dokumentarfilms" [Dziga Vertov: Journalist and Poet of Documentary Films], *Filmwissenschaftlische Mitteilungen* (Berlin), no. 1 (March 1961), pp. 24–5.

Rouch, Jean. "Le film ethnographique" [The Ethnographic Film], *Ethnologie Generale* (Paris: Gallimard, 1968), pp. 37–44.

—"The Cinema of the Future," *Studies in Visual Communication*, no. 1 (Winter 1985), pp. 30–5.

Sadoul, Georges. "Dziga Vertov: Poet du ciné-oeil et prophète de la ciné-oreille" [Dziga Vertov: Poet of the "Film-Eye" and the Prophet of the "Film-Ear"], *Image et Son*, no. 183 (April 1965), pp. 8–18.

—"La notion d'intervalle" [The Notion of the Intervals], *Cahiers du Cinéma*, nos. 220–221 (May–June 1970), pp. 23–4.

—"Kinopravda no. 9," *Cahiers du Cinéma*, nos. 220–1 (May–June 1970), pp. 24–5.

—"Dziga Vertov e i futuristi italiani, Apollinaire e il montaggio delle registrazioni" [Dziga Vertov and the Italian Futurists, Apollinaire and the montage of Sound-Recording], *Bianco e Nero*, no. 7 (July 1964), pp. 1–27. The article is translated as "Les futuristes italianes et Vertov" [The Italian Futurists and Vertov] in *Cahiers du Cinéma*, nos. 220–1 (May–June 1970), pp. 19–22, and in Sadoul's *Dziga Vertov* as "Le montage des enregistrements" [The Montage of Sound-Recording], pp. 15–46.

—"*Kinoks*. Revolution," in *Historie generale du cinéma muet* (Paris: Denoel, 1964); reprinted in revised form in Sadoul's *Dziga Vertov*, pp. 70–100.

—"Bio-Filmographie de Dziga Vertov" [Bio-Filmography of Dziga Vertov], *Cahiers du Cinéma*, no. 146 (August 1963), pp. 21–9; reprinted in Sadoul's *Dziga Vertov*, pp. 145–71.

—"Actualité de Dziga Vertov" [The Reality of Dziga Vertov], *Cahiers du Cinéma*, no. 144 (June 1963), pp. 23–31; translated in Spanish in *Cine Cubano*, no. 72, pp. 98–105.

Sauzier, Bertrand. "An Interpretation of *Man with the Movie Camera*," *Studies in Visual Communication*, 11, no. 4 (Fall 1985), pp. 30–53.

Seton, Marie. "*Three Songs about Lenin*," *Film Art* (London: Winter 1934). Reprinted in Lewis Jacobs' *The Documentary Tradition* (New York: Hopkinson and Blake, 1971), p. 100.

Shklovskii, Viktor. "I 'kinoki' di Dziga Vertov" [The *Kinoks* of Dziga Vertov], *Filmcritica*, no. 201 (Rome: October 1969), pp. 314–15. The article is a translation of the material in *Ikh nastoiashche* [Their Genuineness].

—"Kinoki i nadpisi" [The *Kinoks* and the Intertitles], *Kino*, no. 44 (October 30, 1926), pp. 8–9.

—"Kuda shagaet Dziga Vertov" [Where is Dziga Vertov Marching], *Sovetskii ekran*, no. 32 (1926), pp. 6–7.

Shorin, A. "O tekhnicheskoi baze sovetskogo tonkino" [About the Technological Basis of Soviet Sound Film], *Kino i zhizn'*, no. 14 (1930), pp. 10–11.

Shutko, K. I. "Odinadtsatom" [For the Eleventh Year], *Odinnadtsatyi* (Moscow: Teakinopechat' 1928), pp. 25–7.

—"Chelovek s kinoapparatom" [*The Man with the Movie Camera*], Pravda (March 23, 1929), p. 6.

Skwara, J. "Dziga Wiertow wczoraj i dzis" [Dziga Vertov, Yesterday and Today], *Kino*, no. 8 (August 1973), pp. 41–3. Also in *Young Cinema* (Prague) no. 4 (Winter 1974), pp. 35–41.

Sokolov, Ippolit. "Shestaia chast' mira" [*One Sixth of the World*], *Kinofront*, no. 2 (1927), p. 9.

Svilova, Elizaveta. "V soviete troikh" [In the Council of Three], *LEF*, no. 4 (August 4, 1924), pp. 220–1.

Toti, Gianni. "La 'produttività' dei materiali di Ejzenstejn e Dziga Vertov" [The Productivity of the Materials of Eisenstein and Dziga Vertov], *Cinema e Film*, no. 3 (Summer 1967), pp. 281–7.

Vaughan, Dai. "*The Man with the Movie Camera,*" *Films and Filming*, no. 7 (November, 1960), pp. 18–20.

Verdone, Mario. "Dziga Vertov nell' avanguardia" [Dziga Vertov in the Avant-garde], *Filmcritica*, nos. 139–40 (Rome: November-December 1963), pp. 661–76.

Viazzi, Glauco. "Dziga Vertov et la tendenza documentaristica" [Dziga Vertov and the Documentary Tendency], *Ferrania* (Milano: August-September 1957), pp. 8–9.

"Vystavka Dzigi Vertova v Berline" [The Dziga Vertov Exhibit in Berlin], *Kino*, no. 3 (March 1974), p. 191.

Wienberg, Herman. "*The Man with the Movie Camera,*" *Film Comment*, no. 1 (Fall 1966), pp. 40–2.

Wibom, Anna-Lena. "Tre sanger om Lenin – Dziga Vertov 1934" [*Three Songs about Lenin* – Dziga Vertov 1934], *Chaplin* no. 6, (Stockholm) pp. 217–23.

Williams, Alan. "The Camera-Eye and the Film: Notes on Vertov's Formalism," *Wide Angle*, no. 3 (1979), pp. 12–17.

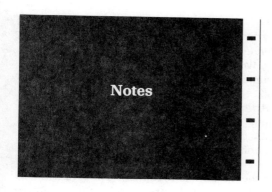

Notes

Chapter I

1. Elizaveta Svilova, "In the Council of Three" [*V Soviete troikh*], *LEF*, no. 4 (August 4, 1924), p. 220. The article is preceded by a brief statement entitled "With the *Kinoks*" [*U kinokov*], signed by Mikhail Kaufman who refers to Svilova as "the first *kinok*-editor."

2. Svilova, ibid., p. 221.

3. Dziga Vertov, "The Basics of 'Film-Eye' " (1924) [*Osnovnoe 'kinoglaza'*], in *Articles, Diaries, Projects* [*Stat'i, dnevniki, zamysli*], ed. Sergei Drobashenko (Moscow: Iskusstvo, 1966), p. 81. Later cited as *Articles*. The translation of the quotations in this book is mine. The existing collection, *Kino-Eye: The Writings of Dziga Vertov* (Berkeley: University of California Press, 1984), trans. Kevin O'Brien, edited and with an introduction by Annette Michelson, is available for additional information about Vertov's work.

4. Vertov, ibid., p. 82.

5. Dziga Vertov, "*Kinoks*. Revolution" (1923), [*Kinoki. Pereverot*], *Articles*, pp. 55–6. Originally published in *LEF* (June 1923), no. 3, p. 135, along with Eisenstein's statement, "Montage of Attractions" [*Montazh attraktsionov*], p. 70. Although the above translation of the title of Vertov's article is widely accepted, it would be more correct to translate it as "*Kinoks*. Overthrow."

6. Naum Gabo and Antonin Pevsner, "A Realist Manifesto," trans. Naum Gabo, in Teresa Newman, *Naum Gabo* (London: Tate Gallery, 1967), p. 34.

7. Vertov, "We. A Variant of a Manifesto" [*My. Variant manifesta*], *Articles*, p. 45. Originally published in *Kinofot* (no. 1, 1922), one of the first Soviet film journals edited by Aleksei Gan and designed by Alexandr Rodchenko.

8. Vertov, ibid., p. 47.

9. Michael Kirby, *Futurist Performance* (New York: Dutton Press, 1971), p. 213.

10. Lev Kuleshov, "Americanitis" [*Amerikanshchina*], (1922), *Kinofot*, no. 1 (1922), pp. 14–15. Also in *Kuleshov on Film*, trans. Ronald Levaco (Los Angeles: University of California Press, 1974), p. 129. The English translation is mine.

11. Vertov, "We. A Variant of a Manifesto," *Articles*, p. 47.

12. Annette Michelson, *Kino-Eye: The Writings of Dziga Vertov*, pp. XLII–XLIII (Introduction).

13. Richard Kostelanetz, ed., *Moholy-Nagy* (New York: Praeger, 1970), pp. 118–23. Also in Istvan Nemeskurty, *Word and Image* (London: Clematis Press, 1961), pp. 62–7. The script "Dynamics of a Metropolis: A Film Sketch" was originally drafted in Berlin, 1921–22.

14. Vertov, "*Kinok*s. Revolution," *Articles*, p. 55.

15. Alexandr Rodchenko, "Warning" [*Predosterezhenie*], *Novyi LEF*, no. 11, 1928, pp. 36–7.

16. See Herbert Eagle, *Russian Formalist Theory* (Ann Arbor: University of Michigan Press, 1981), p. 4–20.

17. See John Bolt, "Alexander Rodchenko as Photographer," *The Avant-Garde in Russia 1910–1930*, eds. Stephani Barron and Maurice Tuchman (Los Angeles County Museum of Art, 1980), p. 55.

18. Camila Gray, *The Russian Experiment in Art: 1863–1922* (New York: Harry N. Abrams, 1962), p. 271.

19. Viktor Shklovsky, "Alexandr Rodchenko: Artist-Photographer" [*Aleksandr Rodchenko: khudozhnik-fotograf*], *Prometei*, no. 1 (1966), p. 402.

20. Unsigned, "The Constructivists" [*Konstruktivisty*], *LEF*, no. 1, (March, 1923), p. 251.

21. Vertov, "We. A Variant of a Manifesto," *Articles*, p. 46.

22. El Lissitzky and Ilya Ehrenburg, "Veshch' / Gegenstand / Objet," an editorial in the journal *Veshch' / Gegenstand / Objet*, no. 1–2 (March–April, 1922), p. 1. After three issues, the journal folded.

23. Vertov, "From 'Film-Eye' to 'Radio-Eye' – From the Alphabet of *Kinok*s" (1929). [*Ot "kinoglaza" k "radioglazu" – Iz azbuki kinokov*], *Articles*, p. 112.

24. Vertov, "*Kinok*s. Revolution." The quotation appears in the paragraph entitled "The Council of Three" [*Soviet troikh*], p. 55.

25. Vertov, "About the Importance of Unstaged Cinema" (1923), [*O znachenii neigrovoi kinematografii*], *Articles*, p. 71.

26. Gan, "Constructivism in Cinema" [Konstruktivizm v fil'me], as quoted in *The Tradition of Constructivism*, ed. Stephen Bann (New York: Viking Press, 1974), p. 130.

27. Vertov, "About the Importance of Unstaged Cinema," *Articles*, p. 71.

28. Vertov, "The Artistic Drama and 'Film-Eye,' " (1924) [*Khudozhestvennaia drama i 'kinoglaz'*], *Articles*, p. 81.

29. Vertov, "About 'Film Truth' " (1924) [*O 'kinopravde'*], *Articles*, p. 78.

30. Gan, "Constructivism in Cinema," *The Tradition of Constructivism*, p. 129.

31. Gan, *Long Live the Demonstration of Everyday Life* [*Da zdravstvuet demonstratsiia byta*] (Moscow: Goskino, 1923), p. 14.

32. Jennifer Oille, " 'Konstruktivizm' and 'Kinematografiya' " *Artforum*, 16, no. 9, May 1978, p. 45.

33. Gan, "Film-Truth: The Thirteenth Essay" [*Kinopravda: trinadtsatyi opyt*], *Kinofot*, no. 5 (December 10, 1922), pp. 6–7.

34. Tamara Selezneva, *Film Thought of the 1920s* [*Kinomysl' 1920kh godov*] (Moscow: Iskusstvo, 1972), p. 32.

35. Gan, *Constructivism*, pp. 2, 3, 18.

36. Vertov, "About Film-Truth," *Articles*, p. 79.

37. Vertov, "Artistic Drama and 'Film-Eye,' " *Articles*, p. 81.

38. Vertov, *"Kinoks*. Revolution," *Articles,* p. 58.

39. Vertov, *"Kinoks*. Revolution," *LEF,* no. 3 (1923), p. 135. In addition to some minor discrepancies, the reprinted essay in *Articles* does not contain the epigraph printed in *LEF* above the text in different letter style.

40. Viktor Pertsov, " 'Play' and Demonstration" [*"Igra" i demonstratsiia*], *Novyi LEF,* no. 11–12 (1927), pp. 35–42.

41. Sergei Ermolinskii, "At the Pushkin Monument" [*U pamiatnika Push-kinu*], in *Dziga Vertov in Recollections of His Contemporaries* [Dziga Vertov v vospominaniiakh sovremenikov], eds. E. I. Vertova-Svilova and A. L. Vinogradova (Moscow: Iskusstvo, 1976), p. 202.

42. Ermolinskii, ibid.

43. *"LEF* and Film" [*LEF i kino*], *Novyi LEF,* no. 11–12 (1927), p. 51. Also in *Screen,* London, no. 4 (Winter 1971–2), p. 74–7.

44. *"LEF* and Film," ibid., p. 52.

45. Vladimir Mayakovsky, "About Film" (1927) [*O kino*], in *Complete Works* [*Polnoe sobranie sochinenii*], XII, (Moscow: Gosudarstvennoe izdatel'stvo khu-dozhestvennoi literatury, 1959), p. 147.

46. "The *LEF* Ring" [*Rink Lefa*], *Novyi LEF,* no. 4, (1928), p. 29. Partially translated in *Screen,* no. 4 (Winter 1971–2), pp. 83–8. The characteristic subtitle of this discussion reads: "Comrades! Hit Each Other With Ideas!" [*Tovarishchi! Shibaites' mneniami!*].

47. Sergei Tretyakov, "The New Tolstoi" [*Novyi Tolstoi*], *Novyi LEF,* no. 1 (1928), p. 1. Following the futurist habit, Tretyakov coined the "verb" from the names Mary Pickford and Henry Ford ("pickfordization").

48. Anatoly Lunacharsky, "Lenin and Film" [*Lenin i kino*] in *Lenin About Culture and Art* [*Lenin o kul'ture i iskusstve*], a collection of articles (Moscow: IZOGIZ, 1938), p. 311.

49. See "Filmography of American Silent Films in Soviet Distribution" [*Fil-mografiia amerikanskykh nemykh fil'mov byvshikh v sovetskom prokate*], *Kino i vremia* [Film and Time], (Moscow: Vsesoiuznyi gosudarstvennyii fond kinofi-l'mov inisterstva kul'tury SSSR, 1960), pp. 212–324; "French Silent Films in Soviet Distribution [*Frantsuzkie nemye fil'my v sovetskom prokate*], and "German Silent Films in Soviet Distribution" [*Nemetskie nemye fil'my v sovetskom prokate*], *Kino i vremia* (Moscow: Gosfil'mfond, 1965), pp. 348–79, 380–476. Overall, the filmography of the foreign silent films distributed in the Soviet Union between 1922 and 1933 includes 956 American, 535 German, and 202 French commercial titles.

50. Vertov, " 'Film-Truth' and 'Radio-Truth' " [*"Kinopravda" i "radiopravda"*] (1925), *Articles,* pp. 84–5.

51. Vertov, "In Defense of Newsreels" (1939), [*V zashchitu khroniki*], *Articles,* p. 153. For a definition of "typage," see note 126.

52. Vertov, "In Defense of Newsreels," *Articles,* p. 153. The sentence reads: "Bor'ba protiv igrovoi fil'my v khronikal'nykh shtanakh."

53. Vertov, *ibid.*

54. Vertov, "About My Illness" (1935), [*O moei bolezni*], *Articles,* p. 190.

55. Vertov, ibid., p. 189.

56. Herbert Marshall, *Masters of the Soviet Cinema: Crippled Creative Bio-graphies* (Boston: Routledge & Kegan Paul, 1983), p. 86.

57. Vertov, "The Latest Experiment" (1935) [*Poslednii opyt*], *Articles*, p. 145.

58. Vertov, "Notebooks" (September 7, 1938), *Articles*, p. 219

59. Vertov, "Autobiography" [*Autobiografiia*], *From the History of Cinema: Materials and Documents* [*Iz istorii kino: materialy i dokumenty*] (Moscow: Akademiia nauk SSSR, 1959), p. 29.

60. Vertov, ibid., p. 85.

61. Mayakovsky, "How to Make Verses" (1926) [*Kak delat' stikhi*], *Complete Works*, XII, p. 85.

62. Mayakovsky, "Morning," (1912) [*Utro*], *Complete Works*, I, p. 34.

63. Edward Brown, *Mayakovsky: A Poet in the Revolution* (Princeton: Princeton University Press, 1973), p. 75.

64. Vertov, "From 'Film-Eye' to 'Radio-Eye,' " *Articles*, p. 114.

65. Osip Brik, "Contributions to the Study of Verse Language," *Readings in Russian Poetics: Formalist and Structuralist Views,"* eds. L. Matejka and K. Pomorska (Cambridge: MIT Press), pp. 117–25.

66. Vertov, "Mouths are Gaping through the Window" [*Rty u vitrin*], as cited by Lev Roshal' in *Dziga Vertov*, p. 35. For more information about the "Great Famine," see note 79.

67. Mayakovsky, "Conversation with a Tax Inspector About Poetry" (1926), [*Razgovor s fininspektorom o poezii*], *Complete Works*, VII, pp. 120–1. The translation is by Herbert Marshall, *Mayakovsky*, pp. 352–53. The original lines read: "Govoria po-nashemu, / rifma – / bochka. / Bochka s dinamitom. / Strochka – fitil'. Stroka dodymit, / vzryvaetsia strochka, –/ i gorod / na vozdukh / strofoi letit."

68. As cited by Mikhail Kaufman in *Dziga Vertov in Recollections of His Contemporaries*, p. 71.

69. Kaufman, ibid.

70. Mayakovsky, "Film and Film" (1922) [*Kino i kino*], *Complete Works*, XII, p. 29. The poem was originally published in *Kinofot*, no. 4, (October 4–12, 1922), p. 2.

71. Mayakovsky, "Theater, Cinematography, Futurism" (1913) [*Teatr, kinematograf, futurizm*], *Complete Works*, I, p. 295. The article was originally published in *Kinozhurnal*, no. 14 (July 14, 1913), p. 3.

72. Mayakovsky, "The Destruction of the 'Theater' by Cinematography as a Sign of a Rebirth of the Theatrical Art" (1913) [*Unichtozhenie kinematografom 'teatra' kak priznak vozrozhdeniia teatral'noga iskusstva*], *Complete Works*, I, p. 278. The article was initially published in *Kinozhurnal*, no. 16, August 1913, p. 5.

73. Mayakovsky, "The Relationship of Today's Theater and Cinematography to Art" (1913) [*Otnoshenie segodniashnego teatra i kinematografii k iskusstvu*], *Complete Works*, I, p. 281. The article was initially published in *Kinozhurnal*, no. 17, Sept 8, 1913, p. 7.

74. Mayakovsky, ibid., p. 284.

75. A note scribbled by Tsar Nikolai II on the margin of a police report, in 1913. Quoted by I. S. Zilbershtein in "Nikolai II About Film" [*Nikolai II o kino*], *Sovetskii ekran*, April 12, 1927, p. 10.

76. Vertov, "We. A Variant of a Manifesto," *Articles*, p. 49.

77. Vertov, "About the Importance of Newsreels" [*O znachenii khroniki*] (1923), *Articles*, p. 67.

78. Tretyakov, *"LEF* and NEP" [*LEF i NEP*], *LEF*, no. 2, April 1923, pp. 70–8.

79. Vertov, "Mouths are Gaping through the Window," as cited by Lev Roshal' in *Dziga Vertov*, p. 35. Although not dated, the poem was probably written between 1932 and 1933, at the time the Ukraine, Kazakhstan, and Volga regions were struck by famine; almost six million people, mostly peasants and their children, died – a fact the official Soviet press has never admitted. See Maksudov, "Geography of the Hunger of 1933" [*Geografiia goloda 1933 goda*], *SSSR: vnutrennie protivorechiia*, no. 7 (New York: Chalidze Publications, 1983), pp. 5–17. Herbert Marshall, on the other hand, doubts that Vertov would have written about the famine of 1932–3, which was man-made by Stalin to crush the Ukrainian "kulaks" and therefore was forbidden to be discussed. In contrast, the natural famine of 1922, was extensively covered by the press, and many artists dealt with it, including Mayakovsky who dedicated to it his 1922 poem "Volga."

80. Mayakovsky, as cited in *Speeches Delivered at a Dispute About the Politics of Sovkino* [*Vstupleniia na dispute o politike Sovkino*] (1927), (Moscow: Iskusstvo, 1954), pp. 441–2.

81. Mayakovsky, "Film and Wine" [*Kino i vino*] (1928), *Complete Works*, IX, p. 64. Originally published in *Kinofot*, no. 4–5 (1922), p. 2. The poem opens with the lines: "Skazal / filosof iz Sovkino: / "Rodnie sestry / kino i vino."

82. Mayakovsky, "Film and Film," *Complete Works*, XII, p. 29. Ivan Mozhukin (1890–1939) was the famous Russian actor who moved to Paris after the revolution. He was known for highly emotional performances in conventional melodramas before 1918. Kuleshov used one of Mozhukin's old close-ups for his montage experiment known as the "Kuleshov effect."

83. Annette Michelson, *Kino-Eye: The Writings of Dziga Vertov*, p. LXI (Introduction).

84. Vertov, "About Mayakovsky" (1934) [*O Maiakovskom*], *Articles*, p. 182.

85. Vertov, "More About Mayakovsky" (1935) [*Eshche o Maiakovskom*], *Articles*, p. 184.

86. Vertov, "Notebooks" (February 29, 1936), *Articles*, p. 200.

87. Sergei Eisenstein, "Word and Image," *The Film Sense*, ed. and trans. Jay Leyda (New York, Harcourt, Brace & World, 1947), p. 63. The original essay, "Montage 1938" [*Montazh 1928*], was changed in the English translation to "Word and Image." Actually, this was the second part of Eisenstein's extensive study on montage which at that time had not yet been published. The other part, written in 1937, was published for the first time in Eisenstein's *Selected Works* [*Izabrannye proizvedeniia*] (Moscow: Iskusstvo, 1964), pp. 329–484.

88. Vertov, *"The Man with the Movie Camera* – A Visual Symphony" [*Chelovek s kinoapparatom – zritel'naia symfoniia*] (1929), *Articles*, pp. 278–9. Vertov wrote several articles explaining this film and its structure. This is the first manifesto related to the film, published in February 1929, at the time of the film's release in Kiev and Moscow. The second manifesto, entitled *"The Man with the Movie Camera:* The Absolute Film and the Radio-Eye" [*Ludina z kinoaparatom: absolutnii kinopis i radio-oko*], was published two months later in the Ukrainian journal *Nova generatsiia* (Khrakov). A detailed analysis of both manifestos can be found in my article, "Dziga Vertov as Theorist," *Cinema Journal*, XVIII, no. 1 (Fall, 1978), pp. 29–47.

89. Mayakovsky, "Conversation with a Tax Inspector about Poetry," in *Complete Works*, VII, p. 121. The translation is by Herbert Marshall, *Mayakovsky*, p. 353. The original lines read: "Poeziia – / ta zhe dobycha / radiia / v gramm dobicha, / v god trudy. / Izvodish' / edinoga slova radi / tysiachi toni / slovesnoi rudy."

90. Vertov, "About Mayakovsky," *Articles*, p. 185.

91. Vertov, ibid., p. 289.

92. Vertov, "A Girl Plays the Piano," *Articles*, p. 291.

93. Vertov, ibid., p. 297.

94. Vladimir Markov, *Russian Futurism: A History* (Berkeley: University of California Press, 1968), p. 185. Another study related to this topic is *Russian Formalism: History – Doctrine,* by Victor Erlich (The Hague, Netherlands: Mouton, 1955), with an excellent chapter entitled "Marxism versus Formalism."

95. Anna Lawton, "Dziga Vertov: A Futurist with a Movie Camera," *Film Studies Annual* (West Lafayette: Purdue University, 1977), Part One, p. 66.

96. For more information about the technique used in the ROSTA posters, see Roberta Reeder, "The Interrelationship of Codes in Mayakovsky's ROSTA Posters," *Soviet Union / Union Sovietique,* no. 7 (1980), p. 41.

97. Mayakovsky, "Cloud in Trousers" (1914–15) [*Oblako v shtanakh*], *Complete Works*, I, p. 185. The translation is by Max Hayward and George Reavey, *The Bedbug and Selected Poetry*, p. 79. The original lines read: "A za poètami – / ulichnye tyshchi: / studenty, / prostitutki, / podriadchiki. / ... "Pomogi mne!" / Molit' o gimne, / ob oratorii! / My sami tvortsy v goriashchem gimne – / shume fabriki i laboratorii."

98. Mayakovsky, "Brooklyn Bridge" (1925) [*Bruklinskii most*], *Complete Works*, VII, p. 83. The translation is by Herbert Marshall, *Mayakovsky*, p. 337.

99. For an extensive discussion of "Zaum," see Marsha Enzensberger, "Dziga Vertov," *Screen*, no. 4 (Winter 1972–3), p. 55; or *Screen Reader* I (London: SEFT, 1977), p. 37. In Russian, the best explanation of "Zaum poetry" [*zaumnaia poezia*], as well as other formalist terms, is provided by Boris Thomashevsky, *Theory of Literature* [*Teoriia literatury*] (Leningrad: Gosudarstvennoe izdatel'stvo, 1925), p. 68.

100. Vertov, "My Last Experiment," *Articles*, p. 144.

101. Fevralsky, "The Forwardlooking" [*Vperedsmotriashchii*], Dziga Vertov in Recollections of His Contemporaries, p. 140–3.

102. Vertov, "More About Mayakovsky," *Articles*, p. 184.

103. Vertov, "The Importance of Newsreels," *Articles*, p. 67.

104. Vertov, "More About Mayakovsky," *Articles*, p. 184.

105. Raymond Durgnat, "*Man with a Movie Camera*," *American Film*, Oct. 1984, p. 79.

106. Vertov, "About the Importance of Unstaged Cinema," *Articles*, p. 71.

107. Esfir Shub, "My Life – Cinema" [*Zhizn' moia – kinematograf*] (Moscow: Iskusstvo 1972), p. 380.

108. As quoted by Boris Thomson, *Lot's Wife and the Venus of Milo* (Cambridge: University of Cambridge Press, 1978), p. 73.

109. Viktor Shklovsky, *Their Genuineness* [*Ikh nastoiashchee*] (Moscow: Kino-pechat', 1927), pp. 24–5. Also in *For Forty Years* [*Za sorok let*] (Moscow: Iskusstvo, 1956), pp. 71–2.

110. Viktor Shklovsky, *Eisenstein* [*Èizenshtein*] (Moscow: Iskusstvo, 1973), p. 142.

111. Sergei Drobashenko, *Phenomenon of Authenticity* [*Fenomen dostovernosti*] (Moscow: Akademiia nauk SSSR, 1972), pp. 48–50.

112. Tamara Selezneva, *Film Thought of the 1920s*, pp. 26–56.

113. Vertov, "In Defense of Newsreels," *Articles*, p. 153.

114. Eisenstein, "Toward the Question of a Materialist Approach to Form" (1925) [*K voprosu o materialisticheskom podkhode k forme*], *Selected Works*, I, (Moscow: Iskusstvo, 1964), pp. 113–14. Translation is mine. Also, in *The Avant-Garde Film*, ed., P. Adam Sitney (New York: New York University Press, 1978), pp. 15–22, translated by Roberta Reeder.

115. Vertov, "The Factory of Facts" (1926) [*Fabrika Faktov*], *Articles*, p. 89. Originally published in *Pravda* (July 24, 1926), p. 6.

116. Shub, in *Close-Up* [*Krupnym planom*] (Moscow: Iskusstvo, 1959), p. 113.

117. Svilova, "A Recollection about Vertov" [*Pamiat' o Vertove*], *Dziga Vertov in Recollections of His Contemporaries*, p. 69.

118. Svilova, ibid.

119. Drobashenko, *Phenomenon of Authenticity*, p. 65.

120. Drobashenko, ibid., p. 66.

121. Drobashenko, ibid., p. 67.

122. Eisenstein, "Through Theater to Cinema" [*Srednaia iz trekh, 1924–9*], in *Film Form*, ed., trans. Jay Leyda (New York: Harcourt, Brace & World, 1949), p. 5.

123. Eisenstein, "Toward the Question of a Materialist Approach to Form," *Selected Work*, I, pp. 113–14.

124. Eisenstein, ibid., p. 114.

125. Shklovsky, "Where is Dziga Vertov Marching?" [*Kuda shagaet Dziga Vertov?*], *Sovetskii ekran* (August 10, 1926), p. 4.

126. "Typage" is a term with several definitions since its meaning evolved in the process of Eisenstein's own theoretical development. In the most general sense, typage implies "casting" both actors and nonprofessionals, insisting on the characteristic facial features that are capable of instantly revealing (on the screen) the typical psychology, social background, and behavior of the characters. Later, Eisenstein emphasized that "*typage* must be understood as broader than merely a face without make-up or substitution of 'naturally expressive' types for professional actors," and proposed that the definition of typage be understood as "the filmmaker's specific approach to the events embraced by the content of the film." *Film Form*, p. 8.

127. Osip Brik, "The *LEF* Ring," *Novyi LEF*, no. 4 (1928), p. 29. In his discussion, Brik also stated: "In order to show Lenin's figure in *October*, Eisenstein opted for the most shameful method, a method below any cultural standard. He found a person, i.e., the worker Nikandrov, resembling Lenin, to play Lenin. The result turned out to be a presumptuous fake which can satisfy only those spectators who are totally insensitive to historical truth" (p. 30). Soon after the discussion about *October*, the practice of impersonating Lenin, Stalin, and other Soviet leaders became common in Soviet cinema. Certain actors even specialized in playing exclusively the roles of important Soviet leaders in feature films.

128. Mayakovsky, "About Film," *Complete Works,* XII, p. 147.

129. Eisenstein, "Montage of Attractions" [*Montazh attraktsionov*], *LEF* (June 1923), no. 3, p. 70. Also, *The Film Sense,* pp. 230–1.

130. Vertov, "Kinoks. Revolution," *LEF* (June 1923), no. 3, p. 135. Also, *Articles,* p. 55.

131. Eisenstein, "On the Question of a Materialist Approach to Form," *Selected Works,* I, pp. 113–14.

132. Eisenstein, ibid., p. 114.

133. Eisenstein, ibid., p. 115.

134. Vertov, "The Factory of Facts" (1926), *Articles,* pp. 88–9.

135. Vertov, ibid., p. 89.

136. Eisenstein, "The Fourth Dimension in Film" (1929), [*Chetvertoe izmerenie v kino*], *Selected Works,* II, p. 51. Also, *Film Form,* p. 73. In the original, the quotation reads: "Podobnym otritsatel'nym primerom mozhet sluzhit *Odinnatsatyi* Dzigi Vertova gde metricheskii modul' nastol'ko matematicheski slozhen, chto ustanovit' v nem zakonomernost' mozhno tol'ko s arshinom v rukakh, to est' ne vospriiatiem a izmereniem."

137. Eisenstein, "Behind the Frame" (1929) [*Za kadrom*], *Selected Works,* II, p. 295. Also, *Film Form,* p. 43. In the original, the quotation reads: "Eshche chasche – prosto formal'nye biriul'ki i nemotirovannoe ozornichan'e kameroi (Chelovek s kinoapparatom)."

138. Eisenstein, "What Lenin Gave To Me" (1932) [*Chto mne dal V. I. Lenin*], *Selected Works,* V, p. 530. The article was published for the first time in *Iskusstvo kino,* no. 4 (1964), pp. 2–8.

139. Andrei Zhdanov (1896–1948) one of the most orthodox party officials, was responsible for the appropriate realization of socialist realism in Soviet art. Throughout the 1930s and 1940s, Zhdanov's power became so strong that this entire period of artistic suppression is known as "Zhdanovism." Already at the First Congress of the Union of Soviet Writers, in 1934, he launched a "practical definition" of the doctrine by demanding that all Soviet artists "produce a truthful and historically concrete representation of reality, combined with the task of ideological transformation and political education in the spirit of Socialist Realism." As quoted by Slonim, *Soviet Russian Literature,* p. 151.

140. Eisenstein, "Pantagruel is Born" (1933) [*Roditsia Pantagruel*], *Selected Works,* II, p. 300.

141. Eisenstein, "Film Directing. The Art of Mise-en-Scène" (1933–4) [*Rezhissura. Iskusstvo mizanstseny*], *Selected Works,* IV, p. 67. It appeared for the first time in Eisenstein's *Selected Works,* published in 1956.

142. Eisenstein, ibid. In the original, the sentence reads: "Gipertrofiiu montazha v ushcherb izobrazheniiu-kadru mozhno bylo by rassmatrivat' kak svoeobraznuiu kinoshizofreniiu."

143. Eisenstein, "The Most Important of the Arts" (1935) [*Samoe vazhnoe iz iskusstv*], *Selected Works,* V, p. 530.

144. Eisenstein, "Twenty" (1940) [*Dvadtsat'*], *Selected Works,* V, p. 104.

145. Eisenstein, "About Stereoscopic Film" (1948) [*O stereokino*], *Selected Works*, III, p. 130.

146. Eisenstein, Pudovkin, Yutkevich, "Statement," *Film Form*, p. 257. The original title was "The Future of the Sound Film – A Statement" [*Budushchee zvukovoi fil'my – Zaiavka*], *Selected Works*, II, p. 315.

147. Vertov, "Let Us Discuss First Sound Film, *Symphony of the Don Basin* Produced by Ukrainfilm" (1931) [*Obsuzhdaem pervuiu zvukovuiu fil'mu Ukrainfil'm, "Simfoniia Donbassa"*], *Articles*, p. 125.

148. Vertov, ibid.

149. As stated by Elizaveta Svilova in an interview with Seth Feldman in *Evolution of Style in the Early Work of Dziga Vertov*, a facsimile reprint of Feldman's dissertation (New York: Arno Press, 1977), p. 166. The interview took place in Stockholm (March 7, 1974).

150. Ippolit Sokolov, "The Potentialities of Sound Cinema" [*Vozmozhnosti zvukovogo kino*], *Kino*, no. 45 (February, 1929), p. 5.

151. Sokolov, ibid.

152. Sokolov, ibid.

153. Eisenstein et al., "Statement," *Film Form*, p. 258.

154. Vertov, "The First Steps," *Articles*, p. 129.

155. Vertov, ibid.

156. Vertov, "In Defense of Newsreels," *Articles*, p. 154.

157. Vertov, "Notebooks" (February 12, 1940), *Articles*, p. 229.

158. Vertov, "Notebooks" (February 12, 1940), *Articles*, p. 228.

159. Vertov, ibid.

160. Vertov, "Stanzas About Myself" [*Stikhi o sebe*], as quoted by Lev Roshal', *Dziga Vertov*, p. 6. The poem is not dated.

161. Vertov, "Notebooks" (February 4, 1940), *Articles*, p. 228. In the original the sentence reads: "Mozhno li umeret' ne ot fizicheskogo a ot tvorcheskogo goloda? Mozhno!"

162. Cited by Osip Brik in his essay "Mayakovsky and the Literary Movement of 1917–30" (1936). The quotation is taken from the English translation of the essay by Diana Matias, published in *Screen*, London, no. 3 (Autumn 1974), pp. 59–81.

163. Brik, ibid., pp. 70–8.

164. Vertov, "Notebooks" (May 17, 1934), *Articles*, p. 178.

165. Vertov, "Notebooks" (May 19, 1934), *Articles*, p. 178.

166. Vertov, "Notebooks" (December 25, 1939), *Articles*, p. 227.

167. Vertov, "Notebooks" (August 14, 1939), *Articles*, p. 224.

168. K. I. Shutko, "*The Man with the Movie Camera*" [*Chelovek s kinoapparatom*], *Pravda*, March 23, 1929, p. 4.

169. Ermolinskii, "At the Pushkin Monument," *Dziga Vertov in Recollections of His Contemporaries*, p. 200.

170. As quoted by Lev Roshal' in his book *Dziga Vertov* (Moscow: Iskusstvo, 1982), pp. 200–4.

171. Roshal', ibid.

172. Roshal', ibid.

173. Roshal', ibid.

174. A. Fedorov-Davydov, "Toward a Realist Art" [*K realisticheskomu is-kusstvu*], *Kino,* March 30, 1936, p. 4.

175. Vertov, "In Defense of Newsreels" (1939), *Articles,* p. 154.

176. Vertov, "Notebooks" (March 26, 1944), *Articles,* p. 253.

177. Vertov, "Notebooks" (August 14, 1943), *Articles,* p. 246.

178. See Georges Sadoul, " 'Film-Truth' and 'Cinéma-Vérité' " [*Kinopravda et cinéma vérité*], Dziga Vertov (Paris: Edition Champ libre, 1971), pp. 108–38; "From Dziga Vertov to Jean Rouch" [*De Dziga Vertov a Jean Rouch*], pp. 139–44.

179. Nikolai Abramov, *Dziga Vertov* (Moscow: Izdatel'stvo Akademii Nauk, 1962), p. 98.

180. Jean Rouch, "Five Views On Vertov" [*Cinq regards sur Vertov*], in Georges Sadoul, *Dziga Vertov,* pp. 11–14.

181. Jean Laude, *L'année 1913* [*The year 1913*] (Paris: Klicksieck, 1971), p. 205. For more information about Zhdanov, see note 139.

182. Gerard Conio, "Debate on the Formal Method," *The Futurists, the Formalists, and the Marxist Critique,* ed., Cristopher Pike (Highland N.J.: Humanities Press, 1979), p. 45.

183. Vertov, "Notebooks" (March 26, 1944), *Articles,* p. 252.

184. Vertov, "Notebooks" (October 11, 1944), *Articles,* p. 261.

185. Vertov, "Notebooks" (September 7, 1938), *Articles,* p. 218.

Chapter II

1. Vertov, *"The Man with the Movie Camera"* (1928), *Articles,* p. 109.

2. Vertov, "From the History of the *Kinoks*" (1929), *Articles,* p. 118.

3. Annette Michelson, *Kino Eye: The Writings of Dziga Vertov,* p. XXIV (Introduction).

4. Stephen Croft and Olivia Rose, "An Essay Toward *Man with the Movie Camera,"* *Screen,* no. 1 (1977), p. 19.

5. Mikhail Kaufman, "Interview," *October,* p. 69.

6. Vertov, *"The Man with the Movie Camera," Articles,* p. 109.

7. Vertov, *"Kinoks* and Montage," p. 97, is a segment of the article "Temporary Instructions to the 'Film-Eye' Groups" (1929), *Articles,* pp. 94–104.

8. Croft and Rose, "An Essay Toward *Man with the Movie Camera," Screen,* no. 1, pp. 15–16.

9. Bertrand Sauzier, "An Interpretation of *Man with the Movie Camera," Studies in Visual Communication,* 11, no. 4 (Fall 1985), pp. 34–53.

10. Vertov, "About 'Film-Truth,' " (1924), *Articles,* p. 78.

11. Eisenstein, see Chapter I, note 137.

12. Vertov, "About the Importance of Unstaged Cinema," *Articles,* p. 71.

13. See, for example, Annette Michelson, *"The Man with the Movie Camera:* From Magician to Epistemologist," *Artforum,* no. 7. (March 1972), pp. 60–72.

14. Noel Burch, "Film's Institutional Mode of Representation and the Soviet Response," *October,* no. 11 (Winter 1979), p. 94. This is the authorized translation of the original paper delivered in French at the International Federation of Film Archives (FIAF) in Varna (Bulgaria), March 1977.

15. Vertov, *"The Man with the Movie Camera* – A Visual Symphony," *Articles,* p. 280.

16. Vertov, "A Letter from Berlin" (1929) [*Pis'mo iz Berlina*], *Articles,* p. 121.

17. Vertov, *"The Man with the Movie Camera* – A Visual Symphony" (1929), *Articles,* p. 280.

18. Vertov, ibid., p. 278.

19. Vertov, "About 'Film-Truth' " (1924), *Articles,* p. 78.

20. Vertov, *"The Man with the Movie Camera* – A Visual Symphony," *Articles,* p. 279.

21. Vertov, *"The Man with the Movie Camera," Articles,* p. 106.

22. Friedrich Engels, *Anti-Dühring,* as quoted in *Marxism and Art,* ed., M. Solomon (New York: Vintage Books, 1974), p. 28.

23. Eisenstein, "Methods of Montage," *Film Form,* p. 83.

24. Eisenstein, "The Filmic Fourth Dimension," *Film Form,* p. 69.

25. Vertov, "About the Importance of Unstaged Cinema," *Articles,* p. 71.

26. Vertov, "The Artistic Drama and 'Film-Eye,' " *Articles,* p. 81.

27. Pudovkin, "Close-Up of Time," *Film Technique and Film Acting,* p. 146.

28. Vertov, "The Birth of 'Film-Eye' " (1924), *Articles,* p. 15.

29. Vertov, *"Kinoks.* Revolution," *Articles,* p. 55.

30. Vertov, "Notebooks" (September 6, 1936), *Articles,* p. 198.

Chapter III

1. Arthur Knight, *The Liveliest Art* (New York: Mentor Books, 1979), p. 86.

2. Vertov, *"The Man with the Movie Camera," Articles,* p. 109.

3. Anna Lawton, "Rhythmic Montage in the Films of Dziga Vertov: A Poetic Use of the Language of Cinema," *Pacific Coast Philology,* Vol. XIII (October 1978), p. 44.

4. Vertov, "About Mayakovsky," *Articles,* p. 183.

5. Vertov, "From 'Film-Eye' to 'Radio-Eye,' " *Articles,* p. 114.

6. Vertov, "We. A Variant of a Manifesto," *Articles,* p. 49.

7. Vertov, ibid.

8. Vertov, ibid., p. 48.

9. Vertov, ibid., p. 47.

10. Eisenstein, "The Cinematographic Principle and Ideogram," *Film Form,* pp. 38–40. The original title of this essay, "Behind the shot" [*Za kadrom*], was published in 1929, the year *The Man with the Movie Camera* was completed.

11. Eisenstein, ibid., p. 47.

12. Vertov, "We. A Variant of a Manifesto" (1922), *Articles,* p. 47.

13. Vertov, "About Love for a Living Man" (1958), *Articles,* p. 159.

14. Vertov, *"The Man with the Movie Camera," Articles,* p. 109.

15. Wilson Bryan Key, *Subliminal Seduction: Ad Media's Manipulation of a Not So Innocent America* (New York: New American Library, 1974), p. 51.

16. Key, ibid., p. 52.

17. N. F. Dixon, *Subliminal Perception: The Nature of a Controversy* (London, McGraw-Hill, 1971), p. 166.

18. Vertov, "Notebooks" (March 26, 1944), *Articles,* p. 254.

19. Maya Deren's statement at "A Symposium With Maya Deren, Arthur Miller, Dylan Thomas, Parker Tyler" (1963), *Film Culture Reader,* ed., P. Adams Sitney (New York: Praeger, 1970), p. 174.

20. Eisenstein, *Film Form,* pp. 67–72, 78–81.

21. Vertov, "From the History of the *Kinok*s," *Articles,* p. 119.

22. Vertov, "We. A Variant of a Manifesto," *Articles,* p. 48.

23. Vertov, "From the History of the *Kinok*s," *Articles,* p. 119.

24. Eisenstein, Pudovkin, Yutkevich, "Statement," *Film Form,* p. 258.

25. Vertov, "From 'Film-Eye' to 'Radio-Eye,' " *Articles,* p. 112.

26. Eisenstein, *Film Form,* pp. 67–72, 78–81.

27. Vertov, *"The Man with the Movie Camera"* (1928), *Articles,* p. 109.

28. Vertov, ibid.

29. Vertov, ibid.

30. Vertov, "About Mayakovsky," *Articles,* p. 182.

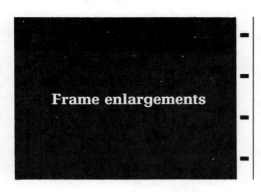

Frame enlargements

1. Giant camera with tiny   (a)   (b)
Cameraman

2. Building with drifting   3. Streetlight pole with drifting
clouds   clouds

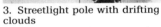

4. Empty movie theater   (a)   (b)

                      (c)   5. Chandeliers and light   (a)
fixtures

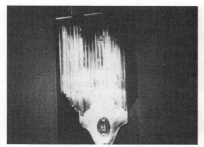

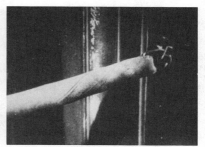

(b)   6. Cordon at theater entrance

7. Cameraman entering movie theater

8. Projector   (a)

(b)   9. Projector and projectionist

10. Film can

11. Projector's reel and projectionist

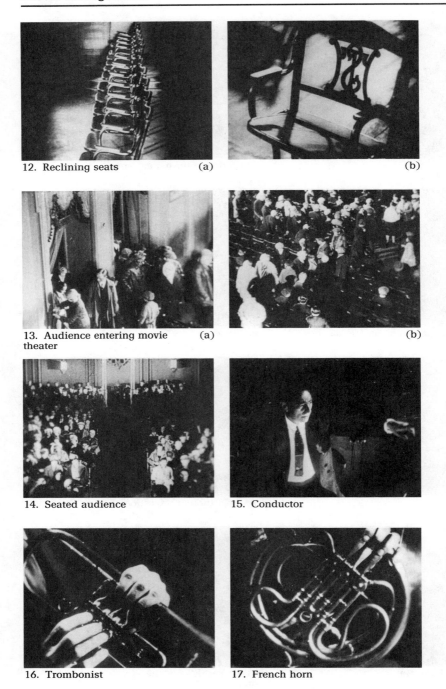

12. Reclining seats   (a)   (b)

13. Audience entering movie   (a)   (b)
theater

14. Seated audience   15. Conductor

16. Trombonist   17. French horn

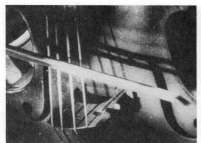

18. Cello

19. Orchestra

20. Trumpet

21. Drummer

22. Violinist

23. Numeral "1"

24. Window   (a)

(b)

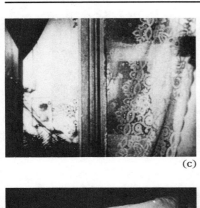

(c)

25. Sleeping young woman (a)

(b)

26. *The Awakening of a* (a)
Woman movie poster

(b)

27. Terrace with trees, and (a)
giant bottle

(b)

28. Derelicts and vagrants (a)

(b)

(c)

(d)　　29. Hosing of streets　　(a)

(b)　　30. Bolshoi Theater

31. Store windows　　(a)　　　　　　　　　　　(b)

(c)

(d)

32. Street at dawn with Gorky banner

33. Traffic signal   (a)

(b)

34. Cameraman going to work   (a)

(b)

(c)

(d)   35. Steel bridge construction
with Cameraman below

36. Pigeons flying backwards –   (a)
reverse motion

(b)

37. Cameraman shooting train   (a)

(b)

38. Speeding train – acceler-   (a)
ated motion

(b)

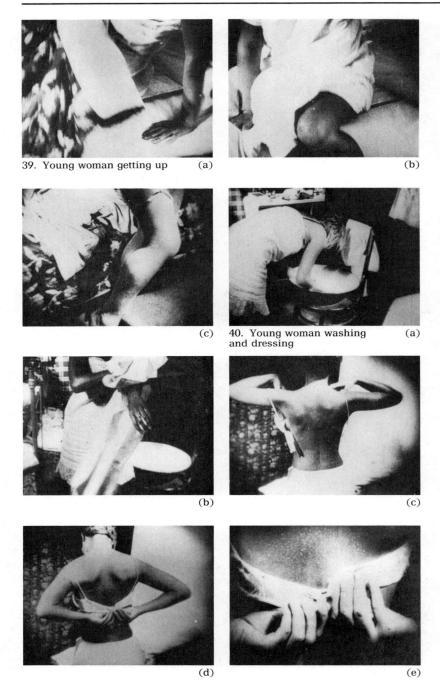

39. Young woman getting up   (a)   (b)

(c)   40. Young woman washing   (a)
             and dressing

(b)   (c)

(d)   (e)

41. Railway tracks – pixilla-   (a)
tion, flickering-effect

(b)

42. Cameraman leaving rail-   (a)
way tracks

(b)

43. Cameraman in convertible
crossing railway tracks

44. Convertible and telephone
poles – accelerated motion

 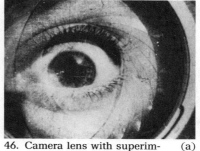

45. Cameraman's hands putting on telescopic lens

46. Camera lens with superim-   (a)
posed eye and reflected
Cameraman

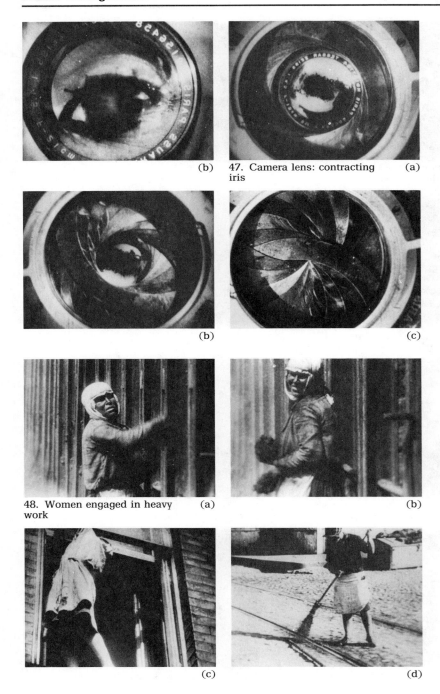

(b)   47. Camera lens: contracting   (a)
      iris

(b)   (c)

48. Women engaged in heavy   (a)   (b)
work

(c)   (d)

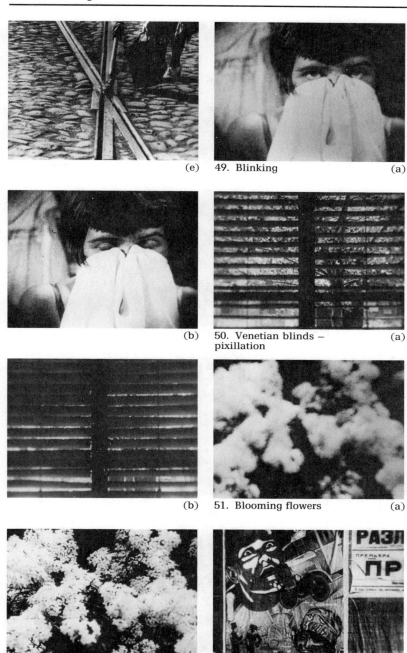

(e)   49. Blinking   (a)

(b)   50. Venetian blinds –   (a)
pixillation

(b)   51. Blooming flowers   (a)

(b)   52. *The Sold Appetite* movie
poster

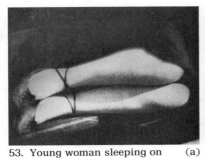

53. Young woman sleeping on   (a)   (b)
bench

                                (c)   54. Passing trolleys   (a)

                                (b)   55. Cameraman and movie
                                       poster

56. Workers pulling carts   (a)   (b)

(c)

57. Cameraman lying on ground

58. Cameraman walking over steel bridge

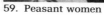

59. Peasant women (a)

(b)

60. Cameraman walking through crowd (a)

(b)

61. Opening of window shutters – overlapping (a)

(b)

(c)

(d)

62. "Glasses – pince nez," opti-   (a)
cian's shop

(b)

63. Reflection in revolving door   (a)

(b)

(c)

(d)

(e)

64. Horse carriages   (a)

(b)

65. Cameraman shooting from   (a)
convertible

(b)

(c)

(d)

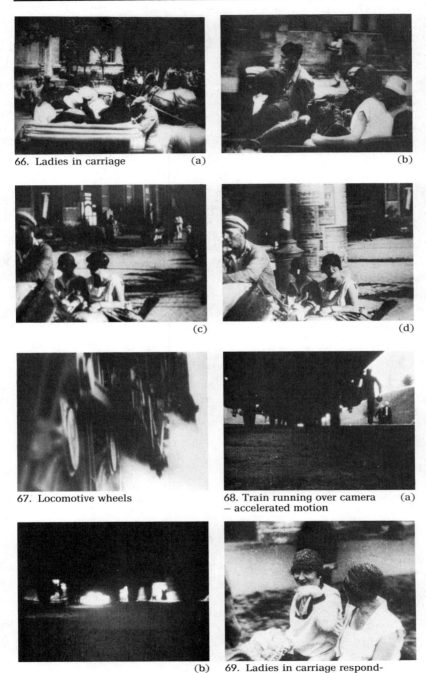

66. Ladies in carriage   (a)   (b)

(c)   (d)

67. Locomotive wheels   68. Train running over camera   (a)
                                         – accelerated motion

(b)   69. Ladies in carriage respond-
       ing to camera

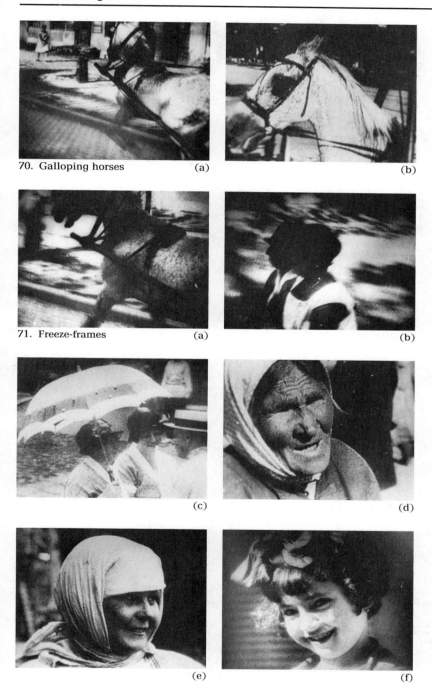

70. Galloping horses   (a)   (b)

71. Freeze-frames   (a)   (b)

(c)   (d)

(e)   (f)

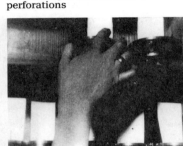

(g)

72. Little girl on filmstrip with perforations

73. Film reels on shelves   (a)

(b)

74. Editor classifying film reels

75. Plate on editing table

76. Filmstrips   (a)

(b)

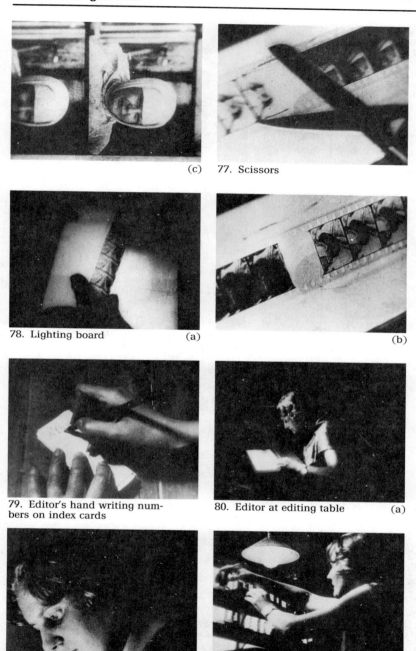

(c)   77. Scissors

78. Lighting board   (a)

(b)

79. Editor's hand writing numbers on index cards

80. Editor at editing table   (a)

(b)

(c)

81. Ladies arriving at their   (a)   (b)
apartment

(c)   82. Cameraman carrying tripod
and camera – lateral view

83. Revolving glass door   84. City square with milling
crowd

85. Telephone operator   86. Street policeman control-   (a)
ling traffic

(b)

(c)

(d)

87. Camera with telescopic (a)
lens shooting from above

(b)

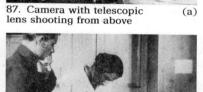

88. Marriage Bureau: first cou- (a)
ple with clerk

(b)

89. Marriage and divorce (a)
certificates

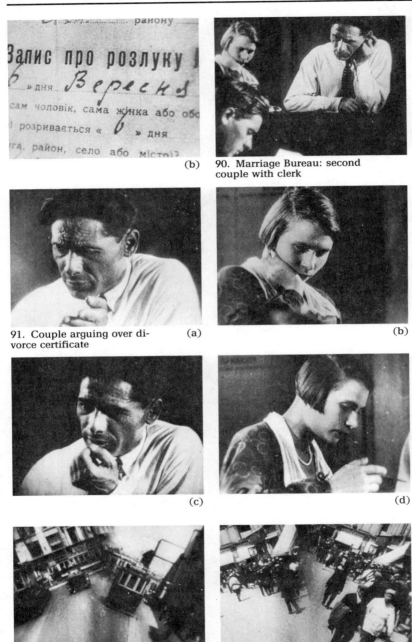

(b)

90. Marriage Bureau: second couple with clerk

91. Couple arguing over divorce certificate (a)

(b)

(c)

(d)

92. Streetcars and pedestrians falling apart – split screen (a)

(b)

93. Marriage Bureau: third (a) (b)
couple with clerk

(c) 94. Trolleys passing each other

95. Old woman weeping over
tombstone

96. Old woman crying over
grave

97. Open casket funeral – lateral view

98. Bride getting out of
carriage

99. Woman in labor

100. Open casket funeral –
frontal view

101. Bride and groom climbing
into carriage

102. Bride and groom carrying
icons

103. Funeral cortege – frontal
view

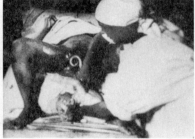

104. Woman giving birth

105. Cameraman shooting over
tall buildings – superimposition

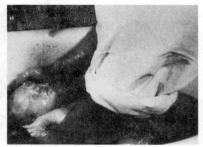

106. Washing baby

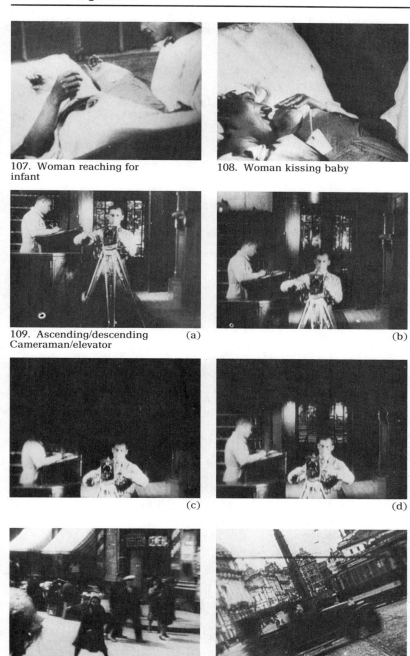

107. Woman reaching for infant

108. Woman kissing baby

109. Ascending/descending Cameraman/elevator   (a)

(b)

(c)

(d)

110. Pedestrians "threatened" by moving camera

111. Oblique view of traffic – accelerated motion   (a)

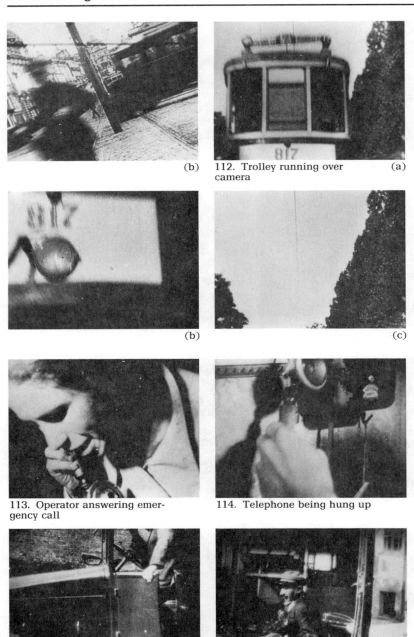

(b)

112. Trolley running over (a)
camera

(b)

(c)

113. Operator answering emergency call

114. Telephone being hung up

115. Ambulance and (a)
paramedics

(b)

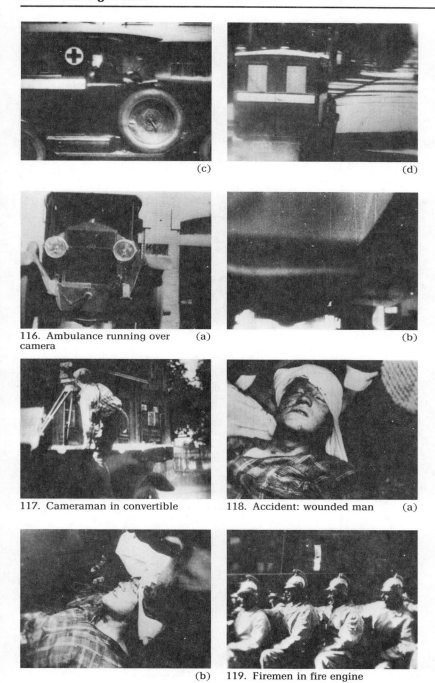

(c)

(d)

116. Ambulance running over (a)
camera

(b)

117. Cameraman in convertible

118. Accident: wounded man (a)

(b)

119. Firemen in fire engine

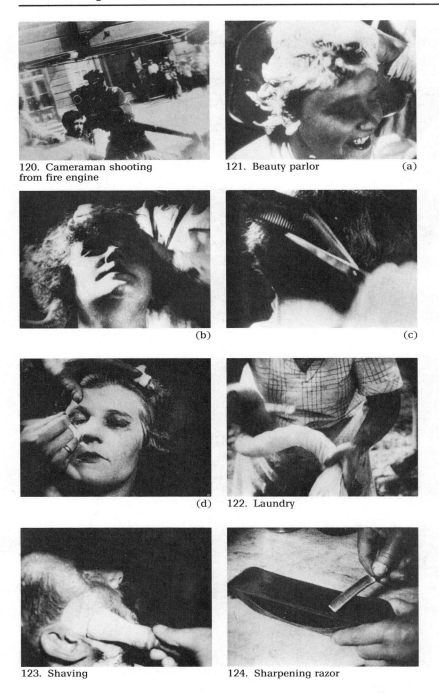

120. Cameraman shooting
from fire engine

121. Beauty parlor (a)

(b)

(c)

(d) 122. Laundry

123. Shaving

124. Sharpening razor

125. Sharpening ax

126. Cameraman reflected in shoemaker's sign

127. Shoeshining

128. Fingernail polishing

129. Splicing film

130. Stitching

131. Sewing

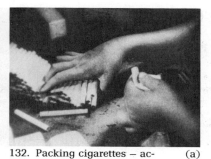

132. Packing cigarettes – accelerated motion   (a)

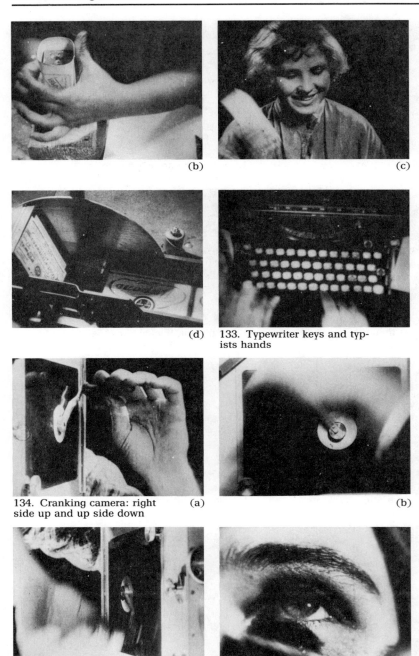

(b)

(c)

(d)

133. Typewriter keys and typists hands

134. Cranking camera: right side up and up side down (a)

(b)

(c) 135. Applying mascara

136. Hand calculating on abacus

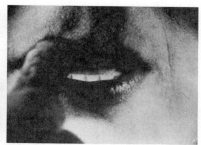

137. Putting on lipstick

138. Hand operating cash register

139. Loading pistol

140. Hand plugging in electric cord

141. Hand pressing telephone buzzer

142. Hand hanging up phone and depressing receiver hook   (a)

(b)

143. Operator's hands at work   (a)   (b)
on switchboard

144. Hands playing piano   145. Cameraman shooting in
                                        mine

146. Cameraman warned by   147. Cameraman at work   (a)
worker

(b)   (c)

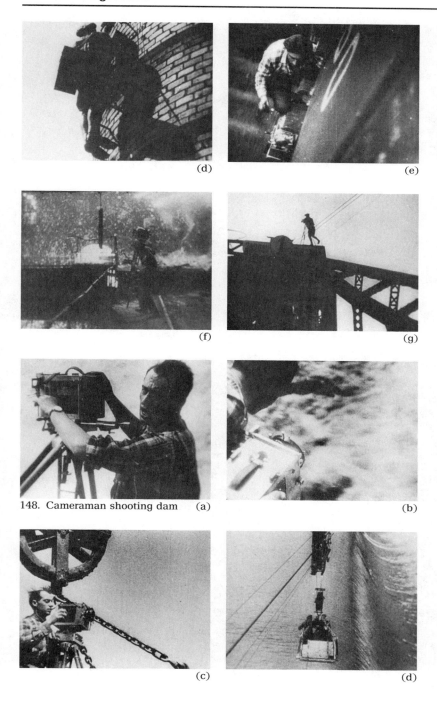

(d)

(e)

(f)

(g)

148. Cameraman shooting dam   (a)

(b)

(c)

(d)

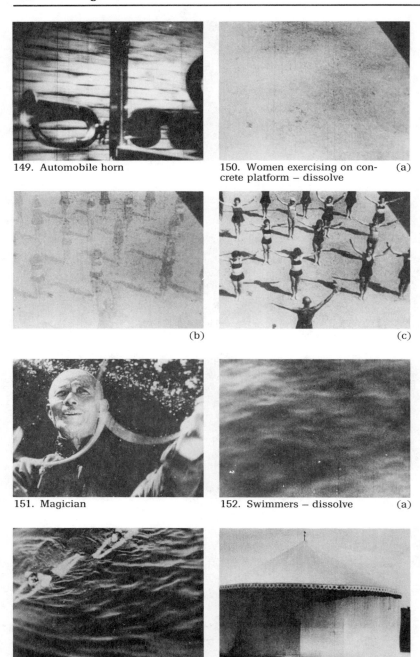

149. Automobile horn

150. Women exercising on con-   (a)
crete platform – dissolve

(b)

(c)

151. Magician

152. Swimmers – dissolve   (a)

(b)   153. Carousel – dissolve   (a)

(b) 154. "Beer hall"/Bierhalle – (a)
dissolve

(b) 155. Moving sticks – animation (a)

(b) 156. Wall newspaper (a)

(b) 157. "About Sports," newspaper article

158. Sports fans   (a)   (b)

(c)   (d)

(e)   (f)

159. Sports events – slow   (a)   (b)
motion

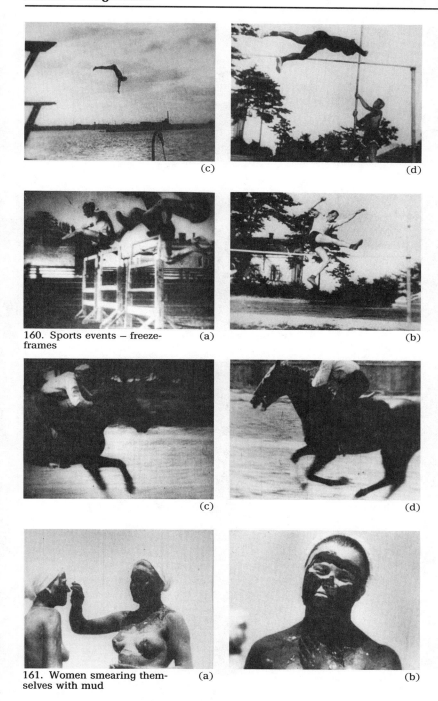

(c)

(d)

160. Sports events – freeze- (a)
frames

(b)

(c)

(d)

161. Women smearing them- (a)
selves with mud

(b)

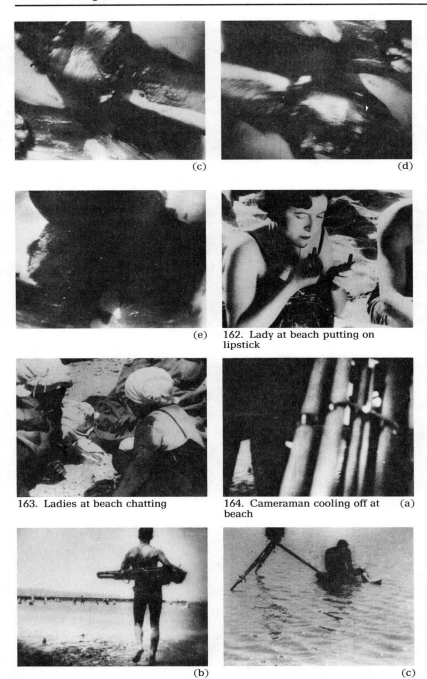

(c)

(d)

(e)

162. Lady at beach putting on lipstick

163. Ladies at beach chatting

164. Cameraman cooling off at beach   (a)

(b)

(c)

(d) 165. Children watching (a)
magician

(b) (c)

166. Magician prestidigitating (a) (b)
mouse – dissolve

(c) (d)

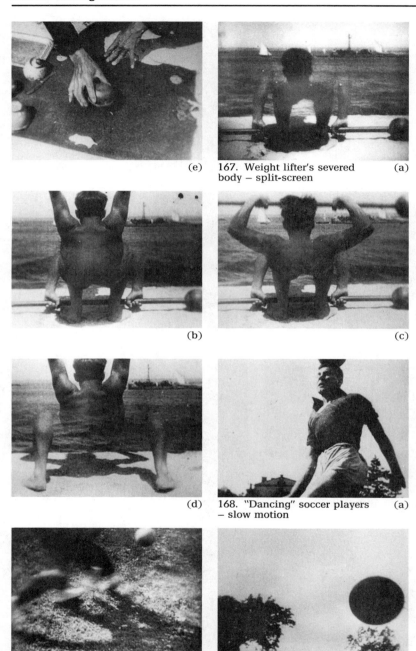

(e)

167. Weight lifter's severed (a)
body – split-screen

(b)

(c)

(d)

168. "Dancing" soccer players (a)
– slow motion

(b)

169. Soccer ball in flight – slow (a)
motion

(b)

170. Athlete throwing javelin

171. Goalkeeper catching ball
– slow motion

172. Somersaulting runner –   (a)
reverse motion

(b)

(c)

(d)   173. Motorcycles   (a)

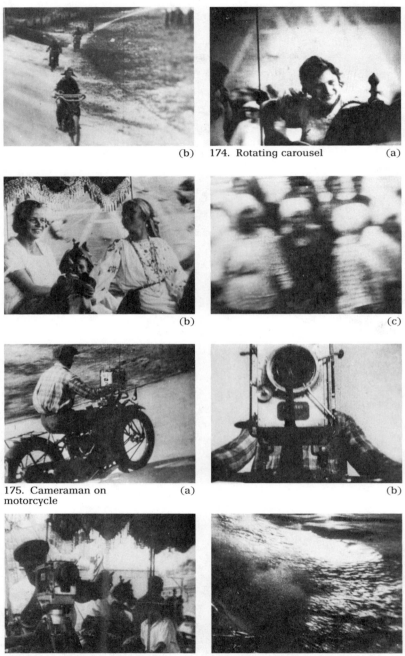

(b)   174. Rotating carousel   (a)

(b)   (c)

175. Cameraman on   (a)   (b)
motorcycle

176. Cameraman on carousel   177. Waves seen from boat

178. Torn filmstrip – freeze-frame, split-screen

179. *Green Manuela* movie (a)
poster – swish pan

(b)

(c)

(d)

(e)

180. Cameraman above city – composite shot

181. People in beer hall (a)

(b) 182. Cameraman "drowned" in (a)
beer mug — superimposition

(b) 183. Beer bottles carried on (a)
tray

(b) 184. Churches turned into (a)
workers' club — swish pan

(b) (c)

(d)

185. Checkers arranging them- (a)
selves – reverse motion

(b)

186. Chess figures arranging (a)
themselves – reverse motion

(b)

187. Workers relaxing in work- (a)
ers' club

(b)

(c)

188. Dziga Vertov playing (a)
chess in workers' club

(b)

189. Young woman holding rifle

190. "Swastika" target

191. "Death to Fascism" target

192. Young woman shooting

193. Beer bottle targets – (a)
animation

(b)

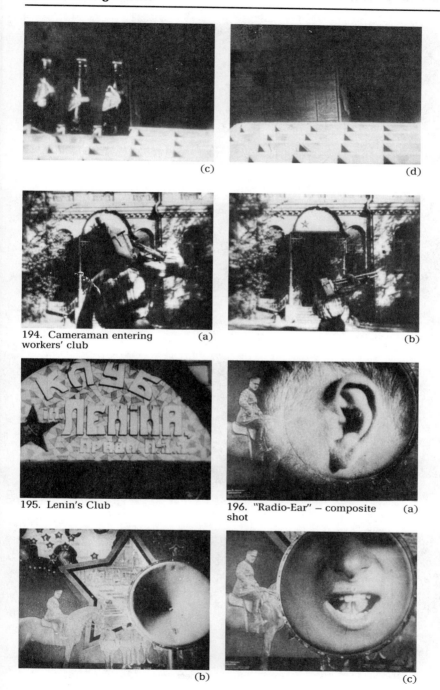

(c)

(d)

194. Cameraman entering   (a)
workers' club

(b)

195. Lenin's Club

196. "Radio-Ear" – composite   (a)
shot

(b)

(c)

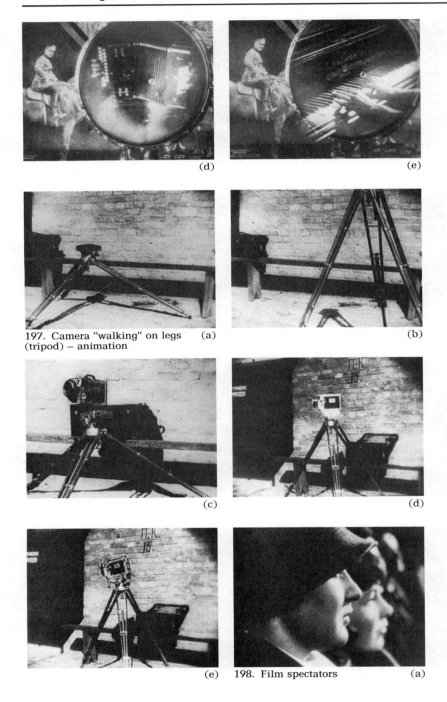

(d)

(e)

197. Camera "walking" on legs (a) (tripod) – animation

(b)

(c)

(d)

(e) 198. Film spectators (a)

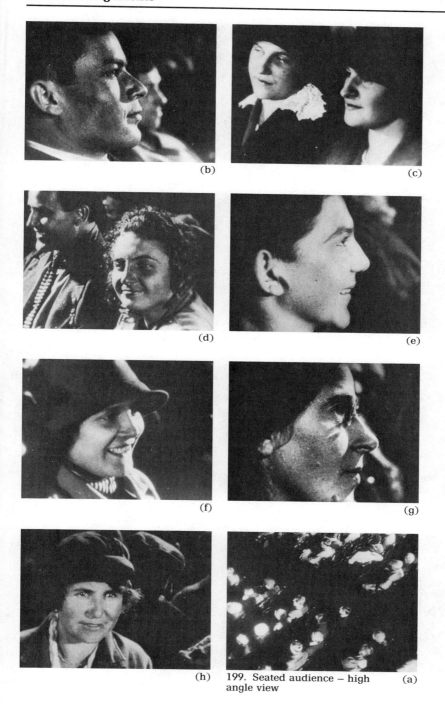

(b)

(c)

(d)

(e)

(f)

(g)

(h)

199. Seated audience – high
angle view

(a)

(b)   200. Rotating spool of wire on real screen

201. Rotating spool on screen-within-screen — composite shot

202. Conversing movie audience

203. Dancers and piano — superimposition, composite shots   (a)

(b)

(c)   204. Audience — frontal view

205. Glittering threads and spinning looms – superimposition

206. Spinning wheel and fe-   (a)
male worker – superimposition

(b)

207. Locomotive wheels on real screen

208. Locomotive on screen-within-screen – composite shot

209. Well-dressed women   (a)

(b)

(c)

(d)

(e)

210. Passing vehicles (a)

(b)

(c)

(d)

(e)

(f)

(g)

(h)

(i)

211. Cameraman shooting crowd – composite shot

212. Pendulum

213. Bolshoi Theater – split screen

(a)

(b)

214. Two ladies and man in white suit in carriage on real screen

215. Two ladies and man on screen-within-screen – composite shot

216. Cameraman on motorcycle on real screen

217. Cameraman on screen-within-screen – composite shot

218. Cameraman shooting with telescopic lens

219. Cameraman shooting planes

220. Trolleys – composite shot

221. Typists – composite shot

222. Switchboard operators –   (a) composite shot

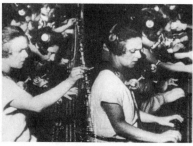

(b)   223. Train on real screen

224. Train on screen-within-
screen – composite shot

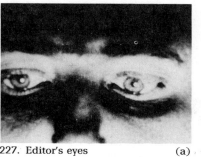

225. Cameraman in convertible
on real screen

226. Cameraman on screen-
within-screen – composite shot

227. Editor's eyes   (a)

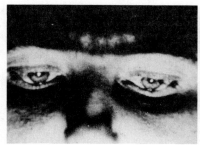

(b)

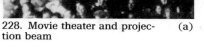

228. Movie theater and projec-   (a)
tion beam

(b)   229. Traffic signal   (a)

(b)   230. Car mounted on tracks,   (a)
running over camera

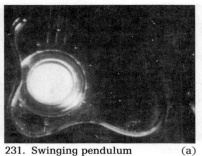

(b)   231. Swinging pendulum   (a)

(b)   232. Trolley running over   (a)
camera

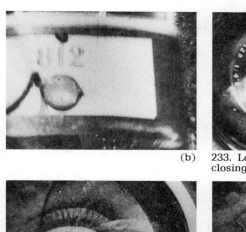

(b)

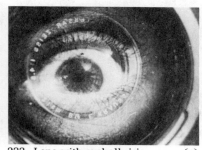

(a)

233. Lens with eyeball: iris closing – superimposition

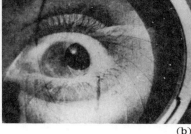

(b)

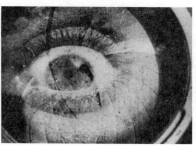

(c)

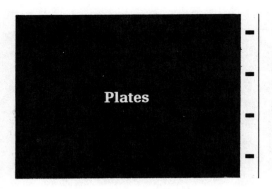

Plates

308

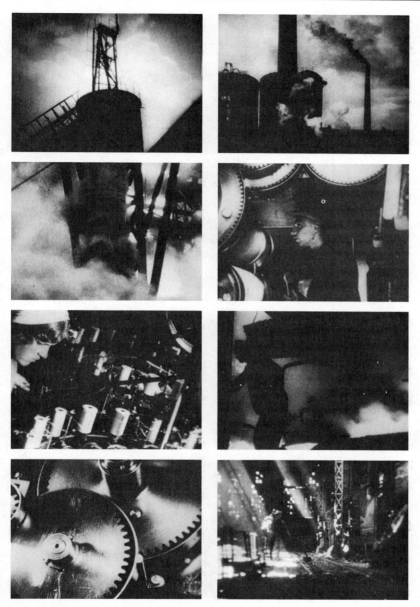

Plate 1. Factory and machines

Plate 2. Traffic and means of communication

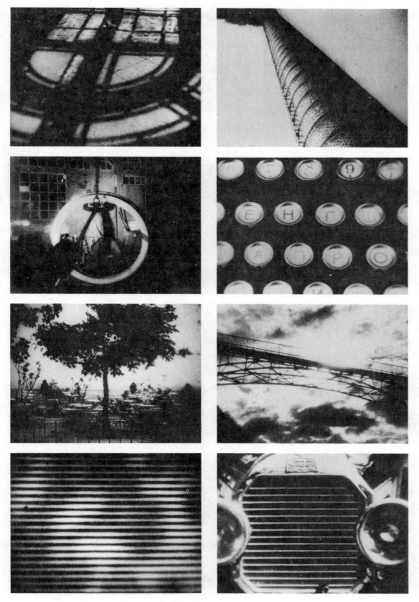

Plate 3. Graphic shot composition

Plate 4. Visual abstraction

Plate 5. "Awakening" sequence (VII)

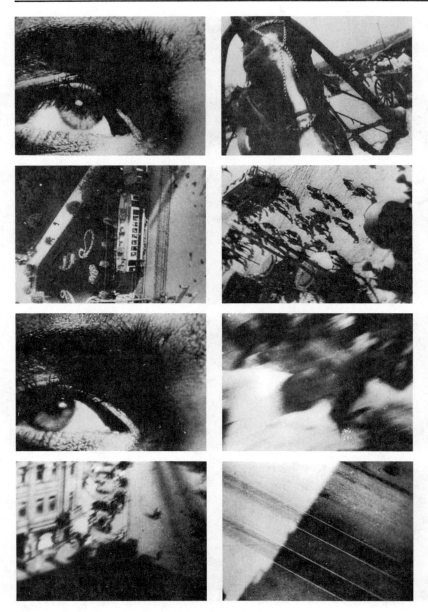

Plate 6. "Street and Eye" sequence (XXII)

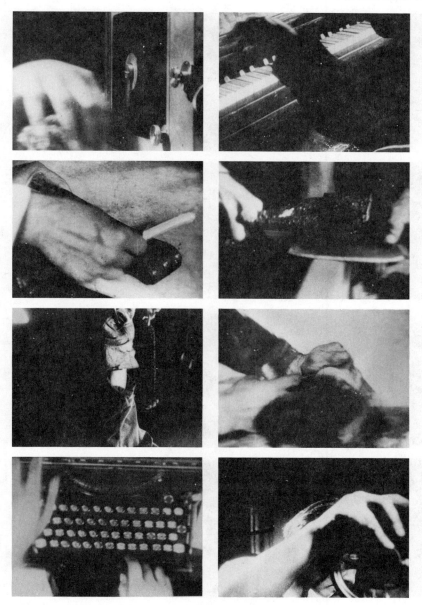

Plate 7. "Working Hands" sequence (XXVII)

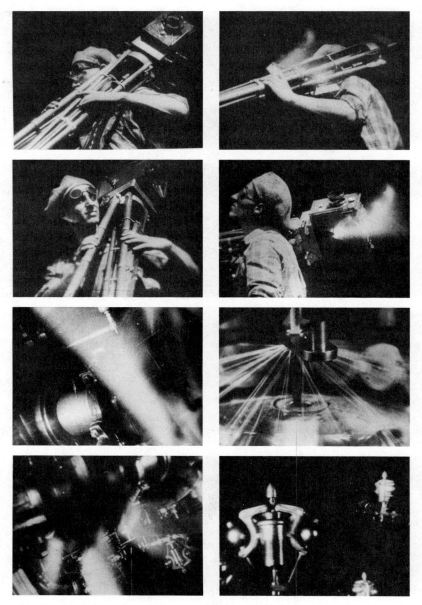

Plate 8. "Cameraman and Machines" sequence (XXXI)

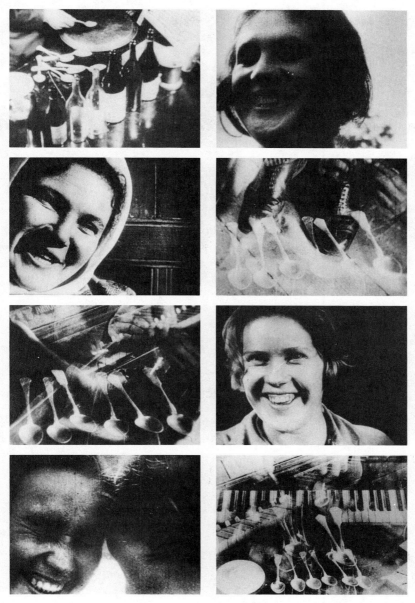

Plate 9. "Musical Performance with Spoons and Bottles" sequence (L)

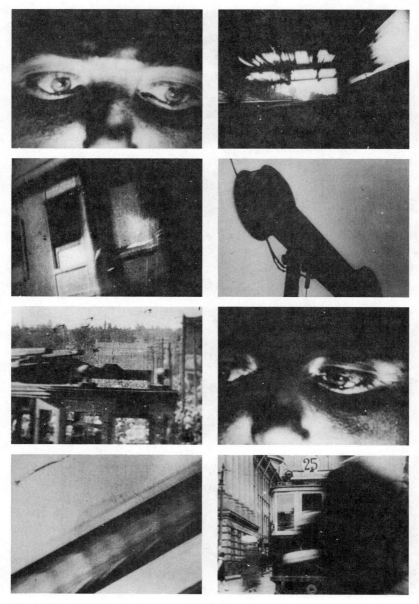

Plate 10. "Editor and the Film" sequence (LV)

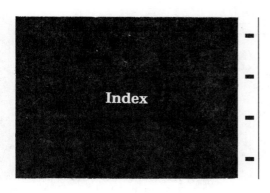

Index

Abramov, Nikolai, 67
"agit-train," 3
Agit-Train, The [*Agitpoezd VTSIK*, 1921],
   3
Alexandrov, Grigori, 183
alienation, 11n, 117; *see also* defamiliarization; estrangement; "making it
   strange"; *Verfremdungseffekt*
animation, 6, 83, 110, 116, 136
Apollinaire, Guillaume, 68
"art as an object," 12
"art of fact," 13–21, 18, 44, 63, 138
Averbakh, G., 76n
*Awakened Sex, The, see Awakening of a
   Woman, The*
Awakening of a Woman, The [*Das Erwachsen des Weibes*, 1927], 86–7

Ballet mécanique, Le (1924), 176
Barantsievich, Boris, 2n
"baring the device," 9, 46, 84, 103, 114,
   119
Barooshian, Vahan, 63
Battleship Potemkin [*Bronenosets Po-
   temkin*, 1925], 50, 55n, 56
Behrendt, Hans, 66n
Beliakov, Ivan, 2n
Berlin: Symphony of a Great City [*Berlin:
   Die Symphonie einer Grossstadt*,
   1927], 71, 79, 152n
Bezhin Meadow [*Bezhin lug*, 1937], 56n,
   66n
biomechanics, 7, 8n
Bolshoi Theater, 85, 90, 132
Bowlt, John, 11
Bowser, Eileen, 114n
Brakhage, Stan, viii
Braun, Edward, 8n, 31n

Brecht, Bertolt, 11n
Brik, Osip, 20, 21, 27, 42n, 54, 63
Brown, Edward, 27
Bulgakov, Mikhail, 47
Buñuel, Luis, 146, 147
Burch, Noel, 78

Cameraman, *see* Kaufman, Mikhail
Cameraman, The (1928), 80
candid-eye, 67; *see also* cinéma vérité;
   compilation film; direct cinema;
   documentary; newsreel
Canudo, Ricciotto, 176
Chaplin, Charles, 63
Chien Andalou, Un (1928), 146
cinema of fact (film of fact), 16, 17, 18,
   20, 21, 23, 30, 33, 35, 51, 56, 110
cinéma vérité, 67; *see also* candid-eye;
   compilation film; direct cinema;
   documentary; newsreel
Clair, René, 176
compilation film, 20; *see also* candid-
   eye; cinéma vérité; direct cinema;
   documentary; newsreel
composite (compound) shot, 105, 106,
   110, 122, 131, 132, 133, 134, 186,
   198
Conner, Bruce, viii
Council of Three, 2, 3, 70, 71
Croft, Stephen, 73
crosscutting, *see* montage, crosscutting

Dali, Salvador, 146
d'Amicis, Edmondo, 32n
defamiliarization, 10, 119; *see also* alienation; estrangement; "making it
   strange"; *Verfremdungseffekt*
Deren, Maya, 155

319

Deserter [*Dezertir*, 1933], 58
dialectical materialism, 15, 41
direct cinema, 67; *see also* candid-eye;
    cinéma vérité; compilation film; doc-
    umentary; newsreel
dissolve, 83, 110, 115, 116, 131, 132, 136
Dixon, N. F., 147
documentary, viii, ix, 3n, 14, 19, 22, 23,
    24, 25, 33, 48, 49, 52, 53, 57, 61, 70,
    71, 79, 87, 88, 128, 145, 176, 200;
    see also candid-eye; cinéma vérité;
    compilation film; direct cinema;
    newsreel
Dos Passos, John, viii
Dostoyevsky, Fyodor, 18
double exposure, 131, 132, 159, 177, 184,
    186; *see also* multiple exposure;
    superimposition
Dovzhenko, Aleksandr, 46
Drobashenko, Sergei, 49–51
Dulac, Germaine, 176
Dupont, E. A., 88
Durgnat, Raymond, 45
Dynamics of a Metropolis [*Dynamik der
    Grossstadt*, 1921–2], 10

Eagle, Steve, xi
editing, *see* montage
Editor, *see* Svilova, Elizaveta
Ehrenberg, Ilya, 12
Eikhenbaum, Boris, 42n
Eisenstein, Sergei, ix, 5, 11, 17, 20, 21,
    22, 23, 24n, 32, 36, 48–60, 66n, 78,
    96, 115, 129, 138, 162, 183
Eleventh Year, The [*Odinnadtsatyi*,
    1928], 21, 56, 57, 183
Engels, Friedrich, 46, 78, 96
Enough Simplicity in Every Wise Man
    [*Na vsiakogo mudretsa dovol'no
    prostoty*, 1922], 49n, 55
*Enthusiasm, see Symphony of the Don
    Basin*
Entr'acte (1924), 176
Epstein, Jean, 9
Erlich, Victor, 42n, 45n
Ermler, Fridrikh, 21
Ermolinsky, Sergei, 20, 65
estrangement, 45n, 117, 119; *see also* al-
    ienation; defamiliarization; "making
    it strange"; *Verfremdungseffekt*

Factory of Facts, 55
Fall of the Romanov Dynasty, The [*Pa-*

denie dinastii Romanovikh, 1927],
    19
Fedorov-Davydov, Aleksei A., 66, 76n
FEKS (Factory of the Eccentric Actor), 55
Feldman, Seth, 73n, 76n
Fevralsky, Aleksandr, 44
"Film-Eye" method, viii, ix, 3, 4, 8, 10,
    13, 14, 18, 19, 24, 27, 30, 35, 37, 39,
    42, 45n, 50, 52, 55, 56, 57, 71, 77, 78,
    79, 84, 94, 105, 110, 111, 116, 117,
    119, 121, 122, 127, 128, 132, 145,
    148, 176n, 183, 188, 199
Film-Eye series (*Film-Eye: Life Caught
    Unawares*, 1924), 11, 21, 40, 51, 52,
    55, 57, 79, 152, 177
"film-fact," 4, 8, 9, 15, 72
"film-image," 14
"Film-Radio-Eye," 183
"film-thing," vii, 4, 13, 14, 70, 76, 77,
    117, 126, 130, 182, 188
"Film-Truth" principle, ix, 4, 8, 13, 14,
    15, 39, 49, 51, 52, 57, 58n, 59, 73, 77,
    79, 82, 84, 86, 88, 92, 109, 110, 118,
    188, 199
Film-Truth series [*Kinopravda*, 1922–5],
    7, 11, 14, 15, 16, 17, 30, 46, 48, 49,
    52, 55, 57, 152n, 177
Fisher, Lucy, 59n
flicker (flickering) effect, 9, 43, 92, 93, 118,
    148, 163, 173, 174
formalism, viii, ix, x, 5, 9, 10, 25, 35–44,
    46, 56, 65, 68, 69, 94, 139, 151, 200
Forward March, Soviet! [*Shagai, Sovet!*,
    1926], 7, 52,
fovea phenomenon, 147, 152, 159, 160
Frantsisson, Boris, 2n, 49n
freeze-frame, 6, 9, 83, 84, 98, 103, 110,
    111, 114, 116, 123, 186
futurism, vii, viii, 5, 6, 8, 25, 35–44, 63,
    68n, 94, 119, 137, 164, 200
    cubo-futurism, 39
    ego-futurism, 40, 41n

Gabo, Naum, 5
Galadzhev, I., 2
Gan, Aleksei, ix, 3, 11, 13–19, 33, 51
Ganly, Raymond, 129
Gaumont newsreel, 30
General Line, The, see Old and New
Ginsburg, Mozes Ia., 8
"Girl Composer, The," [*Devushka-kom-
    pozitor*, 1936], 37n

"Girl Plays the Piano, A," [*Devushka igraet na roiale*, 1939], 37, 39
Glumov's Diary [*Dnevnik Glumova*, 1922], 49n
Godard, Jean-Luc, viii
Goncharova, Nataliya, 6
Gorky, Maxim, 112
Gray, Camilla, 11
Great Road, The [*Velikii put'*, 1927], 19
Green Manuela [*Die Grüne Manuela*, 1923], 88

Hegel, Georg Wilhelm F., 96
hypnagogic (hypnopompic) state, 121, 164, 165n, 175

In Spring [*Vesnoi*, 1930], 71
Instructional Steamer "The Red Star" [*Instruktorskii parokhod "Krasnaia zvezda,"* 1920], 3
"intermediating cinema/film," 22, 23, 49
intervals, ix, 27, 36, 137, 138, 139, 140, 145, 148–55, 159, 164, 165, 183, 184, 196, 199
  oneiric impact of, 164–76
  "Theory of Intervals," 56, 96, 138, 147, 155
Island of the Young Pioneers, The [*Ostrov pionerov*, 1924], 13n
It Cannot Be Bought for Money [*Ne dlia deneg rodivshisia*, 1918], 32n
Ivan (1932), 46
Ivan the Terrible I, II [*Ivan Groznyi*, 1944, 1946/58], 53
Ivanov, Viacheslav V., 126, 127n
Ivanov, Vsevolod, 47n

Jackson, Renata, xi
Joyce, James, viii
jump cut, 84, 98, 117, 166

Kamenev, Lev, 24
Katayev, Valentin, 47n
Katerina Izmailova [*Ledi Makbet Mtsenskogo uezda*, 1926], 56n
Kaufman, Mikhail, x, 2, 6, 12, 13, 30, 70–2, 81, 82, 87, 109, 122, 130, 131, 132, 133, 136, 137, 163, 164
Kaverin, Veniyamin, 47n
Keaton, Buster, 80
Khlebnikov, Velemir (Viktor), 43
kinesthesia (kinesis), x, 27, 40, 89, 91, 112, 117, 119, 130, 136, 137, 138, 139–48, 150, 151, 152, 155, 156, 160, 164, 167, 174, 175, 177, 184, 185, 186, 188, 196, 199
"kinetic resolution," 27n, 138
Kinofot, 11, 13, 17, 33
kinoks, vii, xii, 1–5, 8, 11–15, 18, 19, 22, 29, 30, 33, 35, 44, 46, 49, 50, 52, 54, 55, 57, 58n, 61, 65, 68, 70, 71, 78, 87, 88, 89, 92, 93, 109, 111, 127, 138, 162, 164, 188, 200
Kiselev, Fedor, 61n
Knight, Arthur, 129
Kopalin, Ilia, 2n
Kopp, Anatole, 8n
Kruchenykh, Aleksei, 39
Kuleshov, Lev, 8, 11, 22, 57, 90
"Kuleshov effect," 90, 125

Laboratory of Hearing, 25
Lafargue, Paul, 89
Lapkina, Marpha, 162
Laude, Jean, 68
Lawton, Anna, 39
Leacock, Richard, viii, 67
Lebedev, Nikolai, 60n, 64, 65n
LEF (Left Front of the Arts), viii, 11, 14, 19–23, 33, 53, 55, 57, 63, 68
"*LEF* Ring, The," 21
Leger, Fernand, 176
Lemberg, Aleksandr, 2n
Lenin (Vladimir Ilyich Ulyanov), 4, 16, 21–4, 33, 44, 46, 53, 54, 57, 64, 68n, 78, 85, 86, 89n, 108, 112, 115
Leninist Film-Truth [*Leninskaia kinopravda*, 1924], 50
"Leninist Proportion," 22, 23, 87
"Letter from a Girl Tractor Driver, The" [*Pismo traktoristki*, 1940], 37n
Leyda, Jay, 24n 31n
"Life-As-It-Is," 4, 24, 25, 70, 73, 77, 82, 84, 87, 105, 110, 117, 119, 133, 147, 188, 199
Life-Caught-Unawares series [*Zhizn' v rasplokh*, 1924], *see Film-Eye* series
"life-fact," ix, x, 3, 4, 8, 9, 15, 29, 48, 51, 53, 59, 72, 82, 85–90, 92, 107, 108, 109, 110, 117, 124, 130, 133, 138, 145, 152, 199
"life-unawares" ("life caught unawares"), 4, 14, 21, 59, 70, 79, 89, 103, 104, 115, 122, 126, 145
Lissitzky, El (Lazar), 12

London, Jack, 32n
Lotman, Yuri, 29
Lullaby [*Kolybel'naia*, 1937], 37n, 53
Lunacharsky, Anatoly, 22n, 62n

Macdonald, Dwight, 129
Mach, Ernst, 68n
Machism, 68n
Makavejev, Dušan, viii
"making it difficult," 10, 11, 45, 117
"making it strange," 10, 11n; *see also* alienation; defamiliarization; estrangement; *Verfremdungseffekt*
Malevich, Kazimir, 6, 136, 137
Man with the Movie Camera, The [*Chelovek s kinoapparatom*, 1929] sequences
  "Accelerated Motion" (LIV), 76, 117, 118
  "Accident on the Street" (XXIII), 74, 94, 143, 145
  "Arrested Movement" (XVI), 74, 76n
  "Arrival of the Audience" (III), 74
  "Awakening" (VII), 74, 86, 91, 106, 118, 121, 122, 164–76, 177
  "Basketball" (XLII), 75, 115, 125, 185
  "Beerhall" (XLVI), 75, 89
  "Cameraman and Machines" (XXXI), 75, 135, 137, 148, 155–64
  "Camera Moves on Tripod" (LI), 76, 111, 126, 186, 188
  "Controlling Traffic" (XVIII), 74, 96, 99, 102–5
  "Crowd on the Beach" (XXXIX), 75, 137
  "Death, Marriage, and Birth" (XX), 74, 77, 96, 101–2, 103, 105, 106, 198
  "Editing Room" (XVII), 74, 96, 97–9, 102, 103, 105
  "Editor and the Film" (LV), 76, 117, 121, 184, 188, 189, 190–6
  "Factory and Workers" (XI), 74, 122
  "Fire Engine and Ambulance" (XXIV), 74, 76n
  "Green Manuela" (XLV), 75
  "Introduction" (I), 74
  "Ladies in a Carriage" (XV), 74, 93, 106
  "Lenin's Club – Listening to the Radio" (XLIX), 76
  "Lenin's Club – Playing Games" (XLVII), 75, 85
  "Magician" (XL), 75, 124
  "Manufacturing Process" (XXVI), 75, 148, 149, 155
  "Marriage and Divorce" (XIX), 74, 96, 99–101, 103–6
  "Mine Workers" (XXVIII), 75, 148, 155
  "Morning" (VI), 74, 107
  "Moscow Bolshoi Theater" (LIII), 76
  "Motorcycle and Carousel" (XLIV), 75, 106, 114, 125
  "Movie Theater" (II), 74
  "Musical Performance with Spoons and Bottles" (L), 76, 125, 135, 176–84, 186, 188, 196
  "Opening Shutters and Stores" (XIII), 74
  "Performance" (V), 74, 76n
  "Power Plant and Machines" (XXX), 75, 90, 155
  "Preparation" (IV), 74
  "Recreation" (XXXV), 75, 136
  "Shooting Gallery" (XLVIII), 75, 110, 125, 136
  "Soccer" (XLIII), 75, 83, 115, 125, 185
  "Spectators and the Screen" (LII), 76, 106, 111, 126, 137, 184–6, 188
  "Steel Workers" (XXIX), 75, 155
  "Stoppage of Machines" (XXXIII), 75
  "Street and Eye" (XXII), 74, 77, 95, 124, 135, 140–8, 159, 162, 164, 185
  "Street Traffic" (X), 74, 86
  "Swimming, Diving, and Gymnastics" (XXXVIII), 75, 137
  "Track and Field Events" (XXXVII), 75, 124, 185
  "Traffic Controller and Automobile Horn" (XXXII), 75, 76n, 106, 160, 163, 177
  "Traffic, Elevators, and Cameraman" (XXI), 74, 144
  "Travelers and Pedestrians" (XII), 74, 106
  "Vagrants in the Street" (VIII), 74, 121
  "Various Kinds of Work" (XXV), 75, 106
  "Vehicles and Pedestrians" (XIV), 74, 106
  "Wall Newspaper" (XXXVI), 75, 112
  "Washing and Blinking" (IX), 74, 76n, 122
  "Washing and Grooming" (XXXIV), 75, 106
  "Weight Reducing Exercises" (XLI), 75

"Working Hands" (XXVII), 75, 106, 148–55
Marinetti, Filippo Tommaso (Emilio), 68
Markov, Vladimir, 39
Marshall, Herbert, 45n, 47n, 66n
Marx, Karl, viii, ix, 41, 45, 86, 96
Mayakovsky, Vladimir, viii, ix, 3, 11n, 19, 21, 23, 25–35, 36–42, 44–8, 54, 55, 61–3, 88, 138, 200
Mekas, Jonas, viii
Melody of the World [*Die Melodie der Welt*, 1929], 152
Meyerhold, Vsevolod, 6, 7, 8n, 31
Michelson, Annette, 9, 71, 176n
Moholy-Nagy, Laszlo, 9, 10
montage (editing)
  arithmetic, 183, 187
  associative, 40
  of collisions/conflicts, 36, 138
  crosscutting, 86, 92–5, 108, 110, 124, 126, 175
  dialectical, 96, 107
  disruptive–associative, ix, 95–107, 197
  geometric, 139, 140
  intellectual, 54, 96
  intercutting, 122, 156, 165, 177, 183, 189
  leitmotif, 84
  metric, 183, 184
  overlapping, 84, 148
  overtonal, 54, 162, 199
  parallel, 84, 90, 91
  subliminal, x, 5, 147, 148, 164, 175, 189
"Montage of Attractions," 55
"Montage of Intervals" *see* intervals
"montage way of hearing," 10, 59
"montage way of seeing," 4, 10, 59
Moscow [*Moskva*, 1926], 71
Moscow Art Theater, 56
motion
  accelerated/fast, 9, 46, 56, 77, 80n, 83, 84, 90, 92, 93, 110, 111, 116–18, 124, 148, 163, 176, 189, 190, 191, 193, 194, 195, 198
  decelerated/slow, 9, 10, 56, 83, 84, 110, 116, 148, 176
  reverse, 46, 84, 92, 110, 117, 148, 176n, 189
Moussinac, Leon, 176
Mozhukin, Ivan, 34
multiple exposure, 90, 110, 148, 181, 182, 198; *see also* double exposure; superimposition
Mumu [*Gerasim i Mumu*, 1918], 56n

naturshchik (nonprofessional actor), 53
NEP (New Economic Policy), ix, 21–5, 33, 45, 62, 87, 89, 109
News of the Day series [*Novosti dnia*, 1944–54], 61n
newsreel, 2, 3, 14, 17, 19, 20, 22, 23, 25, 33, 50, 53, 54, 57, 59, 60, 61, 70, 80n, 87, 88; *see also* candid-eye; cinéma vérité; compilation film; direct cinema; documentary
Nicholai II, 19n
Nikandrov, the worker, 54
Novyi LEF, 11n, 20, 21, 22, 63n

Oath of Youth, The [*Kliatva molodykh*, 1944], 61n
October or *Ten Days that Shook the World* [*Oktiabr' ili Desiat dnei kotorye potriasli mir*, 1927–8], 21, 31n, 53, 54, 66n, 115
Okhlopkov, Nikolai, 89
Old and New or *General Line, The* [*Staroe i novoe ili General'naia liniia*, 1929], 162
On the Bloodless Military Front, see Agit-Train, The
One Sixth of the World [*Shestaia chast' mira*, 1926], 7, 11, 19, 51, 52
oneiric cinema, *see* intervals, oneiric impact of
ontological authenticity, 50, 51, 119, 132
OPOYAZ (Society for the Study of Poetic Language), 42
Ostrovsky, Aleksandr, 7, 49n, 55
Our Cinema – Twentieth Anniversary of the Soviet Cinema [*Nashe kino – dvadtsatiletie sovetskogo kino*, 1940], 61
overlapping effect, 115; *see also* montage, overlapping

parallel editing, *see* montage, parallel
Paris qui dort (1923), 176
Pathé Newsreel, 30
Pavlov, Ivan P., 30
Pennebaker, Don, viii
persistence of vision (visual afterimage), 139
Pertsov, Viktor, 19, 20, 21

Pevsner, Antonin, 5
phi-effect, 127, 135, 139–48, 151, 162, 184, 185
photomontage, 10
photoplay, vii, 35
Picture of Dorian Gray, The [*Portret Doriana Greia*, 1915], 31n
pixillation, 84, 117, 148, 168
point-of-view, 94, 119–28
Pravda, 4, 55, 64
"Production Art," x
Proletkult Theater, 55, 68n
Protazanov, Yakov, 31n
Pudovkin, Vsevolod, 21, 22 58, 110n, 116, 129n 183

Radek, Karl, 24
"Radio-Ear," 10, 59, 132, 152n
"Radio-Eye," 10, 27, 35, 58, 59, 103, 152, 183
"Radio-Truth," 58n
Ray, Satyajit, viii
Red Star, see Instructional Steamer
Reed, John, 31n
Reeder, Roberta, xi, 127
"reverse connection," 126, 127n
"Rhythmicosyntactic Theory," 27
Rodchenko, Aleksandr, 10, 11, 12, 14, 16, 19, 131
Rogosin, Lionel, 67
Rose, Olivia, 73
Roshal', Lev, 66n
Rossellini, Roberto, viii
ROSTA posters, 40
Rouch, Jean, viii, 67, 68
Rozanova, Olga, 6
Ruspoli, Mario, 67
Russia of Nicholai II and Lev Tolstoi, The [*Rossia Nikolaia II i Lev Tolstoi*, 1928], 19n
Ruttmann, Walter, 71, 79, 152

Saakov, Lev, 64
Sabinsky, Cheslav, 56
Sadoul, Georges, 68
Sauer, Fred, 87
Sauzier, Bertrand, 73
Scriabin, Aleksandr, 182
Sedgwick, Edward, 80n
Selezneva, Tamara, 17, 18, 49
self-referentiality, 45, 81, 82–4, 88, 93, 103, 104, 116, 119, 121, 123, 125, 126, 128, 131, 132, 133

Sergo Ordzhonikidze (1937), 53
Seton, Marie, 56n, 66n
Severianin, Igor, 41n
Shackled by Film [*Zakovannaia fil'moi*, 1918], 32n
She [*Ona*, 1939], 37n
Shengelaia, Nikolai, 31n
Shklovsky, Viktor, 9n, 10, 11, 20, 21, 34n, 42n, 46, 48, 49, 52
Shloss, Carol, viii
Shub, Esfir (Esther), 19, 20, 21, 32, 33, 46, 50, 51, 53, 54n
Shumyatsky, Boris, 66n
Six Girls Behind the Monastery Walls, see Six Girls in Search of Night Shelter
Six Girls in Search of Night Shelter [*Sechs Mädchen suchen Nachtquartier*, 1927], 66
Slavinsky, Evgeni, 32n
Slonim, Marc, 11n
socialist realism, ix, 11n, 34, 41, 45n, 46, 60, 63, 64, 69
Sokolov, Ippolit, 59
Sold Appetite, The [*Prodannyi appetit*, 1928], 89
Song of a Girl [*Pesnia o devushke*, 1936], 37n
Song of the Liberated Soviet Woman, see Lullaby
split screen, 83, 85, 90, 101, 102, 103, 104, 131, 132, 148, 155, 198
staged film, ix, 3n, 4, 18, 19, 20, 21, 22, 23, 35, 48, 49, 53, 55, 56, 87, 89
Stalin, Iosif (Joseph), 9n, 22, 24, 47n, 53, 57, 62, 64, 66n, 68, 69
Stanislavsky, Konstantin, 6n
stop-trick, *see* animation
Strike [*Stachka*, 1924], 36, 49, 50, 52, 55, 56
Strong Man, The [*Sil'nyi chelovek*, 1916], 31n
Strongin, Barry, xi
subliminal propulsion, 155–64
Suino, Mark, 29n
superimposition, 84, 121, 132, 135, 136, 139, 145, 146, 177, 181, 182, 184, 186, 187; *see also* double exposure; multiple exposure
suprematism, viii, x, 5, 6, 15, 42, 44, 127, 132
Svilova, Elizaveta, x, 2, 3, 12, 13, 27, 29, 37, 50, 70, 71, 77, 79, 81, 82, 90, 94,

96, 97, 102, 107, 109, 111, 115, 117, 119, 122, 123, 124, 125, 127, 135, 137, 150, 151, 155, 156, 157, 160, 163, 164, 177, 183, 189–96, 197
swish pan, 124
symbolism, 26, 40
Symphony of the Don Basin – Enthusiasm [Symfoniia Donbassa – Entuziazm, 1930], 27, 50, 58, 59, 60, 63, 85, 90, 184

Tart, Charles, 164n, 165n
Tatlin, Vladimir, 8, 9, 43n
Taylor, Frederick Winslow, 7, 8n
tectonics, 15
Ten Days that Shook the World, see October
"Theory of Intervals," *see* intervals, "Theory of Intervals"
Three Songs about Lenin [Tri pesni o Lenine, 1934], 23, 24, 43, 44, 53, 57, 64
Tolstoi, Lev, 19n
Tretyakov, Sergei, 11n, 20, 21, 22, 33
trompe-l'oeil, 124
Trotsky, Lev, 24, 35
Turgenev, Ivan, 66n
Turkin, Nikandr, 32n
Twenty-Six Commissars, The [Dvadtsat' shest' komissarov, 1932], 31n
Tynianov, Yuri, 42n
"typage," 22, 23, 36, 53

unstaged film, viii, 3, 19, 20, 21, 22, 25, 49, 58, 60

Verfremdungseffekt, 11n, *see also* alienation; estrangement; "making it strange"
Vernadsky, George, 22n
Vesnin brothers (Aleksandr, Leonid, Viktor), 8
visual afterimage (VAE), *see* persistence of vision
Vorkapich, Slavko, 27n
VTSIK, see Agit-Train, The

Wajda, Andrzej, viii
Weekend [Wochende, 1929], 152n
Where They Trade in Bodies and Souls, see Green Manuela
White Eagle [Belyi orel, 1928], 31n
Whitman, Walt, 38
Wilde, Oscar, 31n
Wise Man, The, see Enough Simplicity in Every Wise Man
Wiseman, Frederick, viii

Yesenin, Sergei, 47
Young Lady and the Hooligan, The [Barishnia i khuligan, 1918], 32n

Zamyatin, Yevgeny, 47n
Zaum (transrational language or metalanguage), 39, 42, 43
Zhdanov, Andrei, 57, 68
Zhdanovism, 68, 69
Zhirmunsky, Vladimir, 42n
Zinoviev, Grigori, 24
Zotov, Petr, 2n